Theories in
INTERCULTURAL
COMMUNICATION

INTERNATIONAL AND INTERCULTURAL COMMUNICATION ANNUAL

Volume XII

1988

Editor
Young Yun Kim
Governors State University

Coeditor
William B. Gudykunst
Arizona State University

Editorial Assistants for Volume XII
Lauren I. Gumbs
Arizona State University

Karen L. Schmidt
Arizona State University

INTERNATIONAL AND INTERCULTURAL COMMUNICATION ANNUAL
VOLUME XII   1988

Theories in
INTERCULTURAL
COMMUNICATION

edited by

Young Yun KIM
William B. GUDYKUNST

Published in Cooperation with
The Speech Communication Association
Commission on International and Intercultural Communication

SAGE PUBLICATIONS
The Publishers of Professional Social Science
Newbury Park   Beverly Hills   London   New Delhi

For information address:

SAGE Publications, Inc.
2111 West Hillcrest Drive
Newbury Park, California 91320

SAGE Publications Inc.
275 South Beverly Drive
Beverly Hills
California 90212

SAGE Publications Ltd.
28 Banner Street
London EC1Y 8QE
England

SAGE PUBLICATIONS India Pvt. Ltd.
M-32 Market
Greater Kailash I
New Delhi 110 048 India

Printed in the United States of America

Library of Congress Cataloging-in-Publication Data

International Standard Book Number 0-8039-3149-2

International Standard Book Number 0-8039-3150-6 (pbk.)

International Standard Series Number 0270-6075

FIRST PRINTING 1988

Contents

Preface

In 1983, the first issue of the *International and Intercultural Communication Annual* (Volume VII) was published under the title *Intercultural Communication Theory* (edited by William B. Gudykunst). The appearance of this volume introduced two firsts: (1) it was the first issue of the *Annual* to focus on a specific theme rather than following the journal format of the earlier issues, and (2) it was the first volume on theory in intercultural communication. Response to this volume has been enthusiastic. The volume went through two printings and has been used as a text in many graduate seminars in the field. It has helped to define the study of intercultural communication and the theoretical perspectives presented in it, and generated a substantial amount of empirical research, which has further stimulated advancements in theorizing intercultural communication.

These advancements, in turn, limit the usefulness of Volume VII today. Hence the present Volume XII, rededicated to the theme of theorizing intercultural communication. Several of the contributors to Volume VII have "updated" their chapters (Applegate & Sypher; Cronen & Pearce; Ellingsworth; Kincaid). A number of new perspectives have been developed for this volume (Collier & Thomas; Gudykunst; Kim & Ruben; Yum). In addition, Giles (in England) and Forgas (in Australia) were invited to write chapters to broaden the scope of this volume beyond work in the United States.

The chapters in this volume cover a wide range of approaches. At the same time, they share a focus on face-to-face communication among members of different cultures and subcultures. Taken together, they represent the major current approaches to the study of intercultural communication, as well as of communication in general. Our special thanks go to Gordon Craigo for his competent assistance in proofreading. We are pleased to present this volume, with a confidence that it will contribute to the continuing theoretical development in the field.

Young Yun Kim
William B. Gudykunst

I

OVERVIEW

1

On Theorizing
Intercultural Communication

YOUNG YUN KIM • *Governors State University*

This chapter introduces the present volume outlining its purpose, scope, and organization. It discusses the conceptual scope of intercultural communication, and identifies theoretical foci of the present theories. The theories are further distinguished from one another based on their respective explanatory forms and underlying metatheoretical orientations. Each theory, then, is identified with one of the three approaches to science: positivist, humanist, and systems. The chapter concludes with a discussion on the need for continued refinement of the existing approaches and increased efforts to find ways to integrate them.

Intercultural communication has achieved a clear visibility in the study of human behavior. The increasingly intercultural reality across linguistic, religious, racial, ethnic, and national boundaries has foregrounded intercultural communication as a topic that bears significant academic and practical merits. The base of the field of intercultural communication has been broadened beyond the group of individuals who have traditionally identified themselves with it. Scholars of various disciplines of human sciences including psychology, sociology, and anthropology in the United States as well as in several other countries have joined in recent publications such as *Interethnic Communication* (Kim, 1986), *Communication and Cross-Cultural Adaptation* (Kim & Gudykunst, 1987), and the second edition of *Handbook of Intercultural Communication* (Asante & Gudykunst, in press).

As the field evolves, we are seeing gradual but increasing consolidation and crystallization of its core concepts. Serious attempts have been made to develop coherent conceptual paradigms of intercultural communication (e.g., Gudykunst & Kim, 1984b; Kim, 1984; Sarbaugh, 1979), based on which systematic inquiries using common terminologies may be advanced. In addition, the first anthology of works that attempted to theorize intercultural communication phenomena was published (Gudykunst, 1983), "pushing" the field forward in the direction of greater coherence and rigor.

Partly updating this 1983 anthology, the present volume offers some of the most current theorizing activities in intercultural communication.

Although the theories presented here are claimed to be neither necessarily "best" nor exhaustive of all the available theoretical works today, they are considered to be most closely assigned with the theoretical mainstreams of the field of communication at large. The editors also assess the present theories as some of the most "visible" and "active" theoretical approaches with a potential for contributing to the development of the intercultural communication field in coming years.

Theorizing endeavors such as the ones in the present volume help us grow beyond the haphazard activities. They help form a sense of direction, an intellectual core, and a consensus among researchers in the field. Although the methodological difficulties we face are complex and place limitations on what we may hope to achieve in the short run, theorizing activities are "soul-searching" efforts that help assess research implications and then act on them in a reasonably concerted fashion.

In introducing the present theories, two interrelated issues are highlighted next, discussing their divergent as well as convergent attributes. First, we will examine the overall conceptual domain of intercultural communication covered by the present theories, and the specific issues or foci addressed by them. Second, the metatheoretical approaches and explanatory forms employed by these theories will be discussed to ascertain their respective theoretical goals.

THE DOMAIN OF INTERCULTURAL COMMUNICATION

All theories are about *something*—the "what" of the description or explanation offered. The theories in this volume are about some aspects of intercultural communication of *individuals* rather than of groups. Because intercultural communication, basically, is not different from all other human communication phenomena, it involves communicators, encoding and decoding of verbal and nonverbal messages, and the physical and social environment. The communicator's behavior at a given time reflects his or her experiential background that, in turn, shapes the attributes of his or her internal meaning system.

The term, *intercultural communication,* is conceived in the present theories primarily as direct, face-to-face communication encounters between or among individuals with differing cultural backgrounds. Culture is viewed in most of the present theories as not limited to the life patterns of conventionally recognizable cultural groups such as national, ethnic, or racial groups. Instead, it is viewed as potentially open to all levels of groups whose life patterns discernibly influence individual

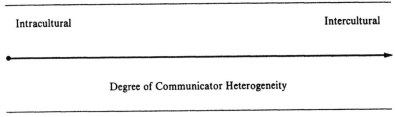

Figure 1:1   The intracultural-intercultural continuum of communication

communication behaviors. All communication, thus, is viewed as "intercultural" to an extent, and the degree of "interculturalness" of a given communication encounter is considered to depend on the degree of heterogeneity between the experiential backgrounds of the individuals involved. The distinction between intercultural and intracultural communication, therefore, is viewed not as a qualitative, categorical distinction, but as a matter of a researcher's particular operationalization of the concepts, or "drawing of a line" between them. (See Figure 1.1.)

This global, inclusive conceptualization of intercultural communication has been widely accepted in the past (see Ellingsworth, 1977; Gudykunst & Kim, 1984a; Samovar & Porter, 1985; Sarbaugh, 1979), and is elaborated by Sarbough in Chapter 2. Sarbaugh presents a taxonomy of intercultural communication in which the degree of "interculturalness" is dependent on the degree of heterogeneity in the participants' worldview, normative patterns of beliefs and overt behaviors, verbal and nonverbal code system, and perceived relation and intent. An underlying assumption here is that individuals who belong to the same cultural group generally share greater commonality. *Intercultural* communication, thus, is a term employed exchangeably with *intergroup* communication by Gudykunst (Chapter 6) and by Gallois, Franklyn-Stokes, Giles, and Coupland (Chapter 7).

THEORETICAL FOCI

Following Sarbaugh's taxonomy, 11 theories are presented to account for issues pertinent to the realm of intercultural communication just described. On the whole, the issues these theories address are roughly organized into three broad questions corresponding to the three parts of the book: How do individuals communicate in different cultures? (Part II); How do individuals experience intercultural communication activities? (Part III); and What are likely consequences of intercultural communication experiences? (Part IV). Within each of these categories, individual theories deal with more specific foci that constitute the "stuff" being described or explained, and are represented by the key *concepts* (or constructs) identified in the theories. The theoretical foci, thus, are the angles from which our theorists "see" intercultural communication phenomena. Collectively, they define features of intercultural communication that currently serve as the main objects of inquiry.

The first theory in Part II is the constructivist theory of Applegate and Sypher (Chapter 3) that describes the influences of culture on individual communication behavior. The theory emphasizes the interpretive nature of communicators and the interrelatedness of culture and the individual's cognitive construction of reality. Following the constructivist theory is a theory by Cronen, Chin, and Pearce (Chapter 4) about the interactive process of "coordinating" and "managing" communicative meaning between individuals. Based on a critical perspective on the study of communication and culture, this theory emphasizes analyzing meaning structure and action of individual communicators that occur in intercultural encounters. In doing so, the theory attempts to illuminate cultural differences and to generate a critical perspective on intercultural behavior. Somewhat relatedly, Collier and Thomas (Chapter 5) propose a theory of cultural identity. In this theory, cultural identity is viewed not as "fixed" by an external criterion (e.g., nationality) but as dependent on the communication competence of the interacting individuals.

The first theory in Part III, by Gudykunst (Chapter 6), focuses on the individual experiences of intercultural encounters, namely uncertainty and anxiety. Gudykunst proposes a set of predictive statements linking a host of factors that are considered to influence the psychological reactions. The theory of communication accommodation by Gallois, Franklyn-Stokes, Giles, and Coupland (Chapter 7) deals with the patterns of speaking behavior and cognitive attribution of individuals in intercultural encounters. This theory offers a system of explanation as to how intercultural communicators' accommodation behavior is influenced by the degree of perceived visibility (or salience) of their group membership.

Forgas's theory of "episode representations" (Chapter 8) provides an explanation of intercultural behavior focusing on the cognitive activity of individuals in intercultural encounters. Specifically, Forgas emphasizes the subjectively perceived nature of a situation, or "communication episode," as the focal point of analysis, and thus proposes a "sociocognitive" approach to studying intercultural behavior. In Chapter 9, Ting-Toomey proposes a theory of intercultural conflict styles. Employing the core concept, "face-negotiation," Ting-Toomey presents a set of propositions explaining cultural differences in individual styles of managing interpersonal conflicts.

The four theories in Part IV deal with changes and adaptation that occur in individuals as a result of intercultural communication experiences. Yum's network theory (Chapter 10) focuses on the structural characteristics of relationship networks of intercultural communicators, and compares them to those of intracultural networks. On the other hand, Ellingsworth (in Chapter 11) attempts to explain the more microscopic, "real-time" process of adaptation that occurs in task-oriented intercultural dyadic encounters.

In addition, Kincaid (Chapter 12) applies the convergence theory of communication to intercultural communication experiences of immigrants. In this theory, Kincaid explains how a greater state of uniformity can occur between the immigrant culture and its host culture, as well as how a greater state of divergence can occur between the immigrant culture and its original culture. In the final chapter (Chapter 13), Kim and Ruben present a theory that explains the gradual transformation of individuals' cognitive, affective, and behavioral attributes toward an increasing level of "interculturalness" as they accumulate their intercultural communication experiences. In doing so, Kim and Ruben attempt to integrate the two existing approaches to intercultural experiences: the "intercultural communication-as-problem" approach and the "intercultural communication-as-learning/growth" approach.

METATHEORETICAL GROUNDING[1]

Overall, these theories, together, paint a revealing (although incomplete) profile of the field of intercultural communication today, by making its key issues visible and concrete. In doing so, each theory presents a set of interrelated statements about the phenomenon under investigation.

The theories, however, differ in their metatheoretical assumptions. Some of the theories seek mainly to promote our *descriptive understanding,* while others are more clearly predictive and thus attempts to increase our ability to *control* the phenomena being theorized (see Dubin, 1969). When such metatheoretical orientations are considered, the 11 theories in this volume can be viewed as generally based on one of the following three traditions: (1) Positivist tradition emphasizing the goal of prediction; (2) Humanist tradition emphasizing the goal of understanding; and (3) Systems tradition emphasizing the goal of understanding and prediction. These metatheoretical orientations are briefly discussed here as they relate to the present chapters.

Positivist Approach

Studies of intercultural communication (including intracultural and cross-cultural studies of communication phenomena) have closely followed what may be loosely characterized as the positivist (or more precisely, "postpositivist") tradition in the philosophy of science. The positivist approach is characterized by *analytic-reductionist-mechanistic-behavioral-quantitative* approaches to research. It embodies the spirit of natural science, and has been strongly identified as *the* scientific approach in communication for the past several decades.

Inquiries in this tradition typically attempt to "isolate" and "detach" separate elements and then bring them together into theoretical relationships. The most theoretically useful units of observation and analysis are assumed to be the smallest units of a given phenomenon, with larger units being simply their aggregate. Typically a proposition consists of one or more "independent" (or explanatory) concepts (or variables) and of one or more "dependent" (or explained) concepts. Once key concepts are identified, their interrelationships are identified according to the "law of association" in the form of "if A then B." In this positivist tradition, theory is commonly viewed as a set of principles, often called axioms or laws, that are taken as "nomothetic" statements, from which a set of probabilistic statements, called propositions or theorems, are derived. In this tradition, causality is essentially one-way and linear, and prediction (and thus control of outcome) is its most desirable goal.

The positivist approach has been profoundly appealing to the majority of the practicing researchers in intercultural communication, as in most of the other human sciences. The "if A then B" logic underlies and characterizes "practical reasoning" in our daily activities, particularly in the North American and Western European societies. This practical logic enables us to simplify, make predictions about, and possibly control, the reality of the phenomenon under observation. In this volume, the theories by Gudykunst (Chapter 6), Gallois, Franklyn-

Stokes, Giles, and Coupland (Chapter 7), Forgas (Chapter 8), Ting-Toomey (Chapter 9), and Ellingsworth (Chapter 11) follow this line of reasoning.

Humanist Approach

The positivist tradition has been recently challenged by a number of alternative approaches including constructivist, rules, critical, and interactionist approaches. These approaches commonly follow the humanist tradition in the philosophy of science. Although distinct from one another, these relatively new approaches commonly view the predominant positivist approach as at least partly inadequate in studying communication phenomena. Instead, they emphasize the *synthetic-holistic-ideographic-contextual* methodology.

Unlike the positivist emphasis on predicting the outcome of a given phenomenon, the humanist tradition concentrates on describing the nature of the phenomenon as it unfolds. Instead of attempting to control the phenomenon, the humanist tradition stresses the "freedom" of individuals and of understanding the course of actions taken by individuals (Gergen & Gergen, 1982, pp. 135-6). Grounded in the phenomenological philosophy, the humanist investigator views the extent of phenomenal reliability fundamentally as a matter of personal, subjective construction and strives to identify the structures of human experience as the organizing principles that give form and meaning to the "lifeworld." Based on the hermeneutic (interpretive) approach, the humanist study concentrates on the historical meaning of experience and its developmental and cumulative effects at both the individual and social levels (Polkinghorne, 1983, p. 203).

The primary theoretical goal in this tradition is, thus, to provide an ideographic description and explanation of a given communication phenomenon. In doing so, a theorist attempts to preserve the structure generated by the individuals participating in the communication event (Delia, 1977), rather than to generate universal lawlike statements imposed by the theorist. This humanist tradition is reflected in the three theories in Part II of the present volume. The perspectives taken by Applegate and Sypher (Chapter 3), Cronen, Chen, and Pearce (Chapter 4), and Collier and Thomas (Chapter 5) emphasize a holistic, contextual investigation of the subjective and intersubjective processes of interpretation and perspective taking in communication.

In addition to the positivist and the humanist approaches, the systems approach provides a major avenue for studying intercultural communication. Systems tradition argues against the "insensitivity" of the positivist approaches in the complex, transactional, dynamic nature of human communication phenomena. Bateson (1972), for example, regarded as committing "heuristic error" the notion of deterministic relationships between independent and dependent variables. Such a systems-based perspective emphasizes that communication phenomena are interactive and that interacting elements of a given entity (system) must be viewed as codetermining the outcome being investigated. The systems perspective further recognizes the structure of a system and the modes of information exchange that occur within the system or that take place between it and its environment.

The systems perspective shares some commonalities with the positivist tradition in that both encourage investigators to identify lawlike principles and patterns of interaction among systems elements. At the same time, the systems approach, like the humanist approach, views that communication is an emergent and interactive process and that a communication system (whether an individual or two or more individuals) must be understood in its totality. As such, the systems perspective integrates both the external "objective" patterns and the internal "subjective" experiences of individuals. These two processes are viewed as inseparable entities operating simultaneously and in concert. Of the theories presented in this volume, the theory of intercultural transformation by Kim and Ruben (Chapter 13) closely follows the systems approach. The network theory by Yum (Chapter 10), the convergency theory by Kincaid (Chapter 12), and the theory of intercultural adaptation in interpersonal dyads by Ellingsworth (Chapter 11) also are grounded in the systems perspective in varying degrees. Additionally, two previously mentioned humanistic theories—coordinated management of meaning theory by Cronen, Chen, and Pearce (Chapter 4) and the cultural identity theory by Collier and Thomas (Chapter 5) use some of the systems theoretic principles.

TOWARD REFINEMENT AND INTEGRATION

Thus far we have examined the domain of intercultural communication as conceptualized in this volume. We have also identified the specific theoretical foci, and differentiated among the range of explanatory forms employed in the theories. Viewing intercultural communication as occurring between individuals of differing experiential backgrounds shaped by their respective group membership (Part I), the present theories look at the interrelatedness of individual and cultural meaning systems (Part II), cognitive experiences of individuals vis-à-vis intercultural encounters (Part III), and the adaptive changes that intercultural communication experiences bring to individuals' interpersonal network structure, behaviors in task-oriented dyads, immigrants' culture, and the internal cognitive-affective-behavioral attributes of intercultural communicators (Part IV). Toward the common goal of enriching our knowledge of intercultural communication, and thus helping intercultural communication activities to be more effective, the present theories raise the salience of these key issues and offer a system of description or explanation for each issue.

Also, it has been pointed out that the positivist theories propose a series of predictive propositions for empirical testing. On the other hand, the humanistic theories in this volume attempt to increase our understanding about the way individuals acquire cultural characteristics in their thought patterns on which they experience intercultural communication encounters. Placing a central emphasis on subjective meaning within individuals and on the intersubjective formation of meanings between individuals, these humanistic theories direct our attention to examining deeper, more subtle dimensions of intercultural communication. Further, the present systems-based theories enable us to look at the dynamic interaction between the internal and the external conditions, the patterns of evolution and change. Also, the systems-based theories examine the nature of information exchanged between individuals in intercultural encounters in relation to the process of change in their psychological and social attributes.

These varied explanatory forms are not necessarily incompatible or inconsistent. As Polkinghorne (1983) pointed out, there is no one method that is *the* correct method for conducting human science research. The diverse approaches, instead, offer systems of inquiry currently available for our selection based on the specific nature of specific intercultural communication issues we may raise. The reality of intercultural communication presents itself as having universalities (regularities, commonalities, consistencies, similarities) *as well as* individualities (irregularities, uniqueness, inconsistencies, spontaneities). To the extent that intercultural communication phenomena share universality, universal measurement would be appropriate. To the extent that human-social phenomena are individually unique, the humanist approach would be useful.

What is called for in the field of intercultural communication, then, appears to be an "integrative pluralism" (Bunge, 1973 cited in Bhaskar, 1982). At least for now, the field of intercultural communication will benefit by the continued development of different theoretical systems. Each approach needs to be further refined in terms of the conventional criteria such as parsimony, heuristics, internal coherence, and aesthetic (see Littlejohn, 1983). The appropriateness, usefulness, and relevance of a given theory in describing and explaining a given phenomenon must be tested against reality. Corresponding research methods must be elaborated and advanced before a given theory can be adequately tested and replicated.

In time, the seemingly conflicting perspectives may solidify their respective vantage points, and the conditions and contexts in which each perspective is most appropriate may be clarified. In the meantime, these possibilities place greater responsibility on individual researchers, requiring that we become something more than mere technicians; that we become methodologists who are familiar with various approaches to scientific investigation (Polkinghorne, 1983, p. 280). In the end, what is acceptable as "knowledge" postulated by "good" theories is what withstands the test of time—through observation, experience, and experiment—and what wins enough of our collective trust.

NOTE

1. The present metatheoretical discussion is based on a review of the various sources including: Blalock (1984), Delia (1977), Dubin (1969), Krippendorf (1975), Littlejohn (1983), Polkinghorne (1983), Secord (1982), and Trenholm (1986).

REFERENCES

Asante, M., & Gudykunst, W. B. (in press). *Handbook of intercultural communication* (2nd ed.). Newbury Park, CA: Sage.

Bhaskar, R. (1982). Emergence, explanation, and emancipation. In P. F. Secord (Ed.), *Explaining human behavior* (pp. 275-310). Beverly Hills, CA: Sage.

Bateson, G. (1972). *Steps to an ecology of mind*. New York: Ballantine.

Blalock, H. M., Jr. (1984). *Basic dilemmas in the social sciences*. Beverly Hills, CA: Sage.

Delia, J. G. (1977). Constructivism and the study of human communication. *Quarterly Journal of Speech, 63*, 66-83.

Dubin, R. (1969). *Theory building*. New York: Free Press.

Ellingsworth, H. (1977). Conceptualizing intercultural communication. In B. D. Ruben (Ed.), *Communication yearbook 1* (pp. 99-106). New Brunswick, NJ: Transaction Books.

Gergen, K. J., & Gergen, M. M. (1982). Explaining human conduct: Form and function. In P. F. Secord (Ed.), *Explaining human behavior* (pp. 127-154). Beverly Hills, CA: Sage.

Gudykunst, W. B. (Ed.). (1983). *Intercultural communication theory*. Beverly Hills, CA: Sage.

Gudykunst, W. B., & Kim, Y. Y. (1984a). *Communicating with strangers: An approach to intercultural communication*. New York: Random House.

Gudykunst, W. B., & Kim, Y. Y. (Eds.). (1984b). *Methods for intercultural communication research*. Beverly Hills, CA: Sage.

Kim, Y. Y. (1984). Searching for creative integration. In W. B. Gudykunst & Y. Y. Kim (Eds.), *Methods for intercultural communication* (pp. 13-30). Beverly Hills, CA: Sage.

Kim, Y. Y. (Ed.). (1986). *Interethnic communication: Current research*. Beverly Hills, CA: Sage.

Kim, Y. Y., & Gudykunst, W. B. (Eds.). (1987). *Cross-cultural adaptations: Current theory and research*. Newbury Park, CA: Sage.

Krippendorf, K. (1975). The systems approach to communication, In B. D. Ruben & J. Y. Kim (Eds.), *General systems theory and human communication* (pp. 138-164). Rochelle Park, NJ: Hayden.

Littlejohn, S. W. (1983). *Theories of human communication* (2nd ed.). Belmont, CA: Wadsworth.

Polkinghorne, D. (1983). *Methodology for the human sciences: Systems of inquiry*. Albany, NY: State University of New York Press.

Samovar, L. A., & Porter, W. E. (Eds.). (1985). *Intercultural communication: A reader*. Belmont, CA: Wadsworth.

Sarbaugh, L. E. (1979). *Intercultural communication*. Rochelle Park, NJ: Hayden.

Secord, P. F. (1982). *Explaining human behavior* (pp. 275-310). Beverly Hills, CA: Sage.

Trenholm, S. (1986). *Human communication theory*. Englewood Cliffs, NJ: Prentice-Hall.

2

A Taxonomic Approach
to Intercultural Communication

LARRY E. SARBAUGH • *Michigan State University*

Participants in a communication event can be classified along a continuum of homogeneity/heterogeneity. This continuum is used to establish levels of interculturalness of a communication event. When participants are highly similar in worldview, normative patterns, code systems, and perceived relationship and intent, then the level of interculturalness is low and communication will proceed with minimal effort and maximum accuracy. Conversely, when participants are highly different on a combination of those four sets of variables, communication will require great effort and the outcome will not match the intent of the participants. The chapter opens with a discussion of conceptualizing and theorizing, and notes that taxonomies are implicit theories. It then summarizes the development of a taxonomy of interculturalness.

As I started to write this chapter, a television talk show was exploring the issue of homeless families in New York City. As I watched, I realized that I was observing, via TV, another world, one with which I could not identify. Even those who were panelists on the show (homeless families and those working with homeless families) displayed a lot of variation in their abilities to conceive of and talk about the situation. There was great variation between the panelists and those in the audience in the way they viewed the world and how to deal with it.

This, I realized, was an intercultural chasm as great as any between me and persons from other countries of the world. And from the cases presented, we obviously are abysmally handling the needs of these persons in the United States. The lack of empathic, or even sympathetic, responses by those in the audience perhaps demonstrated at least one aspect of the difficulty of society doing anything to overcome the problems of homelessness.

Coming back to the world of my word processor in a comfortable carpeted room, with a cool breeze blowing through the window, what can I say about conceptualizing intercultural communication? It's a huge jump from the heady world of academia and the comfort of a middle class home to the world of a mother of six children ages 1 to 14, with no husband present, seeking food and shelter for herself and her children. Add to this the fact that she does not read or write and seemingly has no notion of how or whether she wants to change her situation. In that environment, I find my communication skills woefully inadequate.

That picture of the mother and her children, with no place to go that they can call home, haunts my thoughts as I attempt to write about intercultural communication. I keep wondering whether we are asking the right questions to find solutions to the problems of poverty. Then I wonder if we are asking the right questions to find the solutions to problems of communication among persons in our families, our communities, or our world.

Incidentally, the TV show following the one of the homeless was a game show giving away thousands of dollars for "playing the game"— two different faces of America.

SOME THOUGHTS ON CONCEPTUALIZATION

What is intercultural communication? What is communication? What is culture? What is a concept? And what difference will the answers make in improving the quality of life for those around us, in our communities and in the world? These are questions that one must ask and answer, again and again.

Treatment of these questions here will be quite brief. I hope what is said about them will lead you to reflect on what it is we're about in our building of concepts and theories. I also hope the effort may give us tools to communicate more satisfactorily with the homeless and indigent in our societies, as well as some ways to improve communication among national and international leaders, those making decisions affecting large numbers of people.

It is important to remember that philosophy is a close partner in our scientific undertakings. Philosophy precedes science by examining the concepts and definitions that science takes as a starting point and completes science by attempting to put together the various researchers into a consistent view of the world. It seems important that periodically we should make explicit our philosophy of life, of science, of education, of knowledge, and of ethics. It helps us to clarify the meanings we carry within us and to think about how we use them.

To consider the conceptualizing of intercultural communication, it seems appropriate to reflect on the conceptualizing of concepts (the product) and of conceptualizing itself (the process). Conceptualizing of conceptualizing, that sounds like double talk, but it just might be fruitful. Certainly if one follows one of the axioms of communication, that is, *meanings are in people,* then it behooves us to strive for shared meanings for the labels (symbols) we use for what we write and talk about. That, perhaps, is the most difficult task in all of communication, and the one that even those of use who claim to be communication specialists often overlook in our own message production.

In Webster's *New World Dictionary,* we find *concept* defined as "an idea, especially a generalized idea of a class of objects, a thought, general notion." Howard and Tracy Kendler (1968), writing on concepts in the *International Encyclopedia of Social Sciences,* say, "Our world is filled with sets of objects, events, and ideas that share some common quality while differing in other characteristics. An organism that learns to respond to the common quality of a given set has learned a concept" (pp. 206-211).

They go on to point out that a child has learned the concept of blueness when the child is able to distinguish a blue balloon from a blue ball and to distinguish between blue and other colors of similar objects, for example, blue balloons and red balloons. Similarly, we will have learned the concept of intercultural communication when we have learned to separate the events, ideas, and so on, associated with a given class of communication events and distinguish them from other communication events that are in some way meaningfully different.

Kaplan (1964) refers to the paradox of conceptualization. He points out that proper concepts are needed to form a good theory, but that also one needs a good theory to arrive at proper concepts. Kaplan cites Jevons (1892) who remarked that almost every classification proposed in the early stages of a science will be found to break down as deeper similarities of the objects come to be detected. This emphasizes the stages of successive approximations that are involved in scholarship. It also emphasizes a "process view of reality" that is espoused so widely in communication writing and teaching.

The term *theory* is used here to represent a formulation of apparent relationships and underlying principles based on accumulated observations and speculations. That brief sentence is obviously a shorthand for the concept of theory. The further development of the conceptualization of theory is left to you, with the notion that it is a continuing process. Undoubtedly the other chapters of this book will contribute to that process for you.

Kaplan (1964) also notes that every taxonomy is a provisional and implicit theory or family of theories. The taxonomy of interculturalness reviewed in this chapter derives from a family of theories. It also represents a combination of observational data and speculation as to what distinguishes communication we label intercultural from what we label intracultural. It can provide some bases for theory development. In that process, there can evolve improvements in conceptualizing and theorizing about intercultural communication.

Just as there is interdependence between the conceptual and the theoretical realms, there is interdependence between the observational and the theoretical. The basic point, according to Kaplan, is that there is no observation that is so empirically pure that it is free of any ideational element and no theory that is purely ideational.

It is of interest that the earliest writings in speech communication contain numerous references to the process of conceptualizing. Nancy Harper (1979) reviews some of that history and presents a classical taxonomy of conceptualization developed by the ancient Greeks and Romans. It has two major categories, the inartistic and the artistic, again emphasizing the interplay of sense data and the ideational in our development of the concepts we use.

The terms concept and theory are abstractions, constructions, if you will, to assist us in making our world more meaningful. In this sense, there is a certain uniqueness in their meaning, based on time, place, and the persons by whom they are used. And that is true of the present meager effort at conceptualizing "concept," "conceptualizing," and "intercultural communication."

INTERCULTURAL COMMUNICATION

I define communication as the process of using signs and symbols that elicit meanings in another person or persons for whatever intent, or even without conscious intent, on the part of the person producing the symbols or signs. As will be noted in the conceptualization that follows, I view every communicative act in some sense an intercultural one. I believe the basis for that will become clear as I develop the taxonomy of interculturalness.

Groups can be identified with shared characteristics and given labels to distinguish them from other groups who do not share similar characteristics. Often these identified groups are given racial, national, or ethnic labels. Unfortunately, those labels often conceal more than they reveal, owing to within-group variations, which may be as great or greater than between-group variations. When considering the usefulness of such categorizing to predict and explain what occurs in communication, one must constantly ask how uniform, how homogeneous, are the sets of characteristics of the individuals within the groups so labeled.

The enormity of the task of identifying "cultures" in a manner meaningful for communication analysis becomes apparent when we recognize that Kroeber and Kluckhohn (1952) analyzed 160 definitions of the concept "culture." They concluded that the definitions fell into six major groups based on the emphasis given by the author of the definition. Kroeber and Kluckhohn synthesized the various materials, resulting in the following definition:

> Culture consists of patterns, explicit and implicit, of and for behavior acquired and transmitted by symbols, constituting the distinctive achievements of human groups, including their embodiments in artifacts; the essential core of culture consists of traditional (i.e., historically derived and selected) ideas and especially their attached values; culture systems may, on the one hand, be considered as products of action, on the other as conditioning elements of further action. (p. 181)

There is a difficulty of categorizing persons into groups and labeling the groups according to characteristics noted in such definitions. Culture is considered to be dynamic and constantly changing, but groupings and labels persist beyond their accuracy and usefulness. At one time in history, when natural barriers restricted contact and flow of messages among groups of people in various locations, the characteristics noted in the preceding definition may have been quite stable and resistant to change. Under those conditions, proceeding as though the characteristics of group were stable and relatively unchanging would not cause much difficulty.

Today, with the rapid growth of technologies of communication and transportation, the amount of intergroup contact has increased phenomenally. One example of this is the diffusion of styles of music among the youth in many parts of the world. Another example is the continually increasing economic activity among people in various parts of the world, which adds to the changes in the ways people live as it has in ages past; only now the impact of economic changes becomes visible more quickly as the interdependence of technologically oriented societies require interacting more often and with less time lapse. This increased contact and the increasing pressures for change, I believe, provide a strong argument for a conceptualization of intercultural communication that is readily adaptable to changing environments—technological, sociological, and psychological.

A TAXONOMY OF INTERCULTURALNESS

A taxonomic approach to conceptualizing intercultural communication is presented in *Intercultural Communication* (Sarbaugh, 1987). I believe the taxonomy offers some of the needed flexibility. In discussing the concept of *culture,* it was stated that when we say persons belong to a similar culture, we are saying they share certain psychological, sociological, and technological trappings. That view of culture focuses on those psychological, sociological, and technological aspects of the environment in which they exist. Technology is used as anything that adds to the power available to humans to carry on their daily activities. This can range from the crudest stick or stone instrument to the most complex robot. The product of the technology may function for survival or for artistic gratification.

In the language of the taxonomy, communication events may be classified by level of interculturalness based on the extent to which the participants in the communication event share worldviews, normative patterns of beliefs and overt behaviors, code systems, and perceptions of their relationship and intent. Communication also may be classified as to whether direct or interposed channels are used and how many persons are involved. An interposed channel may be another person, an electronic relay, or a printed page interposed between primary participants in the communication event. In this discussion of the taxonomy, the focus will be on two-person direct channel communication.

The taxonomy is intended to establish the critical similarities and differences among participants in a given communication event, at a given point in time. The degree of difference is referred to as level of homogeneity/heterogeneity of the participants that, in this model, establishes the level of interculturalness of the communication event. As has been noted in earlier writings, the ideas that led to the taxonomy emerged from my own experiences and from discussions in seminars I was teaching. Those elements of sense data, coupled with previous reading, became the basis for the reflective speculation that led to the taxonomy.

Repeated questioning of the differences between what is labeled intercultural communication and all other communication always seemed to lead to asking what the significant differences are among the participants engaged in the communicative act. That also led to asking in what ways people throughout the world are alike.

The questions regarding similarity always settled on experiences with the physical environment and life processes: day-night, hot-cold, wet-dry, growth-decay, birth-death, hunger-thirst, and so on. These are essentially aspects of life pertaining to physical survival. All people also experience a range of feelings: anger, joy, fear, affection, excitement, loneliness, and so on. The nature of these experiences obviously will vary with the physical, social, and psychological environment in which the person(s) exists and will impinge on and influence those environments.

The differences that became apparent were those of prescribed or accepted ways to deal with the physical survival needs and accepted or prescribed ways of relating to other people in the activities of surviving together. There are acceptable and unacceptable foods and acceptable and unacceptable ways to obtain, prepare, and eat the foods. There are proper and improper ways to clothe and adorn one's body, to construct and fit one's shelter, to select a mate, to carry out procreation and child rearing, and to relate to other persons, depending on one's social position and the social position of the other. There are even proper and improper ways to use and think about time, *ad infinitum.* Any deviations from what is proper may become a barrier to communication for the deviant.

Continued reflection suggested it was, in most cases, not just the presence or absence of difference that influenced the communication, but the degree of difference. The amount of difference might range from no detectable difference to the most extreme differences one could imagine. Differences might be small on one dimension of the taxonomy and large on another. This, then, brings into question which differences on which dimensions have the most influence on communication outcomes in which situations.

One advantage of a taxonomy is that it can systematically create new combinations of variables and provide categories for classification of what we're studying. Those combinations can suggest questions and classes of events previously overlooked. That can stimulate refinements in conceptualizing and theorizing. The huge number of potential combinations certainly brings into sharp focus the complexity of communication.

A disadvantage of the taxonomy on levels of interculturalness is that it does not come with ready-made tools of measurement to specify degrees (amount) of difference. And the number of potential combinations is mind boggling. As in any undertaking, one is forced to be arbitrary in choosing which of many potential arrangements one will decide to study. In selecting variables and situations to study so as to maximize the probability of selecting those most likely to make a difference, we have the advantage of access to all the prior communication research that has been done and the associated theories that have been and are being developed.

The theoretic perspectives presented in other chapters of this book give a sampling of theoretic bases for the study and practice of communication at whatever level of interculturalness. The choice of theoretic perspective is dependent on the interests of the user and the situations in which it is used. Ideally one would ask: How would I approach this situation differently using theory A instead of theory B? What differences in prediction or explanation would I expect from using one and not the other? And which yields the most information for the energy expended?

Results from use of the taxonomy have been encouraging. Students and others who have applied it to communication events they considered especially successful or especially unsuccessful report that it brought into clearer focus the elements that contributed to the outcome. In communication they considered unsuccessful, they reported that they were able to correct misperceptions they and the other parties had of one another, after which their satisfaction with their communicating and the outcomes improved.

The concept of mapping from set theory was used in the definitions of variables and in establishing the combinations of variables within the taxonomy to establish levels of interculturalness. Mapping is a systematic way of combining the elements selected for study into all possible combinations. It also provides a mechanism for combining some elements to form new composite elements as will be done later in forming the concept of worldview from the notions of nature of life, purpose of life, and relation of humans to the cosmos.

The underlying assumption in applying the taxonomy to intercultural communication is that as level of interculturalness increases, the energy required to communicate increases, and the likelihood of achieving the intended outcome decreases. The basis for that assumption should become clear as the taxonomy is developed in the following sections.

COMPONENTS OF THE TAXONOMY

The four variables used to construct the taxonomy are actually sets of variables. Elements combined to produce the four variables in the taxonomy and the method of combining them will be summarized. A more complete discussion of the variables and ways of defining them will be found in *Intercultural Communication* (Sarbaugh, 1987).

Worldview

The worldview variable is believed to be the one most resistant to change. It is conceived as encompassing that set of beliefs about the nature of life, the purpose of life, and our relation to the cosmos. These are beliefs that emerge throughout life, often without our being aware that we are acquiring them, and are often difficult to state.

To get at some of those beliefs, Suk Ja Kim (who was a graduate student at Michigan State University) and I asked people, mainly in university communities, to respond to open-ended questions: What do you believe is the purpose of life? What do you believe is the nature of life? (What is it like?) What do you believe is your relationship to the cosmos? (the universe? the totality of things? whatever you want to call that?).

In developing the taxonomy, each of those components was given a code label as follows to facilitate the mapping: nature of life = NL; purpose of life = PL; relation to the cosmos = RC; and worldview = WV. Subscripts were attached to the letter codes to designate levels of homogeneity/heterogeneity so that the lower the number of the subscript the more homogeneity and the higher the number of the subscript the more heterogeneity among the participants. Figure 2.1 shows a sample of combining these three components to create levels of interculturalness in the worldview dimension of the taxonomy.

This pattern of mapping shows the eight logical combinations possible using subscripts one and two to designate the lowest and highest values, respectively, for heterogeneity. There is no logical basis

NL PL RC			WV
1 1 1			1

NL PL RC	NL PL RC	NL PL RC	WV
1 1 2	1 2 1	2 1 1	2

NL PL RC	NL PL RC	NL PL RC	WV
1 2 2	2 1 2	2 2 1	3

NL PL RC	WV
2 2 2	4

Note: WV = World view
NL = Nature of life
PL = Purpose of life
RC = Relation to the cosmos

Figure 2.1 Components of the world view dimension of interculturalness.

for placing any of the three combinations at level WV₂ above either of the other two combinations at that level. If there were empirical data to show that NL, for example, exerted more influence on the communication behavior than PL and RC, then the three combinations on that line of the diagram could be ranked. The same is true for the three combinations at WV₃.

In operationalizing the worldview variable, responses from the three open-ended questions just listed were recorded. Duplications were edited out, producing 76 items. In an unpublished study by Kim and Sarbaugh, these were administered to students from several different countries who were attending Michigan State University. Their responses were factor analyzed to see whether typologies of people on the worldview dimension could be established. The results indicated that the items would discriminate among persons and establish typologies of persons according to their views of the nature of life, purpose of life, and relation of humans to the cosmos.

Later, the items were administered to two groups of students, one from Michigan State University (MSU) and one from a group of Puerto Rican students attending the University of Miami (Roe, Lumanta, & Sarbaugh, 1985). The items were administered in English to the MSU students and in Spanish to the Puerto Rican students. The usual checking of the translations via back translation was followed for the Spanish language version. This group of Puerto Rican students yielded a higher number of consensual items than did the group of students from MSU, suggesting more homogeneity among the Puerto Rican set than among the midwestern set of respondents.

Some findings from an article by Roe, Lumanta, and Sarbaugh (1985) illustrate the kinds of information that can be obtained using the Quanal program with responses to the 76 items. The two groups of students are referred to as Set A (MSU) and Set B (Puerto Rican Students). Consensual items for set B students include: life is dull, monotonous, and meaningless. That same set of items describe those respondents in one of the five people factors for students of set A. In addition, source of control items seemed to be most prominent among those items that identified the differences among the people factors in both sets of students responding to the 76 items. Three sources of control that emerged in this analysis were: control by a deity; control of the environment, including other people by oneself; and working in harmony with other sources of power.

Normative Patterns of Beliefs and Overt Behaviors

Another variable used in the taxonomy is normative patterns of beliefs and overt behaviors. The emphasis here is on beliefs and actions pertaining to what is involved in being a "good" person. The suggested operationalization also involves a set of open-ended questions as a starting point. The questions are: What *must* one do to be a good person? What *ought* one do to be a good person? What *may* one do to be a good person? What is it that one *ought not* do to be a good person? What is it that one *must not* do to be a good person?

Those are the five components for establishing normative patterns. It should be noted that the "must not do" items include taboos. And since some taboos are communicative taboos, communication is practically precluded for persons with those norms on those taboo topics. Walter Gantz (1975), in a paper on taboos, has pointed out that some things are all right to talk about but not do; others one may do but not talk about; and some may not be done or talked about by "good" people. Two examples of such taboo communication are the difficulty of communicating about family planning or the disease AIDS in a society in which sex is a taboo topic.

The basis for establishing the heterogeneity of the participants is whether the participants know the normative patterns of the other person and, if known, whether those patterns would be accepted. The most homogeneous set of participants would be those who knew the normative patterns of the other(s) and accepted those patterns. The most heterogeneous set of participants in a communication event would be those who did not know the normative patterns of the other(s) and, if they could know, would not accept them. The label KA has been used to designate knowing and accepting the normative patterns. It will be used when the four variables are combined later in this chapter to illustrate the composite levels of interculturalness.

With the normative patterns, there is the possibility that sharing an overriding value for encouraging difference may make any other differences in what are acceptable norms of little consequence. One might expect that value to be most prominent among a community of scholars, although one's observations may suggest that that is not always true.

Here again, the potential number of combinations that one can generate is overpowering. The most practical approach would be to take the two ends of the continuum, or at the most the two ends and a middle level, as starting levels for application and study. This will make the operation more manageable.

Code System

Another variable is the code system. Many people believe language is the main barrier to communication. However, anyone who has studied communication recognizes that sharing a common code is a necessary, but not a sufficient condition, for communication to occur.

I prefer the term *code system* to refer to both verbal and nonverbal codes, including time and space. Language often is used to refer only to spoken words or words on a page, and that is too restrictive for our purposes. There are a few scholars writing about pictures as a language, emphasizing the elements of pictorial codes and the way they are structured to elicit meanings. So the term code system is used here to encompass the elements, structures, and psychological and sociological processes that influence the meanings attached to codes.

Following the pattern used with norms, the levels of heterogeneity in relation to the code system variable will be based on the extent to which the participants in a communication event share a common code. Those who are monolingual in a common language community and share common meanings for the codes they possess are the most homogeneous, and their communication would the least intercultural on the code dimensions.

The most heterogeneous would be two persons who are monolingual and do not share any common codes. This situation may be the pure type that does not exist in reality, since it would be difficult to find two persons who cannot use some gestures or facial expressions that would elicit similar meanings. So the most heterogeneous end of the continuum is as near as one can come to no shared code.

An intermediate level would be one in which one person is bilingual and the other is monolingual in one of the code systems of the bilingual person. Placing this as an intermediate level assumes that the additional code system of the bilingual person influences the way that person perceives the world and assigns meaning to stimuli. The label CS will be used to represent code system in the taxonomic sample created.

Perceived Relation and Intent

The last variable to be defined here for the taxonomy will be *perceived relationship and intent,* designated in the taxonomy by the label PRI. Perceived relationship (PR) and intent (I) are defined separately, then combined.

Three components are combined to establish levels of perceived relationships. They are: compatibility of goals (G); hierarchicalness of relationship (H), that is, superior/subordinate versus equals; and positiveness or negativeness of feelings (F) toward the other person. The subscript of 1 (e.g., F_1) designates the most positive feeling while F_2 designates the most negative; G_1 designates compatible goals and G_2 designates incompatible or conflicting goals. H_1 is a relationship in which each perceives the other as an equal; while H_2 is perceived as a strong superior-subordinate relationship. Remember, we're just using the ends of the continuum and the values of 1 and 2 are being used to designate those positions on the continuum.

Homogeneity of participants on the intent dimension is defined as that condition in which each party in a transaction perceives the intent of the other to be sharing and helping. This could involve sharing feelings, beliefs, and materials, or helping with tasks. It would be perceived as positive intent by the participants in the transaction.

Heterogeneity of intent is defined as that condition in which each perceives the intent of the other to be to injure, disrupt, or dominate the relationship through manipulation and "put-downs." The injury could be physical, psychological, or social. It could be attacks on integrity, status, or self-concept. This would be perceived as negative intent and a barrier to communication.

At one time in the development of the taxonomy it seemed that a middle and neutral level would be a perception of intent to ignore. A perception of being ignored, however, can be very damaging when it is interpreted as: You don't exist; or, You're not important. It does seem, however, that being ignored is somewhat less negative than active intent of injuring, so it will be included as a middle level, but tending toward the negative end of the continuum.

As with worldview, the eight combinations of two values each for the three perceived relationship components yield four levels of "FGH" (feelings, goals, and hierarchicalness). Combining FGH with three levels of "I" (perception of intent) yields 12 cells of perceived relationship and intent (PRI).

On inspection, 4 of the 12 cells are assumed to be empty sets. It seemed inconceivable, for example, that two persons who perceive each had positive feelings toward each other, shared compatible goals, and perceived themselves as equals could perceive the other's intent as harmful.

Only the most homogeneous cell and the most heterogeneous cell of the PRI matrix is used in the samples of full taxonomy. Those are labeled PRI_1 and PRI_2, respectively. (For further details on the development of these variables, refer to Sarbaugh, 1987.)

The description of those two cells is as follows: A perceived relationship and intent of PRI_1 would be persons who see themselves operating as equals with compatible goals and positive feelings toward one another and perceive their intent to be one of sharing and helping. A PRI_2 perception of relationship and intent would be persons who perceive themselves in a superior/subordinate relationship with negative feelings toward one another and incompatible goals and a perception of intent to injure or to harm.

LEVELS OF INTERCULTURALNESS

In the classification developed previously, there were 36 combinations created from the four variables. The two end categories in the continuum of interculturalness will be shown here to illustrate the pattern of combining and describing participants in a communication event. The capital letter and number designations will be given first, then the description will be given for that particular set of participants' characteristics.

The most homogeneous set for the least intercultural (i.e., most intracultural) communication event would be:

$$PRI_1 \quad CS_1 \quad KA_1 \quad WV_1$$

The participants in this set perceive themselves operating as equals, with compatible goals and positive feelings toward one another, and an intent of sharing with and helping the other. They share a common code system: and they each know and accept the normative patterns of beliefs and overt behaviors of the other. In addition, their views of the nature of life, purpose of life, and relation of humans to the cosmos are very similar.

The most heterogeneous sets of participants would be:

$$PRI_2 \quad CS_3 \quad KA_3 \quad WV_2$$

These designations show the largest subscripts, the most heterogeneous set. The description of the most heterogeneous set shows participants who perceived the other's intent as one of harming or injuring and a perceived relationship of superior/subordinate, incompatible goals, and negative feelings toward one another. They have no shared codes and they do not know one another's normative patterns of beliefs and overt behaviors and even if they knew them they would not accept the norms of the other; and they are at opposite poles in the worldview beliefs.

This is a condensed treatment of the development of the taxonomy that I created with help from numerous students and colleagues. The other 34 combinations developed in the original formulation suggest five intermediate levels of homogeneity/heterogeneity of participants in addition to the two ends of the continuum just described. Thus, there are seven levels of interculturalness of the communication events established by the 36 combinations of the variables in that original formulation. The levels were established by the sums of the subscripts of the variables in each combination. Those sums ranged from 4 for the most homogeneous to 10 for the most heterogeneous pair of participants.

CONCLUSION

The key notions of the taxonomy and some of the possible uses of it have been illustrated. It may be that its greatest use is heuristic in calling attention, in a different way than formerly, to some of the factors that influence intercultural communication. The key assumption on which it is based is that there is an *inter*dependence among the variables that operate in every communication setting.

My philosophies of life and of science would suggest that there is a uniqueness in every person and situation, as well as elements of similarity. This individual uniqueness leads me to claim that every communication event is to some degree intercultural. It is the elements of similarity that permit us to communicate as well as we do.

The main thesis I have attempted to develop in the taxonomy is that communication difficulty increases as the level of interculturalness increases; that is, as the participants are more heterogeneous along the dimensions presented. Finally, I have attempted to show that by using a taxonomic approach to conceptualize intercultural communication, we can more clearly anticipate where and why communication difficulties may occur. Kaplan (1964) states that every classification serves some purpose or other, but that what makes a concept significant is that the classification it denotes is one into which things fall "naturally."

It dramatizes the complexity of the judgments we make in assessing those with whom we seek to communicate. We must recognize that we make those judgments with or without the aid of some formal schema to guide us. In my experience with the taxonomy, I believe it focuses our attention on the differences among participants that may interfere with achieving the intended outcome in a transaction, so that we may improve our communication.

In evaluating theories, one might use as criteria the accuracy of predictions derived from the theory, the suggestiveness of the theory, and the parsimony of explanation. Accuracy of prediction is easy to state, but is not always easy to achieve in observable terms, wherein independent observers would reach the same conclusion. The explanations generated by the theory should lead to generalizations that have wide applicability; and if not wide applicability, they should make clear the conditions on which one may generalize. A good theory always should be suggestive of new relationships, new ways of looking at the phenomena in question. And of course, the economy of time and energy in using the theory is highly desirable.

The taxonomy is intended to stimulate questions about which sets of variables are most critical in producing what kind of outcomes in which situations, and questions about how we conceptualize intercultural communication. A taxonomy offers a mechanism for classifying and organizing a vast array of materials. It can help identify which variables one can control in the study situation and which variables one must assume are randomly distributed while seeking the effect of a specific variable or set of variables. Further, as it increases our awareness of the complexity of what we are studying and practicing, it can deter the tendency to spawn easy prescriptions for overcoming intercultural communication difficulties.

REFERENCES

Gantz, W. (1975). *The movement of taboos: A message oriented approach.* Unpublished manuscript, Michigan State University.

Harper, N. L. (1979). *Human communication theory.* Rochelle Park, NJ: Hayden.

Jevons, W. S. (1982). *The principles of science.* London.

Kaplan, A. (1964). *The conduct of inquiry.* San Francisco, CA: Chandler.

Kendler, H. H., & Tracy, S. (1968). Concept formation. In *International encyclopedia of the social sciences* (Vol. 14, pp. 206-211). New York: Macmillan/Free Press.

Kroeber, A. L., & Kluckhohn, C. (1952). *Culture: A critical review of concepts and definitions.* Cambridge, MA: Harvard University Press.

Roe, R., C., Lumanata, M. F., & Sarbaugh, L. E. (1985). A taxonomic approach to world view as a sensitizing concept in the process of intercultural communication: A comparison of two data sets. *Michigan Association of Speech Communication Journal, 20*(1), 1-14.

Sarbaugh, L. E. (1987). *Intercultural communication* (rev. ed.). New Brunswick, NJ: Transaction.

II

CULTURE AND MEANING

3

A Constructivist Theory
of Communication and Culture

JAMES L. APPLEGATE ● HOWARD E. SYPHER ●
University of Kentucky

This chapter offers general tenets that the authors believe should guide approaches to inter- and cross-cultural communication. A review of constructivist communication theory and research to date is presented. Implication of this interpretive theory for study of cultural influences on communication and social perception are discussed. Directions suggested by the theory for training also are presented.

Essays forwarding a theoretical framework for studying culture and communication embody assumptions about the nature of theory, the relation of theory and research, the nature of culture and communication, and even differential valuing of alternative modes of communication. Conflicts between theories over these types of assumptions cannot (or at least are unlikely to be) resolved through direct empirical testing. The relative merit of such sets of assumptions as a basis for the construction of theory must be established in rational arguments among members of the scientific community. In the following section we present the general assumptions we believe should guide us in constructing theory-based cultural research programs. An outline follows of a constructivist approach to cultural communication studies embodying these assumptions.

ASSUMPTIONS OF AN INTERPRETIVE APPROACH
TO COMMUNICATION AND CULTURE

First, we argue that what is needed is not a theory of intercultural, cross-cultural, or interracial communication, but at base, a coherent theory of communication whose focus of convenience encompasses the impact of historically emergent forms of group life on the various forms and functions of everyday communication. If theories give no clear, independent conceptualization of the core features of communication, attempts to compare communication across cultural communities are doomed to produce amorphous research results. Researchers are left with little guidance in deciding what to call communication, in generating expectations for which of the myriad facets of cultural life might be expected to influence communication, or for how they would do so. The result is atheoretical variable analysis: a particularly damaging practice in current cross-cultural research. Haphazard selection of variables on which to compare cultural practices has threatened the coherence and heuristic value of this research (see Blumer, 1969; Delia, 1977; Gudykunst, 1985; Sarbaugh, 1979).

Second, we argue that our theories should be interpretive in nature. They should embody a philosophical anthropology that treats people as active interpreters of their social environment: one that rejects determinism and recognizes the falsity of the nature/nurture dichotomy (Furth, 1973; Overton, 1973; Spiro, 1951). Interpretive theories should focus upon the interpenetration of the developing symbolic capacities of human organisms and the historical structures of culture within which the former emerge (Applegate & Delia, 1980; see especially, Manicas, 1980).

Third, following from this interpretive focus we argue that research methods arising from such theories should provide dense and detailed accounts of the everyday interactions of cultural participants. Intimate involvement in the specifics of communication offers the best hope for elaboration and validation of theoretical abstractions that speak to the generic within them. As Geertz (1973) argues,

> Our double task is to uncover the conceptual structures that inform our subjects' acts, the "said" of social discourse, and to construct a system of analysis in whose terms what is generic to those structures. . . will stand out against the other determinants of human behavior. . . . The office of theory is to provide a vocabulary in which what symbolic action has to say about itself—that is about the role of culture in human life—can be expressed. (Geertz, 1973, p. 27)

In short, if we are to assume that people are active interpreters, then we must focus upon their interpretations. It is there that the culture we seek to explain is created and maintained. However, we hasten to add that although the logic of constructivism demands use of methods that naturally capture cultural participants' first-order constructions of reality, it does not preclude the use of a variety of more structured methods of data collection and analysis. This methodological point and the general commitment of constructivism to a reflective empiricism is addressed in detail later.

Fourth, we argue that the focus of our study should not be exclusively, or even primarily, upon comparative studies of cultures, but upon the nature of the relationship between culture and communication. Hence, we forward constructivism as an approach to cultural communication studies rather than to inter- or cross-cultural communication. Comparative studies can throw light on this relationship. They have practical value in explaining and reducing specific problems in encounters between individuals from different cultures. However, to wed studies primarily to comparisons of specific similarities and differences between cultures is to omit the central issue: the relationship between culture and communication (Gudykunst, 1985; Price-Williams, 1980; Sarbaugh, 1979).

Fifth, interpretive approaches to culture and communication need not, and probably should not, adopt a relativist ethical stance in assessing the quality of communication across cultures. Understanding cultural communication systems on their own terms does not prevent us from making "better-worse" arguments. A focus on intercultural studies makes researchers especially sensitive to the never-ending process of weeding our intellectual gardens of ethnocentrism and bias. Nevertheless value arguments should be made and ethical dialogue encouraged if the fear of having biases exposed is not to drive scholars into relativist or nihilist positions. Interpretive theories display the reflexive nature of theory and reality. Interpretive theorists know that a value-free science is impossible. We argue that a value-less science is undesirable if not dangerous. Ethical issues are being raised. More dialogue is needed (see Paige & Martin, 1983; the work of Habermas is relevant, see McCarthy's 1982 review of Habermas's critical theory of communication, especially pp. 272-357).

Sixth, and finally, theory and training should be linked more closely. Embedded in each conception of communication are implications for communication training to enhance the quality of communication generally and intercultural communication specifically. Little constructivist training research has been done to date. We suggest a framework to encourage such research. It is more than appropriate to ask what directions our theories provide us in efforts to enhance the quality of communication across cultures.

Our assumptions can be summarized as follows:

Assumption 1: A theory of communication that focuses on the impact of historically emergent forms of group life on everyday communication is necessary.

Assumption 2: The theory should be interpretive.

Assumption 3: Dense and detailed accounts of everyday interactions of cultural participants are needed.

Assumption 4: The focus of study should be the relationship between culture and communication.

Assumption 5: Value arguments should be made.

Assumption 6: Theory and training should be linked closely.

Having unpacked this much of the assumptive baggage with which we approach the study of the relationships between culture and communication, we now turn to an outline of a constructivist approach to cultural communication studies that builds on these foundations.

A CONSTRUCTIVIST THEORY OF COMMUNICATION

As an approach to the study of communication, constructivism has given central attention to the impact of stable individual differences in social perception processes on development and use of "person-centered" communication behavior: behaviors that recognize and adapt to the autonomy and individuality of other persons in the strategic pursuit of communicative goals (e.g., persuasion, information transmission, comforting, identity management). Constructivist study of social perception is grounded in an integration of George Kelly's personal construct theory (Kelly, 1955) with a Wernerian conception of development (Werner, 1959; Werner & Kaplan, 1963). Communication behavior has been studied using the same developmental logic integrated with symbolic interactionist (Blumer, 1969), sociolinguistic (Bernstein, 1975; Hymes, 1971, 1972, 1974), and rhetorical (Clark & Delia, 1979) concepts. The result of this conceptual integration is a theory of social cognitive and communication development that approaches both from a pragmatic, goal-centered perspective.

As a developmental theory, constructivism embraces the view that development, both social cognitive and communicative, is domain specific and follow Werner's (1957) "orthogenetic" principle: "Wherever development occurs it proceeds from a state of relative globality and lack of differentiation to a state of increasing differentiation, articulation, and hierarchic integration" (p. 126). Werner's theory of development extends Kelly's analysis of the change that occurs in perceptual and behavioral systems with experience and accommodation to the environment.

Differences in the quality of social cognitive schema used to understand people and situations are indexed hierarchically to reflect increasing complexity in organization. While recognizing the multiple forms that schema may take (causal, temporal, spatial) constructivist research has focused on Kelly's theory of bipolar constructs to assess differences in the schema people use to understand other people. Specifically, constructivist researchers have measured the complexity, abstractness, and integration of interpersonal constructs as an antecedent to the construction of more sophisticated communication messages. Since constructivism's central concern has been the relation of interpersonal constructs to communication, we first address the conception of communication. (For reviews reflecting the historical emergence of the theory presented here, see Applegate & Delia, 1980; Burleson, 1987; Clark & Delia, 1979; Delia, 1976, 1977; Delia, O'Keefe, & O'Keefe, 1982.)

Communication as Pragmatic Action

Most basically, constructivism defines communication as occurring when two or more people, with a mutually recognized intention to share, exchange messages. Moreover, that sharing process is goal driven. The organization and quality of the verbal and nonverbal behavior employed in that sharing process can be seen fruitfully as a rationally organized means to some end.

"Rational" here does not mean logical in any formal sense of the word. Rather it means rational in terms of the goals embodied in social situations. To say actors are rational is simply to say they do what they think will accomplish those goals as they understand them. Actors are not always aware of their goals. Sociolinguistic research has documented the fruitfulness of explaining the organization of communication behavior around culturally induced goals of which actors have little or no situated awareness. (For an elaboration of this "rational goals analysis" model of communication, see Brown & Levinson, 1979; O'Keefe, 1988.) This conception of communication has focused constructivist research on identification of central communicative goals and toward development of hierarchic coding systems identifying developmental differences in the quality of communication strategies employed by actors to accomplish goals.

The goals of communication are given in the form and content of typical situational definitions. The concept of the "definition of the situation" as originated in the works of W. I. Thomas (1927, 1928) and elaborated by symbolic interactionist researchers in sociology has influenced heavily the constructivist conception of the organization of communication behavior. Clark and Delia (1979) argue that actors' definitions suggest three important types of goals organizing communication behavior. These are *identity goals* (actors attempt to manage their own and other's identities in the interaction), *relational goals* (organizing the negotiation of such issues as intimacy and dominance) and a variety of *instrumental goals* (e.g., persuasion, comforting, information transmission).

Following this conceptualization of the goal structure for communicative action, researchers have developed a variety of systems for indexing developmental differences in the quality of strategies employed by communicators to (a) manage the identity of others (Applegate, 1982a; Hale, 1986; Kline, 1981a, 1981b, 1982; Leichty & Applegate, 1987), (b) pursue relational goals (Applegate, 1980a; Applegate & Leichty, 1984; Clark, 1979), (c) persuade (Applegate, 1982b; Clark & Delia, 1977; Delia & Clark, 1977; Delia, Burleson, & Kline, 1979; O'Keefe & Delia, 1979), (d) regulate behavior (Applegate, 1980b; Applegate, Burleson, Burke, Delia, & Kline, 1985; Applegate & Delia, 1980), and (e) comfort distressed others (Applegate, et al., 1985; Burleson, 1982a, 1982b, 1983a, 1983b, 1984a, 1984b). Strategic communicative behavior in these contexts is indexed hierarchically to reflect increasing complexity in message behavior.

Message complexity is reflected in the number and types of goals pursued, as well as the situational variables accounted for in the message (including recognition and adaptation to the wants, needs, and dispositions of others), and so on. For example, one message might attempt to persuade another to alter behavior through addressing multiple objections to the proposal held by the person being persuaded, positing advantages tied to his or her specific wants and, at the same time, carefully avoiding threatening the self-image of the person being persuaded. Another simpler message, addressing the same goal, might simply state the persuader's wants as reasons for compliance or invoke a rule that the persuader assumes should govern behavior in the situation. The former message reflects a more differentiated sense of goals present in the situation (persuasive and identity goals) and addresses more communication-relevant features of the situation (in this case the objections and desires of the person being persuaded). Hence, the former message would be indexed as more developmentally advanced. More sophisticated message behavior of this type generally requires speakers to recognize other persons' perspectives and to exploit communication as a means of negotiating the definition of social situations between persons. This more complex message behavior has been labeled "person-centered" communication (Applegate & Delia, 1980; Burleson, 1987). "Person-centeredness" represents a general quality of communication with a variety of separable aspects: (a) the extent to which a message is responsive to the aims and utterances of one's interactional partner, (b) the extent to which a message is adapted or tailored so as to meet the specific characteristics and needs of a particular listener, (c) the extent to which the topic or content of a message deals with persons and their psychological and affective qualities, (d) the extent to which a message implicitly seeks to enhance interpersonal relationships or create positive interpersonal identities, and (e) the extent to which a message encourages reflection by another about his or her circumstance or situation (Applegate, Burke, Burleson, Delia, & Kline, 1985). Person-centered communication reflects an integration of process-oriented communication competencies. Klemp (1979) and Dinges (1983) argue that approaches to intercultural communication competence should focus on such integrative definitions as well as multiple behavioral indicators of such an integration.

Constructivist use of developmentally ordered hierarchic systems tapping these qualities clearly has documented consistent individual differences in the person-centered quality of strategies produced. Clear relations have been drawn between such differences and differences in the quality of the interpersonal construct systems.

The Role of Interpersonal Constructs:
Prediction with a Purpose

As may or may not be obvious at this point, constructivist researchers in communication have altered the basic "person-as-scientist" metaphor common in current social science research. People do operate at times like scientists, seeking to make the blooming, buzzing confusion of reality predictable. Often however, and especially in the interpersonal domain, their inferences and behavior are aimed less at predicting or even understanding self and others than they are designed to accomplish individual or situation-induced goals. O'Keefe (1984) argues for a conception of people as "tool-makers" rather than as scientists (although recognizing our lay person goals may be sciencelike at times). Constructs and communication strategies are key tools in efforts to build bridges from aspirations to accomplishments.

When people respond to other people they typically are less concerned with understanding why others behave as they do (to allow prediction) than in understanding the immediate implications of the behavior for goal accomplishment. Often the goal is simply to respond appropriately and keep the conversation on track. In such situations, people are less "personality theorists" than they are carpenters striving to find the right tools to build and maintain a desirable social environment.

The relation of constructs to communication is the construct's role in generating communication- and goal-relevant beliefs that form the person's definition of the situation. These guide his or her strategic behavior. Differences in the development of constructs are expected to affect what actors define as goals and goal-relevant features of situations. The use of constructs is pragmatically driven: Constructs, like communication strategies, are tools of sociality.

Obviously, some situations require more diligent toolmaking than others. Goals, plans, and strategies are reflexively related to situational definitions through communication. That is, situational definitions generate expectations that help form goals and plans. Communication creates, maintains, or changes situational definitions through the process of emergence (McHugh, 1968; Mead, 1932). However, many situations are extremely routine. Communication is dominated by conventional goals and plans "given" to actors. It is in such situations that the influence of culture and cultural differences on communication is most evident. However, because these conventions are so implicit and routine, intercultural communicators often are unaware of the differences distorting communication.

ANALYZING IMPLICIT CULTURAL COMMUNICATION THEORIES

Sociolinguists have argued that human groups develop linguistic rules at the semantic and pragmatic levels that encourage particular ways of forming and organizing social relationships (i.e., communicating). These rules are seen as organized within "sociolinguistic codes" characterizing particular "speech communities" (e.g., Bernstein, 1975; Gumperz, 1982). Much of the theoretical and empirical analysis in this area is compatible with the logic of contructivism. However, for reasons elaborated elsewhere (e.g., the concept neglects the role of individual psychological processes in communication), constructivist theory avoids use of the "code" concept as traditionally employed. Rather, cultural influences are seen as organized within implicit cultural communication theories. Through socialization, the theory is incorporated actively as an implicit feature of individual worldviews. It is visible in much the same way as one may see the influence of a dominant theory of art embedded in the individual creative works of its period. Cultural rules, conventions, or codes serve as resources in actors' pursuit of implicit and explicit goals. In routine contexts they may be sufficient to the task. Even in these contexts, and certainly in problematic ones, we do best to conceive of cultural prescriptions as used rather than followed (Applegate & Delia, 1980; Jacobs, 1985).

The order of the presentation of foci for research investigating the effect of implicit cultural communication theories on situated communication presented next is dictated by the logical relationship of communication goals, strategic action, and cognition within constructivist theory. However, we subscribe to a modified version of Geertz's (1973) argument that

> one can start anywhere in a culture's repertoire of [communication-relevant] forms and end up anywhere else. One can stay . . . within a single, more or less bounded form, and circle steadily within it. One can move between forms in search of broader unities or informing contrasts. One can even compare forms from different cultures to define their character in reciprocal relief. But whatever the level at which one operates, and however intricately, the guiding principle is the same: societies, like lives, contain their own interpretations. One has only to learn how to gain access to them. (pp. 453)

A goal of research is to make available the nature of and relationship between communication-relevant forms (e.g., goals and strategic action schemes) defined in implicit cultural communication theories implicitly shared by cultural participants. Ultimately, comparisons can be offered of implicit cultural communication theories along dimensions derived from the logic of comparative developmental analysis.

Cultural Influences on the Logic of Communication

In addition to providing the rules, schemas, scripts, and values used in communication, cultures most basically define the logic of communication itself. The latter definition dictates what among all that is social is communication-relevant. Previous research already has shown relations between cultural background and an orientation to person-centered communication. If people must accommodate to a system in which communication is valued as a means of bridging the gap between individual differences and negotiating individual realities, then these people will develop interpersonal schemas and strategic abilities to be successfully social within such an individualistic worldview.

Other more traditional cultural communication systems value conventions and rules as the basis for communication. Within such systems, successful, competent communication is not that which best negotiates individual differences. Rather good communication is "appropriate" communication: communication that successfully enacts the correct cultural conventions. Value orientations such as these are central to a recent and provocative account of the relation of constructs and communication offered by O'Keefe (1988).

O'Keefe (1988) has begun work identifying the different "design logics" embedded in people's communication messages. She is attempting to tie these logics to underlying cultural value orientations for communication and social relations. Such research holds promise for understanding the relation between social perception and communication against the broader backdrop of cultural values and socialization practices.

Cultural Influences on the Goals and Strategic Organization of Action

Cultural communication theories also influence communication by defining the important goals of communication and the most appropriate strategic means of accomplishing those functions. As noted, Clark and Delia (1979) have identified three general types of goals informing the topoi of communication: identity, relational, and instrumental. Halliday (1973, 1978) also argues that language is conceptualized best as a resource capable of use in accomplishing a variety of potential objectives. Halliday and others in sociolinguistics offer their own taxonomies of the major functions guiding human action (also see Bernstein, 1975; Hymes, 1974). A selective list is presented next:

personal/relational	elaborating subjective feelings, motives, needs; negotiating conflicts in perspectives; achieving intimacy, support, dominance

regulative/control	effecting change in others' thinking and behavior
referential	describing objects and objectives relationships in the external world
imaginative	experimenting with language for the sheer enjoyment of creating new ways of seeing the world
identity management	creating a desired self-image; altercasting others

Investigations of such language uses across cultures will enlarge our understanding of the potential objectives of action and the types of strategies that are employed to accomplish them. However, a taxonomy of major functions should not be open to infinite growth (especially when focused on functions emerging across cultures) if we closely tie analyses to situated action. Such a contention is based on the assumption that there is something out there called a social order that is not random and is amenable to abstraction and typification.

Creation of such taxonomies within and across cultures enables us to translate the notion that communication is multifunctional into a powerful analytic tool for strategy analysis "since assumed or already negotiated aspects of social reality culture can be seen as taken for granted . . . constraints upon strategy selection" (Clark & Delia, 1979, p. 199). In analyzing these constraints, we are about the business of unpacking another part of a culture's implicit communication theory. We begin to answer such questions as: What goals of action are most valued by the culture? Are goals differentially valued across social/institutional contexts within the culture? What types of strategies are deemed most appropriate for the accomplishment of particular goals? How do our answers to these questions differ across cultures? What are the implications of such differences for communication across cultures?

Comparative developmental analyses could be done not only of cultural differences in the types of goals valued but also in the degree to which communication is defined as a multifunctional activity in routine cultural definitions of strategies. Cultures may provide and encourage more or less complex situational definitions, including a more complex goal structure. A logical outcome of such differences would be greater or lesser *behavioral complexity* in situated communication. Culture also should influence the level of integration of multiple goals (e.g., identity, relational, instrumental). Cultures may encourage strategies that are not only more sophisticated in their individual logics for accomplishing particular goals (e.g., more person-centered in quality), but also reflect a more sophisticated integration of multiple goals. In short, culture is one factor contributing to the construction of messages that do more or less "work" in social situations. (For examples of work pursuing this line of reasonings, see O'Keefe, 1984; O'Keefe & Delia, 1982; O'Keefe, Murphy, Meyers, & Babrow, 1983; O'Keefe & Shepherd, 1982, 1987; Shepherd & O'Keefe, 1985).

Evidence of cultural influence also can be found in the rules organizing goal-directed interaction. Many such interactions do not represent instances of communication, as that process has been defined here (e.g., the coordination of driving behavior at a busy intersection). Such interactions are certainly worth study and may even be useful in explaining related communicative interactions (e.g., the interaction between two drivers after colliding at the intersection). The focus of constructivist analysis is upon interactions of the latter type. Uncovering consistencies in the nature and hierarchic structuring of rules for communication within a cultural community defines yet another important avenue of cultural influence on communication.

The impact of culture on communication in the form of constraints imposed by rules needs little elaboration here. A variety of positions in communication and sociology have generated a corpus of such rules (e.g., see Cicourel, 1974; Cronen, Chen, & Pearce, this volume; Pearce & Cronen, 1980; Pearce & Wiseman, 1983; Shimanoff, 1980; Wiseman, 1980). Constructivist logic embraces the findings of research identifying particular cultural rules but suggests that the conceptualization of culture as a system of rules is inadequate. Jacob's (1985) analysis is informative here. He convincingly argues a conventional rule-based logic cannot capture (a) the ways actors infer beyond the information given to achieve coherence, (b) generate new patterns of communication, and (c) organize communication functionally (also see Kreckel, 1981). Cultural rules must be seen as resources or constraints that serve both topoi and stasis functions in the pragmatic enterprise of communication.

Cultural Influences on Cognitive Schemes

In fully elaborating an implicit cultural communication theory's influence on individuals' communication, we must include investigations of shared qualities of the cognitive schemes employed by cultural participants to place and organize events within larger contexts of meaning and expectation. As noted, these schemas are the grounding from which particular situational definitions and communication emerge.

Constructivist research to date articulates a complex picture of the nature of cognitive schemes within the interpersonal domain, the course of their structural development, and their impact on strategic action and communication. This work and, more generally, analyses of cognitive schemes provided by schema theorists in psychology (Schank & Abelson, 1977; Sorentino & Higgins, 1986) provide a rich conceptual base to generate what Frake (1969) calls "ethnographies of cognitive systems," particularly of the interpersonal cognitive subsystem (Frake, 1969; for a review see Bock, 1980; Casson, 1983).

Frake's (1969) work and that of others in the area of cognitive anthropology and ethnosemantics offer a starting point for research on cognitive systems. Frake suggests that such ethnographies should include a focus on the differentiation and hierarchic integration of such schemes and argues that such schemes may be fruitfully seen as "contrast sets," a notion very similar to the constructivist conception of a "construct."

Analyses of culture's influence on cognition should include ethnographies outlining the typical structure and quality (i.e., degree of differentiation, integration, abstractness) of cognitive systems. In addition, *content* analysis of schemes employed in particular social domains (e.g., interpersonal, moral, political) may be useful in assessing the impact of culturally shared features of cognition on communication. Casson (1983) reviews research identifying cultural schemata defining (a) object classification systems, (b) events, (c) spatial relations, (d) metaphors, and (e) narrative discourse. More research is needed directly examining the context, structures, and use of clearly communication-relevant cultural schemata (e.g., Ehrenhaus, 1983).

METHODOLOGICAL PRIORITIES

To this point we have focused upon constructivism's philosophical and theoretical underpinnings. We have suggested several substantive questions about the impact of culture on communication to be addressed with this perspective and sought to identify other compatible positions. As all such theoretical discussions must, this one has implied certain methodological priorities.

Wedding Theory and Methodology

Some scholars have viewed constructivism and its tenets as a radical departure from traditional research practices (Miller & Berger, 1978).

However, constructivists endorse many of the canons of traditional research practice. For example, it seems less than radical to contend, as this position does, that one's theory be based upon a firm and consistent philosophical foundation, or that one's research practices and preferences be guided by one's theoretical orientation (Delia, 1977).

Constructivism has been criticized for an overreliance upon free response data collection techniques and interpretive codings methods in its analyses of communicative behavior. However, it should be clear, given the conceptual framework outlined, that such methods are consistent extensions of the theory. They provide a rich understanding of respondents' categories for interpreting the world (rather than the researcher's). However, the position does not require rejection of more structured techniques of analysis.

Delia (1978) has called constructivist methodology "reflective empiricism":

> Such an orientation to research calls on the researcher to become as self aware as possible of the ordering principles embedded in his questions and research tools while recognizing the necessity for commitment to particular points of view and methods in learning anything about the empirical world. (p. 3)

Clearly, constructivism does not reject traditional social science methods (although constructivists have been highly critical of methodological abuses). Constructivists have for some time called upon researchers to recognize the ideological and theoretical assumptions embedded within research questions and procedures. A similar concern has been voiced by scholars who point out the Western bias pervading most intercultural communication research and methodology. However, recognition of this shortcoming does not require that we abandon the techniques and procedures we have been trained to use. Indeed, the realization that our methodological biases need continual reexamination encourages the self-reflection that produces fruitful research.

Methodological Appropriateness

The major methodological question confronting us is not whether to use a method, but which method is the most appropriate for the task at hand. It appears obvious to most that standardized questionnaires developed in one culture are typically not appropriate in another.

Further, one would expect different cultures to value different forms of communication. What methods are appropriate? This requires that we ask, "What is the question?" Some concerns call for psychometric considerations, some for the creation of specific rating scales, others for subject-guided and subject-provided elicitations, whereas naturalistic observation is best suited for others. Constructivist research to date has used a variety of methodological strategies, including experimental manipulations, interaction analysis techniques, naturalistic observation, and standard psychometric test construction methods (see the reviews of Applegate, et al., 1985; Burleson, 1987; Delia, O'Keefe, & O'Keefe, 1982). There has been an overt preference for naturalistic and free-response data collection techniques. This methodological preference lies at the core of constructivists' beliefs about the way that research should be conducted. What is important about these approaches is that a more spontaneous response is elicited. This response is more closely representative of the real-world responses that we seek to generalize. However, constructivists do not advocate "data without structure." Instead, as Delia points out, "the issue is not whether to introduce structure or not, but how much to introduce, when to introduce it in the research process, and the ends to which it is introduced" (Delia, 1978). To date, constructivist researchers have shown a clear preference for using theoretically grounded coding schemes adapted to the emergent quality of respondents' conceptualizations and accounts.

Another major advantage of free response data collection is its flexibility. That is, free response data can be coded in a number of different ways. For example, in one instance, the same data base served in studying strategic elaboration of messages and in establishing the independence of cognitive complexity and loquacity. This type of data lends itself easily to multiple analyses and questions (e.g., Applegate & Delia, 1980; Burleson, Applegate, & Neuwirth, 1981).

What we suggest is that systematic programs of research are hindered if one severs theoretical issues from methodological issues. We believe that such concerns are especially valid in the intercultural context, in which methodology has often preceded theory development (Gudykunst, 1985). Method, theory, and research are interdependent considerations.

Intercultural research especially requires familiarity with the object of study. Lacking such familiarity, researchers are prone to use their own implicit theories of culture. Unfortunately, one often finds that these implicit theories bear only superficial resemblance to the culture being studied. Many central questions about the form and function of communication in differing cultures are just not immediately amenable to investigation with standardized data analysis techniques.

IMPLICATIONS FOR TRAINING AND EDUCATION

Advances in intercultural education and training must be based on advances in our theoretical understanding of the relation of culture and communication. To date the vast majority of training in this area has been atheoretical. However, the lack of theory development in this area should not be of enormous concern. It is no worse here than in other more established areas of training such as human relations, leadership, or general communication skills. That is not to say that the role of theory does not need more attention.

We have emphasized to this point the influence of culture on communication. However, as Samovar, Porter, and Jain (1981) point out, culture can and does change in response to contact with other cultures, particularly when that contact is in the form of education and training programs designed to alter communication practices. Such programs, without ties to a coherent theory, are blind to conflicts in values and worldviews implied by differences between established cultural communication patterns and the innovations introduced by educational programs. Narrow education of this sort may do violence to the integrity of the culture, damage the ability of those trained to maintain identification with their culture, and are unlikely to succeed in effecting meaningful cultural change, even if that is deemed desirable.

Constructivism offers a coherent theoretical base for intercultural educational programs. Grounded in developmental logic, constructivism is committed to hierarchic distinctions in the quality of communication behavior. Hierarchies used have indexed differences in the person-centered quality of communication and more recently in the behavioral complexity and goal integration reflected in situated communication (for examples of the latter work, see O'Keefe, 1984; O'Keefe & Delia, 1982; O'Keefe et al., 1983; O'Keefe & Shepherd, 1982, 1987; Shepherd, 1987; Shepherd & O'Keefe, 1985).

This framework obviously suggests the possibility of training practices to enhance person-centered communication, strategic complexity, multiple goal integration, and so on. The immediate caveat, of course, is that these qualities may or may not be appropriate to encourage in certain cultures.

Conceptually, however, the basic outcome of communication development as defined in the logic of this theory is not a particular form of communication. Development produces process competency, enhancing communicators' ability to flexibly adapt to situations through accessing strategies at multiple levels. For this reason, training enhancing the specific qualities of communication identified in constructivist theory seems particularly appropriate for intercultural education. Flexibility in accommodating to different environmental demands is essential to effective communication across cultural boundaries.

While very limited in scope, and not intercultural in focus, some constructivist research does suggest connections between communication development and certain important outcome variables. Sypher and Zorn (1986), in an impressive longitudinal study, have demonstrated clear relations between construct system development, persuasive communication ability and upward mobility in the corporate setting. Person-centered communication also has been related to more effective leadership in organizational settings (Husband, 1981). Two studies of health care organizations indicate person-centered communication by health care professionals is tied to important health outcome variables including patient compliance (Kasch, 1984; Kline & Ceropski, 1984).

The use of person-centered persuasive and comforting communication strategies is related to the formation of more complex, abstract impressions of speakers using these strategies (Applegate, 1982, 1983; Samter, Burleson, & Basden, 1985). Initial efforts to assess the impact of person-centered parenting communication suggest the person-centered quality of that communication is an important antecedent to social development in children (Applegate et al., 1985; Burleson, 1983a; Delia, Burleson, & Kline, 1979; Jones, Delia, & Clark, 1981; Sarver, 1976).

Individual differences in person-centered communication ability among children are related to peer acceptance in childhood (Burleson, 1986; Burleson, et al., 1986). Children's use of more person-centered persuasive communication affects the willingness of their peers to engage in sharing behavior (Burleson & Fennelly, 1981).

Although this research on outcomes is limited to North American cultural contexts, the research suggests the fruitfulness of extending the constructivist research program into training. Training studies should identify procedures that enhance children's and adult's social perception and person-centered communication skills. Developmental researchers in psychology are paying increasing attention to identifying training procedures that enhance social perception and communication skills in children (see reviews in Dickson, 1981). There also is a substantial body of extant literature on adult communication competence (see the review in Spitzberg & Cupach, 1984). Constructivist research has been much more successful than research in either of these two areas in identifying specific features of social cognition and communication that develop in related and systematic ways. It is, in fact, this specificity that has enabled constructivists to draw consistent linkages between social cognition and communication (Applegate et al., 1985). This same specificity should provide a solid foundation for the development of intercultural training. Clark (e.g., Clark, Willinghanz, & O'Dell, 1985) is pursuing a fruitful line of research at the University of Illinois in developing theory-based training programs.

Future research aimed at developing and assessing the effectiveness of intercultural training should build upon the pragmatic conception of communication embodied in constructivist theory. Such programs could (a) first, and most basically, encourage a view of communication as a rhetorical resource for the negotiation of alternative social realities; a pragmatic rule-using rather than rule-following activity (O'Keefe, 1988), (b) enhance awareness of the goals of communication and the differential valuing of those goals across cultures; (c) encourage development of integrative strategies to address multiple goals; (d) enhance understanding and accessibility of the various levels of strategies available to accomplish goals (flexibility and synchrony should be key concepts guiding training in strategy selection and use); (e) aid in identification of communication-relevant scripts, routines, and common situational definitions (e.g., key speech events) to provide adequate substantive background knowledge to communicators (see Forgas, this volume); and finally (f) enhance the complexity and organization of construct/schema employed to perceive cultural and individual differences in perspectives to enhance perspective-taking skill.

These foci are offered as particularly appropriate directions for future research aimed at developing intercultural training programs using constructivist theory. Again, little has been done to apply constructivist concepts to intercultural training. The theory does hold promise, we believe, given its success in identifying and explaining specific key developments in communication behavior tied to significant social outcomes.

The implications of our position for the study of culture and communication are summarized in the following propositions:

Proposition 1: Communication is goal driven, but actors are not always aware of their goals.

Proposition 2: Strategic communicative behavior is indexed hierarchically to reflect increasing complexity in behavior.

Proposition 3: Person-centered communication reflects an integration of process-oriented communication competencies.

Proposition 4: The influence of culture on communication is most evident in situations in which conventional goals and plans are "given" to actors, but since conventions are implicit and routine; intercultural communicators often are unaware of the differences distorting communication.

Proposition 5: Cultural communication theories are learned through socialization.

Proposition 6: Cultural prescriptions are used rather than followed.

Proposition 7: Culture defines the logic of communication.

Proposition 8: Cultures differentially value communication goals and alternative strategies for reaching these goals.

Proposition 9: Cultural communication theories specify how to place and organize events within larger contexts of meaning and elaboration.

Proposition 10: Intercultural training should focus on developing flexible and integrative strategic means for accomplishing goals.

CONCLUSION

We have presented an outline of a constructivist approach to cultural communication studies. Some current research has successfully applied the theory to the study of specific cultural/situational antecedents to communication development and communication performance (Applegate, 1980b; Applegate & Delia, 1980; Applegate, Coyle, Seibert, & Church, 1987; Jones, Delia, & Clark, 1981; Leichty & Applegate, 1987). The logic of the position allows for, and in fact demands, analyses that abstract from situated communication those shared qualities linked to forms of cultural organization constituting the central interpretive challenge to the developing individual. The general success of applications of constructivist theory to a wide variety of other communication issues argues for its status as a sound general communication theory on which to ground cultural communication studies. Our hope is that this outline will aid in the formulation of theory-based research and training programs designed to enhance flexible, adaptive communication.

Constructivism grants a central role to culture in the process of individuals' social cognitive and communicative development. This essay elaborates how that role may be studied and how differences in the substance of implicit cultural communication theories may be assessed in terms of their influence on the quality of communication within and across cultural boundaries.

This volume reflects an ongoing commitment to theoretical self consciousness by researchers interested in culture and communication. We recognize the need to step back and survey the various theoretical positions available to us: to assess the assumptions they make, the conception of communication they forward, and the foci for cultural research they suggest. This process will aid in the production of programs of theory-based research from a variety of perspectives, providing us with a sound basis for future judgments of the relative usefulness, scope, parsimony, and precision of explanations provided by various theories. Such an approach is essential if we hope to provide any sort of coherent understanding of the "terrible complexity" characterizing the relationship of culture and communication. We must "descend into detail, past misleading tags, past the metaphysical types, past the empty similarities to grasp firmly the essential character of not only the various cultures but the various sorts of individuals within each culture" (Geertz, 1973, p. 53).

REFERENCES

Applegate, J. L. (1980a). Adaptive communication in educational contexts: A study of teachers' communicative strategies. *Communication Education, 29,* 158-170.

Applegate, J. L. (1980b). Person-and position-centered communication in a daycare center. In N. K. Denzin (Ed.), *Studies in symbolic interaction* (Vol. 3, pp. 59-96). Greenwich, CT: JAI.

Applegate, J. L. (1982a, February). *Construct system development and identity-management skills in persuasive contexts.* Paper presented at the Western Speech Communication Association Convention, Denver.

Applegate, J. L. (1982b). The impact of construct system development on communication and impression formation in persuasive contexts. *Communication Monographs, 49,* 277-289.

Applegate, J. L., Burke, J. A., Burleson, B. R., Delia, J. G., & Kline, S. L. (1985). Reflection-enhancing parental communication. In I. E. Sigel (Ed.), *Parental belief systems: The psychological consequences for children* (pp. 107-142). Hillsdale, NJ: Lawrence Erlbaum.

Applegate, J. L., Coyle, K., Seibert, J. H., & Church, S. (1987, August). *Interpersonal constructs and communicative ability in a police environment.* Paper presented at the Seventh International Congress on Personal Construct Psychology, Memphis.

Applegate, J. L., & Delia, J. G. (1980). Person-centered speech, psychological development, and the contexts of language usage. In R. St. Clair & H. Giles (Eds.), *The social and psychological contexts of language* (pp. 245-282). Hillsdale, NJ: Lawrence Erlbaum.

Applegate, J. L., & Leichty, G. (1984) Managing interpersonal relationships: Social cognitive and strategic determinants of competence. In R. N. Bostrom (Ed.), *Competence in communication* (pp. 33-55). Beverly Hills, CA: Sage.

Bernstein, B. (1975). *Class, codes, and control: Theoretical studies toward a sociology of language* (rev. ed.) New York: Schocken.

Blumer, H. (1969). *Symbolic interactionism: Perspective and method.* Englewood, Cliffs, NJ: Prentice-Hall.

Bock, P. K. (1980). *Continuities in psychological anthropology.* San Francisco: W. H. Freeman.

Brown, P., & Levinson (1978). Universals in language usage. In E. N. Goody (Ed.), *Questions and politeness* (pp. 56-289). Cambridge: Cambridge University Press.

Burleson, B. R. (1982a). The development of comforting communication skills in childhood and adolescence. *Child Development, 53,* 1578-1588.

Burleson, B. R. (1982b). The affective perspective-taking process: A test of Turiel's role-taking model. In M. Burgoon (Ed.), *Communication yearbook (Vol. 6, pp. 473-488). Beverly Hills, CA: Sage.*

Burleson, B. R. (1983a). *Interactional antecedents of social reasoning development: Interpreting the effects of parent discipline on children. In D. Zarefsky, M. O. Sillars, & J. R. Rhodes (Ed.), Argument in transition: Proceedings of the third summer conference on argumentation (pp. 597-610). Annandale, VA: Speech Communication Association.*

Burleson, B. R. (1983b). *Social cognition, empathic motivation, and adults' comforting strategies. Human Communication Research, 10,* 295-304.

Burleson, B. R. (1984a). Age, social-cognitive development, and the use of comforting strategies. *Communications Monograph, 51,* 140-153.

Burleson, B. R. (1984b). Comforting communication. In H. E. Sypher & J. L. Applegate (Eds.), *Communication by children and adults: Social cognitive and strategic processes* (pp. 63-104). Beverly Hills, CA: Sage.

Burleson, B. R. (1986). Communication skills and childhood peer relationships: An overview. In M. L. McLaughlin (Ed.), *Communication yearbook* (Vol. 9, pp. 143-180). Beverly Hills, CA: Sage.

Burleson, B. R. (1987). Cognitive complexity. In J. C. McCroskey and J. A. Daly (Eds.), *Personality and interpersonal communication* (pp. 305-349). Beverly Hills, CA: Sage.

Burleson, B. R., Applegate, J. L., Burke, J., Clark, R. A., Delia, J. G., & Kline, S. L. (1986). Communication correlates of peer acceptance in childhood. *Communication Education, 35,* 349-361.

Burleson, B. R., Applegate, J. L., & Neuwirth (1981). Is cognitive complexity loquacity: A reply to Powers, Jordon, and Street. *Human Communication Research, 1,* 212-225.

Burleson, B. R., & Fennelly, D. A. (1981). The effects of persuasive appeal form and cognitive complexity on children's sharing behavior. *Child Study Journal, 11,* 75-90.

Burleson, B. R., & Samter, W. (1985). Consistencies in theoretical and naive evaluations of comforting messages. *Communication Monographs, 52,* 103-123.

Casson, R. W. (1983). Schemata in cognitive anthropology. *Annual Review of Anthropology, 12,* 429-462.

Cicourel, A. V. (1974). *Cognitive sociology: Language and meaning in social interaction.* New York: Macmillan.

Clark, R. A. (1979). The impact of self interest and desire for liking on selection of communicative strategies. *Communication Monographs, 46,* 257-273.

Clark, R. A. & Delia, J. G. (1977). Cognitive complexity, social perspective-taking, and functional persuasive skills in second to ninth-grade children. *Human Communication Research, 3,* 128-134.

Clark, R. A., & Delia, J. G. (1979). Topoi and rhetorical competence. *Quarterly Journal of Speech, 65,* 165-206.

Clark, R. A., Willinghanz, S., & O'Dell, L. (1985). Training fourth graders in compromising and persuasive strategies. *Communication Education, 34,* 331-342.

Delia, J. G. (1976). A constructivist analysis of the concept of credibility. *Quarterly Journal of Speech, 62,* 361-375.

Delia, J. G. (1977). Constructivism and the study of human communication. *Quarterly Journal of Speech, 63,* 66-83.

Delia, J. G. (1978, November). *The research and methodological commitments of a constructivist.* Paper presented at the Speech Communication Association Convention, Minneapolis.

Delia, J. G., Burleson, B. R., & Kline, S. L. (1979, April). *Person-centered parental communication and the development of social-cognitive and communicative abilities.* Paper presented at the annual meeting of the Central States Speech Association, St. Louis.

Delia, J. G., & Clark, R. A. (1977). Cognitive complexity, social perception, and the development of listener-adapted communication in six-, eight-, ten-, and twelve-year-old boys. *Communication Monographs, 44,* 326-345.

Delia, J. G., Kline, S. L., & Burleson, B. R. (1979). The development of persuasive communication strategies in kindergarteners through twelfth-graders. *Communication Monographs, 46,* 241-256.

Delia, J. G., O'Keefe, B. J., & O'Keefe, D. J. (1982). The constructivist approach to communication. In F.E.X. Dance (Ed.), *Human communication theory* (pp. 147-191). New York: Harper & Row.

Dickson, W. P. (Ed.) (1981). *Children's oral communication skills.* New York: Academic Press.

Dinges, N. (1983). Intercultural competence. In D. Landis & R. W. Brislin (Eds.), *Handbook of intercultural training* (Vol. 1, pp. 176-202). New York: Pergamon.

Ehrenhaus, P. (1983). Culture and the attribution process. In W. B. Gudykunst (Ed.), *Intercultural communication theory* (pp. 259-270). Beverly Hills, CA: Sage.

Frake, C. (1969). The ethnographic study of cognitive systems. In Joshua Fishman (Ed.), *Readings in the sociology of language* (pp. 434-446). The Hague, Netherlands: Mouton.

Furth, H. G. (1973). Piaget, IQ and the nature-nurture controversy. *Human Development, 16,* 61-73.

Geertz, C. (1973). *The interpretation of cultures.* New York: Basic Books.

Gudykunst, W. B. (1985). Intercultural communication: Current status and proposed directions. In B. Dervin & M. J. Voight (Eds.), *Progress in communication science* (Vol. 6, pp. 1-46). Norwood, NJ: Ablex.

Gumperz, J. J. (1982). *Discourse strategies.* Cambridge: Cambridge University Press.

Hale, C. L. (1980). Cognitive complexity-simplicity as a determinant of communicative effectiveness. *Communications Monograph, 47,* 304-311.

Hale, C. L. (1982). An investigation of the relationship between cognitive complexity and listener-adapted communication. *Central States Speech Journal, 33,* 339-344.

Hale, C. (1986). Impact of cognitive complexity on message structure in a face-threatening context. *Journal of Language and Social Psychology, 5,* 135-143.

Halliday, M.A.K. (1973). *Explorations in the functions of language.* London: Edward Arnold.

Halliday, M.A.K. (1978). *Language as social semiotic.* Baltimore: University Park Press.

Husband, R. L. (1981). *Leadership: A case study, phenomenology, and social-cognitive correlates.* Unpublished doctoral dissertation, University of Illinois at Champaign-Urbana.

Hymes, D. (1971). Sociolinguistics and the ethnography of speaking. In E. Ardener (Ed.), *Social anthropology and linguistics* (pp. 47-93). London: Tavistock.

Hymes, D. (1972). Models of interaction of language and social life. In J. J. Gumperz and D. Hymes (Eds.), *Directions in socio-linguistics* (pp. 35-71). New York: Holt, Rinehart & Winston.

Hymes, D. (1974). *Foundations in sociolinguistics.* Philadelphia: University of Pennsylvania Press.

Jacobs, C. S. (1985). Language. In M. L. Knapp & G. R. Miller (Eds.), *Handbook of interpersonal communication* (pp. 313-343). Beverly Hills, CA: Sage.

Jones, J. L., Delia, J. G., & Clark, R. A. (1981, May). *Person-centered parental communication and the development of communication in children.* Paper presented at the annual meeting of the International Communication Association, Minneapolis.

Kasch, C. R. (1984, April). *Interpersonal competence, compliance, and person-centered speech: A study of nurses' and para-professionals' communicative strategies.* Paper presented at the Central States Speech Association Convention, Chicago.

Kelly, G. A. (1955). *The psychology of personal constructs* (2 vols). New York: W. W. Norton.

Klemp, G. O. (1979). Identifying, measuring, and integrating competence. In P. Pottinger & J. Goldsmith (Eds.), *New directions in experiential learning* (pp. 41-52). San Francisco: Jossey-Bass.

Kline, S. L. (1981a, November). *Construct system development, empathic motivation, and the accomplishment of face support in persuasive messages.* Paper presented at the annual meeting of the Speech Communication Association, Anaheim, CA.

Kline, S. L. (1981b, May). *Construct system development and face support in persuasive messages: Two empirical investigations.* Paper presented at the annual meeting of the International Communication Association, Minneapolis.

Kline, S. (1982, November). *The effects of instructional set on the provision of face-support by persons differing in construct system development.* Paper presented at the annual meeting of the Speech Communication Association, Minneapolis.

Kline, S. L., & Ceropski, J. M. (1984). Person-centered communication in medical practice. In J. T. Wood & G. M. Phillips (Eds.), *Human decision-making* (pp. 120-141). Carbondale: Southern Illinois University Press.

Kreckel, M. (1981). *Communicative acts and shared knowledge in natural discourse.* New York: Academic.

Leichty, G. & Applegate, J. L. (1987, May). *Social cognitive and situational determinants of face support in persuasive contexts.* Paper presented at the annual meeting of the International Communication Association, Montréal.

Manicas, P. (1980). The concept of social structure. *Journal for the Theory of Social Behavior, 10,* 65-82.

McCarthy, T. (1982). *The critical theory of Jurgen Habermas.* Cambridge: MIT Press.

McHugh, P. (1968). *Defining the situation.* New York: Bobbs-Merrill.

Mead, G. H. (1932). *The philosophy of the present.* Chicago: Open Court.

Miller, G. R. & Berger, C. R. (1978). On keeping the faith in matters scientific. *Western Journal of Speech Communication, 42,* 44-57.

O'Keefe, B. J. (1984). The evolution of impressions in small working groups: Effects of construct differentiation. In H. E. Sypher and J. L. Applegate (Eds.), *Communication by children and adults* (pp. 262-291). Beverly Hills, CA: Sage.

O'Keefe, B. J. (1988). The logic of message design. *Communication Monographs, 55,* 80-103.

O'Keefe, B. J., & Delia, J. G. (1979). Construct comprehensiveness and cognitive complexity as predictors of the number and strategic adaptation of arguments and appeals in a persuasive message. *Communication Monographs, 46,* 231-240.

O'Keefe, B. J., & Delia, J. G. (1982). Impression formation and message production. In M. E. Roloff & C. R. Berger (Eds.), *Social cognition and communication* (pp. 33-72). Beverly Hills, CA: Sage.

O'Keefe, B. J., Murphy, M. A., Meyers, R. A., & Babrow, A. S. (1983, May). *The development of persuasive communication skills: The influence of developments in interpersonal constructs on the ability to generate communication-relevant beliefs and a level of persuasive strategy.* Paper presented at the annual meeting of the International Communication Association, Dallas.

O'Keefe, B. J., & Shepherd, G. (1982, November). *Defining the communication situation: Consequences for perception and action.* Paper presented at the annual convention of the Speech Communication Association, Washington, DC.

O'Keefe, B. J., & Shepherd, G. (1987). The pursuit of multiple objectives in face-to-face persuasive interactions: Effects of construct differentiation on message organization. *Communication Monographs, 54,* 396-419.

Overton, W. F. (1973). On the assumptive base of the nature-nurture controversy. *Human Development, 16,* 74-89.

Paige, R. M., & Martin, J. N. (1983). Ethical issues and ethics in cross-cultural training. In D. Landis & R. W. Brislin (Eds.), *Handbook of intercultural training* (Vol. I, pp. 36-60). New York: Pergamon.

Pearce, W. B., & Cronen, V. E. (1980). Communication, action, and meaning. New York: Praeger.

Pearce, W. B., & Wiseman, R. L. (1983). Rules theories. In W. B. Gudykunst (Ed.) *Intercultural communication theory* (pp. 79-88). Beverly Hills, CA: Sage.

Price-Williams, D. (1980). Toward the idea of a cultural psychology. *Journal of cross-cultural psychology, 11,* 75-88.

Samovar, L. A., Porter, R. E., & Jain, N. C. (1981). *Understanding intercultural communication.* Belmont, CA: Wadsworth.

Samter, W., Burleson, B. R., & Basden, L. (1985). *Effects of comforting strategy type, sex, and cognitive complexity on impressions of a speakers.* Unpublished manuscript, Purdue University, West Lafayette, IN.

Sarbaugh, L. E. (1979). *Intercultural communication.* Rochelle Park, NJ: Hayden.

Sarver, J. L. (1976). *An exploratory study of the antecedents of individual differences in second- and seventh-graders' social cognitive and communicative performance.* Unpublished doctoral dissertation, University of Illinois at Champaign-Urbana.

Schank, R. & Abelson, R. (1977). *Scripts, plans, goals, and understanding.* Hillsdale, NJ: Lawrence Erlbaum.

Shepherd, G. J. (1987). Individual differences in the relationship between attitudinal and normative determinants of behavioral intent. *Communicative Monographs, 54,* 221-231.

Shepherd, G. J., & O'Keefe, B. J. (1985, November). *Securing task, interactional, and relational objectives in interpersonal persuasive interactions.* Paper presented at the Speech Communication Association Convention, Denver.

Shimanoff, S. (1980). *Communication rules.* Beverly Hills, CA: Sage.

Sorentino, R. M. & Higgins, E. T. (Eds.) (1986). *Motivation and cognition.* New York: Guilford.

Spiro, M. E. (1951). Culture and personality. Psychiatry, 4, 19-41.

Spitzberg, B. H., & Cupack, W. R. (1984). *Interpersonal communication competence.* Beverly Hills, CA: Sage.

Sypher, B. D. & Zorn, T. E. (1986). Communication abilities and upward mobility: A longitudinal investigation. *Human Communication Research, 12,* 420-431.

Thomas, W. I. (1927). Situational analysis: The behavior pattern and the situation. Reprinted in Morris Janowitz (Ed.) (1966). *W. I. Thomas on social organization and social personality* (pp. 154-167). Chicago: University of Chicago Press.

Thomas, W. I. (1928). *The child in America.* New York: Knopf.

Werner, H. (1959). The concept of development from a comparative and organismic point of view. In D. B. Harris (Ed.), *The concept of development* (pp. 125-146). Minneapolis: University of Minnesota Press.

Werner, H., & Kaplan, B. (1963). *Symbol formation: An organismic- developmental approach to language and the expression of thought.* New York: John Wiley.

Wiseman, R. L. (1980). Toward a rules perspective of intercultural communication. *Communication, 9,* 30-38.

4

Coordinated Management of Meaning
A Critical Theory

VERNON E. CRONEN ● VICTORIA CHEN ● W. BARNETT
PEARCE
University of Massachusetts, Amherst

The coordinated management of meaning (CMM) theory provides a critical perspective on the study of communication and culture. It differs from "mainstream" work in communication because it is in the tradition of North American Pragmatist philosophy and thus opposed to the Cartesian commitments of logical positivism as well as much of interpretive research. CMM takes communication to be the primary process rather than basing critique on individual rights, class relationships, or other sources. This chapter sets forth nine propositions providing the basic orientation of the theory. The theory's method of analyzing structure and action to illuminate cultural differences and generate a critical perspective on cultural practices also are described. The example of a Chinese family at dinner is used to describe CMM methods and differentiate these methods from the mainstream.

One of the consequences of the technological revolution is that it has brought us into close contact with widely differing ways of carrying on everyday life. North American social scientists, accustomed to teenage self-assertion in their own country, find that a Chinese teenager will most likely remain silent when an older relative states a position strongly opposed to the teenager's own. Are Chinese teenagers "repressed?" Do they care less about their own ideas? Are they less mature, or do they value talk less than North American teenagers? What are we to make of such differences?

A story from Jewish folklore helps orient our response. In the mythical town of Chelm, a man saw his friend riding his horse-drawn cart rapidly through town. Curious to see why his friend was in such a hurry, he ran after him and shouted, "Where are you going and why so fast?" His friend replied, "I'm going to Minsk!" "But you should be going the other way! You are headed toward Pinsk, not to Minsk!" "I know," he said as his voice faded away in the distance, "but I can't stop now because I'm making such good time."

The obvious point of the story is that we can get so involved in the progress we are making that we fail to recall just where we are and where we intend to go. In dealing with social phenomena such as differences in silence/verbosity between Chinese and North American teenagers, various theories of communication begin from different orientations and sometimes have different views of what a theory should do. The "mainstream" of intercultural communication research is informed by a worldview deriving from Descartes. Both positivist and subjective-interpretive approaches take the individual as the fundamental unit of analysis and employ a series of dualisms. The most fundamental is that of mind and body. This dualism is elaborated into others, such as subjective and objective, interpretation and sensation, society and individuals, values and facts. The Cartesian tradition has produced a large body of data and served particular interest well. It has "made good time," but perhaps on the way to Pinsk.

The coordinated management of meaning (hereafter CMM) theory is based on North American Pragmatist philosophy. Deliberately non-Cartesian, it is designed to serve an alternative set of interests while meeting appropriate standards of rigor and generating a robust body of research. Because CMM differs so much from the mainstream, researchers in the discipline have sometimes found it confusing. Some have labeled its theoretical commitments mystifying. Others have misunderstood it. We think that these readings are owing to the fact that CMM is "going the other way."

Our procedure in this chapter is to describe the theoretical commitments of CMM, showing how these inform a set of studies that differ markedly from the mainstream of intercultural work in communication. The "interests" served by CMM may be expressed in three objectives.

First, CMM seeks to understand who we are, what it means to live a life, and how that is related to particular instances of communication. We take it as sufficiently well substantiated that all communication practices point beyond themselves to (and derive their meaning from) sets of contexts. We also take it as sufficiently substantiated that the process of living a life differs in various cultures. The combination of these two assumptions require CMM researchers to deal with intercultural communication and comparative patterns of communication.

Second, CMM seeks to render cultures comparable while acknowledging their incommensurability. Intercultural comparisons can serve the useful function of illuminating our common humanity while at another level of analysis showing how different we are. However, the most significant results of the study of other cultures may be for one's own culture. Such studies enhance awareness of the peculiarities of our own taken-for-granted condition—the familiar is made strange. In addition, awareness of the vast array of sophisticated ways to lead a human life is itself liberating. It sparks the realization that the way things are is not the only way they can be.

Third, CMM seeks to generate an illuminating critique of cultural practices, including the researchers' own. A social science that claims to reveal underlying principles or capture the native point of view, but has nothing to say about the possibilities for enhancing the conditions of human life, does not take on its full share of responsibility. This is not merely to say that all social scientists should do their work and then consider the moral dimension of the findings. For a theory to have a critical focus the same set of principles that guide description and interpretation must guide critique.

FUNDAMENTAL COMMITMENTS: AVOIDING PINSK

Comparison Without Objectivity or Relativism

In the Cartesian tradition, knowledge claims are either "objective" or "subjective." To be "objective" they have to be based on a "foundation" that is beyond doubt. Descartes thought that such foundational knowledge was to be found in distinct ideas, located in the individual mind, and of such character that to doubt them would be self-contradictory. Empiricists like Bacon and Locke sought foundational knowledge in sensations stamped upon individual minds. Kant searched for a foundation in transcendental categories of mind that each individual used to make a unified personal whole of experience. All of these western philosophies share the assumptions that the individual is the primary unit of social analysis and that knowledge must rest on a secure foundation outside of culture, history, and action. Without an objective foundation, it was thought, nothing was left but a relativism in which no knowledge claim could be adjudicated as better than another. This frightful image, dubbed the "Cartesian anxiety" by Richard Bernstein (1983), has shaped intellectual endeavors in more far-reaching and subtle ways than usually is acknowledged.

The tradition of North American pragmatism offers an alternative in which knowledge claims refer to lived experience rather than to ahistorical, acultural substances. Claims that proceed from lived experience are neither "objective" nor "subjective," because the Cartesian dualisms that separate mind and body, subject and object are themselves set aside. Emancipated from the Cartesian anxiety, pragmatists such as Dewey (1920, 1922, 1925, 1929), Mead (1934, 1938), Bernstein (1983), and Rorty (1979) argue that thoughts cannot be "inside" our heads and actions "outside." Rather, thought must always arise in action and take its distinctively human cast through transactions with other persons. By the same token, thought cannot be "outside" the mind because people appropriate thought from the social talk around them (Bruner, 1075; Dewey, 1922; Vygosky, 1962), but do so from a unique position in space, time, and relationship. The possibility for individuality derives in part from being at a unique nexus of social realities. Thus, objectivity and subjectivity are dimensions of thought and of action.

Terms for Comparing Cultural Systems

If lived experience is the closest thing to a "foundation" that we can expect to have, then the existence of culture constitutes a problem for communication and for knowledge. Although there are various ways of describing culture, by definition, the forms of lived experience differ across cultures. This being the case, how is it possible for people in one culture to understand those in another? Where might one stand in order to compare two or more cultures?

Bernstein (1983) offers three terms that facilitate this discussion: *incompatibility, incommensurability,* and *incomparability.* When we say two systems (of lived experience) are compatible, we assert that they have a common logical framework and a common language in which the two systems can be expressed without distortion. In this common language, it is possible to create a yardstick by which to measure the products of the two systems. For those old enough to remember, the war over attitude theories in the 1960s was a case of incompatibility. A social situation that closely resembles the war of the attitude theories is that in which Fundamentalist Christians argue among themselves over the proper interpretation of scripture. They share the same idea about the inerrancy of the texts, the nature of their activity, and many other matters. They also share a common logic for decision. Theirs is not the logic of the classic social science experiment, but that of scriptural citation and analogy.

Two systems are incommensurable when there is no neutral language that can provide a point-by-point comparison without distorting one system or another. Thus there is no single algorithm for comparison. Newtonian and Einsteinian physics are examples of incommensurable systems. Thomas Kuhn (1970) explains that Einstein's theory did not simply extend Newton's by showing Newton's dynamical equations to be a special case. Only approximations of Newton's system can be derived from Einstein. Their conceptions of time, space, and observation are so different that one cannot be simply mapped on the other.

What is to be said if two social systems are incommensurable as are those of Java, Bali, China, and Canada? Bernstein observes that while profound differences preclude a neutral observation language for comparison, this does not make comparison impossible. Thus while no single algorithm for judging difference can exist it does not mean that moral judgments must be nonrational. There is a great difference between the claim that two systems are incommensurable and the claim that they are incomparable. For example, the conclusion that the Confucian and Aristotelian concepts of the "mean" are different requires some ability to compare—at least enough to recognize the magnitude of the difference. Indeed, Kuhn argues in the postscript to his famous book that theories like Newton's and Einstein's are definitely comparable. And he explicitly states that one is rationally to be preferred because it is an advance over the other. Incommensurable worldviews, however, must be compared in multiple ways because no single yardstick will do.

The means available for comparison come from the diverse resources of cultural traditions. These include literature, folkways, art, histories, music, technologies, and so on. The means also include theories and research projects. As traditions develop and encounter other traditions, the means of comparison expand. We believe that *in principle* all systems are comparable, but the means of comparison have to be created. In this sense CMM is a cultural achievement, although it is neither the product of work in a single culture nor the work of persons from a single cultural heritage. CMM theory is a cultural product designed to facilitate comparisons of incommensurable systems, and it continues to develop in the course of multicultural contact.

BASIC PROPOSITIONS: HEADING TO MINSK

CMM is intended to function as a lens through which the social world can be interpreted and critiqued. Because it derives from a pragmatic rather than a Cartesian philosophy, its "propositions" serve a different purpose than those in mainstream communication theory. From a pragmatist's point of view, developing theory is itself a practice. Theories are developed under real social, historical, and institutional conditions. As Lentricchia (1986) observes, there are ironic aspects to theory from a pragmatist perspective. Theory must emerge from a world of practices, institutions, and points of view, yet theory claims to transcend that world. Theories with wide ranging applicability tend toward a totalizing of experience, yet pragmatists since James (1975) have recognized the world to be "diffused and distributed" (p. 126). In Lentricchia's (1986) phrase, "a cacophony of stories" (p. 10). Still, theory is not impossible. It does productive work precisely because it has a reflexive relationship with the material conditions in which it develops and in which it is used. Thus the following propositions are *not* statements untainted by history and culture. They are orienting statements that *taken together* sketch out the perspective we think most useful in light of past practice.

Not only do CMM propositions differ in purpose from those of mainstream theories, they differ in content. CMM is opposed to the procedure of treating culture as a set of dimensions or variables on which people differ. It does not accept behavioral norms, attitudinal tendencies, or common beliefs and values as providing sufficient insight into cultural differences. Stated positively, the key insight embraced by CMM may be expressed in the form of metaphysical claim:[1] *Communication is the primary social process.* The apparently stable social world—dinners and dates, commodity exchanges and capital creation, emotion and thought—is deceptive. It does not consist of "found things" but rather is created, maintained, and transformed in the process of communication. It sometimes seems that individuals communicate to express their emotions and to refer to the world around them. But whence come these "individuals," "emotions," and "event/objects"? They are constructed in the process of communication.

Proposition 1: Persons communicating constitute the smallest unit of social analysis. The emphasis is on person*s* communicating. Two persons communicating are not three basic units but one (Harre, 1984). This proposition stands in opposition to the Enlightenment concept of the individual. Western individuality is best understood as a social achievement rather than a natural form of being (Geertz, 1973; Lukes, 1985; Mauss, 1985). One of the interesting aspects of the western form of individuality is that it entails a form of consciousness that obscures its social origins. Communication is not something that humans choose to do. There never was a time when individuals lived "in nature" without ongoing communication. Communication is part of the natural condition of mammals, particularly primates (Bateson, 1972). As studies of feral children show, our humanity does not exist outside of communication with other persons.

Proposition 2: Communicating persons are physical beings that endure in real space-time. This proposition states our commitment to the form of realism. We are satisfied by Strawson's (1959) argument that no coherent form of social life is possible without assuming that persons as material bodies occupy locations in real time/space, and that they can endure and be recognized beyond the course of a particular episode or story. In this proposition we also acknowledge that persons have a physiological make-up that opens diverse opportunities for being human. While emotions vary across culture and history (Averill, 1980; Harre, 1984), persons in all cultures have physiological responses that are part of communication.

Proposition 3: All human communication is both idiosyncratic and social. Descartes reframed Plato's problem of the senses in a highly individualized way. The problem he created is reflected in such dilemmas as this: "How can I know that there is a tree in front of me when all I can know is what my senses tell me and my senses can be wrong?" This sort of thinking is based on the inside-outside distinction that has been part of western culture since Descartes, but is not common to other cultural traditions or to our Greco-Roman predecessors. The inside-outside dichotomy gives rise to the subjective-objective dichotomy and the individual-society dichotomy. This problem can be discarded if we reject the ideas that a sensation is a self-contained mark in Newtonian time. Dewey treated sensation and perception as aspects of a process. Any perception, Dewey said, must be rooted in real world physicality or it could not arise. Yet human perception is never untouched by human minds.

In no sense does this social emphasis imply the deemphasis of individuality. A culture can encourage consciousness of individual differences and stress the elaboration of particular kinds of distinctions. Just what differences are to be identified and how they are to be elaborated will differ across cultures. A social theory that is relevant to cultural differences ought to identify practices that produce and sustain certain forms of selfhood and offer a critique of those forms and practices.

Proposition 4: Communication entails a reflexive relationship between structure and action. This proposition challenges the common dichotomy that divides meaning and action. It is expressed in both the attempt to reduce action to the problems of knowing what people think (e.g., personal constructs theory) or to reduce mind to the problem of what people do (e.g., radical behaviorism). In our view, mind is formed in the course of social interaction. Forms of mind open a variety of possibilities for minded action.

When we speak of minds we are referring to the densest loci of structure that guides action. Structures are resources organized by rules (Giddens, 1979). At the level of persons, structure includes that which has been traditionally called mind. The person's resources include: (1) hierarchically and reflexively organized meanings and (2) physical-neurological capabilities. At the personal level, rules organize resources into forms of consciousness, emotional roles, intentionality, and activity. At the level of society, resources include not only the physical environment and institutions, but also the socially produced objects that make a human world. Examples include means of economic exchange, buildings, clothing, art, machines, and, of course, the texts that objectify history, technology, ritual, and so on (Arendt, 1958). Rules that connect these societal resources must be held by persons or they would not exist at all. These rules can, for example, connect history to art, constitute money as a means of exchange and constitute a means of transportation as a means commodity.

All structure, personal and societal, arises through and is sustained and altered by practice. Conversely, practice is guided by structure. All structure that is human bears the marks of meaning, intentionality, consciousness, and physicality. Similarly, these human characteristics will be reflected in the activity of communication.

Proposition 5: Punctuated historicity is endemic to human communication. The focus of this proposition is epistemological because it addresses the question of how to support practical judgments. CMM theory takes the stand that intelligent reflection on experience provides the essential rational grounds for action. This assertion is in direct contrast to one that is deeply entrenched in Western tradition—more deeply entrenched than Cartesianism that assumes it.

Parmenides argued that reliable knowledge has to be of unchanging things. He held this to be so because as soon as a knower understood a changing object, that object would have changed, thus obviating the knowledge. The effect of this argument in intercultural communication research is shown by efforts to find some unchanging set of dimensions or exhaustive set of variables that will render all cultures commensurable. But Parmenides' argument is only telling if we assume that (1) building social theory is a quest for ultimate certainty, and (2) the problem of meaning and truth is that of mapping (or picturing) a reality external to the knower. If, however, social theory is a quest for *useful* understanding under particular historical and social conditions, and if meaning itself arises from communication, we can then pass on from Parmenides' problem to that of understanding how it is that social actors (scientists included) reach useful judgments.

In a recent paper, Kenneth Gergen (1983) asserted that the real meaning of any utterance or action is in principle unknowable. By the "real" meaning, he refers to the quest for absolute knowledge about an utterance. To make his point, Gergen takes a bit of text and demonstrates that by assuming different contexts we can rationally assign radically different meanings to it. What Gergen fails to emphasize is the temporal aspect of any context. Social actors are rarely in the predicament of finding that an almost infinite array of meanings can be assigned to what is happening. Even when they cannot decide which of certain competing interpretations should be acted upon, they usually think they know what the limited array of viable competing interpretations contains. The absence of a constant existential *angst* does not mean that social actors are naive. They make useful judgments from the flow of action and interpretation. The situation is not essentially different in scientific work. Nelson Goodman (1979) has argued in a classic paper that the justification of inductive moves in science ultimately lies in the history (or histories) of practice and not in *a priori* logical principles.

In our view the current state of knowledge requires standing Parmenides on his head. It is not repeatable reflection on static objects that renders human activity rational, but the ever changing flow of minded activity that is unified and realized in communication.

Proposition 6: Human communication is inherently imperfect. After stating this proposition we hasten to add that the great power of human communication lies precisely in its imperfection. Descartes's work was part of the more general Western "quest for certainty" (Dewey, 1929). This quest is based on the conviction that perfection of form (as exhibited by mathematics and formal logic) is of the highest value, whereas that which is informal, incomplete, or ambiguous is of less value. For us *clarity, mutual understanding, accuracy,* and *consensus* have value depending upon the situation. None of those terms capture the quiddity of human communication is the unfinished quality of communication that opens up the multiplicity of the human condition. Our claim that communication is inherently imperfectable by technological standards is based on seven lines of arguments. Although space does not permit us to develop these here, proposition six is so essential to our position that we shall briefly identify these arguments:

(1) There are internal limits to formalizing. In our century two events have challenged the value of the mathematical-logical model of knowledge. The first was the development of noneuclidean geometry, followed by the creation of additional forms of mathematics and logics. If several formal systems can be equally well formed but incommensurable, what formal standards can be used to decide among such systems? The possibility of logic of logics was removed by the second event, Gödel's (see Nagel & Newman, 1958). Gödel was able to show that all formal systems are based on axioms that cannot be proven within the system. Thus, all formal systems are inherently incomplete.

(2) Symbols always point beyond themselves. Mead (1934), Wittgenstein (1953), Vygosky (1962), and others have argued persuasively that meaning arises in social action. If the meaning of symbols arises in the course of patterned activity, then meaning is never finished. John Shotter (1984) recently has expressed this idea by saying that language always points beyond itself. Recall that proposition four stipulated a reflexive relationship between structure and action. Read in that light, the statement "symbols always point beyond themselves" may be read "structure and action are always unfinished."

(3) Patterns of communication are always conjointly produced by two or more actors. The important theoretical aspect of this argument is that an actor's interpretation and behavior is contingent on the activity of other actors. Further, as Bateson (1972) observed, there is a double contingency involved because each actor's structure is evolving in the course of social interaction. That evolution is contingent upon, but not fully determined by, other's acts. (For a demonstration of this using a simplified symbol system see Pearce & Cronen, 1980.)

(4) Mutual understanding is only one avenue of productive coordination. CMM research has shown that misunderstanding, confusion, and ambiguity can, under particular circumstances, be very productive (see especially the "Jan and Dave" study in Pearce & Cronen, 1980.)

Although CMM does not endorse misunderstanding as a universal cure, we think that the more dominant problem in our culture has been the single-minded quest for perfection.

(5) Ends evolve as organic aspects of structure. The ends humans pursue are transformations of higher order contexts. Anscombe (1957), for example, talks about intention as what we aim at, and motive as a higher order conception that creates and justifies the aim. Thus as structure evolves, different motives and intentions (ends) evolve. The CMM view is very close to Dewey's (1922). We take ends to be orientation points constructed in action, not the termination points of completed action. When certain ends and motives are commonly pursued in a culture, CMM theory poses the questions: How did they evolve? What is their part in various patterns of practice? How are they changing? Are persons "stuck" in the pursuit of destructive ends? and How are ends reconstituted in action?

(6) There is an ineffable dimensions to communication. Language is but one aspect of communication. Patterning talk into contexts, feeling in touch with reality, the arousal of physiological responses, producing emotional roles, and connecting phrases with imagery are a few examples of other factors that are part of human communication. As Pearce and Branham (1978) have argued, to strip communication of all aspects that cannot be satisfactorily reduced to propositional form is to remove its very human character. A theory without interest in the ineffable dimension of communication is uninterested in probing deeply into what it means to live a life.

(7) There is no linear relationship between the degree of self-consciousness and the quality of communication. Without the ability to disattend to the structural sources of one's own action, many emotional roles would be impossible (Averill, 1980). Moreover, many complex skilled performances demand a form of consciousness that is not self-reflective, for example, the body language involved in courtship. In nature, perfections are mere epiphenomena, says Jay Gould (1987); they are evolutionary dead ends. CMM theory holds that this is also true in social life.

Proposition 7: Moral orders emerge as aspects of communication. Since enlightenment social theory has tended to separate facts and even theories from values. However, it can be observed that all communication systems are intrinsically moral orders. Cultures vary considerably in the way selfhood and responsibility are organized, but all entail ideas about what one must do, can do, may not do, and what is outside one's responsibility. They all involve patterns of consciousness that organize and legitimate responsibilities.

An illustration serves to vivify the claim. Recently, Cronen, Pearce, and Tomm (1985) presented a case analysis of a family that included a daughter with an eating disorder. When asked what he thought the problem in the family was, the father said, "My daughter is the cause of our problems, but she has an illness—she can't be blamed. When she acts the way she does I have to do certain things because that's what's right. Then the family gets upset with me and you can't really blame them." Father's brief statement is interesting because of the moral order implied in it. Ultimately no one is to blame. Daughter's actions are caused, not chosen. Father's actions are conscious choices, but wholly obligated by his role relationship. Other family members' responses to father are described as legitimate in light of father's obligatory acts. Forms of consciousness are part of the process by which acts are legitimated.

Proposition 8: Communication is the process by which the dual modes of liberation may be materialized. Paulo Freire (1986) said, "Freedom is a moment in the process of liberation." For CMM theory there are two distinguishable sorts of moments in which freedom is experienced (Cronen, 1986). One is seeing the possibility of elaborating seminal ideas into sophisticated structure through action. The other is seeing the possibility of moving beyond problem-ridden aspects of structure to a new point of view. Bateson (1972) referred to these two sorts of moments as representing rigor and imagination.

The moral implications should be clear. Movement from periods of rigorous elaboration to periods of imaginative reconstruction together constitute the process of liberation. This process is unique to human beings because they are constituted as selves and societies through communication. This perspective gives a modern day answer to an old question posed by Aristotle, who asked that if playing well is that for the sake of which one is a harpist, then what is it for the sake of which one lives a human life? CMM suggests that it is participation in the process of liberation that makes us distinctively human. It is that for the sake of which we live human lives individually and communally (Cronen, 1986). Rational discussion about the desirability of any cultural practice ought to start with the worth of a practice within the process of liberation. Any such analysis must employ means with sufficient heuristic power to identify how opportunities for creative elaboration and imaginative reconstitution are materialized or undermined.

Proposition 9: Diversity is essential to elaboration and transforma-tion through communication. It is traditional in Eastern culture to seek the "correct" methods and eliminate incorrect ones. Here the techno-logical metaphor and the quest for certainty appear. The attempt to expunge "wrong" ways of thinking has been a factor in the awful moral record the West has compiled. In contrast to the tendencies within the quest for certainty, CMM stresses the crucial importance of preserving diversity. Probably the most important contribution that intercultural study can make is not reassurance of some underlying unity, but an idea of the range of possibilities for being human in different but productive ways. Consider the fact that all Western painting was profoundly affected by Picasso's discovery of African masks. Creative practice in both its elaborative and transformative phases depends on the encour-agement and preservation of diversity. Because of the inherently imperfect incomplete nature of the primary social process, it is impossible to know in advance how different forms of practice may enrich each other.

COROLLARIES FOR CROSS-CULTURAL AND INTERCULTURAL STUDIES: ROAD SIGNS TO MINSK

The foregoing propositions are elaborated below into a set of three corollaries specifically to guide cultural studies.

Corollary 1: Cultures are patterns of coevolving structures and actions. A culture is conceptualized best as everyday activities practiced by its members. It is not a static entity to be dissected but rather is always in the process of becoming. Geertz (1973) nicely articulated it this way, "Culture provides the link between what men are intrinsically capable of becoming and what they actually . . . in fact become" (p. 52). Static conceptions of culture are rejected by CMM. By static conceptions we include those that treat culture as the finished end product of ethnic heritage, a fixed set of routinized behaviors, beliefs, and values, or a set of projections along some standardized dimension.

Suppose we find that on a reliable scale Chinese women are significantly more reticent than North American women. What do we still not know? We don't know anything about context. Where and how is this reticence displayed? Is it displayed in intimate relationships, in student street demonstrations, in university classes, in a street market, in meeting with older persons, or where? Is reticence experienced as an emotion that comes over one or as a consciously enacted role? We do not know to which settings and experiences Chinese women refer when answering most questionnaires. Consider some other things we would not know about the reticence of Chinese women. How is it related to forms of personhood and social relationships? What does its enactment legitimate and obligate in the actions of *others* and in what context? In addition to these unanswered questions, we still know nothing about the evolution and change of reticence displays. We believe that understanding the meaning of Chinese reticence depends on answering questions like these.

Corollary 2: Cultures are polyphonic. Curtis (1978) used the provocative metaphor polyphony to describe culture in light of its technical meaning in music. The *Oxford Companion to Music* says that the terms *polyphony* and *polyphonic* refer to

"many-sound" or "many-voiced" music, i.e., to music in which instead of the parts marching in step with one another, and without particular interest in their individual melodic curves, they move in apparent independence and freedom though fitting together harmonically (cited in Curtis, 1978, p. vii).

Following this musical metaphor, we think the polyphonic nature of culture can be rendered in three senses. First, on a broad scale, any culture has a variety of resources that include traditions of art, literature, technology, forms of leisure, modes of production, patterns of relationship, and so on. Within each of these general types of resources we find variety. In music a Westerner can listen to the older work of Bach, Mozart, and Armstrong, or the modern work of Bartok, Shostokovich, and Parker. This diversity may be less pronounced in some cultures but it is there. The practices of the men's hunting lodge are not the same as the practices of the family group, and neither is the same as those in women's food gathering activities.

A second sense of polyphony is derived from the different forms of selfhood within a culture. When we talk about Western selfhood later in this chapter we are really talking about the middle class form. But we know that working-class women have a variant of the form that differs in some ways from working-class men or the middle class. Rubin's classic study *Worlds of Pain* (1976) highlights these differences.

A third sense to extract from the polyphony metaphor is the

individuality of interpretation. Because all human activity combines individuality and sociality, no two enactments or interpretations will be exactly the same. This third feature of polyphony also reflects the fact that critique is not the privileged right of social theorists. We must recognize not only the natives' interpretations of action, but also unique critical voices within their own culture.

The polyphonic character of culture preserves the very heart of identity and judgment. Hannah Arendt (1958) observes that when people act so that each multiplies and prolongs the experience of their neighbors, they become, in effect, entirely private. They are deprived of seeing, hearing, and being heard by others. They become collectively "imprisoned in the subjectivity of their own singular experience which does not cease to be singular if the same experience is multiplied innumerable times" (Arendt, 1958, p. 58). It is only in distinction that the one can be identified.[2]

Corollary 3: Research activity is part of social practice. From the CMM perspective research is a practice, a part of social life. The position of observer or participant-observer is an orientation *within* social structure and action that is afforded by and created in structure and action. As Hofsteadter (1979) noted, one cannot step outside a system to observe it. Observations must be made from a vantage point within it. If research is a social practice then it must have the essential features of the primary process on which all practices are based. Furthermore, based on the propositions that we have offered, it would follow that the action carried on between social researchers and their cultural informants must be under the contingent and conjoint control of all parties. From those conversations emerge some objectification— objects that can be somehow stored and observed by others. These objects include sets of data, written analyses, and theoretical texts such as this chapter. These objects are conjointly made. Thus as Clifford (1983) observes, we must come to view our cultural informants much like coauthors.

In truth, more than joint authorship is involved. Participation induces change for both researcher and informant. The informant may be asked, for example, to articulate and bring to consciousness features of taken-for-granted practice. Changes in the form of consciousness may have profound effects. The idea that cross-cultural and intercultural studies can be simply descriptive or interpretive and therefore politically benign is probably naive.

ANALYSIS OF SOCIAL EPISODES: WHAT TO DO IN MINSK

CMM is most widely known in communication as a "rules" theory (Cushman & Sanders, 1982). Unlike other "rules" theories, CMM rules do not state normative behavior patterns or general modes of inference making. Rather, each rule we write reflects structure and action for a particular actor in a material circumstance. There are two kinds of rules in CMM. The rules that guide action we call regulative rules. Detailed discussions of CMM rule analysis are available elsewhere (Pearce & Cronen, 1980; Cronen, Johnson, & Lannaman, 1982; Cronen, Pearce, & Tomm, 1985). Here we shall provide a brief presentation of how we analyze conversation. The example we will use is the one presented at the beginning of this chapter. We will consider part of an episode of talk around a Chinese family's dinner table and then make some comparisons to a similar looking episode at a North American dinner table. We will be concerned with how CMM analysis goes beyond descriptive work to attain a critical stance toward its object of study.

Interpretive Work

At the Chinese family's dinner table are a mother and father, their teenage daughter, and daughter's uncle and aunt. The family begins to discuss whether young people are as dedicated to their studies as they were in former times. Uncle makes a comment that he and everyone else knows to be one with which the teenager disagrees. He says "I think Western ideas about gratification through consumer goods have a very bad effect on young people and the way they attend to their studies." Toward the end of his statement he makes eye contact with the teenager. As he is finishing his statement, she returns the eye contact, smiles slightly, then looks back to her place setting. Her father responds to her uncle while she remains silent.

One way of dealing with this event is to subsume it under a general description of the value different cultures place on talk and silence. We could simply say that Chinese women are more reticent than North Americans. However, this fails to account for our observations of the amount of talk in a Chinese market where Chinese women are considerably more verbal than their North American counterparts. It is more illuminating to view this event as historically situated within the contexts of the culture, relationships, and autobiography. We do this by

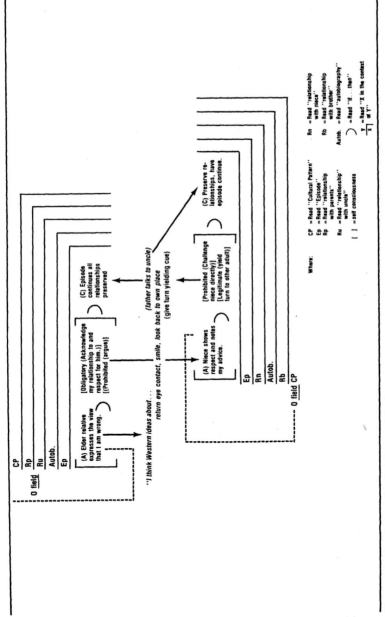

Figure 4.1 Regulative rules for niece and uncle.

using a CMM rules analysis to see how structure generates conversation and how conversation reconstitutes or alters structure.

Regulative rules depicted in Figure 4.1 describe certain aspects of the event. In the niece's rule are a set of embedded contexts. The highest context is that of cultural pattern (CP) within which forms of relationship emerge. We need to study this episode in light of the fact that the teenager's understanding of the cultural pattern and her relationship to her parents (R_p) have both social and idiosyncratic features and are unfinished. They emerge in action and are reconstituted and changed in action. The next two levels of context shown in Figure 4.1 are the teenager's relationship to her uncle (R_u) and her own autobiography (Autob). The two lowest levels of context are the episode (E_p) and a triad of acts. The triad of acts includes the antecedent act of condition (A), her own possibilities for action (SpAct), and an anticipated consequence or responding act (C). At this lowest level we also insert deontic operators (DO). These indicate whether an action is experienced as obligatory, legitimate, prohibited, or of undertermined status. If the action is experienced as outside of conscious control, then the appropriate operator would be from the set "caused," "probable," "blocked," and "random." No reflexive loops are indicated between levels of the teenager's structure. If there were, they would be symbolized ⌐⌐.

In Figure 4.1 we included the "I" as distinguished from auto-biography. Our use of it is very similar to that developed by Mead (1934). Here we have placed the "I" at the level R_p. In doing so we are claiming that the daughter's point of view is her relationship to her parents, and that this is the highest level of context of which she is consciously aware. The "I" is also indicated to have a field as opposed to an observer orientation (Nigro & Neisser, 1983). This means she is experiencing the action from a first or second person perspective, that of a fully engaged participant, not as a third person seeing the action as if looking over his or her own shoulder. The "I" is a location in structure to which other elements of structure and action can be reported creating self-consciousness. This structural description is intended only to describe a phase of this particular episode. It is not static or traitlike.

To understand this little bit of the Chinese family's structure and action, we need to know several more things about the teenager's role. We want to know how strongly various levels of context prefigure her choice of action ("prefigurative force" in CMM). We want to know whether her choice of action depends on the effectiveness the act is thought to have for obtaining a particular consequence, or whether the act must be performed regardless of its result ("practical force" in CMM). It is very important to consider how much a particular kind of consequence is needed to reconstitute aspects of structure ("reflexive needs" in CMM). We do not assume that because a certain kind of response is greatly needed, the actor is necessarily conscious of it at the moment of action. Neither do we assume that the actor is being strategic when reflexive needs are great. Finally, we want to know about the effects that responsive acts have on someone's structure, for those effects constitute the conditions under which subsequent actions are taken ("reflexive effects" in CMM).

In our Figure 4.1 example, we would expect to find that the prefigurative force of relationships (R_p, R_u) is very strong. We would also predict that our teenager would say that she must remain silent regardless of what happens next. In other words, there is a weak practical force. Yet we expect that she can predict quite well what her uncle will do. Her uncle's acceptance of her silence functions to reconstitute her cultural understandings, relationships, autobiography, and the progress of the episode, but this does not mean the structure is static. She has interacted with her uncle in the presence of her parents in a particular way on a new and sensitive topic. We would predict that our teenager is not conscious of reflexive needs or subtle reflexive effects. We do not think that she probably would be able to report prefigurative factors and tell us that her silence is obligatory, a conscious requirement.

Thus far, our analysis has been focused on the individual and that is clearly insufficient. We need to know how the niece's silence and nonverbal behavior form part of the context for her uncle's response. We are sure, based on ethnographic work (Chen, 1987), that the niece's act creates important constraints for her uncle. It is prohibited for him to challenge her views personally and directly. Her silence and nonverbal behavior have the reflexive effect of confirming the nature of the niece-uncle relationship and that relational context has strong prefigurative force for him.

Let us briefly compare this event to a supposedly similar event in a North American home. A North American teenager would more likely respond to her uncle's challenge of her views. At first glance the North American teenager seems "liberated," whereas the Chinese teenager seems "dominated," but a closer examination yields a more complex story. In the North American situation, if uncle challenges his niece's viewpoint, he would either have to treat her view as personal possession or demean it further by either saying she just "picked up" the ideas, or by treating her as "just a typical teenager." Thus the North American teenager elicits a personal challenge to part of her identity, or an attack on the existence of her individuality. This is serious because in North American culture developing individuality is prerequisite to competence and maturity.

The situation for the Western teenager is further complicated by the fact that in some North American subcultures she is expected to defend herself *and show respect for the adult at the same time!* In many North American homes parents' requirement to respect elders would certainly limit the extent and kind of response their daughter can make. At the same time, acts that could be read as disrespectful legitimate further efforts by uncle to "put her in her place." These efforts are likely mandated by uncle's autobiography, which prefigures the assertion of his superiority, and by his reflexive need to sustain his autobiography. The struggle over which generation is in charge is intrinsic to a culture that lauds change and youth but has difficulty finding a useful role for older people.

If the North American teenager comes from a home that demands both personal assertiveness and respect for authority, she faces a paradoxical situation (see Figure 4.2). The paradox in Figure 4.2 should be read like this: In the context of answering back competently, the teenager is displaying disrespect (arrow a). To act disrespectfully is a sign of social incompetence (arrow b). In the context of being socially immature, the teenager lacks the ability to answer back disrespectfully (arrow c). In the context of not answering back, the teenager is being respectful, and being respectful is socially mature (arrow d). In the context of social maturity, the teenager should be able to answer back (arrow e). Of course it could be argued that the North American teenager simply has to learn how to disagree respectfully. This may, however, be quite difficult because the sheer act of disagreeing legitimates a strong response from an elder, while the requirement to be respectful places real limits on what she can do.

If our analysis is generally correct, the North American uncle is also in a paradoxical situation. His paradox is shown in Figure 4.3. In the context of personalizing the challenge, he is threatening an aspect of who his niece is—her identity. In the context of a possible threat to the identity of his niece, it is required that he back off and depersonalize the challenge, attributing the view to "a typical teenager's response," or "just some ideas she picked up." In the context of depersonalizing the view,

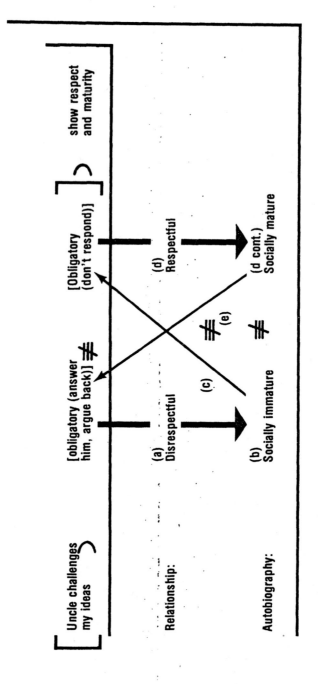

Figure 4.2   American teenager's paradox.

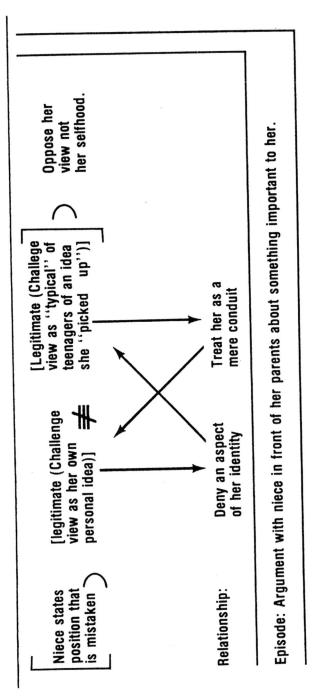

Niece states position that is mistaken ⌒ [legitimate (Challenge view as her own personal idea)] ≢ [Legitimate (Challenge view as "typical" of teenagers of an idea she "picked up")] ⌒ Oppose her view not her selfhood.

Deny an aspect of her identity

Treat her as a mere conduit

Relationship:

Episode: Argument with niece in front of her parents about something important to her.

Cultural Pattern: The Western concept of a sealed-off, container view of self.

Figure 4.3   American uncle's paradox.

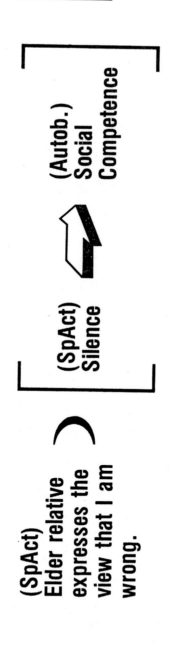

Contexts: Ep, Ru, Rp, CP

(SpAct)
Elder relative
expresses the
view that I am
wrong.

(SpAct)
Silence

(Autob.)
Social
Competence

Where:

= Read "counts as"

Figure 4.4 Example of a constitutive rule.

his niece counts as a nonindividual—she is just a conduit for ideas not her own. In the context of a threat to the individuality of his niece, it is obligatory to personalize the challenge.

Now return to the Chinese example. The Chinese teenager does not face this sort of paradox. Moreover, she has done nothing that implies to anyone that she has conceded her position. These structure relationships, of course, require much further analysis. All she has done is to affirm a set of understandings about her relationship to certain adults.

The rules shown in Figure 4.1 are regulative rules that organize action over time. The existence of constitutive rules has been implicit in our discussion. Think of constitutive rules as operating vertically through the rules shown in Figure 4.1. One of the constitutive rules that operates to integrate structure in our Chinese example is this: Within the contexts C_p, R_p, R_u, and E_p, and after uncle states his differing view, the speech act "silence" counts as "competence" at the level of autobiography. This constitutive rule is often expressed in CMM as shown in Figure 4.4. In this way the constitutive rule explains the prefigurative force. Other constitutive rules explain other forces in the structure. Silence for a North American teenager might count as a demonstration of one's own immaturity and incompetence.[3]

When we make such comparisons across cultures we must be careful to observe just how different the two situations are. The North American would have different concepts at all levels of context. Autobiography would be differently positioned in the hierarchy, and consciousness would be differently organized. The North American and the Chinese are not merely doing different things in the same situation. The relationship of a person to his or her elder relatives, the significance of eating together, the organization of conversation, and the forms of selfhood are some of the differences at work here. The situations are incommensurable though they may be compared using our knowledge of the two cultures guided by CMM.

Critical Work

At this point we want to demonstrate how the concepts embodied in CMM can generate a critical focus on this situation. The Chinese example provides a point of contrast that sensitizes us to many taken-for-granted features of our own situation. We shall concentrate on the North American situation here because more of our readers are familiar with it, not because the Chinese situation requires no critique.

Many scholars share a concern for the problematic features of the western Cartesian self (see Carbaugh, in press, Geertz, 1973; Harre, 1984; Horkheimer, 1972; Rorty, 1979; Sampson, 1983). The effort to solve all problems by blaming or "fixing" the individual leaves us blind to the social aspect of our problems. CMM's historicity proposition is consistent with the thrust of Marx's famous aphorism: "Men [and women] make history but not under conditions of their own choosing."

Briefly, the western concept of a self is that of a bounded and unique person, set contrastingly against others and society, possessing an independent and integrated consciousness (Geertz, 1983, p. 59). In the West, the individual is thought to possess their uniqueness as a set of ideas, processes, categories, and so on, for which the individual is a container (Rorty, 1979).

How is the western view a self reconstituted and changed in real episodes of interaction? We think that the North American dinner table example described here illustrates a material case of such reconstitution. We are not that profoundly disturbed by the mere fact that there is paradox involved. Paradox can produce creativity as well as disturbance (Kafka, 1971). We are much more concerned with how the experience of the paradox reconstitutes the Western conception of self. We do not think that the teenager is likely to be conscious of the form of the paradox, but we do think that she may experience a powerful tension between satisfying personal and social requirements. What she experiences is that when the two requirements are somehow connected, the effort to satisfy either one results in obstructing both. With such experiences, is it any wonder that Westerners find it hard to accept that individuality and sociality are aspects of our condition, not choices? Part of the "proof" for the "reality" of the dichotomy is the emotional pain that is experienced in the effort to affirm both individuality and sociality.

Next consider the uncle's paradox in Figure 4.3. Observe that the source of his paradox lies in another aspect of Western selfhood. Self is a "container of beliefs." If beliefs (or attitudes, values, or whatever) are not personal, then what is left of personhood? Whichever choice uncle makes, the response he will get from his niece will probably be either an effort to defend the challenged belief or an effort to take possession of the challenged belief. In either case the two, while in conflict, coconspire to reconstruct the container view of self.

We think that this sort of critical analysis is very important. Indeed some of us who work within the CMM perspective would argue that the most fundamental contradiction in Western society is not, as Marx claimed, the contradiction of socialized labor and private ownership. We think there is a deeper contradiction that is between the communication patterns for the production and reconstitution of Western selfhood and a form of selfhood that cannot recognize communication among persons as the foundation of its existence.

Methods of Collecting Data

CMM embraces a number of research strategies for the analysis of communication including statistical procedures, interviews, analyses of texts and transcripts, and field observation. Quantitative methods have been used mainly to assess the strength of connections within actors' rules. In these studies scales are used to measure prefigurative force, practical force, reflexive needs, reflexive effects, and other aspects of structure. These quantitative studies of rule structure can be used in case studies as well as in more traditional statistical designs.

CMM has used interviews both to set the ground work for quantitative studies and as an independent means of illuminating rule structure. One method was developed by Harris (1979, 1980). It involves asking couples or groups to work both individually and together to construct episodes and describe them. Another form of interview used in CMM research is based on the method called circular questioning. Circular questioning was developed originally for use in family therapy by the Milan Team (see Selvini Palazzolli et al., 1978). In the course of our work with Boscolo and Cecchin of the Milan team, and with Karl Tomm of the University of Calgary, the circular questioning method has been expanded to more explicitly reflect elements of the rule structure analysis described in the previous section of the paper (see Tomm, 1985). The most extensive work on the adaptation of circular questioning for use with CMM has been done by McNamee (1983, 1985).

When social scientists consider the study of different cultures, the approach most likely to come to mind is ethnography. The increasing number of studies on ethnography of communication based on Hymes's (1972) descriptive framework has offered us many insights into communication from a cultural perspective. Communication scholars have also made useful extensions of the Hymesian method (see Carbaugh, 1986; Stewart & Philipsen, 1984). Ethnography of communication encompasses a variety of research techniques organized around certain assumptions about communication. CMM is compatible with many of the assumptions on which the ethnography of communication is based.

It differs from the ethnography of communication tradition in three ways.

First, the ethnographer may choose any specific theory to guide his or her work and then use the results of their study as a critique of the "borrowed" theory. Obviously CMM mandates the use of a particular theory, though we hope that working with our theory can lead to a critique of it. Using CMM as part of an ethnographic study can lead to a critique of other theories as well. Consider, for example, what the implications of our "dinner table" analysis are for communication apprehension research as carried on by the West Virginia group (see McCroskey, 1977, 1984).

Second, in practice, most ethnographic work on communication does not emphasize the production of particular episodes or their reflexive features. Emphasis is on the discovery of broad cultural patterns that account for and illuminate practices. This is a laudable achievement, but not sufficient if one accepts all of the propositions stated earlier in the paper. The deemphasis of reflexivity brings in its wake another difference in practice. Ethnographic work usually does not move from interpretation to critique. Although CMM began in the interpretive tradition, it has evolved into a critical approach. We do not see critique as a secondary consideration, although we know that sound critique cannot come from poor description and interpretation. The distinction lies here: We think that the selection of a theory to guide ethnographic work ought to be based on its critical potential, and its descriptive and interpretive power ought ultimately to serve the critical interest. (CMM has been used in a growing number of cross-cultural and intercultural studies employing a range of data collection methods as we have described here. These studies are marked in the reference list.)

PROSPECT: FUTURE TRAVELS FROM CHELM

At the beginning of this chapter we failed to tell you one thing about the story of our traveler from Chelm and his frustrated friend who tried to redirect him. The detail we left out is that in the folk tradition, Chelm is a mythical place where *all* the inhabitants are either crazy or fools. To be sure, if one assumes the Cartesian tradition, then all that we have suggested is indeed crazy. If society is no more than normal distributions of behavior, the kind of work we suggest then is foolish. Obviously, we don't think so. But be warned, to travel our way is to take a very different path and run the risk of looking a bit crazy or foolish to some in the mainstream. Just where do we expect to go in our study of communication and culture? Earlier in this chapter we said that CMM has evolved from an interpretive orientation to encompass a critical stance. Hopefully, our work can illuminate deep cultural problems by providing a way to analyze the processes by which episodes of communication are produced and how those episodes partially reconstitute and alter social structure. The criteria for critique grow out of our analysis of the fundamental social process—communication. If concepts such as diversity, imperfectability, and the dual modes of liberation capture the quiddity of the primary process, we have some useful things to say about demands to "purify" cultural practices. Such demands are becoming more strident world wide. The instability and threat associated with living in the modern world seems to have set off an intensified "quest for certainty" (Dewey, 1929). We hear its echoes in the Soviet Union's intolerance for cultural diversity, and in the North American Right's determination to stamp out anything Marxist. We hear it in the Fundamentalist's demand that Christianity be taught in public schools and non-Christian ideas be banned. We hear it in Fundamentalist Islam's demand for return to a "perfected" ninth-century form, and in remarkably similar demands from Israel's religious right for return to the Judaism of the Middle Ages. CMM bases its opposition to all such "quests" not on the much discredited doctrine of natural individual rights, but on an analysis of communication. In CMM theory, communication is not something individuals choose to do. It is the most fundamentally human feature of lived experience. Efforts opposed to the intrinsically liberating character of communication strike at the heart of what it means to be human.

CMM offers more than a general defense of human freedom. Its analytic apparatus is designed to be useful for assessing the potential of cultural features. Implicit in our earlier discussion are these questions: Is the Chinese conception of selfhood capable of useful elaboration under modern circumstances? Is the North American form of selfhood still productive? In the North American case, we are coming to the conclusion that the Cartesian self is so fundamentally flawed that efforts to elaborate it may be futile and a very radical transformation required. Judgments of this kind must be based on a detailed analysis of how cultural achievements like the Cartesian self enter into the conduct of actual practices. CMM is intended to generate such analyses, but it cannot do so within a monocultural setting. If CMM lacks the power to render incommensurable social realities comparable, it will be blind to the range of human possibility and lose its sensitivity to the character of its own cultural birth place.

Much needs to be done. Hitch up your cart! See you in Minsk!

NOTES

1. The authors recognize that some contemporary pragmatists have argued against the connection of pragmatism to theory-building and even to social criticism. This "against theory" approach championed by Rorty (1979) seems to us antithetic to the work and spirit of James, Dewey, and Mead. See Rosenthal (1986), Margolis (1986), and Lentricchia (1986).

2. CMM does not agree with the Marxists that every society has an underlying base that gives rise to social distinctions and institutions. Nor do we agree that class as defined by Marx is universally useful as a way to identify major social divisions. While Marxists recognize contradictions in a cultural order, we do not think that they recognize the full extent to which cultures are polyphonic. Although many aspects of structure and action may be interdependent, we do not think they are usually so integrated that if the single node is identified the whole cultural system can be transformed. An example of Marxist overemphasis on the unifying properties of "base" may be found in the history of the Soviet Union. In spite of radical change in organization for production, much remains the same. Russian nationalism, anti-Semitism, labor camps, the secret police, and many other less onerous features of prerevolutionary Russia remain. Indeed, Russian culture and tradition seem to have swallowed the revolution.

3. Constitutive rules also integrate the hierarchy by connecting conceptions to physiologic conditions. An example of a constitutive rule (CR) that performs this integration is stated as follows: In the context of a romantic episode, when the music is soft, lights low, and another smiles at me; sensations x, y, z count as sexual excitement. One final caution about the analysis of rules. Consider how fully this rule depends on an appropriate form of consciousness for competent social action. In our culture it is almost impossible to produce the experience of being in love while maintaining an observer's orientation and detailed self-consciousness of one's own behaviors.

REFERENCES

*Studies employing the CMM approach

*Alexander, A., Cronen, V. E., Kang, K., Tsou, B., & Banks, B. J. (1986). Patterns of topic sequencing and Information Gain: A comparative study of relationship development in Chinese and American Cultures. *Communication Quarterly, 34,* 66-78.

Anscombe, G.E.M. (1957). *Intention.* Ithaca, NY: Cornell University Press.
Arendt, H. (1958). *The human condition.* Chicago: The University of Chicago Press.
Averill, J. (1980). A constructive view of emotion. In R. Plutchik & H. Kellerman (Eds.), *Theory of emotion.* New York: Academic Press.
Bateson, G. (1972). *Steps to an ecology of mind.* New York: Ballantine.
Bernstein, R. (1983). *Beyond objectivism and relativism.* Philadelphia: University of Pennsylvania Press.
Bruner, J. (1975). From communication to language—a psychological perspective. *Cognition, 3,* 255-287.
Carbaugh, D. (1986). Some thoughts on organizing as cultural communication. In L. Thayer (Ed.), *Organizational communication: Emerging perspectives* (pp. 85-101). Norwood, NJ: Ablex.
Carbaugh, D. (in press). *Talking American: Cultural discourses on DONAHUE.* Norwood, NJ: Ablex.
*Chen, V. (1986). Hyphenated competence: A case study of a Chinese-American's 'world.' Paper presented at the Annual Conference on Culture and Communication, Philadelphia.
Chen, V. (1987). "Mien-tzu" at the Chinese dinner table: An ethnography of the public enactment of "face." Unpublished manuscript, Department of Communication, University of Massachusetts; Amherst.
*Chuang, E. N. (1983). Intercultural sensitivity: An exploratory study of the relation between intercultural sensitivity and logical force in problematic situations. Unpublished master's thesis, University of Massachusetts, Amherst.
Clifford, J. (1983). On ethnographic authority. *Representation, 1,* 118-146.
Cronen, V. E. (1986). The individual in a systemic perspective. Keynote address delivered at the fifteenth anniversary of the founding of Interaktie Akademie, Antwerp, Belgium.
Cronen, V. E., Johnson, K. M., & Lannamann, J. W. (1982). Paradoxes, double binds, and reflexive loops: An alternative theoretical perspective. *Family Process, 20,* 91-112.
Cronen, V. E., Pearce, W. B., & Tomm, K. (1985). A dialectical view of personal change. In K. J. Gergen & K. E. Davis (Eds.), *The social construction of the person* (pp. 203-244). New York: Springer-Verlag.
*Cronen, V. E., & Shuter, R. (1983). Initial interactions and the formation of intercultural bonds. In W. B. Gudykunst (Ed.), *Intercultural communication theory.* Beverly Hills, CA: Sage.
Curtis, J. (1978). *Culture as polyphony: An essay on the nature of paradigms.* Columbia: University of Missouri Press.
Cushman, D. P., & Sanders, R. E. (1982). Rules theories of human communication processes: The structural and functional perspectives. In B. Dervin & M. J. Voigt (Eds.), *Progress in communication sciences* (pp. 49-83). Norwood, NJ: Ablex.
Dewey, J. (1920). *Reconstruction in philosophy.* New York: Holt.
Dewey, J. (1922). *Human nature and conduct.* New York: Holt.
Dewey, J. (1925). *Experience and nature.* Chicago: Open Court Press.
Dewey, J. (1929). *The quest for certainty.* New York: Minton, Baloh.
Freire, P. (1986). Remarks made at a colloquium under the auspices of the Center for Advanced Study in the Humanities, University of Massachusetts, Amherst.
Geertz, C. (1973). *The interpretation of cultures.* New York: Basic Books.
Geertz, C. (1983). *Local knowledge.* New York: Basic Books.

Gergen, K. J. (1983). *Social construction, psychology, and science*. Paper presented at the American Psychological Association convention.

Giddens, A. (1979). *Central problems in social theory*. Berkeley: University of California Press.

Goodman, N. (1979). *Fact, fiction, and forecast*. Cambridge, MA: Harvard University Press.

Gould, J. (1987). The panda's thumb of technology. *Natural History, 96*, 14-23.

Harre, R. (1984). *Personal being*. Cambridge, MA: Harvard University Press.

Harris, L. M. (1979). Communication competence: Empirical tests of a systemic model. Unpublished doctoral dissertation, University of Massachusetts, Amherst.

Harris, L. M. (1980). The maintenance of a social reality: A family case study. *Family Process, 19*, 19-33.

Hofsteadter, D. R. (1979). *Godel, Escher, Bach: An eternal golden braid*. New York: Basic Books.

Horkheimer, M. (1972). *Critical theory*. New York: Seabury.

Hymes, D. (1972). Models of the interaction of language and social life. In J. J. Gumperz & D. Hymes (Eds.), *Directions in sociolinguistics: The ethnography of communication* (pp. 35-71). New York: Holt, Rinehart & Winston.

James, W. (1975). *Pragmatism and The meaning of truth* (Introduction by A. Ayer). Cambridge, MA: Harvard University Press. (Original works published in 1907 and 1909)

Kafka, J. (1971). Ambiguity for individuation: A critique and reformulation of the double-bind theory.

*Kang, K. & Pearce, W. B. (1983). *Transculturation: A conceptualization of the process of confronting a novel culture*. Paper presented at the fifth International Conference on Culture and Communication, Philadelphia, Pennsylvania.

*Kang, K. & Pearce, W. B. (1984). The place of transcultural concepts in communication theory and research, with a case study of reticence. *Communication, 9*, 79-96.

Kuhn, J. (1970). *The structure of scientific revolutions*. Chicago: University of Chicago Press.

Lentricchia, F. (1986). The return of William James. *Cultural Chinese, 4*, 5-31.

Lukes, S. (1985). Conclusion. In M. Carrithers, S. Collins, & S. Lukes (Eds.), *The category of the person* (pp. 282-301). Cambridge: Cambridge University Press.

Margolis, J. (1986). *Pragmatism without foundations*. Oxford: Basil Blackwell.

Mauss, M. (1985). A category of the human mind: The notion of the person; the notion of self. In M. Carrithers, S. Collins, & S. Lukes (Eds.), *The category of the person* (pp. 1-25). Cambridge: Cambridge University Press.

Mead, G. H. (1934). *Mind, self and society*. Chicago: University of Chicago Press.

Mead, G. H. (1938). *The philosophy of the act*. Chicago: University of Chicago Press.

McCroskey, J. C. (1977). Oral communication apprehension: A summary of recent theory and research. *Human Communication Research, 4*, 78-96.

McCroskey, J. C. (1984). The communication apprehension perspective. In J. A. Daly & J. C. McCroskey (Eds.), *Avoiding communication* (pp. 13-38). Beverly Hills, CA: Sage.

McNamee, S. (1983). *Therapeutic change in family systems: A communication approach to the study of convoluted interactive patterns*. Unpublished doctoral dissertation, University of Massachusetts, Amherst.

McNamee, S. (1985). *Theory and practice integration: Social change as research, clinical* practice, and daily interaction. Paper presented to the Eastern Communication Association, Providence, RI.

*McNamee, S. & Pearce, W. B. (1984). *The therapeutic use of culture—in and out of therapy.* Paper presented to the Eastern Communication Association, Philadelphia.

Nagel, E., & Newman, J. (1958). *Godel's proof.* New York: New York University Press.

*Nakanishi, M. (1986). Perceptions of self-disclosure in initial interaction. *Human Communication Research,* Vol. 13, 167-190.

*Nakanishi, M., & Johnson, K. M. (1985). *Implications of self-disclosure on conversational logics, perceived communication competence, and social attraction: A comparison of Japanese and American cultures.* Paper presented at the International and Intercultural Communication Division, Speech Communication Association, Denver, CO.

*Narula, U., & Pearce, W. B. (1986). *Development as communication: The case of India.* Carbondale: Southern Illinois University Press.

Nigro, G. & Neisser, U. (1983). Point of view in personal memories. *Cognitive Psychology, 15,* 467-482.

*Norden, M. F., & Wolfson, K. (1986). Cultural influences on film interpretation among Chinese and American students. In B. A. Austin (Ed.), *Research on Film: Audiences, Economics, Law* (Vol. II). Norwood, NJ: Ablex.

Pearce, W. B., & Branham, R. J. (1978). The ineffable: An examination of the limits of expressibility and means of communication. In B. Ruben (Ed.), *Communication yearbook 2* (pp. 345-350). New Brunswick, NJ: Transaction.

*Pearce, W. B., & Chen, V. (in press). "Translation" and "interlocution": The representational rhetorics of Clifford Geertz and James Clifford. In K. J. Gergen & J. Shotter (Eds.), *Perspectives on the rhetoric of the human sciences.* London: Sage.

Pearce, W. B., & Cronen, V. E. (1980). *Communication, action and meaning: The creation of social realities.* New York: Praeger.

*Pearce, W. B., & Kang, K. (1986). Acculturation and communication competence: A case study. In *Communication theory from Eastern and Western Perspective,* edited by Larry Kincaid. Albany: SUNY Press. (Also to be published by Akira Tsujimura, in Japanese, title uncertain.)

*Pearce, W. B., & Kang, K. (in press). Conceptual Migrations: Implications of "travelers' tales" for communication theory. In Y. Y. Kim & W. B. Gudykunst (Eds.), *Cross-cultural adaptation: Current theory and research.* Newbury Park, CA: Sage.

*Pearce, W. B., & Lannaman, J. W. (1978). Modernity makes immigrants of us all: Communication competence and intercultural communication. *Journal of Asian-Pacific and World Perspectives, 6,* 27-34.

*Pearce, W. B., & Narula, U. (1984). *Learned dependency and "confusion" in the development dialogue in India: An analysis from a communication perspective.* Paper presented at the Communication of Culture Conference, Philadelphia.

*Pearce, W. B., Stanback, M., & Kang, K. (1984). Cross-cultural studies of the reciprocal causal relation between communication and culture. In S. Thomas (Ed.), *Studies in communication theory and interpersonal interaction.*

*Pearce, W. B., & Wiseman, R. (1983). Rules theories: Varieties, limitations, and potentials. In W. B. Gudykunst (Ed.), *Intercultural communication theory.* Beverly Hills, CA: Sage.

Rorty, R. (1979). *Philosophy and the mirror of nature.* Princeton, NJ: Princeton University Press.

Rosenthal, S. (1986). *Speculative pragmatism.* Amherst, MA: University of Massachusetts Press.

Rubin, L. (1976). *Worlds of pain: Life in the nothing class family.* New York: Basic Books.

Sampson, E. (1983). *Justice and the critique of pure psychology.* New York: Plenum.

Selvini Palazzoli, M., Boscolo, L., Cecchin, G., Prata, G. (1978). *Paradox and counterparadox.* New York: Jason Arronson.

Shotter, J. (1984). *Social accountability and selfhood.* Oxford: Basil Blackwell.

*Stanback, M., & Pearce, W. B. (1981). "Talking to the man": Some communication strategies used by subordinates and their implications for intergroup relations. *Quarterly Journal of Speech, 67,* 21-30. Reprinted in L. A. Samovar & R. E. Proter (Eds.) (1985). *Intercultural communication: A reader* (4th ed.). Belmont, CA: Wadsworth.

Stewart, J., & Philipsen, G. (1984). Communication as situated accomplishment: The cases of hermeneutics and ethnography. In B. Dervin & M. J. Voigt (Eds.), *Progress in communication sciences* (Vol. 5, pp. 177-217). Norwood, NJ: Ablex.

Strawson, P. F. (1959). *Individuals.* London: Methuen.

*Su, F. (1985). *The politics of "normalization": The process and the creation of social reality.* Unpublished master's thesis, University of Massachusetts, Amherst.

Tomm, K. (1985). Circular interviewing: A multifaceted clinical tool. In D. Campbell & R. Draper (Eds.), *Applications of systemic family therapy: The Milan Method* (pp. 33-46). London: Academic Press.

*Wolfson, K., & Norden, M. (1984). Measuring responses to filmed interpersonal conflict: A rules approach. In W. B. Gudykunst & Y. Y. Kim (Eds.), *Methods for intercultural communication research.* Beverly Hills, CA: Sage.

*Wolfson, K., & Pearce, W. B. (1983). A cross-cultural comparison of the implications of self-disclosure on conversational logics. *Communication Quarterly, 31,* 249-256.

Vygosky, L. (1962). *Thought and language.* Cambridge: MIT Press.

Wittgenstein, L. (1953). *Philosophical investigations.* New York: Macmillan.

5

Cultural Identity
An Interpretive Perspective

MARY JANE COLLIER • *California State University, Los Angeles*
MILT THOMAS • *University of Washington*

Cultural identity typically has been operationalized by researchers as an independent variable and defined a priori. *In this chapter, cultural identity is argued to be one level of multiple identities that are formed and managed in intercultural communication. Communication is said to be more intercultural to the extent that intersubjective cultural interpretations are revealed in discourse. Culture is defined as a historically transmitted system of symbols and meanings, identifiable through norms and beliefs shared by a people. This approach to cultural identity is based on an interpretive philosophy of inquiry. Because cultural identity is based on the extent to which one is communicatively competent, rules/systems theory is argued to be an ideal approach to the study of identity in intercultural communication. Finally, a research program is overviewed and implications are discussed.*

Intercultural communication often is approached by defining cultural difference *a priori* and then predicting from cultural identities to behavior. In many cases, assumptions about culture are based on overgeneralizations, overly simplistic categorizations, or inappropriate assumptions in conversations and research. These conceptualizations of cultural identification and intercultural communication consequently oversimplify and perhaps misrepresent the phenomena. The parameters of what counts as intercultural communication remain vague as well, and the experience of participants is ignored largely.

We think that grounded theory needs to be developed in which actual discourse between interlocutors is examined for its intercultural quality. The intercultural status of a communication episode would then be determined by the discursive interpretations of the participants, as they attribute and acknowledge each other's different cultural identities from one another. Thus in this chapter we propose a model for studying cultural identity in intercultural communication based in an interpretive perspective to inquiry.

We begin by presenting characterizations of intercultural communication and interpersonal communication. After laying out basic terms, we discuss the epistemological and ontological assumptions that guide our perspective on inquiry and compare it to other general perspectives. Third, the rules/systems theoretical approach is outlined, illustrated, and applied to the study of cultural identity.

Cultural identity then is described and compared to and contrasted with other types or levels of identity we believe to be operative in intercultural communication. Finally, implications for intercultural communication theory development and research are discussed.

INTERCULTURAL AND
INTERPERSONAL COMMUNICATION

We characterize *intercultural communication* as *contact between persons who identify themselves as distinct from one another in cultural terms*. We are concerned most with direct, person-to-person contact in which the operative cultural identities of interlocutors are revealed in discourse. Interlocutors may explicitly reveal cultural frames or may refer to, for example, homelands, backgrounds, or communities. In a conversation, to the extent that persons relate to themselves and the other as members of different cultural groups, contact can be said to be intercultural. A continuum of cultural differences exist, but we are interested in contact in which the participants conduct themselves as if the other person is culturally different.

Our conceptualization of intercultural communication is orthogonal to standard definitions of interpersonal communication (Ting-Toomey, 1986). Although there is general agreement that contextual definitions of interpersonal communication are limited, alternative characterizations also present problems. Miller (1978), for example, has argued that communication is based on cultural, sociological, and psychological data. Relationships are said to "develop" along with changes in the types of data used to predict others' behavior. Although Miller describes this trend as only general, we think important communication processes are glossed by an overemphasis on "development."

People orient toward one another in variable, multiple, yet synchronistic ways, as well as move in some sort of progression. Intimates, for example, can be heard referring to one another's heritage as well as personality.

Stewart (1986), following philosophers of dialogue such as Buber, has suggested that communication becomes more interpersonal insofar as the distinctiveness or uniqueness of the communicators is brought to the fore. As with Miller, the number of participants and the message media are not discriminating variables for determining whether or not the communication is interpersonal. Apart from how communication tends to "progress," Stewart (1986) and Cissna and Sieburg (1986) note that interpersonal communication is more confirming than noninterpersonal contact. Nonetheless, we also believe that in communication perceived to be intercultural, confirmation is primarily obtained when avowed and ascribed identities match; these identities may operate at a personal, social, or cultural level (Tajfel & Turner, 1979).

If, for example, an interlocutor is defining himself or herself as a "Chicano" or "Chicana," then his or her fellow interlocutors would do well to use a cultural frame in order to cater to his or her preferences at that time. If communication is most validating when persons feel confirmed, then culturally oriented demeanor should be met with culturally oriented deference (Cissna & Sieburg, 1986; Goffman, 1967).

In order to reconcile our view of intercultural communication with the dilemmas created by the multiplicity of communicator identities, we will demarcate direct, person-to-person contact as the context in which we are most interested for studying intercultural communication. "Interpersonal communication" will refer to contact in which the distinctiveness or uniqueness of a person is emphasized, especially person-specific qualities. "Interpersonal competence" will be conceptualized as mutually appropriate and effective; for example, identity-validating conduct. "Intercultural competence" will refer to contact in which one's ascriptions of cultural identities appropriately and effectively match those that are avowed. Communication can therefore be more or less interpersonal and simultaneously more or less intercultural.

People may or may not communicate with an intercultural frame. One person in an intercultural encounter may act on and thematize cultural differences, and the other person may not. The extent to which both persons perceive cultural difference is evident in the discursive text. When one person perceives the encounter as intercultural, then the encounter can be defined as such. When both persons consider the encounter to be intercultural, then the encounter is "more intercultural."

We believe that intercultural communication occurs as the interface between two culture systems, in other words, two separate systems of rules and meanings. We believe that participants, however, experience intercultural contact primarily through definitions of personhood. Communication is therefore intercultural when participants identify themselves and their interlocutors as representing different culture groups. To explicate our model, we will define *culture* as it pertains to intercultural communication and cultural identity, and delineate the context that we believe is most amenable to the study of cultural identity.

Culture

"Culture" has been conceptualized in varying ways by various scholars in cultural and intercultural communication. Many definitions provide lists of shared background characteristics, such as histories, institutions, core values, beliefs and attitudes or world views, heritage and traditions, technologies, as well as shared behavioral characteristics, such as verbal and nonverbal message styles (Dodd, 1987; Samovar, Porter, & Jain, 1981; Sarbaugh, 1979).

These kinds of conceptualizations are problematic for several reasons. First, it is difficult to determine when communication is intracultural and when it is intercultural. The question is raised as to how many of the characteristics need to be different in order to posit cultural difference. Second, the characteristics vary in their degree of importance and impact on certain cultures, and the salience of the characteristics is not typically given attention in communication research. Geertz (1973) makes a similar argument when he criticizes "eclectic" definitions of culture. For example, a history of oppression may be a highly salient and immediate cultural characteristic for Blacks in the United States and may be relatively unimportant for Anglos in the United States. Although researchers conceptualize culture as similarities in the variables listed, seldom do researchers measure all the variables to ascertain the cultural identity of their respondents. Finally, such definitions may not capture the experience of the participants.

Because we argue that the experience of the participants is the basis for conduct, the participants' communication about and identification with particular cultural groups is our focus. Whatever identity label is self-selected in discourse can be correlated with conduct within, across and between those labeled groups.

We define culture as *a historically transmitted system of symbols and meanings, and norms.* Our definition of culture is liberal yet definitive, entailing a broad understanding of what may constitute intercultural communication. "Culture" can refer to ethnicity, gender, profession, or any other symbol system that is bounded and salient to individuals. This definition co-opts Schneider's (1976) definition, which highlights the systematicity of a communication code by emphasizing Geertz's (1973) attention to tradition and to how human interaction becomes a discursive text (the saying becomes the said as soon as it has occurred). We also distinguish two aspects of culture, or dimensions of conduct: the moral or normative dimension (the "should" or "ought") and the constitutive or meaning dimension (the "is"). Thematizing these two dimensions of culture points to the importance of potential differences in both rules and meanings in intercultural communication.

Norms/Rules. Cultural systems or subsystems can be analyzed in terms of the rules that covary with patterns of action. When these norms or rules are the focus of study, emphasis is on the "how to" of coordinated activity; that is, the motions to make or avoid in order to get along or get by. Data include prescriptions, proscriptions, and social sanctions—stories that are told related to norm violations (Ragan, 1983; Shimanoff, 1980).

Meanings. When meanings are the focus, then the structures of co-occurring terms as they recur in discourse are analyzed for systematicity. Metaphors, stories, and myths reveal important themes and dimensions of understanding communicated by members of a culture group (Philipsen, 1980). Schneider (1976) has pointed out that symbols tend to pervade cultures broadly, forming symbol "galaxies" that cluster around core symbols. Norms tend to function, however, within contexts that he calls normative "institutions," such as the church, the family, or the workplace. Because of their contextuality, Schneider argues that normative statements provide specific symbols that can direct inquiry toward core symbols.

An example of inquiry consonant with Schneider's (1976) descriptions, and which identifies meanings and norms, is Katriel and Philipsen's (1981) ethnography of the use of the word *communication* in popular North American speech. *Communication* was examined as a core symbol that systematically co-occurs with the terms *self* and *relationship.* Predominant metaphors revealed that communication is considered the labor of love in a work metaphor, and the fertilizer that helps organic selves and relationships "grow." Analysis revealed that three dimensions of meaning consistently were imposed in "communication" discourse, so that "real communication," as opposed to "small talk," is *close, supportive, flexible* speech. Norms for how to communicate and pay ritual due to "selves" were discovered around a cluster that Katriel and Philipsen called the "communication ritual."

Core symbols. Schneider (1976) contends that cultures can be differentiated from one another by core symbols. He describes core symbols in the following way:

> I have called a cluster of symbols and their meanings a galaxy.... If a cluster of symbols and their meanings can be shown to have some features which distinguish it from other clusters, then the probability arises that a total system may be discerned which is distinct from other total systems. This is to say that a total cultural system is an analytic possibility.... Each galaxy has its central, core, key, master, unifying, dominant or epitomizing symbol. (p. 214)

He adds that all meanings are to some extent context-defined or context-determined within the framework of norms.

Core symbols can be differentiated from one another on a variety of dimensions and can be used to compare and contrast cultures. An example is Hofstede's (1983) research on dimensions of culture. Hofstede identifies four dimensions of culture: individualism-collectivism, power distance, uncertainty avoidance and masculinity-femininity. Core symbols can represent dimensions of cultural communication, and core symbols about communication patterns and norms can be compared across groups. For example, a core symbol for collectivistic cultures such as Mexico's may be bondedness, whereas a core symbol for a more individualistic culture, such as mainstream culture in the United States, may be individual accomplishment.

When core symbols are linked to notions of personhood, they may be thought of as emblems in talk. DeVos (1982) describes the process of culture and ethnic groups using symbolic emblems to differentiate themselves from other groups. An emblem can be anything from a mode of dress to a code of language or a key term or reference in conversation. We believe that these types of emblems and core symbols should be generated by researchers from the participants' perspectives and then tested or posited as potential etic categories across cultures (Pike, 1966).

Our definition of culture is consistent with popular definitions such as that offered by Gudykunst and Kim (1984). Typically, however, intercultural communication is studied as though cultural status is determined by birth rather than one's subscription to a system of symbols and meanings.

Consistent with our definition of culture, we believe that communication is rendered intercultural whenever the process takes the form of an interface between different systems of rules and meanings. Communication may "turn intercultural" in a moment and then turn or drift back again. We are arguing that cultural identity as a variable revealed in discursive texts is an indicator of intercultural communication.

PHILOSOPHICAL ASSUMPTIONS

Epistemological Assumptions

Our approach to cultural identity is founded in an interpretive philosophy of inquiry. We assume that interlocutors' conduct is "driven" by or covaries with their interpretations revealed in discourse. These interpretations appear as discursive texts that can be "read" or examined for normative patterning and symbolic structuring (Geertz, 1983). Themes may be derived from the observation of naturally occurring discourse as well as from solicited reflections about contexted interaction.

Our epistemological stance is, therefore, that abstractions from "local" interpretations best reveal cultural identity (Geertz, 1983). Our phenomena of interest are part of the lay epistemology of participants. The question is, "What does one need to know to do cultural membership?" Cultural competence is recursive with cultural identity; a person is a core member of a culture to the extent that he or she coherently articulates and understands symbols and follows norms. Identity can be interpreted as a continuous variable by tracking the systematic similarities and differences between persons who are said to "belong" in some way to a culture group.

The knowledge in which we are interested is intersubjective. "Intersubjectivity" has been used to refer to agreements across a community of researchers, private meaning transmitted from one subject to another, a "web of significance" (Geertz, 1973) in which cultural members are "caught" or is cocreated, and processual understanding that is fused in dialogue (Grossberg, 1982). "Intersubjectivity" is used here to fuse the third and fourth notions just described, to refer to the web of meaning revealed in structured relations between persons, so that levels of identity can be ascertained by subtracting variations in narratives from common themes.

Insofar as a person talks "the party line" of Hispanics, for example, she or he can be said to be a core member of a culture group. Others who diverge from the most general group in ways consistent with one another are members of more specific identity groups, as in the rhetoric of Chicanos. This discursive distillation process may be continued until relatively idiosyncratic rules and meanings are derived. Even in these cases, however, the knowledge a person "has" is generated and evolves intersubjectively.

With an emphasis on intersubjective knowledge, culture both constrains and facilitates conduct. Schneider (1976) refers to these two functions respectively as the regnant and generative functions. It is within the web of significance that persons manage general cultural identities and from it that they negotiate more particular ones.

Ontological Assumptions

The basic ontological assumption guiding our approach is that everywhere persons negotiate identity (Brown & Levinson, 1978). In other words, personhood varies contextually. Not only does a primary identity emerge in a given context, but also identity is experienced (i.e., occurs in discourse) at a variety of levels across situations. Intimates we know, for example, often thematize "personality" while simultaneously talking about gender and heritage factors as cultural influences on personal choice.

We make no claim here as to the ultimate "generative mechanism" that guides behavior in intercultural communication. We argue only that various types of identity revealed in talk covary with other communication and contextual variables in systematic ways. Interpretive inquiry is often most concerned with describing and explaining phenomena rather than explaining "causal" relationships and predicting behavior, and we believe that cultural identity is important in describing and explaining intercultural communication.

Another way to conceptualize our perspective is that it is sociolinguistic (Gumperz & Hymes, 1972). We are interested in the relationships between the linguistic variables of social identity and sociocontextual factors. This perspective can be contrasted with psycholinguistic perspectives in which cognitive phenomena are inferred and correlated with linguistic variables. For example, variables measured in Intergroup research include attitudes, perceived similarity, uncertainty, and attributions (Gudykunst, 1985) while Giles and Johnson (1981, 1986, in press) give attention to variables such as group vitality, ethnic boundaries, and status. Cultural identity is assumed *a priori* and then linked with such variables as those listed, or the variables listed are approached as predictors of linguistic strategies used to reflect ethnic identity. In summary, our perspective on cultural identity is based on identity formation and management in intercultural contact. Metatheoretically, the epistemological and ontological assumptions that ground the theory are characterized by a theme of intersubjectivity. Theoretical statements in the form of assumptions can be made to summarize our perspective. The assumptions are presented as fundamental definitions and descriptions upon which subsequent theoretical axioms and theorems are based.

Assumption 1: Persons negotiate multiple identities in discourse.

Assumption 2: Communication is rendered intercultural by the discursive ascription and avowal of differing cultural identities.

THE RULES/SYSTEMS APPROACH

Any theoretical approach used to explore cultural identity must be consistent with the epistemological and ontological assumptions. The rules/systems theoretical approach is compatible with an interpretive philosophy of inquiry, thematizes intersubjectivity, and has been shown to be appropriate for tracking the normative dimension of culture. Rules/systems can also provide a systematized, contextualized method for analyzing meaning.

Systems

The construct of system is the foundation upon which the rules/systems theoretical approach is built. Systematicity is inherent in conceptualizations of culture by both Geertz (1973) and Schneider (1976). Collier, Ribeau, and Hecht (1986) conceptualize cultural and intercultural systems by defining systems as interdependent, interacting components with an identifiable structure and function (Berrien, 1968; Boulding, 1956; Farace, Monge, & Russell, 1977; Fisher, 1978; Monge, 1977; Ruben, 1972; Thayer, 1968; Watzlawick, Beavin, & Jackson, 1967). Thus cultures are composed of systems of messages the structure of which can be identified through core symbols or norms, for example, and the function of which can be identified by described outcomes. Intercultural contact is also, by definition, systemic; delineation of the system versus the sub- or suprasystem is arbitrary for the researcher

(Farace, Monge, & Russell, 1977). Given the focus of this volume on intercultural contact, our preference here is to study cultural identities as core symbols in the cultural systems and compare and contrast them within the intercultural suprasystem.

Systems can be studied by identifying patterned interactions and through describing the structure and function of those patterns. Essentially, a system is maintained when the structure or "what to do, how to act" is clear and the outcomes are positive or system enhancing. One way to study how cultural systems maintain themselves and interface with one another is through the description of communication competencies.

Intercultural Competence

We define *communication competence* as *behaviors (social actions) perceived to be appropriate and effective in particular contexts,* following Spitzberg and Cupach (1984). People with similar cultural identities are viewed as a system, the members of which share common verbal and nonverbal conduct patterns, common rules, and common goals/positive outcomes.

Intercultural competence is defined as the demonstrated ability to negotiate mutual meanings, rules, and positive outcomes. In order to create intercultural competence, discursive meanings must be shared; for example, an encounter might be mutually understood as a social gathering. People must negotiate relational meanings, concepts of time, activities, and so forth, throughout the gathering.

People who are highly competent in intercultural encounters are those who can mutually agree upon and follow rules for appropriate conduct, and who experience positive outcomes, the most important of which is confirmation of the preferred identity. A central outcome from competent intercultural encounters is the confirmation of whichever identity is salient in the given context, a process achieved through sharing meanings and following mutually agreed-upon rules of conduct.

Rules. Because we propose that one useful way to study cultural systems is to study cultural competence, we suggest that scholars begin by giving attention to the structure of the system, and hence, the norms and rules.

We define *rules* as *communicative prescriptions that specify when and how actions are to be performed* (Harre & Secord, 1972). Rules are participants' perceptions of behavior that is deemed to be appropriate or inappropriate. For example there are rules for politeness, for offering proper evidence, and for how to be properly assertive. Rules are conceptualized here as consistent with Searle's (1969) regulative rules in the sense that they are prescriptions that are used to regulate and evaluate and predict, if not guide conduct. We agree with Shimanoff (1980) who defines rules as followable prescriptions for obligated, preferred, or prohibited behavior.

We use *norm* and *rule* interchangeably in this chapter.

Norms are not being defined as the standard or average behavior (Kolb, 1964) but rather as rules (contexted prescriptions) that apply to a specific social group in a specific situation (Hymes, 1972; Shimanoff, 1980).

Actions that conform to mutually shared rules are more predictable (Shimanoff, 1980), more self-concept affirming (Collier, 1986a), and more affirming of cultural identity (Collier, 1986a, 1986b, in press). Rule-following conduct is also perceived to be more effective with regard to goal accomplishment (Collier, in press). Therefore, rules merit attention from intercultural communication scholars.

Because rules are so central to identity, and because identities vary in such dimensions as scope, salience, and intensity, it follows that rules also vary along these dimensions. Collier (1986a) has argued that rules can be categorized from broad to specific in generality.

Different rules, also varying in scope and salience, have been identified for intercultural conversations among acquaintances (Collier, in press). Interestingly, Mexican-Americans were found to hold similar rules for appropriate conduct whether they were conversing with another Mexican-American or an Anglo, whereas Black- and Anglo-North Americans used different rules for intra- and intercultural conversations with acquaintances. Mexican-American students preferred relationally friendly and bonding messages early in advisement meetings with Anglo advisers, while Asian-American students preferred role-related, more formal conduct (Collier, in press).

Outcomes. In addition to rules, communication competence includes attention to the outcomes of rule conformity or violation in particular conversations. In this way, the function or outcome of the system processes, and results of rule conformity or violation, are given attention. Specifically, we are referring to the consequences or effects of communication. Communication is functional to the extent that positive outcomes are experienced, regardless of whether or not the "intended" goal was accomplished (Spitzberg & Cupach, 1984).

Communication competence includes not only following mutually appropriate rules for conduct, but also conducting oneself in a way that allows interlocutors to experience positive outcomes from a particular interaction. Outcomes are an important source of data in intercultural inquiry because they reveal the "force" of particular rules (Pearce & Cronen, 1980). Also, relationships that are perceived to be contexts that produce positive outcomes will more likely be maintained or escalated (Collier, in press). Finally, outcomes also can be compared and contrasted across dimensions such as scope, salience, and intensity.

Different types of outcomes already have been identified in cultural and intercultural inquiry. Positive outcomes include self-concept reinforcement (Collier, 1986a), affirmation of cultural identity (Collier, 1986b, in press), desire to maintain the relationship (Collier, 1986a; Collier, Ribeau, & Hecht, 1986), and goal accomplishment (Collier, 1986a; Collier, Ribeau, & Hecht, 1986).

Competencies—rules and preferred outcomes—have been identified in a variety of relationships and conversational contexts. The various levels of rules and different types of outcomes have been identified in both intra- and intercultural conversational settings. Rules and preferred outcomes have been identified among acquaintances (Collier, 1988; Collier, Ribeau, & Hecht, 1986), among friends (Collier, 1986a; 1986b), and within more formal relationships, such as adviser-advisee (Collier, in press) and instructor-student settings (Powell & Collier, 1987). In each of these particular studies, nationality rules, ethnic rules, gender rules, and relational rules differed. Various outcomes were experienced as well.

Meanings. We have noted the importance of a major dimension of culture, that of meaning, "worldview," or the constitutive. We are positing that the rules/systems approach can be expanded to include the identification of beliefs and core symbols. Beliefs are found in systems of meanings in the text (Geertz, 1973). The meanings associated with particular cultural or ethnic labels can be described intersubjectively by interlocutors. In other words, the galaxies of meanings around the label *Chicano* could be charted and patterns and recurring symbols could be identified from conversational text by persons who consider themselves Chicano. The beliefs associated with certain roles can also be tracked, such as "adviser" or "professor" (Kerssen, 1987).

The rules/systems approach therefore has been successful in identifying different types of rules and preferred outcomes perceived to be relevant by interlocutors. This approach enables researchers to identify intercultural as well as intracultural communication competencies and to ultimately compare intra- to intercultural communication competencies (Collier, 1988).

Rules/systems is establishing a "track record" in the identification of competencies in general, and cultural/ethnic competencies in particular. It has been applied primarily to the identification of the normative dimension of culture. Collier (1986b) argued that core symbols could be postulated from intra- and intercultural competencies. An example is that of "demeanor" that was a core symbol identified as characterizing Asian-American competence.

Finally, the rules/systems approach is appropriate here because the ontological and epistemological assumptions are consistent. We believe that researchers should give attention to the experience of the interlocutors. Identifying the normative and constitutive dimensions of culture intersubjectively in talk are consistent with this research goal.

Methodologically, there are a variety of ways that researchers can identify competencies and beliefs. Collier has used recent recalled conversations as one text from which competencies have been identified (Collier, 1986a, 1986b, 1988; Collier, Ribeau, & Hecht, 1986). Research by Hecht and Ribeau (1984), as well as Collier's work, has shown that recalled conversation is an appropriate and reliable method of inquiry when persons are asked to describe a recent conversation and they are asked to describe the other person's behavior instead of their own. Powell and Collier (1987) asked respondents to describe an effective instructor in college classrooms and then content-analyzed the descriptions to identify beliefs about and preferences for instructor conduct. Transcripts or videotapes of entire conversations could be analyzed for constitutive and normative themes. Core symbols could thus be inferred from competencies revealed in the text, or from beliefs articulated in the text, or both.

We have argued that the rules/systems theoretical approach is an appropriate way to study the formation and management of cultural identity. This theoretical approach focuses on two sets of concepts that are relevant to cultural identity, meanings and norms. Meanings and norms are subsumed under the umbrella concept of cultural core symbols; core symbols can be inferred from meanings and norms.

The contributions that we see the rules/systems theoretical approach making to the study of cultural identity are summarized in the assumptions and axioms that follow. The axioms listed are consistent with the conceptualization of an axiom discussed by Gibbs (1967), as well as Hawes (1975), and illustrated by Shimanoff (1980). The axioms here are general in scope, and are descriptive statements about relationships between constructs.

Assumption 3: Intracultural communication competence involves the coherent management of meanings and competencies—appropriate (rule-following) and effective (positive outcome-producing) conduct.

Assumption 4: Intercultural competence is created by the negotiation of mutual meanings, rules, and positive outcomes.

Assumption 5: Intercultural competence is a process in which cultural identities are validated.

Axiom 1: The more that norms and meanings differ in discourse, the more intercultural the contact.

Axiom 2: The higher the degree of intercultural competence, the higher the likelihood that the relationship will be developed or maintained.

CULTURAL IDENTIFICATION

In the preceding discussions, we have argued for an interpretive perspective in studying the process of intercultural communication competence in which the communication code is the most general unit of analysis. We have offered interpretive characterizations of culture, intercultural communication and communication competence. We believe, however, that the nucleus around which these phenomena revolve is cultural identity. What follows is a characterization of the most specific unit of analysis that we find significant in intercultural communication—cultural identity—and an explanation of the role we believe cultural identity plays in communication.

According to DeVos (1982), a sense of common origin and survival has bound humans into groups throughout time. We notice that in discourse, persons' cultural and other group identities are complex, multivariate, and dynamic. Identities are formed, negotiated, modified, confirmed, and challenged through communication and contact with others (Goffman, 1967; McCall, 1976; Scotton, 1983). Ting-Toomey (1986) posits that individuals are constantly negotiating identities such as social role and personal identity.

DeVos and Ross (1982) argue that identities are negotiated through a process of contrast of self to others and one's group to other groups. The cultural identities of interlocutors are a function of their self- and alter-ascriptions in cultural terms (McCall, 1976). DeVos and Ross

(1982) note that identities function to define rules of comportment, create a moral commitment, and reinforce a sense of common origin. When individuals identify a conversational partner as culturally different, the negotiation process becomes more complex. Intercultural communication is a process of comparisons, judgments, ascriptions, and negotiations of both persons' identities. One's own cultural identity may include stereotypes, opinions and meanings, and norms about other cultural groups that have been passed down and are then modified and negotiated in intercultural contact.

We subscribe to a liberal conceptualization of culture, and are most interested in "cultural" identities. We define *cultural identity* as *identification with and perceived acceptance into a group that has shared systems of symbols and meanings as well as norms/rules for conduct* (following conceptualizations of culture by Geertz, 1973; Schneider, 1976). Cultural identity is created through symbolic and normative competence. In other words, when individuals identify with cultural groups they are able to manipulate and understand systems of symbols and beliefs and are able to enact culturally appropriate and effective behavior with members of that group. Identity is a combination of ideas about "being" and norms for "acting." Core symbols and emblems reify cultural identity for interlocutors.

Cultural identity is dynamic and fluid because it is constituted and rendered in interaction, but it also has substance that is transmitted from generation to generation, or from cultural group member to newcomer. One or more particular cultural identities may become salient in a given conversational encounter.

Dimensions of Cultural Identity

We believe that various levels or types of identity are operative in intercultural communication. Cultural identities differ with regard to several dimensions. For example, identities differ in their scope—the breadth and generalizability of the identity. Some identities such as nationality are quite broad in scope and apply to large numbers of people, while others, such as personality, tend to be narrow in scope and apply to specific persons. Cultural identity has relatively broad scope, beyond that of family membership or personality, because of the emphasis on culture and the historically transmitted system of meanings and norms. Thus, an idiosyncratic identity or role would not be "cultural." The discursive form cultural identity takes is an explicit interpretation of conduct in which a claim is made about personhood, the origins of which are attributed to a culture group.

Identities also differ on the salience of the particular identities relative to other potential identities in particular contexts (Ting-Toomey, 1986). For example, in a professional setting, one's identity as a nontenured college professor may be most important, whereas at a social gathering, one's identity as spouse may be most important and evident in dialogue. For a detailed overview of some variables that correlate with and predict salience of group identity in intergroup communication see Giles and Johnson (1981, 1986, in press).

In addition to scope and salience, identities vary in the intensity with which they are communicated. A person who identifies himself or herself as a Pan-African, for example, may use a stronger voice tone, may be more likely to speak Ebonics, may use more "we" terms, and may include more talk about "actions that are needed by the community" than a person who identifies himself or herself as a North American of African descent.

Atkinson, Morten, and Sue (1983) detail a minority development model that suggests that a person's development of a cultural or minority identity occurs in a process over time. Minority identity is formed through contact with individuals from one's own group, as well as through contact with individuals from the dominant culture. At various stages of development, a person may identify him or herself as a member of the dominant culture, at other stages may strongly proclaim membership in a minority culture and may openly criticize the dominant culture, and at still other stages take on a more pluralistic, and individual identity. Thus, the intensity with which the group member openly and explicitly defines himself or herself changes.

Conditions Covarying with Cultural Identity

At this point, it is reasonable to assume that any aspect of social context may systematically covary with the discursive presence of cultural identities. Hymes (1972) describes a framework useful for identifying features of social context that are likely to covary with linguistic features such as cultural identity labels. Some probable sociocontextual variables are the number and relationship(s) of participants, speech event, and topic. We believe, however, that identity negotiation is fluid and narrative in nature, and that multiple identities are likely to be negotiated in a single episode, so that a method such as interpretive ethnography (Geertz, 1973, 1983) may be most appropriate for at least preliminary investigations. Social context may be a canvas woven from a number of features on which multiple cultural identities are painted. If so, efforts to draw linear relationships may be premature.

Ethnic Identity

Ethnic identity is a particularly important cultural identity because of the diversity in scope, salience, and the intensity with which it is communicated. Ethnic groups in the United States, for example, are large to small in number, adhere to their ethnic heritage and customs in vastly different degrees, and view the importance of their ethnic identity in dramatically different strengths.

Ethnic identity is a primary source of identification for many individuals (Banks, 1984). *Ethnic identity is identification with and perceived acceptance into a group with shared heritage and culture* (Collier, 1986b). DeVos (1982) summarizes the difference between other general identities and ethnic identity by noting that ethnic identity includes an emphasis on the past heritage and roots over present or future orientations.

Identity formation and management occurs in communication. The discursive text created between interlocutors reflects and influences identities that are salient at a given time. The text reflects symbols about "what is" and "what should be." The identity frames and texts for an individual may differ significantly from context to context. For example, the identity that is managed for a student may be "American" when friends visit from outside the country, "Mexican" at home with the extended family, "Chicano" with friends at college, "minority" when registering for courses, and "student" in class. In each context, the identity frames, core symbols, and norms are identifiable in the discursive text.

Axioms and theorems can be proposed at this point in order to summarize our theoretical perspective and approach to the study of cultural identity in intercultural communication. A theorem is a secondary statement and, although general in scope, contains constructs that can be operationally defined and empirically observed (Hawes, 1975).

> *Assumption 6:* Cultural identity varies along three central, interdependent dimensions: scope, salience, and intensity.
> *Axiom 3:* The more that cultural identities differ in the discourse, the more intercultural the contact.

Axiom 4: The more the consistency in each individual's ascription of the other's cultural identity matching the other's avowed cultural identity, the higher the intercultural competence.

Axiom 5: Linguistic references to cultural identity systematically covary with sociocontextual features such as participants, type of episode, and topic.

Theorem 1: The more intensity with which cultural identities are avowed in discourse, the higher the salience of those particular identities relative to others.

IMPLICATIONS

Several implications can be drawn from our model of cultural identity and intercultural communication. Our model of interpretive inquiry is a viable alternative to other psycholinguistic and social-psychological perspectives. This perspective on research in intercultural communication strengthens the validity of conclusions from research because of the basis in human experience. We argue that a focus on symbolic activity and discourse is primordial to communication research. Finally, our perspective is a coherent mode of inquiry and begins to represent the complexities and processual nature of cultural identity development as experienced by interlocutors.

When intercultural communication is conceptualized according to operative cultural identities, then we can begin to distinguish intercultural from nonintercultural communication, either by explicit references to differing cultural identities or by inappropriate or incoherent conduct. With an attention to levels of cultural identity, we can track cultural systems and subsystems and begin to identify meanings and rules that reflect membership in particular groups. For example, we can distinguish when a Hispanic is primarily defining himself or herself as a man or woman or as primarily a "Chicano."

Cultural identity is a fluid process residing in discourse rather than a discrete dependent or independent variable. Because cultural identities differ in scope, salience, and intensity, *a priori* predictions from cultural identity based on birth or nationality, for example, may be oversimplified. It may not be appropriate to predict from or to "Anglo-American" since Anglo-American may not be salient in some situations, may be defined differently by different individuals, may be intensely claimed in contexts with individuals who are defined as minorities, and may be weakly claimed in contexts with international visitors. Studying scope, salience, and intensity of cultural identities in discourse is therefore theoretically useful, because if one participant ascribes a more general or inappropriate identity to the other, disconfirmation and dissatisfaction may be the outcome. When researchers and practitioners alike have a framework with which to describe and understand cultural identity avowal, ascription, and negotiation, knowledge is advanced. Cultural identity as conceptualized here, as systems of core symbols, meanings and norms provides such a framework. We can thus begin to understand when two persons are less than satisfied with an encounter (e.g., a Chinese female defines her Anglo friend as a liberal "pal" who happens to be male, and presents herself as an "acculturated feminist," while her Anglo male friend is presenting himself as a potential spouse and ascribes to her the role of a more traditional, nonassertive female).

Perhaps most importantly, we believe that our model of inquiry and our conclusions should be applicable to the improvement of the quality of human contact. Therefore, attention to intercultural competence and appropriate and effective identity validation is warranted. Intercultural competence is not a set or list of skills that can guarantee success and positive outcomes. Intercultural competence is a mutually negotiated process with varying degrees of appropriateness and varying outcomes. When people are able to understand the identities that are manifest and able to describe differences in meanings or norms, they can begin to negotiate what would be more appropriate and effective for both of them.

CONCLUSION

We believe that the extent to which communication is intercultural is in large part decided by the operative interpretations of the persons present in a given discursive event. These interpretations of identities vary contextually, and cultural identities are always a potential frame in which interlocutors may interpret communication. Cultural identity can be revealed in the discursive texts created by talk about systems of meanings and norms. The better a person is able to manage coherent discourse and comply competently with norms, the more she or he can be said to identify with a cultural group.

Core symbols about cultural identity are revealed in normative talk about intra- and intercultural competence. The rules/systems approach was designed to access communicative competence, therefore it is amenable to the study of cultural identity. Preliminary inquiry about cultural identity has indicated that the rules/systems approach does produce norm statements that contain not only core symbols and general prescriptions but also a range of norms and meanings that suggests operative levels of identity. We believe that in interlocutors' discursive identity formation and management lies an important key to our understanding of intercultural communication.

REFERENCES

Atkinson, D. R., Morten, G., & Sue, D. W. (1983). Minority group counseling, an overview. In D. Atkinson, G. Morten, & D. W. Sue (Eds.), *Counseling American minorities* (2nd ed., pp. 11-32). Dubuque, IA: William C. Brown.

Banks, J. A. (1984). *Teaching strategies for ethnic studies* (3rd. ed.). Boston: Allyn and Bacon.

Berrien, F. K. (1968). *General and social systems.* New Brunswick, NJ: Rutgers University Press.

Boulding, K. (1956). General systems theory—the skeleton of science. *Management Science, 2,* 197-208.

Brown, P., & Levinson, S. (1978). Universals in language usage: politeness phenomena. In E. N. Goody (Ed.), *Questions and politeness: Strategies in social interaction* (pp. 56-289). Cambridge: Cambridge University Press.

Cissna, K.N.L., & Sieburg, E. (1986). Patterns of interactional confirmation and disconfirmation. In J. Stewart (Ed.), *Bridges not walls* (4th ed., pp. 230-239). New York: Random House.

Collier, M. J. (1986a). Culture and gender: Effects on assertive behavior and communication competence. In M. McLaughlin (Ed.), *Communication yearbook 9* (pp. 576-592). Beverly Hills, CA: Sage.

Collier, M. J. (1986b). *Core symbols and the ethnic identification process.* Unpublished manuscript.

Collier, M. J. (1988). A comparison of conversations among and between domestic culture groups: How intra- and intercultural competencies vary. *Communication Quarterly, 36,* 122-144.

Collier, M. J. (in press). Competent communication in intercultural advisement contexts. *Howard Journal of Communications.*

Collier, M. J., Ribeau, S. & Hecht, M. L. (1986). Intracultural communication rules and outcomes within three domestic cultures. *International Journal of Intercultural Relations, 10,* 439-458.

DeVos, G. (1975). Ethnic pluralism: Conflict and accommodation. In G. DeVos & L. Ross (Eds.), *Ethnic identity* (pp. 5-41). Chicago: The University of Chicago Press.

DeVos, G., & Ross, L. (1975). Ethnicity: Vessel of meaning and emblem of contrast. In G. DeVos & L. Ross (Eds.), *Ethnic identity* (pp. 363-390). Chicago: The University of Chicago Press.

Dodd, C. (1987). *Dynamics of intercultural communication.* Dubuque, IA: William C Brown.

Farace, R. V., Monge, P. R., & Russell, H. M. (1977). *Communication and organizing.* Reading, MA: Addison-Wesley.

Fisher, B. A. (1978). *Perspectives on human communication.* New York: Macmillan.

Geertz, C. (1973). *The interpretation of cultures.* New York: Basic Books.

Geertz, C. (1983). *Local knowledge.* New York: Basic Books.

Gibbs, J. P. (1967). Identification of statements in theory construction. *Sociology and Social Research, 52,* 72-87.

Giles, H., & Johnson, P. (1981). The role of language in ethnic group relations. In J. Turner & H. Giles (Eds.), *Inter- group behavior* (pp. 169-198). Chicago: University of Chicago Press.

Giles, H., & Johnson, P. (1986). Perceived threat, ethnic commitment, and interethnic language behavior. In Y. Kim (Ed.), *Interethnic communication* (pp. 91-116). Newbury Park, CA: Sage.

Giles, H., & Johnson, P. (in press). Ethnolinguistic identity theory: A social psychological approach to language maintenance. *International Journal of the Sociology of Language.*

Goffman, E. (1967). On face-work. In *Interaction ritual: Essays on face-to-face behavior* (pp. 5-45). Garden City, NJ: Anchor.

Grossberg, L. (1982). Intersubjectivity and the conceptualization of communication. *Human Studies, 5,* 213-235.

Gudykunst, W. B. (1985). A model of uncertainty reduction in intercultural encounters. *Journal of Language and Social Psychology, 4,* 79-98.

Gudykunst, W. B., & Kim, Y. Y. (1984). *Communicating with strangers.* New York: Random House.

Gudykunst, W. B., & Lim, T. (1986). A perspective for the study of intergroup communication. In W. Gudykunst (Ed.), *Intergroup communication* (pp. 1-9). Baltimore: Edward Arnold.

Gumperz, J., & Hymes, D. (Eds.). (1972). *Directions in sociolinguistics: The ethnography of communication.* New York: Holt, Rinehart and Winston.

Harre, R., & Secord, P. (1973). *The explanation of social behavior.* Totowa, NJ: Littlefield, Adams.

Hawes, L. C. (1975). *Pragmatics of analoguing: Theory and model construction in communication.* Reading, MA: Addison-Wesley.

Hecht, M. L., & Ribeau, S. (1984). Ethnic communication: A comparative analysis of satisfying communication. *International Journal of Intercultural Relations, 8,* 135-151.

Hofstede, G. (1983). Dimensions of national cultures in fifty countries and three regions. In J. B. Deregowski, S. Dziurawiec, & R. C. Annis (Eds.), *Explications in cross-cultural psychology* (pp. 335-355). Lisse, the Netherlands: Swets & Zeitlinger.

Hymes, D. (1972). Models of the interaction of language and social life. In J. Gumperz & D. Hymes (Eds.), *Directions in sociolinguistics: The ethnography of communication* (pp. 1-72). New York: Holt, Rinehart & Winston.

Katriel, T., & Philipsen, G. (1981). What we need is "communication": "Communication" as a cultural category in some American speech. *Communication Monographs, 48,* 301-317.

Kerssen, J. (1987, February). Accuracy in academia? "Professor" as a problematic cultural term: An ethnographic study. Paper presented at the annual meeting of the Western Speech Communication Association, Salt Lake City.

Kolb, W. L. (1964). Norm. In J. Gould & W. Kolb (Eds.), *Dictionary of the social sciences* (pp. 472-473). New York: Free Press of Glencoe.

McCall, G. J. (1976). Communication and negotiated identity. *Communication, 2,* 173-184.

Miller, G. R. (1978). The current status of theory and research in interpersonal communication. *Human Communication Research, 4,* 164-168.

Miller, G. R., & Steinberg, M. (1975). *Between people.* Chicago: Science Research.

Monge, P. (1977). The systems perspective as a theoretical basis for the study of human communication. *Communication Quarterly, 25,* 19-29.

Pearce, W. B., & Cronen, V. E. (1980). *Communication, action and meaning.* New York: Praeger.

Philipsen, G. (1980). *The prospect for cultural communication.* Paper presented at the Seminar on Communication Theory from Eastern and Western Perspectives, East-West Communication Institute, East-West Center, Honolulu.

Pike, K. L. (1966). *Language in relation to the unified theory of the structure of human behavior* (2nd ed.). The Hague: Mouton.

Powell, R., & Collier, M. J. (1987, May). *The effect of student culture/ethnicity on judgments of instructional communication: A replication and extension.* Paper presented at the annual meeting of the International Communication Association, Montréal.

Ragan, S. (1983). Alignment and conversational coherence. In R. Craig & K. Tracy (Eds.), *Conversational coherence* (pp. 157-171). Beverly Hills, CA: Sage.

Ruben, B. (1972). General system theory: An approach to human communication. In R. Budd & B. Ruben (Eds.), *Approaches to human communication* (pp. 120-144). New York: Spartan.

Samovar, L., Porter, R., & Jain, N. (1981). *Understanding intercultural communication.* Belmont, CA: Wadsworth.

Sarbaugh, L. E. (1979). *Intercultural communication.* Rochelle Park, NJ: Hayden.

Schneider, D. (1976). Notes toward a theory of culture. In K. Basso & H. Selby (Eds.), *Meaning in anthropology* (pp. 197-220). Albuquerque, NM: University of New Mexico Press.

Scotton, C. M. (1983). The negotiation of identities in conversation: A theory of markedness and code choice. *International Journal of the Sociology of Language, 44,* 115-136.

Searle, J. (1969). *Speech acts.* Cambridge: Cambridge University Press.

Shimanoff, S. (1980). *Communication rules: Theory and research.* Beverly Hills, CA: Sage.

Spitzberg, B., & Cupach, W. (1984). *Interpersonal communication competence.* Beverly Hills, CA: Sage.

Stewart, J. (1986). Introduction. *Bridges not walls* (4th ed.). New York: Random House.

Tajfel, H., & Turner, J. C. (1979). An integrative theory of intergroup conflict. In W. Austin & S. Worchel (Eds.), *The social psychology of intergroup relations* (pp. 33-48). Monterey, CA: Brooks/Cole.

Thayer, L. (1968). *Communication and communication systems.* Homewood, IL: Irwin.

Ting-Toomey, S. (1986). Interpersonal ties in intergroup communication. In W. Gudykunst (Ed.), *Intergroup communication* (pp. 114-126). Edward Arnold.

Watzlawick, P., Beavin, J. H., & Jackson, D. (1967). *Pragmatics of human communication.* New York: Norton.

III

INTERCULTURAL BEHAVIOR

6

Uncertainty and Anxiety

WILLIAM B. GUDYKUNST • *Arizona State University*

The purpose of this chapter is to proffer an explanation of intergroup communication that is based, in part, on uncertainty reduction theory. Initially, the basic assumptions of the theory are explicated. Axioms then are generated relating ethnolinguistic identity, expectations, group similarity, shared networks, interpersonal salience, second language competence, self- monitoring, cognitive complexity, and tolerance for ambiguity to attributional confidence and the reduction of intergroup anxiety. Next, attributional confidence and the reduction of intergroup anxiety are used to explain intergroup adaptation and effectiveness. Finally, cultural variability is incorporated in the theory by linking individualism-collectivism to attributional confidence and uncertainty avoidance to the reduction of intergroup anxiety. The current status and future direction for the theory also are examined.

Uncertainty reduction theory is one of the few communication theories systematically extended to explain cross-cultural variations in communication, as well as intercultural and intergroup communication (see Berger, 1987; Berger & Gudykunst, in press, for recent reviews of the theory). Underlying the theory is the assumption that individuals attempt to reduce uncertainty in initial interactions with strangers when they will be encountered in the future, can provide rewards, or act in a deviant fashion (Berger, 1979). Uncertainty reduction involves the creation of proactive predictions about others' attitudes, beliefs, feelings, and behavior, as well as retroactive explanations about others' behavior. Berger and Calabrese's (1975) initial formulation of the theory posited seven axioms and 21 theorems specifying the interrelations among uncertainty, amount of communication, nonverbal affiliative expressiveness, information seeking, intimacy level of communication

AUTHOR'S NOTE: *The chapter benefited from the comments and suggestions of Charles Berger, Young Yun Kim, Ronald Perry, and Michael Sunnafrank. Mitchell Hammer, coauthor of an earlier special version of the theory applied to intercultural adaptation, agreed to the use of portions of that version of the theory here, and provided a valuable critique of this chapter as well. The chapter was presented at the November 1987 Speech Communication Association Convention in Boston in its present form.*

content, reciprocity, similarity, and liking. Berger (1979) elaborated the theory by outlining three general strategies individuals use for reducing uncertainty: passive, active, and interactive. More recently, Berger and Bradac (1982) emphasized the influence of language and the general similarity construct on uncertainty reduction processes, while Parks and Adelman (1983) linked shared communication networks to the reduction of uncertainty.

Cross-cultural studies suggest that the theory generalizes initial interactions between low- and high-context cultures (Gudykunst, 1983c; Gudykunst & Nishida, 1984; Gudykunst, Nishida, Koike, & Shiino, 1986), as well as to acquaintance, friend, and dating relationships across cultures (Gudykunst, Yang, & Nishida, 1985). Recent research (Gudykunst & Hammer, 1987) also reveals that the theory can account for ethnic differences in initial interactions between blacks and whites in the United States. Intercultural research (Gudykunst, 1985a, 1985c; Gudykunst, Chua, & Gray, 1987; Gudykunst, Nishida, & Chua, 1986) further indicates that uncertainty reduction theory is useful in explaining communication between people from different cultures and interethnic communication in the United States (Gudykunst, 1986a).

Gudykunst (1985a) tested a preliminary model of uncertainty reduction in intercultural encounters and suggested an extension to intergroup situations that partially integrated ethnolinguistic identity theory (Beebe & Giles, 1984). Essentially the model suggests that ethnolinguistic identity influences second language competence and intergroup attitudes/stereotypes. In combination with interpersonal factors (e.g., the use of uncertainty reduction strategies, attraction, frequency of communication, intimacy of relationship, and attitude similarity), group similarity, intergroup attitudes/stereotypes, knowledge of the other group, shared networks, and second language competence influence uncertainty reduction (attributional confidence).

Gudykunst and Hammer (1988) also applied uncertainty reduction theory to intercultural adaptation. They argued that reducing uncertainty and reducing/controlling anxiety are necessary and sufficient conditions for intercultural adaptation. Eight variables were related to reducing both uncertainty and anxiety: knowledge of host culture, shared networks, intergroup attitudes, favorable contact, stereotypes, cultural identity, cultural similarity, and second language competence; four influenced only uncertainty reduction: intimacy, attraction, display of nonverbal affiliative expressiveness, and the use of appropriate uncertainty reduction strategies; and four were associated only with reducing anxiety: strangers' motivation to live permanently in the host culture, host nationals' intergroup attitudes, host culture policy toward strangers, and strangers' psychological differentiation.

The purpose of the present chapter is to modify Gudykunst's (1985a) model and Gudykunst and Hammer's (1988) theory of intercultural adaptation to proffer an explanation of intergroup communication based on uncertainty reduction and ethnolinguistic identity theories.[1] The focus is on intergroup communication in general, rather than intercultural communication in particular, because intercultural communication is a form of intergroup communication (Gudykunst & Lim, 1986; e.g., the specific case of intergroup communication when participants come from different cultures). Gudykunst and Kim (1984) argue that communication can be viewed as varying along a continuum from involving total strangeness to total familiarity. At the total strangeness end of the continuum, individuals are communicating with strangers (in the sense that Simmel, 1950, used the concept; discussed next), basing their communication on categorical (i.e., group membership) information. At the total familiarity end, in contrast, little categorical data is used. Focusing on intergroup communication allows the theory proffered to be integrated with a major line of research in social psychology (i.e., the study of intergroup relations) and it avoids the quagmire of terminology for related processes (e.g., interethnic, interracial, interclass).

FOUNDATIONS OF THE THEORY

Uncertainty and Anxiety

To understand intergroup communication, it is necessary to recognize that at least one of the individuals involved is a "stranger" (Gudykunst & Kim, 1984). Simmel (1950) introduced the concept in his classic essay "Der Fremde" ("The Stranger," published in 1908 in German), arguing that strangers are physically present and participating in a situation (i.e., interacting with the ingroup), but at the same time, are outside the situation because they are from a different place (i.e., an outgroup). Schuetz (1944) views a stranger as "an adult individual . . . who tries to be permanently accepted or at least partially tolerated by the group which he [or she] approaches" (p. 499). Because strangers lack "intersubjective understanding," or an understanding of the social world inhabited by the members of the ingroup, their interactions with members of the ingroup can create anxiety and often are experienced as a series of crises. This suggests:

> *Assumption 1:* At least one participant in an intergroup encounter is a stranger vis-à-vis the ingroup being approached.

Herman and Schield (1961) point out that "the immediate psychological result of being in a new situation is lack of security. Ignorance of the potentialities inherent in the situation, of the means to reach a goal, and of the probable outcomes of an intended action causes insecurity" (p. 165). Attempts to adapt to the ambiguity of new situations involves a cyclical pattern of tension-reducing and information-seeking behaviors (Ball-Rokeach, 1973). Information seeking is directed toward individuals increasing their ability to predict or explain their own and others' behavior in the environment; that is, reducing cognitive uncertainty. Tension reduction, on the other hand, is directed toward reducing the anxiety individuals experience. Stephan and Stephan (1985) argue that "anxiety stems from the anticipation of negative consequences. People appear to fear four types of negative consequences: psychological or behavior consequences for the self, and negative evaluations by members of the outgroup and the ingroup" (p. 159). These observations imply:

> *Assumption 2:* Strangers' initial experiences with a new ingroup are experienced as a series of crises; that is, strangers are not cognitively sure of how to behave (i.e., cognitive uncertainty) and they experience the feeling of a lack of security (i.e., anxiety).

Before proceeding, the relationship between uncertainty and anxiety needs to be addressed. For the purpose of the present formulation, it is assumed that uncertainty and anxiety are independent aspects of the communication process. While social cognitive processes (i.e., uncertainty reduction) and affective processes (i.e., reducing anxiety) are related, the influence of social cognitive processes on intercultural communication is mediated through behavioral intentions and the influence of affective processes is not (Gudykunst, 1987a). It is possible for strangers to reduce uncertainty, but still have high levels of anxiety and vice versa. A third assumption, therefore, is needed:

> *Assumption 3:* Uncertainty and anxiety are independent dimensions of intergroup communication.

Group Membership and Communication

Strangers are socialized members of one culture (outgroup), but are confronting a new, "foreign" culture or subculture (ingroup). To explain their communication, it is necessary to examine how culture influences behavior. Keesing (1974) borrows the distinction between "competence" and "performance" from linguistics to explain how culture influences behavior:

> It is his [or her] *theory of what his [or her] fellows know, believe, and mean*, his [or her] theory of the code being followed, the game being played ... It is this theory to which a native actor refers in interpreting the unfamiliar or the ambiguous, in interacting with strangers ... the actor's "theory" of his [or her] culture, like his [or her] theory of his [or her] language, may be in large measure unconscious. Actors follow rules of which they are not consciously aware. (p. 89)

This conceptualization suggests that culture forms an "implicit" theory that individuals use to guide their behavior and interpret others' behavior. Much behavior in which individuals engage in their own culture is habitual. Habits "are situation-behavior sequences that are or have become automatic, so that they occur without self-instruction. The individual is not usually 'conscious' of these sequences" (Triandis, 1980, p. 204). Individuals become conscious of their habitual behavior, however, when they enter new situations (e.g., interact with a member of another culture) because they are interacting with individuals who do not share their implicit theories. Gudykunst and Kim (1984) contend that this heightened awareness makes individuals more conscious of their behavior when communicating with people from other cultures than when communicating with someone from their own. This suggests:

Assumption 4: Strangers' behavior takes place at high levels of awareness.

Communication between members of an ingroup and strangers is based, at least in part, upon group membership. Sherif (1966) argues that "whenever individuals who belong to one group interact collectively or individually, with another group or its members *in terms of their group identification*, we have an instance of intergroup behavior" (p. 12). Tajfel and Turner (1979) describe behavior as varying along a continuum from purely interpersonal (i.e., no behavior is based on group membership) to purely intergroup (i.e., all behavior is based on group memberships). Gudykunst and Lim (1986), however, argue that both interpersonal and intergroup factors are salient in every encounter, and therefore, two dimensions are needed: low-to-high intergroup salience and low-to-high interpersonal salience. Billig's (1987) argument that both categorization and particularization occur in intergroup encounters supports the contention that interpersonal and intergroup salience are orthogonal dimensions. This implies:

> *Assumption 5:* Both intergroup and interpersonal factors influence intergroup communication.

When intergroup factors are salient, research suggests that strangers do not give the "proper" weight to situational factors in predicting or explaining outgroup members' behavior; that is, they tend to underestimate its influence. Jaspars and Hewstone (1982) argue the tendency is to attribute positive behavior of ingroup members (other strangers) to dispositional factors and positive behavior from an outgroup member (member of ingroup being approached) to situational factors. Negative behavior by ingroup members, in contrast, is attributed to situational factors, while outgroup members' negative behavior is attributed to dispositional factors. Strangers' attributions during the process of intercultural adaptation are influenced highly by cultural differences and, therefore, the dispositional factor used to explain host nationals' behavior often is culture. A sixth assumption, therefore, emerges:

> *Assumption 6:* Strangers overestimate the influence of group membership in explaining members of other groups' behavior.

FORMULATION OF THE THEORY

To formulate the theory, axioms that state the relationships between primary variables were generated. Blalock (1969) states that axioms are "propositions that involve variables that are taken to be directly linked causally; axioms should therefore be statements that imply direct causal links among variables" (p. 18, italics omitted). When combined, the axioms form a "causal-process" theory (Reynolds, 1971) that attempts to explain two outcomes of intergroup communication: intergroup adaptation and intergroup communication effectiveness. To preview, the argument presented is that these outcomes are a function of uncertainty reduction and the reduction of intergroup anxiety. Uncertainty and anxiety reduction, in turn, are influenced by ethnolinguistic identity, second language ability, expectations, group similarity, shared networks, interpersonal salience, self-monitoring, cognitive complexity, and tolerance for ambiguity. Finally, uncertainty and anxiety reduction, as well as the relationship of other variables to these two, are influenced by culture. The remainder of this section is devoted to presenting the basic evidence for the axioms.

Ethnolinguistic Identity

Social identity theory (Tajfel, 1978; Turner, 1987) assumes that individuals seek positive social identities in intergroup encounters. Social identity is "that *part* of an individual's self-concept which derives from his [or her] knowledge of his [or her] membership in a social group (or groups) together with the value and emotional significance attached to that membership" (Tajfel, 1978, p. 63). That part of the self-concept not accounted for by social identity is personal identity. Giles and Johnson (1981) argue that language is a vital aspect of the social identity of any group, particularly ethnolinguistic groups.

Giles and Byrne (1982) extended Giles and Johnson's (1981) analysis to provide an intergroup model of second language competence. They argue that second language competence is increased when there is weak ingroup identification, quiescent intergroup comparisons are made, ingroup vitality is perceived as low, ingroup boundaries are open/soft, and members of the ingroup identify with other social categories strongly. Giles and Johnson's (1987) research supported the proposed linkages between weak ingroup identification, quiescent intergroup comparison, open/soft ingroup boundaries, and second language competence. Results of Hall and Gudykunst's (1986) study are consistent with the intergroup model in general, with the strongest support emerging for the effect of soft/open boundaries.

Recent work by Gudykunst, Sodetani, and Sonoda (1987) and Gudykunst and Hammer (in press) applied this line of research to uncertainty reduction. Both studies demonstrated that ethnolinguistic and social identity are related to uncertainty reduction processes in general and that they are related positively to interethnic attributional confidence. While inconsistent with the initial version of Giles' (e.g., Giles & Byrne, 1982) intergroup theory of second language acquisition, this finding is consistent with a recent revision (Giles, Garrett, & Coupland, 1987). Gudykunst and Hammer's finding is consistent with Hall and Gudykunst's (1986) results, which indicated that the stronger the ingroup identification, the greater the perceived competence in the outgroup language. Their data also are compatible with Lambert, Mermigis, and Taylor's (1986) study, which suggests that the more secure and positive members of a group feel about their identity, the more tolerant they are of members of other groups. Similar observations emerge from other studies (e.g., Bond & King, 1985; Pak, Dion, & Dion, 1985).

Gudykunst and Hammer's (in press) research further revealed that social identity influences uncertainty reduction only when members of the outgroup are perceived as typical of their group. When members of the outgroup are perceived as atypical, social identity does not affect uncertainty reduction. Gudykunst and Hammer also found that social identity influences uncertainty reduction only when ethnic status is activated. These findings are consistent with Gerard's (1963) research, which indicated that uncertainty produces a desire in individuals to compare themselves with others. It also appears that ethnic identity influences the anxiety strangers experience in new cultures; the stronger the identification with the native culture, the more anxiety (Dyal & Dyal, 1981; Padilla, 1980). Treating ethnolinguistic identity as one variable, the first axiom emerges:

> *Axiom 1:* An increase in the strength of strangers' ethnolinguistic identities will produce an increase in their attributional confidence regarding members of other groups' behavior and an increase in the anxiety they experience when interacting with members of other groups. This axiom holds *only* when members of the outgroup are perceived as "typical" and when ethnic status is activated.

Expectations

Expectation states theory (e.g., Berger & Zelditch, 1985) posits that the expectations individuals form for each other influence their behavior. Expectations involve looking forward or anticipating something (positive or negative) in the future. Expectations are a function of knowledge, beliefs/attitudes, stereotypes, self-conceptions (including ethnolinguistic identity), roles, prior interaction, and status characteristics. Status characteristics are activated by external factors (e.g., race, ethnicity, sex, physical attractiveness, education, occupation) and expressive (e.g., dialect, eye contact, speech styles, skin color) or indicative (e.g., "I am a Chicano") cues (see Berger, Webster, Ridgeway, & Rosenholz, 1986, for an overview of cues that reflect status characteristics).[2] The first factor involved in the formation of expectations to be examined is knowledge of the other group.

Miller and Steinberg (1975) argue that individuals use three types of data when making predictions about others' behavior: cultural, sociological, and psychological. People in any culture generally behave in a regular fashion because of shared norms, rules, and values, and this regularity allows for making predictions on the basis of "cultural" data. Miller and Sunnafrank (1982) elaborate by pointing out that "knowledge about another person's culture—its language, dominant values, beliefs, and prevailing ideology—often permits predictions of the person's probable response to certain messages" (p. 226). "Sociological" predictions are based on memberships in or aspirations to particular social groups. Miller and Sunnafrank (1982) argue that sociological data are the principal kind used to predict the behavior of people from the same culture. At the "psychological" level predictions are based on the specific people with whom strangers are communicating. At this level strangers are concerned with how individuals are different from and similar to other members of the host culture and of the groups to which they belong. The preceding analysis suggests that intergroup attributional confidence (the inverse of uncertainty) is affected by the expectancies created from knowledge of the other group. Stephan and Stephan's (1984) research also suggests that lack of knowledge of the other group is one of the major causes of intergroup anxiety.

Intergroup expectancies also are formed on the basis of intergroup attitudes such as prejudice (Pettigrew, 1978) and social representations (Hewstone, Jaspars, & Laljee, 1982). There is conflicting evidence, however, with respect to ethnocentrism. O'Driscoll and Feather's (1983) study indicated that ethnocentrism influences the social distance between members of different ethnic groups. Taylor and Jaggi (1974) also found that ethnocentrism influences attributions Hindus make about Muslims, but research by Hewstone and Ward (1985) suggests that this may not be a universal tendency. Their research revealed that the influence of ethnocentrism may be mediated by the stereotypes of the outgroup or social identity vis-à-vis the ingroup. Negative intergroup attitudes also influence the knowledge strangers have about an outgroup (Stephan & Stephan, 1984) and intergroup anxiety (Stephan & Stephan, 1985). In addition to strangers' attitudes toward the ingroup, ingroup attitudes toward strangers influence the degree of anxiety strangers experience (Dyal & Dyal, 1981; Gudykunst, 1983b).

Information used in making predictions about members of other groups is generated by inferences based on observations. Once strangers obtain information about members of other groups, an impression of individuals or "typical" members of the group is made through inferences about expected relationships. Research suggests that the need to make inferences is greater when dealing with people who are unfamiliar than when dealing with those who are familiar (Koltuv, 1962). When strangers deal with members of other groups there is limited information available and many gaps must be filled and, therefore, extreme inferences often are necessary.

Berger (1979) isolated three major strategies individuals use to gain information (which creates expectancies) about others: passive, active, and interactive. Strangers can use all three strategies prior to interacting with members of other groups and after meeting members of another group to gain information. The passive strategies strangers use to reduce uncertainty about members of other groups' behavior include, but are not limited to, reading books, watching television or movies, and observing them interacting with each other.

Observing members of other groups, either personally or through mass media, is one way of gaining information. The mass media provide most of the information for those who have not had contact with other groups (Hartmann & Husband, 1972). Individuals who have had little contact also tend to perceive the media's content to be "real" (Murray & Kippax, 1979). The media, therefore, provide strangers who have had little experience with other groups stereotypes that are perceived to be accurate (Rothbart, Dawes, & Park, 1984). Stereotypes influence several aspects of strangers' communication with members of other groups. Drawing on Hewstone and Giles's (1986) analysis of stereotypes, at least four generalizations appear to be warranted: (1) stereotyping is the result of cognitive biases stemming from illusory correlations between group membership and psychological attributes; (2) stereotypes influence the way information is processed, i.e., more favorable information is remembered about ingroups and more unfavorable information is remembered about outgroups; (3) stereotypes create expectancies (hypotheses) about others and individuals try to confirm these expectancies; and (4) stereotypes constrain others' patterns of communication and engender stereotype-confirming communication, that is, they create self-fulfilling prophecies. Stephan and Stephan's (1985) research also indicated that negative stereotypes are related to anxiety experienced during intergroup contact.

Active strategies (i.e., asking other strangers about the group), in contrast, can play a role in changing attitudes and increasing the accuracy of stereotypes. Hamilton and Bishop (1976), for example, found that whites in an integrated housing area changed their racial attitudes as a function of indirect methods of collecting information about blacks; that is, discussion with other whites. When contact takes place, information can be obtained using interactive strategies such as interrogation, self-disclosure, and deception detection (Berger, 1979). Downs and Stea (1977) argue that information, not necessarily understanding, emerges from contact. Accurate information, however, can be obtained only if the contact occurs under favorable conditions (i.e., conditions that do not increase prejudice or ethnocentrism; see Amir, 1969; Hewstone & Brown, 1986; Miller & Brewer, 1984; for reviews). Although actual intergroup contact is not likely to meet these "favorable" conditions (Rose, 1981), Stephan and Stephan (1985) demonstrate that when previous contact has occurred under favorable conditions, the anxiety experienced in new contact situations is reduced. Favorable conditions should produce positive expectations, while "unfavorable" conditions should produce negative expectations. Knowledge of the other group, intergroup attitudes, stereotypes, and prior contact create intergroup expectancies. This contention is consistent with expectation states theory (e.g., Berger & Zelditch, 1985).[3] Current research (Honeycutt, 1986) also suggests that situational expectancies have a direct influence on uncertainty. Given the relationships among these variables and attributional confidence and anxiety, a second axiom is proposed:

Axiom 2: An increase in strangers' positive expectations will produce an increase in their attributional confidence regarding members of other groups' behavior and a decrease in the anxiety they experience when interacting with members of other groups.

Group Similarity

Gudykunst's (1983a) research indicates that people ask more questions when others are culturally dissimilar and self-disclose more when others are culturally similar. Simard's (1981) study suggests that people are more confident in predicting the behavior of culturally similar individuals than they are in predicting the behavior of culturally dissimilar individuals. Gudykunst's (1983a) and Simard's (1981) studies also reveal that individuals know how to get to know others when they come from the same culture, but are not sure how to do this when people come from different cultures. Wilder and Allen's (1978) research further indicates that individuals tend to seek out information about dissimilarities for members of outgroups. Blau and Schwartz's (1984) research revealed that the greater the degree of cultural similarity, the more networks overlap. Chance and Goldstein (1981) also found that individuals are more willing to draw inferences about subjective attributes of culturally similar others than they are for culturally dissimilar others. Moreover, there is data to suggest the more similar two groups are, the easier it is for members of one group to learn the other group's language (Gudykunst, 1985a; Whyte & Holmberg, 1956).

With respect to anxiety, Stephan and Stephan's (1985) research revealed that the greater the perceived cultural dissimilarities, the more anxiety individuals experienced during intergroup contact. Research further suggests that small cultural differences in assimilationist societies produce stress in strangers, while large cultural differences in pluralist societies produce less stress in strangers (Berry, 1975; Murphy, 1973). The following axiom, therefore, emerges:

> *Axiom 3:* An increase in the similarity between strangers' ingroups and other groups will produce an increase in their attributional confidence regarding members of other groups' behavior and a decrease in the anxiety strangers experience when interacting with members of other groups.

Shared Networks

Parks and Adelman's (1983) study revealed that shared networks are related to uncertainty reduction. Gudykunst's (1985a) research indicated that attraction and shared networks are related to attributional confidence, even when the communicators are culturally dissimilar. Similarly, Gudykunst, Chua, and Gray (1987) found that all three variables are correlated with uncertainty reduction under conditions of cultural dissimilarity. Research further suggests that shared networks reduce the anxiety strangers experience in interacting with members of other groups (Dyal & Dyal, 1981; Katz, 1974). This suggests:

> *Axiom 4:* An increase in the networks strangers share with members of other groups will produce an increase in their attributional confidence regarding members of other groups' behavior and a decrease in the anxiety strangers experience when interacting with members of other groups.

Interpersonal Salience

The interpersonal salience of the relationships strangers develop with members of other groups also moderates the influence of cultural dissimilarities on intergroup relationships. Interpersonal salience is one of the two dimensions of all relationships isolated in Assumption 5 (the other is intergroup salience, which is subsumed under group similarity and ethnolinguistic identity in the present formulation). This dimension can be conceived to include the intimacy of a relationship, as well as Sunnafrank's (1986) predicted outcome value of a relationship (Gudykunst, Nishida, & Schmidt, 1987).

Most interpersonal relationships (i.e., acquaintances, role relationships) are guided by cultural norms. Friendships, in contrast, are less influenced by normative expectations. Altman and Taylor (1973) contend that cultural stereotypes do not influence communication in friendships. Since cultural stereotypes are broken down in friendships and not in earlier stages of relationships, the level of cultural similarity has a differential impact on uncertainty reduction processes in different relationships. This position is supported by several studies (Gudykunst, 1985a, 1985b; Gudykunst, Chua & Gray, 1987; Gudykunst & Hammer, in press; Gudykunst, Nishida, & Chua, 1986). Recent research also indicates that an increase in the intimacy of relationships leads to a decrease in anxiety (Prager, 1986). This implies:

Axiom 5: An increase in the interpersonal salience of the relationship strangers form with members of other groups moderates the effect of group dissimilarities and will produce an increase in their attributional confidence regarding members of other groups' behavior, as well as a decrease in the anxiety strangers experience when interacting with members of other groups.[4]

Second Language Competence

Research indicates that second language competence increases individuals' ability to cope with uncertainty (Naiman, Frohlich, Stern, & Todesco, 1978). Gudykunst's (1985a) model of uncertainty reduction during intercultural encounters further posits a direct impact of second language competence on attributional confidence. Gardner (1985) summarizes research on the relationship between anxiety and second language learning. He concludes that anxiety specific to the second language inhibits learning the language. Stephan and Stephan (1985) argue that the relationship also goes the other way; that is, lack of knowledge of other groups' subjective culture, which includes their language, increases the anxiety associated with interaction with members of those groups. Another axiom emerges from this work:

> *Axiom 6:* An increase in strangers' second language competence will produce an increase in their attributional confidence regarding members of other groups' behavior and a decrease in the anxiety experienced when interacting with members of other groups.

Personality Factors

Several personality factors influence uncertainty reduction processes, including self-monitoring, psychological differentiation, tolerance for ambiguity, uncertainty-certainty orientation, and cognitive complexity. Snyder (1974) characterized self-monitoring as "self-observation and self-control guided by situational cues to social appropriateness" (p. 526). Previous research has revealed that, in comparison to low self-monitors, high self-monitors are better able to discover appropriate behavior in new situations, have more control over emotional reactions, and create the impressions they wish (Snyder, 1974), modify their behavior to changes in social situations more (Snyder & Monson, 1975), make more confident and extreme attributions (Berscheid, Graziano, Monson, & Dermer, 1976), seek more information about others with whom they anticipate interacting (Elliott, 1979), initiate and regulate conversations more, as well as have a greater need to talk (Ickes & Barnes, 1977).

Recent work by Berger and his associates (Berger & Douglas, 1981; Berger & Perkins, 1978) suggests that self-monitoring also influences the use of passive uncertainty reduction strategies. Berger and Douglas, for example, discovered differences in perceptions of how informative formal and informal situations are in reducing uncertainty. Intercultural research by Gudykunst and Nishida (1984) revealed that self-monitoring has an impact on attributional confidence, intent to self-disclose, and intent to interrogate. Gudykunst's (1985c) research also indicated that self-monitoring has a multivariate influence on all uncertainty reduction processes. These findings suggest:

> *Axiom 7:* An increase in strangers' self-monitoring will produce an increase in their attributional confidence regarding members of other groups'

behavior and a decrease in the anxiety experienced when interacting with members of other groups.

There are fewer studies of other personality factors, but there appears to be sufficient research to generate axioms. McPherson's (1983) research, for example, indicates that individuals with a lower tolerance for ambiguity have a greater tendency to seek supportive rather than objective information. Ruben and Kealey's (1979) research revealed that tolerance for ambiguity is related to culture shock (i.e., anxiety) among Canadian technical advisers in Kenya. Nishida (1985) observed a similar relationship for Japanese students studying English in the United States. Sorrentino and Hewitt (1984) also discovered that uncertainty-oriented individuals seek cognitive information more than certainty-oriented individuals. Witkin and Berry (1975) found that field-independents experience less stress upon entering a new culture than field-dependents, no matter what the degree of cultural dissimilarity. Downey, Hellriegel, and Slocum's (1977) research further suggested that there is a negative association between cognitive complexity and perceived uncertainty. Finally, Detweiler (1975) found that narrow categorizers make stronger and more confident attributions about members of outgroups who cause a negative outcome than do wide categorizers. Psychological differentiation and category width are both related to the complexity of cognitive systems and, accordingly, can be incorporated into the more general construct, cognitive complexity. Two axioms, therefore, emerge:

Axiom 8: An increase in strangers' cognitive complexity will produce an increase in their attributional confidence regarding members of other groups' behavior and a decrease in the anxiety experienced when interacting with members of other groups.
Axiom 9: An increase in strangers' tolerance for ambiguity will produce an increase in their attributional confidence regarding members of other groups' behavior and a decrease in the anxiety experienced when interacting with members of other groups.

Outcomes: Adaptation and Effectiveness

Two major outcomes of intergroup communication are adaptation to new intergroup situations and increased effectiveness of communication. Research suggests that these two "outcomes" are correlated with respect to the adjustment of sojourners (Ruben & Kealey, 1979). Uncertainty reduction and anxiety can be related to each of these outcomes.

Gudykunst and Hammer (1988) assumed that uncertainty reduction and controlling/reducing anxiety are necessary and sufficient conditions for strangers' adaptation to new cultural environments. No research has been conducted to date on this assumption, but the posited relationships appear plausible. If *adaptation* is defined as "a consequence of an ongoing process in which a system strives to adjust and readjust itself to challenges, changes, and irritants in the environment" (Ruben, 1983, p. 137), then the affect of uncertainty and anxiety reduction becomes obvious. Specifically, it is impossible to adjust successfully to changes in the environment if high levels of anxiety or uncertainty exist. Support for the posited relationship between uncertainty reduction and adaptation emerges from recent applications of the theory to organizational socialization (Lester, 1986; Wilson, 1986) and organizational assimilation (Jablin & Krone, 1987). The relationship between anxiety and adaptation is bolstered by research on social support (see Albrecht & Adelman, 1984).

Triandis (1976, 1977) argues that influencing the behavior of a person from another culture involves the ability to understand the causes of their behavior (e.g., reduce uncertainty). Stated differently, effective intercultural communication requires that individuals from one culture can make attributions that are isomorphic with individuals from the target culture. Hammer and his associates' (Hammer, 1987; Hammer, Gudykunst, & Wiseman, 1978) research with sojourners from the United States also demonstrates that there are three behavioral dimensions to intercultural effectiveness: the ability to establish interpersonal relationships, the ability to effectively communicate, and the ability to deal with psychological stress. Abe and Wiseman's (1983) research in Japan tends to support the existence of these dimensions for sojourners from Japan (Gudykunst & Hammer, 1984). Cross-cultural research suggests that the same dimensions are used in determining effectiveness of intracultural communication in the United States and Japan (Hammer & Nishida, 1985) and Mexico (Hammer, 1986). The use of the same dimensions intra- and interculturally gives weight to the argument that these dimensions are related to effectiveness. This contention is supported further by Downey and Slocum's (1979) research, which revealed a negative relationship between perceived uncertainty and effective performance. This work thereby suggests two additional axioms:

Axiom 10: An increase in strangers' attributional confidence regarding members of other groups' behavior will produce an increase in their intergroup adaptation and effectiveness.

Axiom 11: A decrease in the anxiety strangers experience when interacting with members of other groups will produce an increase in their intergroup adaptation and effectiveness.

Cross-Cultural Variations

The preceding axioms focus on intergroup communication within one culture and constitute the basic theory. Some would consider the theory complete if it stopped here. It, however, would not have cross-cultural generalizability and its scope would have to be limited to the United States. There are at least two ways cross-cultural generalizability of the theory can be established: either the theory can be tested cross-culturally or culture can be integrated as a variable in the theory. The later option is used here. The remainder of this section, therefore, is devoted to integrating cultural variability with the major constructs in the theory, uncertainty and anxiety.[5]

There are cross-cultural variations in interpersonal and intergroup communication (see Gudykunst, in press; Gudykunst & Ting-Toomey, in press; for reviews). Culture, however, must be treated as theoretical variables in axioms isolated regarding cultural differences. Foschi and Hales (1979) argue that when culture is treated as a theoretical variable "culture X and culture Y serve to operationally define a characteristic a, which the two cultures exhibit to different degrees" (p. 246). Cultural differences per se, therefore, are not important; rather, it is necessary to treat culture as an operationalization of a dimension of cultural variability. Foschi and Hales' position is consistent with Doise's (1986) contention that different levels of analysis (e.g., kinds of explanation) must be "articulated" (i.e., interlinked) in order to provide the most complete account of any specific process.

Individualism-collectivism is the major dimension of cultural variability isolated by theorists across disciplines that influences intergroup processes (e.g., Hofstede, 1980; Kluckhohn & Strodtbeck, 1961; Marsella, DeVos, & Hsu, 1985; Triandis, 1986). In individualistic cultures, individuals take care of themselves and members of their immediate family; while in collectivistic cultures, the ingroups to which individuals belong take care of them in exchange for loyalty (Hofstede, 1980). People in individualistic cultures tend to be universalistic and apply the same value standards to all, while people in collectivistic cultures tend to be particularistic and apply different value standards for members of their ingroups and outgroups. Triandis (1986) sees the key distinction between individualistic and collectivistic cultures as the focus on the ingroup in collectivistic cultures. Collectivistic cultures emphasize goals, needs and views of the ingroup over those of the individual; the social norms of the ingroup, rather than individual pleasure; shared ingroup beliefs, rather than unique individual beliefs; and a value on cooperation with ingroup members, rather than maximizing individual outcomes.

Several other dimensions of cultural variability also can influence intergroup processes. Hofstede (1980), for example, empirically derived four dimensions: individualism-collectivism (just discussed), power distance, uncertainty avoidance, and masculinity-femininity. High power distance cultures value an order of inequality with everyone having a rightful place where the hierarchy reflects existential inequality. Uncertainty avoidance involves the lack of tolerance in a culture for uncertainty and ambiguity. Cultures high in uncertainty avoidance have high levels of anxiety, a great need for formal rules, and a low tolerance for groups that believe in a deviant manner. High masculinity, according to Hofstede, involves valuing money, assertiveness, and unequal sex roles, while cultures in which people, quality of life, nurturance, and equal sex roles prevail are feminine.

To begin, there appears to be cultural variations in dealing with uncertainty. Wright and his colleagues (1978), for example, found that British students have a finely differentiated (i.e., calibrated) view of uncertainty. Students from Hong Kong, Malaysia, and Indonesia, in contrast, have less differentiated views and tend to use more extreme responses (i.e., total certainty or total uncertainty) than the British. The four cultures have similar scores on two of Hofstede's (1983) dimensions of culture (uncertainty avoidance and masculinity) and differences on two (power distance and individualism). The three Asian cultures, however, differ on power distance. The only dimension consistent with the findings is individualism. There also are cross-cultural studies that have examined communication in ingroup and outgroup relationships. Noesjirwan (1978), for example, found that the rule guiding behavior with respect to the ingroup in Indonesia (collectivistic) is that members of the group should adapt to the group so that the group can present a united front. In Australia (individualistic), on the other hand, members are expected to do their own thing even if they must go against the group. Similarly, Argyle and his associates (1986) discovered that rules regarding ingroups, such as maintaining harmonious relations, are endorsed highly in collectivistic cultures (Japan and Hong Kong), but not in individualistic cultures (England and Italy). Related research indicates that ingroup relationships are perceived as more intimate in collectivistic cultures than in individualistic cultures (Gudykunst & Nishida, 1986b). Gudykunst, Yoon, and Nishida (1987) also observed that members of collectivistic cultures (Japan and Korea) perceive greater social penetration (personalization and synchronization) in their ingroup relationships than do members of individualistic cultures (United States). Their data further revealed greater perceived personalization in outgroup relationships in collectivistic cultures than individualistic cultures. Finally, Gudykunst, Nishida, and Schmidt (1988) found that there is a difference between ingroup and outgroup uncertainty reduction processes (e.g., attributional confidence) in collectivistic cultures, but not in individualistic cultures. An additional axiom appears warranted:

> *Axiom 12:* An increase in collectivism will produce an increase in the differences in attributional confidence between ingroup and outgroup communication.

Affective reactions also are one of the major by-products of intergroup communication (Pettigrew, 1986; see Gudykunst & Ting-Toomey, 1988, for a review of cross-cultural research on affective communication). Bobad and Wallbott's (1986) report of cross-cultural research in eight cultures, for example, reveals that there is greater fear associated with interactions with people who are unfamiliar (e.g., members of outgroups) than with people who are familiar (e.g., members of ingroups). Their research also demonstrates that there is less verbalization and less control over expressing anger with people who are unfamiliar than with people who are familiar. There were cultural differences across the emotions experienced with strangers and in whether emotions were experienced with familiar or unfamiliar people (see Appendix D of Scherer, Wallbott, & Summerfield, 1986), but the researchers did not examine culture by familiarity interaction effects, so specific predictions cannot be generated from the data. A comparison of the eight cultures across Hofstede's (1980) dimensions of cultural variability, however, allows for a potential theoretical explanation to be derived. The eight cultures are all moderate to high in individualism, moderate in masculinity, low to moderate in power distance, while five of the eight are high in uncertainty avoidance and the remaining three are low to moderate. Given that uncertainty avoidance is the dimension that affects the expression of emotion (Hofstede, 1980), the following axiom is plausible:

> *Axiom 13:* An increase in uncertainty avoidance will produce an increase in the anxiety strangers experience when interacting with members of other groups.

DISCUSSION

Current Status of the Theory

The theory proffered in this chapter is an initial attempt to formally state a general theory of intergroup communication based, in part, upon uncertainty reduction and ethnolinguistic identity theories. A total of 13 axioms were generated. The only axiom that may be problematic is Axiom 1. This axiom posits a negative relationship between uncertainty reduction and strength of ethnolinguistic identity, but a positive relationship between reducing anxiety and strength of ethnolinguistic identity. All other axioms suggest the same relationship between uncertainty reduction and anxiety reduction and the other variables involved. While the relationship between strength of ethnolinguistic identity and the two dependent variables (reducing anxiety and uncertainty) may be different, the inconsistency in Axiom 1 also may suggest a curvilinear relationship. It may be, for example, that low and high strength of ethnolinguistic identity lead to uncertainty and anxiety reduction. Moderate strength of ethnolinguistic identity, in contrast, may not lead to the reduction of uncertainty and anxiety.

The presentation of evidence to support the axioms is truncated in several places because of space limitations (the theory will be articulated more fully in Gudykunst, in progress). All axioms, nevertheless, appear plausible given past research and theorizing. Additional axioms might be warranted. Support for other possible relationships, however, is not as direct as that used to generate the axioms and they, therefore, were omitted in the present version of the theory.

Theorems can be deduced from the axioms isolated. By combining Axiom 1, an increase in the strength of strangers' ethnolinguistic identity will produce an increase in their attributional confidence and an increase in their anxiety, and Axiom 6, an increase in strangers' second language competence will produce a decrease in their attributional confidence and anxiety, Theorem 1 can be deduced: Strangers' second language competence is associated positively with their attributional confidence regarding members of other groups' behavior. A large number of theorems can be generated from the 13 axioms. Some theorems (e.g., similarity and interpersonal salience are associated positively) are consistent with Berger and Calabrese's (1975) original formulation of the theory. Several theorems (e.g., strength of ethnolinguistic identity is associated negatively with shared networks with outgroup members) are compatible with ethnolinguistic identity theory (Beebe & Giles, 1984; Giles & Johnson, 1987). Other theorems (e.g., expectations are associated positively with strength of ethnolinguistic identity) provide hypotheses for future research because they have not been investigated. Many theorems, in contrast, are not supported by previous research or involve the "fallacy of the excluded middle." Space, however, does not permit a complete listing of either the plausible theorems or those not supported in previous research (see Gudykunst & Hammer, 1987a, for a listing of many theorems that could be derived from the present axioms).

The number of statements included in the theory is somewhat large, but not excessive. Reynolds (1971) argues that "in dealing with logical systems that are completely abstract . . . a common criterion is to select the smallest set of axioms from which all other statements can be derived, reflecting a preference for simplicity and elegance. There is reason to think that this is inappropriate for a substantive theory, particularly when it makes it more difficult to understand the theory" (p. 95).

An initial simplification of the theory has been attempted by incorporating expectations and interpersonal salience. As used herein, expectations derive from status cues, knowledge of the other group, intergroup attitudes, stereotypes, and prior contact. Following Lieberson (1985), these factors are conceived of as "superficial" causes of attributional confidence and anxiety, while expectations are viewed as the "basic" cause. Similarly, interpersonal salience consists of intimacy and nonverbal affiliative experiences, which are "superficial" causes, while interpersonal salience is conceived as a "basic" cause of attributional confidence and anxiety reduction. Consistent with Gudykunst and Hammer (1988), only two basic causes (i.e., attributional confidence and anxiety) of intercultural adaptation are posited. A similar argument also is made for intercultural effectiveness. The explanation of the outcomes, therefore, is consistent with Leiberson's argument that most dependent variables are the result of only a few basic causes. Given this position, further simplification should occur in future versions of the theory (i.e., isolating the basic causes of attributional confidence and anxiety), but such simplification must be based on additional research.

The theory proffered overcomes several of the major problems in previous work on intergroup relations. Pettigrew (1986) argues that all of the major criticisms of social psychological theory in general apply to work on intergroup contact:

(1) they are more often loose frameworks than testable theories
(2) they have centered on cold cognition to the relative exclusion of affective considerations
(3) they stress similarities (mechanical solidarity) to the virtual exclusion of differences (organic solidarity) as social bonds
(4) they focus largely on isolated, noncumulative effects
(5) they too glibly assume universality across time, situations, and cultures
(6) they are narrow- to middle-range in scope with bold generic theory that links various levels of analysis conspicuous by its absence. (p. 179)

The axioms and theorems presented form a testable theory of intergroup communication. The theory also incorporates affective factors (i.e., ethnolinguistic identity and anxiety) as both major independent and dependent variables. Ethnolinguistic identity involves an affective reaction to group membership and anxiety is an affective response to intergroup communication. Similarities and differences also are recognized as major forces in intergroup relationships. Finally, the theory articulates (Doise, 1986) all four major levels of analysis: intrapersonal (e.g., cognitive complexity, self-monitoring), interpersonal (e.g., interpersonal salience), intergroup (e.g., group similarity), and cultural (e.g., individualism-collectivism).

Future Directions

There are several issues future work on the theory must address. The most critical issue that needs to be addressed is the focus on uncertainty reduction. Planalp and Honeycutt's (1985) intracultural research indicates that an increase in uncertainty has negative consequences for interpersonal relationships. Sodetani and Gudykunst's (1987) intercultural study, in contrast, reveals both positive and negative outcomes for interpersonal relationships between members of different cultures following an increase in uncertainty. While these are potential methodological explanations for the different results of the two studies (e.g., Planalp and Honeycutt gave only negative examples of uncertainty increase, and Sodetani and Gudykunst did not provide examples), another plausible explanation involves differences in intracultural and intercultural relationships. Given findings of these two studies and Berger's (1987) argument that initial affective responses to observable attributes such as skin color and age (e.g., cues to group membership) can either impede or propel attempts to reduce uncertainty, it appears advisable for future work on the theory to focus on uncertainty in general, rather than uncertainty reduction in particular. Uncertainty might best be conceived as a dialectical process, with continual shifts from increase to decrease and back to increase occurring throughout a relationship (see Altman, Vinsel, & Brown, 1981, for an application of the dialectical notion to social penetration processes). Future theorizing also should integrate or examine the role of the use of ambiguity in general (Levine, 1985) and strategic ambiguity in particular (Eisenberg, 1984), as well as the role of "second guessing" (Doelger, Hewes, & Graham, 1986) on uncertainty.

Another issue that needs to be addressed in future work on the theory is the effect of anticipated interaction on uncertainty change. Berger (1979) argued that anticipated future interaction was one of the major conditions under which individuals try to reduce uncertainty. Kellermann's (1986) research, however, suggests that anticipated future interaction does not increase attempts to reduce uncertainty. Honeycutt's (1986) study, in contrast, indicates that situational expectancies (e.g., friendly, unfriendly, or no-expectancy) influences uncertainty. Given that intergroup communication often is associated with unfriendly expectancies, the influence of the expected outcome should be examined in future research. This position is consistent with Sunnafrank's (1986) argument that "predicted outcome value" of a relationship plays a major role in uncertainty reduction processes. The importance of predicted outcome value was demonstrated in Gudykunst, Nishida, and Schmidt's (1988) study of ingroup and outgroup communication in Japan and the United States. Their research, however, suggested that it can be incorporated under interpersonal salience. Given that predicted outcome values also create expectancies, future versions of the theory need to address how interpersonal salience and expectancies are different, or combine them into one variable.

This line of argument suggests that expectation states theory (Berger & Zelditch, 1985) should be integrated more completely with the theory proffered. Such an integration should provide a powerful heuristic because expectation states theory focuses on how status characteristics (e.g., group memberships) influence expectations, which in turn affect behavior. This line of argument is supported by Gudykunst and Hammer's (in press) finding that social identity affects uncertainty reduction processes only when ethnic status is activated. Turner's (1985, 1987) theory of group behavior also appears compatible with the present formulation and could profitably be incorporated since it focuses on self-categorization and the self-concept and its integration would refine those aspects of the theory dealing with ethnolinguistic identity.

Finally, future work on the theory should incorporate Gudykunst and Hall's (1987) integration of ethnolinguistic identity theory with Berger and Bradac's (1982) work on the relationship between language and uncertainty. Berger and Bradac suggest four alternative models regarding the relationship between language and uncertainty reduction that are influenced by ethnolinguistic identity. Model 1 specifies that people use others' language to develop hypotheses about their group affiliations, and on the basis of these hypotheses, judgments of similarity are made. The greater the similarity, the more uncertainty is reduced. Model 2 is similar except that a "judgment of psychological trait or state" replaces the judgment of group membership as the mediator for judging similarity. Model 3 posits that language leads to a judgment of group membership, which in turn leads to a judgment of psychological trait or state, which then forms the basis of a judgment of similarity. Similarity then leads to uncertainty reduction. Model 4 posits that only a judgment of similarity intervenes between language and uncertainty reduction.

Each of the four models "is probably valid in particular circumstances" (Berger & Bradac, 1982, p. 55), however, Berger and Bradac do not specify under which circumstances each model might be valid. Gudykunst and Lim's (1986) argument that the interpersonal intergroup salience of encounters are orthogonal dimensions provides a way to define the circumstances under which each of Berger and Bradac's models should be valid. Four quadrants can be isolated: (I) high interpersonal and high intergroup salience, (II) high interpersonal and low intergroup salience, (III) low interpersonal and high intergroup salience, (IV) low interpersonal and low intergroup salience. The major generative mechanism for intergroup behavior is ethnolinguistic identity, whereas the major generative mechanism for interpersonal behavior is personal identity.

Gudykunst and Hall (1987) suggest that when intergroup salience is high and interpersonal low (Quadrant III) and ethnolinguistic identity is a major generative mechanism for behavior, individuals use language to make judgments of group affiliation on which judgments of similarity are made and uncertainty is reduced (Model 1). When the intergroup salience is high and interpersonal also is high (Quadrant I) and both ethnolinguistic and personal identity are generative mechanisms for behavior, it is plausible that judgments of group membership are used to make judgments of psychological traits that form the basis for the judgment of similarity, which reduces uncertainty (Model 3). When intergroup salience is low and interpersonal salience is high (Quadrant II), and personal, *not* ethnolinguistic, identity is the major generative mechanism for behavior, language should lead directly to judgments of psychological traits that form basis of judgments of similarity that are used to reduce uncertainty (Model 2). Finally, when both interpersonal and intergroup salience are low (Quadrant IV), language may only cue similarity judgment (Model 4) because the interaction is of relatively low importance. Integrating this perspective with the theory proffered is beyond the capacity of this chapter, but future work may reveal that scope and boundary conditions are necessary for some of the axioms based upon the interpersonal/intergroup salience of the encounter.

To conclude, the theory proffered is an initial attempt to state an uncertainty reduction-based theory of intergroup communication in "causal-process" form. While the formulation is complex and involves a large number of theoretical statements, it is empirically testable. The complete theory (assumptions, axioms, and theorems) ideally should be tested and modified as necessary. Future versions of the theory also should be simplified by removing unnecessary axioms; that is, the theory should be as parsimonious as possible without distorting the causal processes operating. To accomplish this, higher order concepts such as expectations must be isolated and linked to the concepts included in the present version of the theory.

NOTES

1. Portions of this chapter are drawn from Gudykunst and Hammer (1988).
2. Status cues incorporate Berger and Calabrese's (1975) display of nonverbal affiliative expressiveness.

3. While the contention is consistent with expectation states theory, the overall theory presented is not, in its present form. Expectation states theory is limited (by a scope condition) to task-oriented situations that have success or failure outcomes. The present theory is not designed to be limited to task-oriented situations, but should apply in these situations.

4. Interpersonal salience here includes attraction and intimacy as used in Berger and Calabrese's (1975) original theory.

5. For the purpose of the initial statement of the theory, only cultural variabilities related to attributional confidence and anxiety are isolated. Many other relationships relevant to the theory (e.g., cultural variability influences ethnolinguistic identity, Gudykunst, 1987b) could be proffered. Also cultural variability can influence the relationship between other variables and uncertainty reduction processes (i.e., culture serves as a moderating variable). Gudykunst and Nishida (1986a), for example, found that amount of communication is associated with both low- and high-context attributional confidence in the United States, but not Japan. Shared networks was correlated with high-context attributional confidence in Japan, but not in the United States. Low-context attributional confidence, however, was associated with shared networks in both cultures.

REFERENCES

Abe, H., & Wiseman, R. L. (1983). A cross-cultural confirmation of the dimensions of intercultural effectiveness. *International Journal of Intercultural Relations, 7*, 53-67.

Albrecht, T. L., & Adelman, M. B. (1984). Social support and life stress. *Human Communication Research, 11*, 3-32.

Altman, I., & Taylor, D. (1973). *Social penetration: The development of interpersonal relationships.* New York: Holt, Rinehart and Winston.

Altman, I., Vinsel, A., & Brown, B. (1981). Dialectical conceptions in social psychology: An application to social penetration and privacy regulation. In L. Berkowitz (Ed.), *Advances in experimental social psychology* (Vol. 14). New York: Academic Press.

Amir, Y. (1969). The contact hypothesis in ethnic relations. *Psychological Bulletin, 71*, 319-342.

Argyle, M., Henderson, M., Bond, M., Iizuka, Y., & Contarello, A. (1986). Cross-cultural variations in relationship rules. *International Journal of Psychology, 21*, 287-315.

Ball-Rokeach, S. J. (1973). From pervasive ambiguity to a definition of the situation. *Sociometry, 36*, 378-389.

Beebe, L. M., & Giles, H. (1984). Speech accommodation theories: A discussion in terms of second-language acquisition. *International Journal of the Sociology of Language, 46*, 5-32.

Berger, C. R. (1979). Beyond initial interactions. In H. Giles & R. St. Clair (Eds.), *Language and social psychology.* Oxford: Basil Blackwell.

Berger, C. R. (1987). Communicating under uncertainty. In M. E. Roloff & G. R. Miller (Eds.), *Interpersonal processes.* Newbury Park, CA: Sage.

Berger, C. R., & Bradac, J. J. (1982). *Language and social knowledge: Uncertainty in interpersonal relations.* London: Edward Arnold.

Berger, C. R., & Calabrese, R. (1975). Some explorations in initial interactions and beyond. *Human Communication Research, 1*, 99-112.

Berger, C. R., & Douglas, W. (1981). Studies in interpersonal epistemology III: Anticipated interaction, self-monitoring, and observational context selection. *Communication Monographs, 48,* 183-196.

Berger, C. R., & Gudykunst, W. B. (in press). Uncertainty and communication. In B. Dervin (Ed.), *Progress in communication sciences.* Norwood, NJ: Ablex.

Berger, C. R., & Perkins, J. (1978). Studies in interpersonal epistemology I: Situational attributes in observational context selection. In B. Ruben (Ed.), *Communication yearbook 2.* New Brunswick, NJ: Transaction Books.

Berger, J., Webster, M., Ridgeway, C., & Rosenholz, S. (1986). Status cues, expectations, and behavior. *Advances in Group Processes, 3,* 1-22.

Berger, J., & Zelditch, M. (Eds.). (1985). *Status, rewards and influence.* San Francisco: Jossey-Bass.

Berry, J. W. (1975). Ecology, cultural adaptation, and psychological differentiation. In R. Brislin, S. Bochner, & W. Lonner (Eds.), *Cross-cultural perspectives on learning.* Beverly Hills, CA: Sage.

Berscheid, E., Graziano, W., Monson, T., & Dermer, M. (1976). Outcome dependency: Attention, attribution, and attraction. *Journal of Personality and Social Psychology, 34,* 978-989.

Billig, M. (1987). *Arguing and thinking.* Cambridge: Cambridge University Press.

Blalock, H. H. (1969). *Theory construction: From verbal to mathematical formulations.* Englewood Cliffs, NJ: Prentice Hall.

Blau, P., & Schwartz, J. (1984). *Cross-cutting social circles.* New York: Academic Press.

Bobad, E. Y., & Wallbott, H. G. (1986). The effects of social factors on emotional reaction. In K. Scherer, H. Wallbott, & A. Summerfield (Eds.), *Experiencing emotion: A cross-cultural study.* Cambridge: Cambridge University Press.

Bond, M. H., & King, A.Y.C. (1985). Coping with the threat of westernization in Hong Kong. *International Journal of Intercultural Relations, 9,* 351-364.

Brewer, M., & Campbell, D. (1976). *Ethnocentrism and intergroup attitudes.* New York: Wiley.

Burstall, C. (1975). French in the primary schools: The British experiment. In H. Stern, C. Burstall, & B. Harley (Eds.), *French from age eight or eleven.* Toronto: Ontario Studies in Education.

Chance, J. E., & Goldstein, A. (1981). Depth of processing in response to own- and other-race faces. *Personality and Social Psychology Bulletin, 7,* 475-480.

Detweiler, R. (1975). On inferring the intentions of a person from another culture. *Journal of Personality, 43,* 591-611.

Doelger, J. A., Hewes, D. E., & Graham, M. L. (1986). Knowing when to "second-guess": The mindful analysis of messages. *Human Communication Research, 12,* 301-338.

Doise, W. (1986). *Levels of explanation in social psychology.* Cambridge: Cambridge University Press.

Downey, H. K., Hellriegel, D., & Slocum, J. W. (1977). Individual characteristics as sources of perceived uncertainty variability. *Human Relations, 30,* 161-174.

Downey, H. K., & Slocum, J. W. (1979). *Uncertainty and performance.* Unpublished manuscript, Oklahoma State University.

Downs, R., & Stea, D. (1977). *Maps in minds.* New York: Harper and Row.

Dyal, J. A., & Dyal, R. Y. (1981). Acculturation, stress, and coping. *International Journal of Intercultural Relations, 5,* 301-328.

Eisenberg, E. (1984). Ambiguity as a strategy in organizational communication. *Communication Monographs, 51,* 227-242.

Elliott, G. (1979). Some effects of deception and level of self-monitoring on planning and reacting to a self-presentation. *Journal of Personality and Social Psychology, 37,* 1282-1292.

Feldman, R. E. (1968). Response to compatriot and foreigner who seek assistance. *Journal of Personality and Social Psychology, 10,* 202-214.

Foschi, M., & Hales, W. H. (1979). The theoretical role of cross-cultural comparisons in experimental social psychology. In L. H. Eckensberger, W. J. Lonner, & Y. H. Poortinga (Eds.), *Cross-cultural contributions to psychology.* Lisse, Netherlands: Swets & Zeitlinger.

Gardner, R. C. (1985). *Social psychology and second language learning.* London: Edward Arnold.

Gerard, H. G. (1963). Emotional uncertainty and social comparison. *Journal of Abnormal and Social Psychology, 66,* 568-573.

Giles, H., & Byrne, J. L. (1982). An intergroup approach to second language acquisition. *Journal of Multilingual and Multicultural Development, 3,* 17-40.

Giles, H., Garrett, P., & Coupland, N. (1987). *Language acquisition in the Basque country: Invoking and extending the intergroup model.* Paper presented at the Basque Conference, Madrid, Spain.

Giles, H., & Johnson, P. (1981). The role of language in ethnic group relations. In J. Turner & H. Giles (Eds.), *Intergroup behavior.* Chicago: University of Chicago Press.

Giles, H., & Johnson, P. (1987). Ethnolinguistic identity theory. *International Journal of the Sociology Language, 68,* 69-99.

Gudykunst, W. B. (1983a). Similarities and differences in perceptions of initial intracultural and intercultural encounters. *Southern Speech Communication Journal, 49,* 40-65.

Gudykunst, W. B. (1983b). Toward a typology of stranger-host relationships. *International Journal of Intercultural Relations, 7,* 401-415.

Gudykunst, W. B. (1983c). Uncertainty reduction and predictability of behavior in low- and high-context cultures. *Communication Quarterly, 31,* 49-55.

Gudykunst, W. B. (1985a). A model of uncertainty reduction in intercultural encounters. *Journal of Language and Social Psychology, 4,* 79-98.

Gudykunst, W. B. (1985b). An exploratory comparison of close intracultural and intercultural friendships. *Communication Quarterly, 33,* 270-273.

Gudykunst, W. B. (1985c). The influence of cultural similarity, type of relationship, and self-monitoring on uncertainty reduction processes. *Communication Monographs, 52,* 203-217.

Gudykunst, W. B. (1986a). Intraethnic and interethnic uncertainty reduction processes. In Y. Kim (Ed.), *Current research in interethnic communication.* Beverly Hills, CA: Sage.

Gudykunst, W. B. (1986b). Toward a theory of intergroup communication. In W. B. Gudykunst (Ed.), *Intergroup communication.* London: Edward Arnold.

Gudykunst, W. B. (1987a). Cross-cultural comparisons. In C. Berger & S. Chaffee (Eds.), *Handbook of communication science.* Newbury Park, CA: Sage.

Gudykunst, W. B. (1987b, July). *Cultural variability in ethnolinguistic identity.* Paper presented at the Social Identity Conference, University of Exeter, England.

Gudykunst, W. B. (in press). Culture and intergroup processes. In M. Bond (Ed.), *The cross-cultural challenge to social psychology*. Newbury Park, CA: Sage.

Gudykunst, W. B. (in progress). *Strangeness and similarity: A theory of interpersonal and intergroup communication*. Clevendon, England: Multilingual Matters.

Gudykunst, W. B., & Hall, B. J. (1987, July). *Ethnolinguistic identity and uncertainty reduction in interpersonal and intergroup encounters*. Paper presented at the Third International Conference on Language and Social Psychology, Bristol, England.

Gudykunst, W. B., & Hammer, M. R. (1984). Dimensions of intercultural effectiveness: Culture specific or culture general. *International Journal of Intercultural Relations, 8*, 1-10.

Gudykunst, W. B., & Hammer, M. R. (1988). Strangers and hosts: An uncertainty reduction based theory of intercultural adaptation. In Y. Y. Kim & W. B. Gudykunst (Eds.), *Intercultural adaptation*. Newbury Park, CA: Sage.

Gudykunst, W. B., & Hammer, M. R. (in press). The influence of social identity and intimacy of interethnic relationships on uncertainty reduction processes. *Human Communication Research*.

Gudykunst, W. B., & Hammer, M. R. (1987). The effect of ethnicity, gender and dyadic composition on uncertainty reduction in initial interactions. *Journal of Black Studies, 18*, 191-214.

Gudykunst, W. B., & Kim, Y. Y. (1984). *Communicating with strangers: An approach to intercultural communication*. New York: Random House.

Gudykunst, W. B., & Lim, T. S. (1986). A perspective for the study of intergroup communication. In W. Gudykunst (Ed.), *Intergroup communication*. London: Edward Arnold.

Gudykunst, W. B., & Nishida, T. (1984). Individual and cultural influences on uncertainty reduction. *Communication Monographs, 51*, 23-36.

Gudykunst, W. B., & Nishida, T. (1986a). Attributional confidence in low- and high-context cultures. *Human Communication Research, 12*, 525-549.

Gudykunst, W. B., & Nishida, T. (1986b). The influence of cultural variability on perceptions of communication behavior associated with relationship terms. *Human Communication Research, 13*, 147-166.

Gudykunst, W. B., & Ting-Toomey, S. (1988). Culture and affective communication. *American Behavioral Scientist, 31*, 384-400.

Gudykunst, W. B., & Ting-Toomey, S., with E. Chua. (in press). *Culture and interpersonal communication*. Newbury Park, CA: Sage.

Gudykunst, W. B., Nishida, T., & Chua, E. (1986). Uncertainty reduction in Japanese-North American dyads. *Communication Research Reports, 3*, 39-46.

Gudykunst, W. B., Nishida, T., & Schmidt, K. L. (1988). *The influence of cultural variability on uncertainty reduction in ingroup vs. outgroup and same- vs. opposite-sex relationships*. Paper presented at the International Communication Associate Convention, New Orleans.

Gudykunst, W. B., Nishida, T., Koike, H., & Shiino, N. (1986). The influence of language on uncertainty reduction: An exploratory study of Japanese- Japanese and Japanese-North American interactions. In M. McLaughlin (Ed.), *Communication yearbook 9*. Beverly Hills, CA: Sage.

Gudykunst, W. B., Sodetani, L., & Sonoda, K. (1987). Uncertainty reduction in Japanese-American-Caucasian relationships in Hawaii. *Western Journal of Speech Communication, 51*, 256-278.

Gudykunst, W. B., Wiseman, R., & Hammer, M. (1977). Determinants of sojourners' attitudinal satisfaction. In B. Ruben (Ed.), *Communication yearbook 1.* New Brunswick, NJ: Transaction.

Gudykunst, W. B., Yang, S. M., & Nishida, T. (1985). A cross-cultural test of uncertainty reduction theory: Comparisons of acquaintance, friend, and dating relationships in Japan, Korea, and the United States. *Human Communication Research, 11,* 407-455.

Gudykunst, W. B., Yang, S. M., & Nishida, T. (1987). Cultural differences in self-consciousness and self-monitoring. *Communication Research, 14,* 7-34.

Gudykunst, W. B., Yoon, Y. C., & Nishida, T. (1987). The influence of individualism-collectivism on perceptions of communication in ingroup and outgroup relationships. *Communication Monographs, 54,* 295-306.

Gudykunst, W., Chua, E., & Gray, A. (1987). Cultural dissimilarities and uncertainty reduction processes. In M. McLaughlin (Ed.), *Communication yearbook 10.* Beverly Hills, CA: Sage.

Hall, B. J., & Gudykunst, W. B. (1986). The intergroup theory of second language ability. *Journal of Language and Social Psychology, 5,* 291-302.

Hall, E. T. (1976). *Beyond culture.* New York: Doubleday.

Hamilton, D. L., & Bishop, G. D. (1976). Attitudinal and behavioral effects of initial integration of white suburban neighborhoods. *Journal of Social Issues, 32,* 47-67.

Hammer, M. R. (1986, November). *A cross-cultural comparison of the behavioral dimensions of communication competence: An extension to Mexico.* Paper presented at the Speech Communication Association Convention, Chicago.

Hammer, M. R. (1987). Behavioral dimensions of intercultural effectiveness: A replication and extension. International Journal of Intercultural Relations, 11, 65-88.

Hammer, M. R., Gudykunst, W. B., & Wiseman, R. L. (1978). Dimensions of intercultural effectiveness: An exploratory study. *International Journal of Intercultural Relations, 2,* 382-392.

Hammer, M. R., & Nishida, H. (1985, November). *A cross-cultural comparison of the dimensions of interpersonal effectiveness.* Paper presented at the Speech Communication Association Convention, Denver.

Hartmann, P., & Husband, C. (1972). The mass media and racial conflict. In D. McPhail (Ed.), *Sociology of mass communication.* Hammondsworth, England: Penguin.

Herman, S., & Schield, E. (1961). The stranger group in a cross-cultural situation. *Sociometry, 24,* 165-176.

Hewstone, M., & Brown, R. (Eds.). (1986). *Contact and conflict in intergroup encounters.* Oxford: Blackwell.

Hewstone, M., & Giles, H. (1986). Social groups and social stereotypes in intergroup communication. In W. Gudykunst (Ed.), *Intergroup communication.* London: Edward Arnold.

Hewstone, M., Jaspars, J., & Laljee, M. (1982). Social representations, social attribution, and social identity. *European Journal of Social Psychology, 12,* 241-269.

Hewstone, M., & Ward, C. (1985). Ethnocentrism and causal attribution in Southeast Asia. *Journal of Personality and Social Psychology, 48,* 614-623.

Hofstede, G. (1980). *Cultures consequences.* Beverly Hills, CA: Sage.

Hofstede, G. (1983). Dimensions of national cultures in fifty countries and three regions. In J. Deregowski, S. Dziurawiec, & R. Annis (Eds.), *Expiscations in cross-cultural psychology.* Lisse, Netherlands: Swets and Zeitlinger.

Honeycutt, J. M. (1986, May). *Processing information about others and attributional confidence in initial interaction on the basis of expectancies.* Paper presented at the International Communication Association Convention, Chicago.

Ickes, W., & Barnes, R. (1977). The role of sex and self-monitoring on unstructured dyadic interaction. *Journal of Personality and Social Psychology, 35,* 315-330.

Jablin, F. M., & Krone, K. J. (1987). Organization assimilation. In C. R. Berger & S. Chaffee (Eds.), *Handbook of communication science.* Newbury Park, CA: Sage.

Jaspars, J., & Hewstone, M. (1982). Cross-cultural interaction, social attribution, and inter-group relations. In S. Bochner (Ed.), *Cultures in contact.* Elmsford, NY: Pergamon.

Katz, P. (1974). *Acculturation and social networks of American immigrants in Israel.* Doctoral dissertation, State University of New York at Buffalo.

Keesing, R. (1974). Theories of culture. *Annual Review of Anthropology, 3,* 73-97.

Kellerman, K. (1986). Anticipation of future interaction and information exchange in initial interaction. *Human Communication Research, 13,* 41-75.

Kim, Y. Y. (1977). Communication patterns of foreign immigrants in the process of acculturation. *Human Communication Research, 41,* 66-76.

Klein, W., & Dittmar, N. (1979). *Developing grammars: The acquisition of German syntax by foreign workers.* New York: Springer-Verlag.

Kluckhohn, F., & Strodtbeck, F. (1961). *Variations in value orientations.* New York: Row, Peterson.

Koltuv, B. (1962). Some characteristics of intrajudge trait intercorrelations. *Psychological Monographs, 76*(33), Whole No. 552.

Lambert, W. E., Mermigis, L., & Taylor, D. M. (1986). Greek Canadian's attitudes toward own group and other Canadian ethnic groups: A test of the multiculturalism hypothesis. *Canadian Journal of Behavioural Sciences, 18,* 35-51.

Larson, D. N., & Smalley, W. A. (1972). *Becoming bilingual: A Guide to language learning.* South Pasadena, CA: William Carey Library.

Lester, R. E. (1986). Organizational culture, uncertainty reduction and the socialization of new organizational members. In S. Thomas (Ed.), *Culture and communication.* Norwood, NJ: Ablex.

Levine, D. N. (1985). *The flight from ambiguity.* Chicago: University of Chicago Press.

Lieberson, S. (1985). *Making it count: The improvement of social research and theory.* Berkeley: University of California Press.

Marsella, A. J., DeVos, G., & Hsu, F.L.K. (Eds.). (1985). *Culture and self: Asian and Western perspectives.* New York: Tavistock.

McPherson, K. (1983). Opinion-related information seeking. *Personality and Social Psychology Bulletin, 9,* 116-124.

Mehrabian, A. (1971). *Silent messages.* Belmont, CA: Wadsworth.

Miller, N., & Brewer, M. (Eds.). (1984). *Groups in contact.* New York: Academic Press.

Miller, G. R., & Steinberg, M. (1975). *Between people.* Chicago: Science Research Associates.

Miller, G. R., & Sunnafrank, M. J. (1982). All is for one but one is not for all. In F. Dance (Ed.), *Human communication theory.* New York: Harper and Row.

Murphy, H.B.M. (1973). The low rate of hospitalization shown by immigrants to Canada. In C. Zwingemann & M. Pfister-Ammende (Eds.), *Uprooting and after.* Heidelberg: Springer-Verlag.

Murray, J. P., & Kippax, S. (1979). From the early window to the late night show:

International trends in the study of television's impact on children and adults. In L. Berkowitz (Ed.), *Advances in experimental social psychology* (Vol. 12). New York: Academic Press.

Naiman, N., Frohlich, M., Stern, H., & Todesco, A. (1978). *The good language learner.* Toronto: Ontario Institute for Studies in Education.

Nishida, H. (1985). Japanese intercultural communication competence and cross-cultural adjustment. *International Journal of Intercultural Relations, 9,* 247-270.

Noesjirwan, J. (1978). A rule-based analysis of cultural differences in social behavior: Indonesia and Australia. *International Journal of Psychology, 13,* 305-316.

O'Driscoll, M., & Feather, N. (1983). Perception of value congruence and interethnic behavioral intentions. *International Journal of Intercultural Relations, 7,* 239-252.

Padilla, A. M. (1980). The role of cultural awareness and ethnic loyalty in acculturation. In A. Padilla (Ed.), *Acculturation: Theory, models, and some new findings.* Boulder, CO: Westview.

Pak, A., Dion, K. L., & Dion, K. K. (1985). Correlates of self-confidence with English among Chinese students in Toronto. *Canadian Journal of Behavioural Sciences, 17,* 369-378.

Parks, M., & Adelman, M. (1983). Communication networks and the development of romantic relationships. *Human Communication Research, 10,* 55-80.

Pettigrew, T. (1978). Three issues in ethnicity. In J. Yinger & S. Cutler (Eds.), *Major social issues.* New York: Free Press.

Pettigrew, T. F. (1986). The intergroup contact hypothesis reconsidered. In M. Hewstone & R. Brown (Eds.), *Contact and conflict in intergroup encounters.* Oxford: Basic Blackwell.

Planalp, S., & Honeycutt, J. (1985). Events that increase uncertainty in interpersonal relationships. *Human Communication Research, 11,* 593-604.

Prager, K. J. (1986). Intimacy status: Its relationship to locus of control, self-disclosure, and anxiety in adults. *Personality and Social Psychology Bulletin, 12,* 91-109.

Reynolds, P. D. (1971). *A primer in theory construction.* Indianapolis: Bobbs- Merrill.

Rose, T. L. (1981). Cognitive and dyadic processes in intergroup contact. In D. Hamilton (Ed.), *Cognitive processes in stereotyping and intergroup behavior.* Hillsdale, NJ: Lawrence Erlbaum.

Rothbart, M., Dawes, R., & Park, B. (1984). Stereotyping and sampling biases in intergroup perception. In J. Eiser (Ed.), *Attitudinal judgement.* New York: Springer-Verlag.

Ruben, B. (1983). A system-theoretic view. In Gudykunst (Ed.), *Intercultural communication theory.* Beverly Hills, CA: Sage.

Ruben, B., & Kealey, D. J. (1979). Behavioral assessment of communication competency and the prediction of cross-cultural adaptation. *International Journal of Intercultural Relations, 3,* 15-48.

Scherer, K. R., Wallbott, H. G., & Summerfield, A. B. (Eds.). (1986). *Experiencing emotion: A cross-cultural study.* Cambridge: Cambridge University Press.

Schuetz, A. (1944). The stranger. *American Journal of Sociology, 49,* 499-507.

Selltiz, C., Christ, J. R., Havel, J., & Cook, S. W. (1963). *Attitudes and social relations of foreign students in the United States.* Minneapolis: University of Minnesota Press.

Sherif, M. (1966). *Group conflict and cooperation.* London: Routledge and Kegan Paul.

Simard, L. (1981). Cross-cultural interaction. *Journal of Social Psychology, 113,* 171-192.

Simmel, G. (1950). The stranger. In K. Wolff (Ed. & Trans.). *The sociology of Georg Simmel.* New York: Free Press.

Snyder, M. (1974). Self-monitoring of expressive behavior. *Journal of Personality and Social Psychology, 30,* 526-537.

Snyder, M., & Monson, T. (1975). Persons, situations, and the control of social behavior. *Journal of Personality and Social Psychology, 32,* 637- 644.

Sodetani, L. L., & Gudykunst, W. B. (1987). The effects of surprising events on intercultural relationships. *Communication Research Reports, 4.*

Sorrentino, R. M., & Hewitt, E. C. (1984). The uncertainty reducing properties of achievement tasks revisited. *Journal of Personality and Social Psychology, 47,* 884-899.

Stephan, W. G. (1985). Intergroup relations. In G. Lindzey & E. Aronson (Eds.), *The handbook of social psychology* (3rd ed., Vol. II). New York: Random House.

Stephan, W. G., & Stephan, C. W. (1984). The role of ignorance in intergroup relations. In N. Miller & M. Brewer (Eds.), *Groups in contact.* New York: Academic Press.

Stephan, W. G., & Stephan, C. W. (1985). Intergroup anxiety. *Journal of Social Issues, 41*(3), 157-176.

Sunnafrank, M. (1986). Predicted outcome value during initial interactions: A reformulation of uncertainty reduction theory. *Human Communication Research, 13,* 3-33.

Tajfel, H. (1978). Social categorization, social identity, and social comparison. In H. Tajfel (Ed.), *Differentiation between social groups.* London: Academic Press.

Tajfel, H., & Turner, J. C. (1979). An integrative theory of intergroup conflict. In W. Austin & S. Worchel (Eds.), *The social psychology of intergroup relations.* Monterey, CA: Brooks/Cole.

Taylor, D. M., & Jaggi, V. (1974). Ethnocentrism and causal attributions in a South Indian context. *Journal of Cross-Cultural Psychology, 5,* 162-171.

Triandis, H. C. (1976). *Interpersonal behavior.* Monterey, CA: Brooks/Cole.

Triandis, H. C. (1977). Subjective culture and interpersonal relations across cultures. *Annals of the New York Academy of Sciences, 285,* 418-434.

Triandis, H. C. (1980). Values, attitudes, and interpersonal behavior. In M. Page (Ed.), *Nebraska symposium on motivation 1979* (Vol. 27). Lincoln: University of Nebraska Press.

Triandis, H. C. (1986). Collectivism vs. individualism. In C. Bagley & G. Verma (Eds.), *Personality, cognition, and values: Cross-cultural perspectives of childhood and adolescence.* London: Macmillan.

Turner, J. C. (1985). Social categorization and the self-concept: A social cognitive theory of group behavior. *Advances in Group Processes, 2,* 77-121.

Turner, J. C. (1987). *Rediscovering the social group: A self-categorizing theory.* London: Basil Blackwell.

Weick, K. E. (1979). *The social psychology of organizing* (2nd ed.). Reading, MA: Addison-Wesley.

Whyte, W., & Holmberg, A. (1956). Human problems of U.S. enterprises in Latin America. *Human Relations, 15,* 1-40.

Wilder, D. A., & Allen, V. L. (1978). Group membership and preference for information about others. *Personality and Social Psychology Bulletin, 4,* 106-110.

Wilson, C. (1986, November). *Uncertainty reduction, communication networks, and organizational socialization.* Paper presented at the Speech Communication Association Convention, Chicago.

Witkin, H. A., & Berry, J. W. (1975). Psychological differentiation in cross- cultural perspective. *Journal of Cross-Cultural Psychology, 6,* 4-87.

Wright, G. N., Phillips, L. D., Wholley, P. C., Choo, G. T., Ng, K. O., Tan, I., & Wisudha, A. (1978). Cultural differences in probablistic thinking. *Journal of Cross-Cultural Psychology, 9,* 185-299.

Yum, J. O., & Wang, G. (1983). Interethnic perceptions and the communication behavior among five ethnic groups in Hawaii. *International Journal of Intercultural Relations, 7,* 285-308.

7

Communication Accommodation in Intercultural Encounters

CYNTHIA GALLOIS • *University of Queensland*
ARLENE FRANKLYN-STOKES • *HOWARD GILES* •
University of Bristol
NIKOLAS COUPLAND • *University of Wales, Institute of Science & Technology*

This chapter combines propositions from speech accommodation theory and ethnolinguistic identity theory into one communication accommodation theory that is applicable to intercultural settings. The role of the situation in constraining both speaker behavior and receiver attributions is stressed and the importance of interpersonal and intergroup salience is highlighted. A model of the progress of two participants in an intergroup interaction through the decisions they must make about communication is presented.

When two people from different cultural groups come together, sometimes the encounter is as smooth as silk. The people simply seem to get onto the same wavelength, and all goes well. At other times, though, this sort of encounter can seem a series of obstacles and incompatibilities and can end in misunderstanding, hostility, and an increase in prejudice. For many years, researchers in intergroup encounters have been aware that mere contact between cultural groups is not enough to reduce prejudice (e.g., Allport, 1954). Both Allport and Cook (1984), on the basis of laboratory and field work, have maintained that the *type* and the *context* of contact are important determinants of whether prejudice will increase or decrease after an intergroup encounter. Clearly, then, the outcomes and communicative character of intercultural encounters can be predicted only by a model that integrates considerations of code and context, by examining how they determine and are determined by the strategic initiatives of interactants.

Speech Accommodation Theory (SAT), with its recent emphasis on discourse, paralanguage and nonvocal behavior—and thereby recently renamed Communication Accommodation Theory (CAT) (see Giles, Mulac, Bradac, & Johnson, 1987)—is concerned primarily with the communicative moves speakers make in interactions relative to the social and psychological contexts that are operating, and relative to each other's communicative characteristics. CAT, therefore, is particularly relevant to analyzing the complex processes underlying intercultural communication. In describing CAT, as well as its linguistic characteristics and social outcomes, this chapter has two main aims. First, we will relate CAT to relevant theory on intergroup encounters, drawing especially on the work of Hewstone and Brown (1986). In the course of doing this, we will briefly review the history of CAT. Our second aim is to elaborate CAT by combining Speech Accommodation Theory (see Giles et al., 1987) and Ethnolinguistic Identity Theory (ELIT; see Giles & Johnson, 1987), to present a more complete theory of communication in intercultural settings. We will also draw heavily on the further elaboration of SAT in an intergenerational context formulated by Coupland, Coupland, Giles, and Henwood (1988). Throughout, we will highlight both the intergroup and the interpersonal aspects of intercultural encounters.

INTERGROUP AND INTERPERSONAL ASPECTS OF INTERCULTURAL ENCOUNTERS

Hewstone and Brown (1986) recently developed a model for describing intergroup contact that stresses the importance of whether individuals in the encounter see each other as typical or atypical of their groups. They also pay at least lip service to the notion that the situation has a *sociolinguistic* aspect that has been little studied from a prejudice-reduction perspective. Hewstone and Brown point out, that if participants in intergroup contacts see the encounter mainly in interpersonal terms, it is unlikely that any attitude change resulting from it will generalize to the outgroup as a whole. Thus, they suggest, an attitude change toward an individual participant is most likely to generalize to the outgroup as a whole when intergroup differences, including communicative differences, are obvious.

The expectations or stereotypes that members of one group have about members of another are important in determining what are perceived as the similarities and differences between the groups, and thus the representativeness of individuals' behavior. These stereotypes also include views of one's *own* group (Turner, 1986). In a review of this literature, Hewstone and Giles (1986) specify the ways that stereotypes affect communication in intergroup settings and may contribute to communication breakdown. As we will point out later, CAT makes specific predictions about how stereotypes and initial attitude affect speaker and listener behavior, and about the consequences of this behavior for evaluations of the encounter by participants.

Beginning with the work of Tajfel (1978), interpersonal or intergroup salience has been viewed as a crucial dimension of any encounter between people. In an interpersonally-salient encounter, the unique features of participants are attended to. When group identity is salient, however, participants often minimize individual, and maximize group differences (see Tajfel & Turner, 1979). Most researchers and theorists in the intergroup area have described intergroup and interpersonal salience as lying along a single continuum (e.g., Ball, Giles, & Hewstone, 1985; Hewstone & Brown, 1986). As a number of scholars have now pointed out, however, intergroup and interpersonal really represent two orthogonal dimensions that encompass four quadrants: *high intergroup/high interpersonal,* of which a good example is an interaction between spouses (sex as intergroup, but each spouse as an individual); *high intergroup/low interpersonal,* such as a meeting between strangers from two ethnic groups with a history of political rivalry; *low intergroup/high interpersonal,* exemplified by a meeting between friends of the same age, sex, and ethnic group; and *low intergroup/low interpersonal,* of which a good example is a ritualized encounter between strangers (e.g., buying a stamp at the post office), where all goes as expected (Giles & Hewstone, 1982; Gudykunst, 1986). As a matter of fact, these two dimensions are probably negatively correlated, which may explain the tendency to view them as a single continuum. Nonetheless, we must recognize that, even in encounters in which group membership is highly salient, participants may also react to each other as individuals, and vice versa. In addition, interpersonal and intergroup salience can, and often do, change within the duration of a single encounter (Coupland, 1980; Stephenson, 1981).

Intercultural encounters always have the potential to represent any of the four quadrants described previously. Therefore, we have paid special attention to these dimensions. This chapter takes up individual differences in the tendency to approach intercultural encounters as high-intergroup, high-interpersonal, or both, as well as situational constraints that encourage everyone to perceive a given encounter in intergroup or interpersonal terms. In addition, later sections deal with intergroup and interpersonal communication strategies within an interaction, and with the attributions and evaluations receivers make in relation to them. Very often, the verbal and nonverbal behaviors of participants in an interaction give us the best clue about whether intergroup factors, interpersonal factors, or both, are salient, and in which direction (positive or negative). Here again, CAT makes explicit predictions.

COMMUNICATION ACCOMMODATION THEORY

It is beyond the scope of this chapter to give more than a sketch of the theoretical and empirical developments in CAT since its original presentation by Giles (1973). Giles introduced the concepts of *convergence* and *divergence* (and later, *maintenance,* see Bourhis, 1979) as strategies that speakers could use to signal their attitudes toward each other. Convergence involves changing one's linguistic (language, dialect, vocabulary, speech style) or paralinguistic behavior (tone of voice, speech rate, and so on) so as to be more similar to one's conversational partner, in order to seek approval, enhance comprehension, or show solidarity. Divergence is the opposite of this; speakers emphasize differences between their own and their partners' speech. Maintenance refers simply to continuing in one's own style, sometimes without reference to the partners' speech and sometimes as a deliberate reaction to it. Evaluative responses to maintenance are said to be similar to those to divergence: generally negative, just as those to convergence are, within limits, generally positive.

Giles and Powesland (1975) related SAT to similarity-attraction theory (Byrne, 1971), arguing that convergence should increase attraction and divergence inhibit it. Later work related SAT to the attributions that conversational partners make of each other's accommodating language (Simard, Taylor, & Giles, 1976) and to Tajfel's (1974; Tajfel & Turner, 1979) theory of social identity and intergroup relations (Giles, Bourhis, & Taylor, 1977). Giles and Johnson (1981), working within the framework of SAT, expanded into the intercultural context (with what was later called Ethnolinguistic Identity Theory) by proposing that members of subordinate ethnic groups are more likely to retain their linguistic style if they see language as an important dimension of their group, see their group boundaries (especially linguistic boundaries) as hard and closed, and see their group as having high ethnolinguistic vitality (e.g., high numbers, high status, and institutional support; see Giles et al., 1977). In this case, subordinate group members are less likely to want to learn the language/dialect/accent of the dominant group, or to accommodate to it (see Giles & Byrne, 1982).

Several studies have pointed to the importance of interactants' *perceptions* of their own and others' communicative behavior (e.g., Beebe & Giles, 1984; Street & Giles, 1982; Thakerar, Giles, & Cheshire, 1982). In fact, it is pointed out that speakers do not converge to (or diverge from) the *actual* behavior of others, but rather to what they *think* are the communicative behaviors of their conversational partners. Platt and Weber (1984) showed some of the ways that *subjective accommodation* can be inappropriate, and can be attributed as patronizing, ingratiating, or humiliating by receivers. Finally, a number of researchers (Ball, Giles, Byrne, & Berechree, 1984; Bourhis & Genessee, 1980; McKirnan & Hamayan, 1984a, 1984b) have highlighted the importance of norms for correct behavior in a situation to the occurrence and evaluation of accommodation. Generally speaking, researchers have found that when convergence is norm-violating it is evaluated as negatively as divergence.

In addition to the recent elaborations of SAT (Giles et al., 1987) and ELIT (Giles & Johnson, 1987), there have been two other important developments. First, Gudykunst (1985) attempted an integration of ELIT with uncertainty reduction theory (Berger, 1979; Berger & Bradac, 1982). Gudykunst stressed the influence of the development of the relationship between interactants on intergroup encounters. In particular, when people contemplate a closer relationship with a conversational partner, they use uncertainty reduction techniques, including questioning, self-disclosure, and deception detection, in order to fit themselves and the partner into roles and social categories, reduce uncertainty about the partner as a person, and increase confidence in explaining the partner's behavior. Thus the person can make a decision about whether to make the relationship closer or to keep the partner at a distance. As with all accommodation processes, however, there is no simple relationship between initial orientation, strategy, and consequence. For example, speakers who wish to reduce uncertainty may use overdisclosive behavior, which can be alienating and can confirm negative intergroup stereotypes (Coupland, Coupland, Giles, & Wiemann, in press).

The second development involves work by Coupland et al. (1988), which situates SAT more clearly in the sociolinguistic domain. They suggest that SAT, in attempting to explain the ways interlocutors attune their behavior to each other, has concentrated on a limited set of strategies involving *approximations,* including convergence, divergence, and maintenance as discussed previously. All these approximation strategies focus upon the behavior, or *productive performance,* of the other person, as it actually is, is perceived, or is stereotyped.

Coupland et al. (1988) introduced three other concerns and sets of strategies. They argue that these strategies, like the approximation ones, relate to the *addressee focus* taken; that is, the aspect of the other's talk that is attended to. The first addressee focus they consider involves attending to other's *interpretive competence* or ability to understand (as it is, is perceived, or is stereotyped). This concern leads to a set of *interpretability* strategies that can be used to modify the complexity of speech (for example, by decreasing diversity of vocabulary or simplifying syntax, as in "foreigner talk"), to increase clarity (by changing pitch, loudness, or tempo), or to influence the selection of conversational topics (staying in "familiar areas" for the other person). In addition, interlocutors attend to each other's *conversational needs.* This leads to a set of *discourse management* strategies, including topic choice (maintaining coherence and thematic development), sharing topic selection, and sharing the management of turn-taking. Finally, participants attend to *role relations,* which leads to a set of *interpersonal control* strategies. These strategies either increase or decrease the discretion of the other person to change roles, and can be encoded through forms of address, interruptions, directive talk, and so forth. Like the approximation strategies, these three types of behavior can be used either to maintain social distance (lower solidarity or emphasize status differences) or, alternatively, can bring the other person closer and make the interaction richer, procedurally smoother, or more equal-status. In addition, the strategies can stem from beliefs (or stereotypes) about the other person's group, the other person as an individual, or both. It is, therefore, the perceptions of participants about each other and about their interaction, or the *subjective* elements of accommodation, that are crucial in explaining sociolinguistic behavior and its consequences.

With these new developments, and in view of the predictions it makes about behavior in intercultural encounters, we turn now explicitly to CAT. The basic communicative elements of an intercultural interaction are presented schematically in Figure 7.1. People come to an encounter with a certain initial orientation that may be high intergroup, high interpersonal, high on both dimensions, or low on both. Initial orientation, as Figure 7.1 indicates, is influenced strongly by social and personal identity (see Tajfel & Turner, 1979), and represents a general

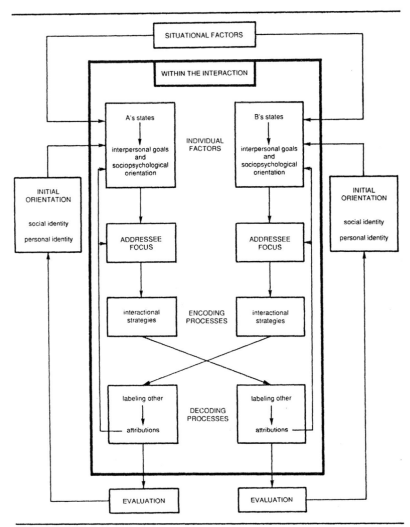

Figure 7.1 A model of communication accommodation in intercultural encounters.

tendency to view intergroup encounters in a particular way. Propositions 1 to 8 in the next sections deal with individual differences in *initial* orientation.

Once they are in an interaction, the initial orientation of participants may change, at least to some extent. First, each interaction brings its own situational constraints. These include situational norms about status and formality, as well as aspects of the interaction such as topic and competitiveness, that are likely to increase or decrease the perception of threat. Propositions 9 and 10 deal with aspects of the situation that are likely to qualify initial orientation significantly, and to have a large influence on addressee focus.

During the encounter itself, participants employ various strategies as speakers and react to their partners. Here, the microlevel features of the situation become the major influence on both speaker and listener behavior. Thus, addressee focus, speaker strategies, and listener attributions may shift, and the influence of initial orientation and other macrolevel variables becomes more indirect. Propositions 11 to 14 deal with speaker variables, and Propositions 15 and 16 with listener reactions.

Finally, participants in an intercultural interaction evaluate their own and their partners' behavior. This process may change the intergroup or interpersonal salience of the interaction for them, as well as their orientation to their partner. They take this evaluation away from the encounter with them, thus changing or reinforcing their initial orientation in the next interaction, and their view of their partners' group (see Hewstone & Brown, 1986).

INITIAL ORIENTATION IN INTERCULTURAL SETTINGS

As previously noted, no matter how well interactants in intercultural encounters know and like each other, group membership is always potentially salient because of different values, codes, and background characteristics. Individual interactants, however, are influenced by these factors in quite different ways.

Subordinate Groups

Sociolinguists have for many years noted the way that members of subordinate class, ethnic, and cultural groups signal solidarity with their group by selective use of ingroup language, dialect, accent, or vocabulary (see Giles, 1977; Labov, 1972; Romaine, 1982). Research within the framework of CAT has focused upon individual differences in the tendency to use ingroup markers. Empirical research is beginning to show support for predictions and their implications for ethnic language maintenance (Giles & Johnson, 1987; Hall & Gudykunst, 1986). Once again, however, there is reason to believe that it is the *perceived* vitality of a group, rather than objectively measured vitality that influences behavior (Bourhis & Sachdev, 1984; Giles, Rosenthal, & Young, 1985; Young, Giles, & Pierson, 1986). In addition, if members of a subordinate group think that their group or its linguistic identity is threatened—that is, its perceived vitality is dangerously low—they may use their ingroup's speech style more frequently and show stronger loyalty to it (e.g., Giles & Johnson, 1987).

Over time, members of subordinate groups arrive at a habitual level of accommodation to the dominant group's speech style that reflects their initial orientation in intergroup encounters. For example, Shockey (1984) found high levels of accommodation by North American residents in England to British English, particularly when comprehension was affected. Clyne (1982) has related a language switch by Australian immigrants to English (the dominant language) versus maintenance of the ethnic language, to the importance of the first language as a group symbol, and to vitality. Other Australian research (Gallois & Callan, 1987) has found that Italian and British speakers converge to Australian nonverbal behavior after a number of years' residence in the country, at least in public settings where communicative clarity is an issue. Indeed, Trudgill (1986) has proposed long-term accommodation as a major mechanism of dialect change.

Taking all this research into account, Giles and Johnson (1987) proposed individual differences in the way subordinate group members view their sociolinguistic situation, which influences the initial orientations of these speakers in any encounter with members of the dominant outgroup. We have reformulated their propositions here for clarity and parsimony, and we have added specific references to intergroup and interpersonal salience. Propositions 1 to 4 describe four categories of individuals who differ in relative dependence on their ingroup or independence from it, and who show strong or weak solidarity with their group (see Thibaut & Kelley, 1959). *Dependence* is defined in terms of the available alternatives outside the ethnic ingroup and the person's relative status inside and outside it. *Solidarity* is defined in terms of identification with the ethnic ingroup and satisfaction with it. Solidarity is also related to threat; in general, the more one's group is threatened, the more one tends to act in solidarity to it or in defense of it.

Different psychological and communicative orientations in intercultural situations are predicted for each of the four categories. First, people in different categories tend to view interactions with members of the dominant group differently in terms of intergroup and interpersonal salience. In addition, they are motivated differently to adopt addressee foci and speaker strategies that either attune their behavior strongly to their partner (e.g., along the approximation discussion they converge), do not attune their behavior (e.g., they maintain their own style), or counter-attune (e.g., they diverge). Attuning can occur either with respect to group markers in the interaction, such as language, accent, or the selection of salient topics for one group or the other, or it can involve more interpersonal aspects of the interaction, such as matching in nonverbal behavior, sharing responsibilities for topic development, and so forth. Finally, people are motivated to evaluate the encounter in different ways. It must be remembered, of course, that these initial orientations may change once participants actually enter an intergroup encounter.

(1) *High dependence, high solidarity.* Members of a subordinate group that has language and speech as important dimensions of its identity, and who

  (a) belong to few other social categories (including the outgroup) whose norms and values do not overlap with those of their ingroup, perceive the social identities deriving from these as relatively inadequate, and perceive their status within their ingroup to be higher than their status in the larger society (high dependence on the ingroup);
  (b) identify strongly with their ethnic ingroup (high solidarity);
  (c) feel that their group situation is threatened and could become better or worse as a result of social change (high solidarity resulting from threat);
  (d) perceive threat to their ethnic ingroup resulting from soft and open boundaries *or* low vitality, but not both (as for c, preceding);

  are likely to be initially oriented in intergroup encounters to

  (i)   defining the situation as having high intergroup salience and low interpersonal salience, and evaluating it in intergroup terms;
  (ii) not attuning or counter-attuning to the distinctive communicative features of the outgroup;
  (iii) not attuning or counter-attuning to outgroup members interpersonally.

(2) *High dependence, low solidarity.* Members of a subordinate group that has language and speech as important dimensions of its identity, and who

  (a) belong to some other social categories (including the outgroup) whose norms and values do not overlap with those of their ingroup, perceive the social identities deriving from these as relatively inadequate, and perceive their status within their ethnic ingroup to be higher than their status in the larger society (high dependence on the ingroup);

(b) identify moderately or weakly with their ethnic ingroup and aspire to increase contact with the outgroup (low solidarity);

(c) feel that their ethnic ingroup situation is threatened and could become better or worse as a result of social change (some solidarity resulting from threat);

(d) perceive their ethnic ingroup boundaries to be hard and closed and their group to have high vitality (high dependence resulting from vitality);

are likely to be initially oriented in intergroup encounters to

(i) defining the situation as having moderate or low intergroup salience and high interpersonal salience, and evaluating the encounter in interpersonal terms;

(ii) not attuning to the distinctive communicative features of the outgroup, especially when there is pressure from the ingroup or the situation not to do so;

(iii) attuning strongly to outgroup members interpersonally.

(3) *Low dependence, high solidarity.* Members of a subordinate group who

(a) belong to many other social categories (including the outgroup) whose norms and values do not overlap with those of their ingroup, perceive the social identities deriving from these as relatively adequate, but perceive their ingroup status to be as high as their status in the larger society (low dependence);

(b) identify strongly with their ethnic ingroup (high solidarity);

(c) do not feel their group is threatened by changes to the *status quo* (solidarity does not result from threat);

(d) do not perceive their ethnic ingroup to be threatened by soft and open boundaries or by low vitality (as for c above);

are likely to be initially oriented in intergroup encounters to

(i) defining the situation as high in both intergroup and inter-personal salience;

(ii) attuning strongly to the distinctive communicative features of the outgroup unless their ethnic group is threatened by some aspect of the encounter;

(iii) attuning strongly to outgroup members interpersonally.

(4) *Low dependence, low solidarity.* Members of a subordinate group who

(a) belong to many other social categories (including the outgroup) whose norms and values do not overlap with those of their ingroup, perceive the social identities deriving from these to be relatively

adequate, and perceive their status within their ethnic ingroup to be lower than there status in the larger society (low dependence);
(b) identify moderately or weakly with their ethnic ingroup (low solidarity);
(c) do not feel that their ethnic group is threatened by changes or are indifferent to their group's status to the *status quo* (low solidarity resulting from threat);
(d) see their group as having soft and open boundaries and low vitality, but do not feel threatened by this (as for c above);

are likely to be initially oriented in intergroup encounters to

(i) defining the situation as low in intergroup salience and high in interpersonal salience;
(ii) attuning strongly to the distinctive communicative features of the outgroup (if they have not already adopted these habitually);
(iii) attuning strongly to outgroup members interpersonally.

Thus, people in Category 1, because of their high ingroup solidarity and feeling of defensiveness for their group, are likely to let intergroup considerations override interpersonal ones in encounters with the dominant group, while people in Category 4, who are relatively indifferent to the fate of their ethnic ingroup, are likely to view the situation in interpersonal terms. They may, indeed, aspire to join the dominant group if this possibility is open to them, as may people in Category 2. Individuals in the latter category, however, because of their dependence on their ethnic ingroup, are still likely to be oriented to maintain their group's communication style (unless they feel they can get away with convergence), although they may view intergroup encounters in interpersonal terms. Finally, people in Category 3 are most likely to let the specific features of an encounter dictate their behavior, as both group and interpersonal factors are salient to them.

These four categories of people can be usefully characterized with respect to their feelings of *relative deprivation* (Dube-Simard, 1983; Walker & Pettigrew, 1984); that is, the extent to which they feel that they as individuals are disadvantaged (egoistic deprivation) or that their group is disadvantaged (fraternal deprivation). People in the first category are likely to see their ingroup as deprived relative to the larger society, and to perceive social injustice toward their group. Thus we would predict that members of subordinate groups who feel fraternally deprived will be oriented to show strong ingroup communication marking. People in Category 2 are deprived egoistically, however. These people also are oriented to show ingroup marking, but this is because they do not perceive good alternatives to complying with group norms, rather than because they feel solidarity for the group. People in Categories 3 and 4 are characterized as egoistically advantaged by the larger society, rather than deprived; hence their strong interpersonal orientation.

Members of subordinate groups, then, are likely to be differentially disposed to use convergent or divergent approximation strategies in intercultural encounters. Because uncertainty reduction and interpretability, discourse management, and interpersonal control strategies have been studied mainly among majority (or dominant) group members and or in ingroup settings, it is more difficult to make predictions about the reactions of subordinate group members. This is, therefore, an important area for future research. We might expect that people in Category 1 generally tend to *under-accommodate*; that is, they may not take sufficiently into account the communicative needs of the other person. As yet, however, there are no tests of this hypothesis.

Dominant Groups

There is a very large body of literature on the reactions of members of dominant groups to the communicative behaviors of subordinate cultural, ethnic, class, sex, and age groups (for reviews, see Ryan & Giles, 1982; Gudykunst, 1986). As a general rule, members of dominant groups downgrade the speech and language of subordinate groups, especially on traits related to social status (there are, of course, exceptions to this). Nonetheless, we would expect the same processes underlying the reactions of subordinate group members to play a role in the accommodative behavior of members of the majority. We can, thus, extend the propositions put in the last section to dominant groups.

One difference between members of dominant and subordinate groups, however, is that the former are always likely to see their ingroup as having high vitality. Even so, members of dominant groups may feel threatened because they feel the status of a subordinate group is rising too quickly, or that too many members of the subordinate group are passing into their group (see Taylor & McKirnan, 1984).

The four types of individuals from dominant groups presented next match types I to IV in the previous section in terms of dependence and solidarity.

(5) *High dependence, high solidarity.* Members of majority or dominant groups in this category can be characterized like members of subordinate groups in the preceding Category 1, except that they

(a) perceive their group's boundaries to be soft and open, but perceive their group to have high vitality; and their initial orientation is like that of people in Category 1.

(6) *High dependence, low solidarity.* Members of majority or dominant groups in this category can be characterized like members of the preceding Category 2, and their initial orientation is the same.

(7) *Low dependence, high solidarity.* Members of majority or dominant groups in this type can be characterized in many ways like members of the preceding Category 3, *except for the fact that the absence of threat and ingroup allegiance would orient them to maintaining* their distinctive dominant group style.

(8) *Low dependence, low solidarity.* Members of majority or dominant groups in this category can be characterized like members of category 4, except that they do not perceive that their group has low vitality, and their initial orientation is the same.

People in Categories 5 and 6 can be expected to allow intergroup considerations to override interpersonal ones in many interethnic or intercultural encounters. People of Category 5, indeed, probably come closest to showing high fraternal deprivation. In addition, they are likely to be high ethnocentrics, a group that McKirnan and Hamayan (1984a) found to have stricter and less tolerant norms for minority group speech. Members of Category 6, on the other hand, are disadvantaged by the lack of alternatives to their own group. They, like members of Category 2, may be oriented to maintain their group's style and status, but may be more susceptible to reacting to outgroup members as individuals.

Because they are somewhat threatened by the subordinate group, people in Categories 5 and 6 may also have salient negative stereotypes (see Hewstone & Giles, 1986). On the other hand, if they do change their attitude as the result of an intergroup encounter, they may be likely to generalize the change to the outgroup as a whole. For people in Category 7, both intergroup and interpersonal factors are likely to be salient, and in the same direction. Finally, people in the last category are likely to address most intercultural situations in interpersonal terms, and not to generalize their reactions to the outgroup as a whole.

As a final point, it should be noted that members of dominant groups (with the possible exception of Category 8) are most likely to maintain their group's linguistic and speech style. They may induce hostility among members of subordinate groups either by underaccommodating or by engaging in foreigner talk (assuming the incompetence of the other person), or by *overaccommodating* in other ways (see the following), even including mimicking the subordinate group's speech in extreme cases. On the other hand, they may show friendliness by matching the nonverbal behavior of their conversational partner, by attuning appropriately (or even perhaps excessively, i.e., overaccommodate) to interpretability, conversation needs, and role relations, and by making clear their positive attitude toward the other person (thus reducing uncertainty). Again, while there is much research that supports these predictions indirectly, this is an area that can be usefully explored and clarified much further. In addition, measures of language attitudes and behavior, which are the province of CAT, usually can be linked to social measures like relative deprivation, as well as to personality measures such as ethnocentrism.

SITUATIONAL CONSTRAINTS

Most theory on intergroup encounters has recognized that the particular situation in which the encounter occurs puts constraints on the behaviors available to speakers and the attributions made by receivers. Initial orientation, as we pointed out earlier, clearly is modified by situational factors, particularly by participants' perceptions of situational norms and of threat coming from other participants (or other aspects of the situation).

As Argyle, Furnham, and Graham (1981) pointed out, each situation, in addition to having its own goals, also has its own set of roles and rules or norms. Norms vary in the extent to which they are salient in the particular situation, agreed upon by a speech community, and in the strictness or tolerance with which they are applied (McKirnan & Hamayan, 1984b). On balance, research into communication norms suggests that norms are stricter and more salient, and outgroup deviations are more negatively evaluated, in status-marked situations (formal situations like interviews, or competitive settings such as work or school). Many studies have found that the accent and language of minority ethnic and cultural groups is downgraded in status-marked situations, especially on traits that have to do with social status and prestige (see Ryan & Giles, 1982, for a review). Ball et al. (1984), indeed, found that convergence to a working-class accent in a job interview setting was rated as negatively as divergence; in this case, situational norms overrode the positive effects of attuning.

Norms in other situations often have more flexibility. In general, researchers have found smaller evaluative differences between ethnic and cultural groups in informal or friendly settings (e.g., Gallois & Callan, 1985; Ryan & Carranza, 1975). To the extent that this is the case, there is more latitude to show solidarity with one's own cultural group in these situations. We still know very little, however, about what the norms are in various situations and how strictly they are applied. One study that did look at this (McKirnan & Hamayan, 1984a) found that the strictest norms held by Anglo-Americans about Mexican-American speech had to do with lexical intrusions from Spanish.

The role of threat in an intergroup situation seems to be to heighten sensitivity to group memberships (Giles & Johnson, 1986). Threat may come from the topic under discussion and how strongly participants feel about it, as Giles and Johnson (1986) found, or it may come from other participants, their group memberships, or their behavior (Bourhis & Giles, 1977; Gallois, Callan, & Johnstone, 1984; Giles & Johnson, 1987). Indeed, threat to one's ingroup can override considerations of vitality, as pointed out previously. More research needs to be done on this important situational variable.

Giles and Johnson (1987) presented two propositions about the effect of situational constraints, especially status-related norms and threat, on speaker behavior. We generalize them to receiver reactions and reformulate them here. These situational constraints apply to all eight categories just described, although people in Categories 3 and 7, to whom both intergroup and interpersonal considerations are salient in the initial-orientation to intergroup encounters, may be especially susceptible to them.

(9) In the intergroup situations when they

    (a) are not strongly committed in general to an attitude position on which an outgroup interactant opposes them, or they perceive the topic to be peripheral to their social identity (that is, they do not perceive their group to be threatened by the topic of conversation);

    (b) do not perceive the situation or the behavior of outgroup members to be competitive (that is, their group is not threatened by the behavior of another person); or

    (c) perceive a number of features of the situation to emphasize status-stressing dimensions;

few people are likely to define the situation in intergroup terms, to counter-attune their behavior on group-salient communicative features, or to interpret the behavior of others in intergroup terms.

Under these circumstances, most people are likely to follow social norms and preserve their status as polite, cooperative, and sociable people. They are also likely to define the situation in either interpersonal or role-related terms (depending upon the prevailing norms), and to attune their behavior accordingly. On the other hand, the last proposition describes situations that are more likely to be defined in intergroup terms, because they are threatening.

(10) In intergroup situations when they

(a) are strongly committed in general to an attitude position on which an outgroup member opposes them or they perceive the topic to be central to their social identity (i.e., they perceive their group to be threatened by the topic of conversation);

(b) perceive the situation or the behavior or outgroup members to be competitive or to violate social norms; or

(c) perceive few features of the situation to emphasize status-stressing dimensions;

many people are likely to define the situation in intergroup terms, not to attune or to counter-attune their behavior on group-salient communicative features, and to interpret the behavior of others in intergroup terms.

In these circumstances, people are likely to diverge on behaviors salient to ingroup identity (especially linguistic behaviors). They may also be likely to make their own discourse less interpretable, less cooperative, and tolerate or promote conflicting degrees of control.

THE IMMEDIATE INTERACTION AND ITS CONSEQUENCES

It is within the interaction itself that intergroup and interpersonal factors begin to play different, and sometimes contradictory, roles. The preceding propositions give us some clues about how to describe initial orientation and situational factors. On the other hand, once people are in an interaction, their developing reaction to the person or persons with whom they are interacting and the details of how talk proceeds also influence them. As we pointed out earlier, speakers in any intergroup interaction have a number of strategies by which they can signal intergroup solidarity, interpersonal attraction, or the converse. We suggest that speakers may use different behaviors to signal the intergroup and interpersonal aspects of their attitudes and the addressee focus they are attending to. As receivers, in addition, they may use different behaviors as a basis for attributing the interpersonal and intergroup attitudes of the other participants. Behaviors used to signal and infer intergroup attitudes should be the more important determinants of whether the other participants are seen as typical or atypical of their groups.

The following propositions, then, assume an initial orientation and a set of situational factors, and are concerned with the process of the interaction itself.

Speakers' Behavior

CAT proposes a number of motives for attuning in an interaction, among them desire for social approval, communication efficiency, and desire to show solidarity or identification with the other person's group. Speakers counter-attune, of course, for the opposite motives. Giles et al. (1987) have formulated several propositions about the sociopsychological orientation underlying the use of approximation strategies within an interaction. We reformulate them here to take more account of the intergroup and interpersonal aspects of interaction, and to add propositions relating to addressee foci other than attention to productive performance (Coupland et al., 1988).

(11) When speakers in an intercultural encounter

    (a) desire recipients' social approval (and the perceived costs of acting in an approval-seeking manner are proportionally lower than the perceived rewards) (all sociolinguistic dimensions);

    (b) desire a high level of communication clarity and comprehension (interpretability);

    (c) desire to meet the perceived communication needs of recipients as individuals (discourse management);

    (d) desire a self-presentation shared by recipients (approximation); or

    (e) desire equal-status role relations with recipients (interpersonal control);

they attempt to attune positively, along the sociolinguistic dimensions indicated, to the communicative characteristics they *believe* to belong to their message recipients, whether they are considered as individuals or as representatives of their groups.

(12) When speakers in an intercultural encounter

- (a) desire to communicate a contrastive self- or group-image (approximation);
- (b) desire to dissociate personally from the recipients or the recipients' definition of the situation (approximation);
- (c) desire to signal differences in experience/knowledge/intellectual capability/communicative style (interpretability); or
- (d) desire to achieve or maintain a high-status role relative to recipients (interpersonal control);

they attempt to counter-attune or not to attune to the perceived communicative characteristics of their message recipients, whether recipients are seen as typical or atypical of their groups.

Empirical evidence so far suggests that speakers choose different behaviors to encode the intergroup and interpersonal aspects of their communication. In principle, the four address foci we have mentioned can be motivated by either intergroup or interpersonal considerations. Nonetheless, we predict that some strategies are more used when there is high intergroup salience and others on more interpersonally salient occasions. Proposition 13 thus deals with the *form* of attuning.

(13) When interpersonal concerns are salient in an intergroup encounter, people attempt to attune their behavior (or not to attune or to counter-attune) using primarily

- (a) *approximation* strategies involving behaviors relevant to idiolectal (personal identity) or ongoing stylistic features, including idiosyncrasies of phrasing or vocabulary, formality levels and key, and most nonverbal behaviors;
- (b) *discourse management* strategies involving behaviors relevant to the immediate conversation, including sharing of topic selection and turn-taking, back-channeling, and face-maintaining;
- (c) *interpersonal control* strategies such as interruptions, correcting and evaluating moves, and so on;
- (d) *interpretability* strategies including speech rate (in which it has no intensive group-marking function), loudness, framing and focusing moves, and so on, whereas when intergroup concerns are salient, people attempt to attune their behavior to or away from their recipients using
- (e) *approximation* strategies involving behaviors relevant to dialectal features (social identity), including language, dialect, accent, socially-marked vocabulary, and group-marked nonverbal behavior;

(f) *interpersonal control* strategies involving behaviors relevant to group and role relations, including forms of address;

(g) *interpretability* strategies involving behaviors relevant to group differences, including syntax, lexis, and topic selection.

Finally, the extent to which speakers are able and motivated to attune their behavior is influenced by several factors. Proposition 14 takes up the *degree* of attuning.

(14) The degree of attuning depends upon

(a) the extent of speakers' repertoires;

(b) norms about the minimal and maximal limits of conversational attuning in the speech community;

(c) the magnitude of individual, social, and contextual factors that may increase the level of intergroup salience, interpersonal salience, or both; and

(d) the extent to which the recipients' actual communication in the situation matches the beliefs that speakers have about it.

Note that (a) refers to the capacities speakers bring into an interaction with them (these capacities, however, do not form a part of speakers' initial orientation, which is motivational). Part (b) is related to situational norms, but refers to general rules about holding *any* conversation. It is only with reference to such rules that certain styles of *attuned* talk can attract *negative* evaluations, as either inadequately (under-accommodation) or excessively (over-accommodation) attuned. Finally, parts (c) and (d) relate to changeable features of the ongoing interaction.

There is very little research that looks at the intergroup and interpersonal aspects of communication accommodation. What there is, however, suggests that in encounters in which interpersonal salience is high (for example, in ingroup encounters), speakers tend to attune (or match) particularly on nonverbal behaviors, such as speech rate, response latency, amount of gaze, and so forth (see Cappella, 1983; Giles et al., 1987). Thus, as Proposition 13 predicts, attuning on nonverbal behavior is a good measure of interpersonal attraction, while low attuning (or counter-attuning) is an indication of hostility. We predict that discourse management and uncertainty reduction strategies also have a strong interpersonal focus, either promoting or discouraging close personal relationships.

On the other hand, within intergroup settings, research has generally shown that convergence and divergence occur on group-marked behaviors like those listed in Proposition 14 (e) (e. g., Bourhis & Giles, 1977; Bourhis, Giles, Leyens, & Tajfel, 1979). We suggest that it is specifically these, mainly linguistic, behaviors that give clues to the intergroup attitudes of participants in intercultural encounters. In addition, interpersonal control strategies are likely to be salient in intergroup settings, as are interpretability strategies (although, again, both dimensions can be used to attune to the competence of a particular individual).

Receivers' Reactions

Most of the research using the matched guise technique (Lambert, Hodgson, Gardner, & Fillenbaum, 1960) has examined receiver or observer reactions to users of ingroup or outgroup language or style (i.e., convergent or divergent speakers; see Ryan & Giles, 1982, for a review). The studies that have looked directly at receiver reactions to accommodation have obtained similar findings to these (e.g., Bourhis & Genessee, 1980; Ball et al., 1984; Doise et al., 1976). The general finding, as expected, has been that divergent speech is evaluated less favorably, especially when it comes from subordinate groups and in status-marked settings, although this depends on the political relations between the groups.

Recently, it has become apparent that receivers have expectations about the optimal level of accommodation to their speech. Argyle (1982), for example, suggested that foreigners usually are expected to converge on some behaviors but not others, and Collett (1982) pointed to the confusion that can arise in intercultural settings when one participant is not sure of whether another is converging or not. Platt and Weber (1984) found that inappropriate convergence is interpreted negatively, even when it is well-intentioned. As noted, *overaccommodation* (see Coupland et al., 1988) is one category of evaluative response to inappropriate convergence or other inappropriate attuning (which is usually based on stereotypes about another's group, rather than on actual behavior). On the other hand, insufficient attuning, or inappropriate maintenance of one's own speech style, may be evaluated as inconsiderate or unhelpful. Coupland et al. (1988) refer to this as *underaccommodation*. Finally, emphasis on the distinctive aspects of one's own group's communication (maintenance or divergence), and obstructive or conflictual style in general, are liable to be evaluated as *contraaccommodation,* and generally interpreted as having hostile intent. All these evaluations of inappropriate speaker behavior can be distinguished from evaluatively appropriate attuning or *accommodation.*

Given this basis, the reactions of receivers (labeling and attributions in Figure 7.1) can be predicted fairly straightforwardly from the factors we have mentioned. Again, we have elaborated on two propositions taken from Giles et al. (1987).

(15) When recipients perceive message senders' behavior to be well attuned (accommodation); that is, when they perceive a sender's communication to be

(a) a match to (or a shift toward) their own communicational style;
(b) a match to (or a shift toward) a communication stereotype for a group in which they perceive themselves to have valued membership;
(c) optimally distant sociolinguistically;

or they perceive

(d) the sender's style to adhere to a valued norm;

especially when they attribute to the sender

(e) high effort;
(f) high choice; and
(g) an altruistic or benevolent intent;

the recipients explain the sender's behavior positively (i.e., as friendly, attractive, and so on).

(16) When recipients perceive message sender's behavior to be badly attuned;

that is, when they perceive a sender's communication to be

(a) a mismatch to their own communicational style;
(b) a match to a communication stereotype for a group in which they perceive themselves *not* to have valued membership;
(c) encoded so as to achieve a minimal fit with their own code or style; or
(d) the sender's style to depart from a valued norm;
especially when they attribute to the sender
(e) high effort;
(f) high choice;
(g) a selfish or malevolent intent;

the recipients explain the sender's behavior negatively.

Evaluation of the Interaction

A number of studies have shown that members of subordinate groups evaluate ingroup and outgroup speech in ways we would expect, given the initial orientations described in Propositions 1 to 4. Giles and Johnson (1987), drawing on work on ethnic language attitudes (Ball, Gallois, & Callan, 1988; Giles & Ryan, 1982), have characterized some of the types. Individuals in Category 1 (see Proposition 1) are likely to upgrade users of ingroup speech (whether they belong to the ingroup or not) and the ingroup speech style itself, particularly on traits related to solidarity, such as friendliness, warmth, and integrity, and other salient ingroup dimensions. People in Category 2 may not downgrade the ingroup style and its users on traits relating to solidarity, but are likely to downgrade them on status-related traits, such as intelligent, confident, and ambitious. People in Category 4 are likely to downgrade their ingroup style and its users, especially on status-related traits. Finally, we add that people in Category 3 may not see many differences between their ingroup style and the style of the dominant group. For example, Callan and Gallois (1982) found that Italo-Australians, a group well-assimilated into the larger society but who still show strong solidarity to the Italian community, do not evaluate Italian and English very differently. This was in contrast to Greek-Australians, who upgraded Greek relative to English on solidarity-related traits.

Hewitt's (1986) ethnography of racism and racist discourse between black and white youths in central London suggests further refinements. His data show that intergroup and interpersonal salience are in part *dictated by* sociolinguistic features called into play. Hence, Hewitt argues that peer-group solidarity can be emphasized by whites through creole use (to blacks), but only when ethnically nonsalient forms are used. On the other hand, whites adopting creole pronunciation—a slang marker of black ethnic group membership—meet with hostility from blacks, because it is perceived as devaluing a culturally significant marker. Once again, the context can defuse this perception (e.g., when the activity in which it occurs involves joking, competitive talk, or verbal display).

Little research has examined individual differences in how members of dominant groups downgrade subordinate speakers and their styles, especially on status-related traits. Nonetheless, we would expect individual differences among them to parallel those previously described.

In general, then, we would expect that when an interaction has high intergroup salience (e.g., emphasizes the communicational differences between groups, or has a threatening topic), and speakers either do not attune to each other or counter-attune on the group-related dimensions mentioned in Proposition 13, participants are likely to walk away from the interaction evaluating each other (negatively) as typical of their groups. In these same circumstances, when speakers do attune their behavior interpersonally, but maintain the distinctive features of their groups, they are likely to be evaluated more positively as individuals, but as atypical of their groups. Finally, when the encounter has high interpersonal salience, but low intergroup salience, participants are unlikely to be representative of their groups at all (see Hewstone & Brown, 1986).

CONCLUSION

It is beyond the scope of this chapter to develop fully the idea that receivers have expectations about the level of accommodation speakers will encode, have expectations (or stereotypes) about their own communicational style, and use both sets of expectations in making attributions about speakers. In addition, the complex possibilities of contradictory strategies being adopted in the same sequence of discourse (e.g., over- *and* underaccommodation along different dimensions) cannot be elaborated here. We refer readers to Coupland et al. (1988), Giles et al. (1987), and Hewstone and Giles (1986) for fuller discussions of these issues. Once again, however, it is likely to be nongroup-marked nonverbal behavior that influences receiver attributions about the speaker as an individual, and group-marked linguistic behavior that determines how typical a group member the speaker is seen to be (and thus generalizable from the encounter to the speaker's group as a whole).

This chapter has had a major objective to combine propositions from SAT and ELIT into one Communication Accommodation Theory that is applicable to intercultural settings. We have stressed the role of the situation in constraining both speaker behavior and receiver attributions, and have highlighted the importance of interpersonal and intergroup salience to every intergroup encounter. Figure 7.1 has put forward a simple model of the progress of two participants in an intergroup interaction through the decisions they must make about communication. A brief summary *reconsideration of the model* is in order.

First, consider the initial orientation of participants in an encounter. *Group factors* in the figure include such things as A's and B's cross-group membership, the extent to which each identifies with his or her ingroups, perceived vitality and boundaries, and perception that relations between the groups could change. To these, we must add each participant's *personal identity,* including salient personal dimensions of comparison with others and of self-presentation. *Situational factors* include norms and roles, emphasis on status or solidarity, and threat to individuals and their groups.

Both these sets of factors influence the attitudes and behavior of participants once they are in an interaction. Here, *individual factors* involve A's and B's states (cognitive, affective, behavioral), as well as their goals in the interaction (for example, to obtain social approval or to promote ingroup distinctiveness). In addition, they include the participants' psychological orientation to each other (positive, negative, or neutral). Next, *addressee focus* refers to the aspect of the other person's communication that is attended to (productive performance, interpretive competence, conversation needs, or role relations between participants). *Encoding processes* refer to the sociolinguistic strategies mentioned earlier (approximation, interpretability, discourse management, and interpersonal control) and the behaviors (linguistic, discoursal, or nonverbal) to which they give rise. *Decoding processes* include the labeling of speaker behavior by the receiver as accommodative, or as over-, under-, or contraaccommodative. In addition, they include attributions about speaker effort, choice, and intent, made on the basis of this labeling. Finally, *evaluation* includes whether the encounter is viewed in intergroup or interpersonal terms (or both), whether the behavior of the other person is seen as a typical or atypical group member. Participants take this away with them, and they may generalize it to the partner's group as a whole.

We have not dealt in any detail here with the role played by uncertainty reduction in intercultural interactions. Logically, a desire for uncertainty reduction forms part of participants' initial orientation, as well as part of their sociopsychological orientation to each other within an interaction (see Figure 7.1). As such, it is likely to affect the addressee focus chosen, as well as the sociolinguistic strategies used by speakers and the attributions made of them by receivers. It must be left to future research, however, to explicate these relationships in intergroup contexts.

One more future priority that this model implies is a test of the causal path. In addition, we need to know more about how people perceive group factors and situational factors in intergroup encounters. Lastly, little research to date has examined the specific behaviors that may signal intergroup or interpersonal attuning. Overall, CAT provides a rich framework in which intercultural encounters can be studied and evaluated.

REFERENCES

Allport, G. W. (1954). *The nature of prejudice.* Cambridge/Reading, MA: Addison-Wesley.

Argyle, M. (1982). Intercultural communication. In S. Bochner (Ed.), *Cultures in contact* (pp. 61-80). Oxford: Pergamon.

Argyle, M., Furnham, A., & Graham, J. A. (1981). *Social situations.* Cambridge: Cambridge University Press.

Ball, P., Gallois, C., & Callan, V. J. (1988). Language attitudes: A perspective from social psychology. In D. Blair & V. Collins (Eds.), *Studies in Australian English* (pp. 1-14).

Ball, P., Giles, H., Byrne, J. L., & Berechree, P. (1984). Situational constraints in the evaluative significance of speech accommodation: Some Australian data. *International Journal of the Sociology of Language, 46,* 115-130.

Ball, P., Giles, H., & Hewstone, M. (1985). Interpersonal accommodation and situational constraints: An integrative formulation. In H. Giles & R. St. Clair (Eds.), *Recent advances in language, communication, and social psychology* (pp. 263-286). London: Lawrence Erlbaum.

Beebe, L., & Giles, H. (1984). Speech accommodation theories: A discussion in terms of second-language acquisition. *International Journal of the Sociology of Language, 46,* 5-32.

Berger, C. (1979). Beyond initial interaction: Uncertainty, understanding and the development of interpersonal relationships. In H. Giles & R. St. Clair (Eds.), *Language and social psychology* (pp. 122-144). Oxford: Basil Blackwell.

Berger, C., & Bradac, J. J. (1982). *Language and social knowledge.* London: Edward Arnold.

Bourhis, R. Y. (1979). Language in ethnic interaction: A social psychological approach. In H. Giles & R. St. Jacques (Eds.), *Language and ethnic relations* (pp. 117-141). Oxford: Pergamon.

Bourhis, R. Y., & Genessee, F. (1980). Evaluative reactions to code-switching strategies in Montréal. In H. Giles, W. P. Robinson, & P. Smith (Eds.), *Language: Social psychological perspectives* (pp. 335-343). Oxford: Pergamon.

Bourhis, R. Y., & Sachdev, I. (1984). Vitality perceptions and language attitudes. *Journal of Language and Social Psychology, 3,* 97-126.

Callan, V. J., & Gallois, C. (1982). Language attitudes of Italo-Australian and Greek-Australian bilinguals. *International Journal of Psychology, 17,* 345-358.

Cappella, J. (1983). Conversational involvement: Approaching and avoiding others. In

J. Wiemann & P. R. Harrisson (Eds.), *Non-verbal interaction* (pp. 113-148). Beverly Hills, CA: Sage.

Clyne, M. (1982). *Multilingual Australia: Resources—needs—policies.* Melbourne: River Seine.

Collett, P. (1982). Meetings and misunderstandings. In S. Bochner (Ed.) *Cultures in contact* (pp. 81-98). Oxford: Pergamon.

Coupland, J., Coupland, N., Giles, H., & Wiemann, J. (in press). My life in your hands: Processes of self-disclosure in intergenerational talk. In N. Coupland (Ed.), *Styles of discourse.* London: Croom Helm.

Coupland, N. (1980). Style-shifting in a Cardiff work-setting. *Language in Society, 9,* 1-12.

Coupland, N., Coupland, J., Giles, H., & Henwood, K. (1988). Accommodating the elderly: Invoking and extending a theory. *Language in Society, 17.*

Doise, W. (1978). *Groups and individuals.* Cambridge: Cambridge University Press.

Dube-Simard, L. M. (1983). Genesis of social categorisation, threat to identity, and perceptions of social injustice: Their role in intergroup communication. *Journal of Language and Social Psychology, 2,* 183-206.

Gallois, C., & Callan, V. J. (1985). Situational influences on perceptions of accented speech. In J. P. Forgas, (Ed.), *Language and social situations* (pp. 159-193). New York: Springer-Verlag.

Gallois, C., & Callan, V. J. (1987, July). *Social situations and accommodation: Anglo-Australians' perceptions of ingroup and outgroup speakers.* Paper presented at the Third International Conference on Social Psychology and Language, Bristol, England.

Gallois, C., Callan, V. J., & Johnstone, M. (1984). Personality judgements of Australian Aborigine and white speakers: Ethnicity, sex, and context. *Journal of Language and Social Psychology, 3,* 39-57.

Giles, H. (1973). Accent mobility: A model and some data. *Anthropological Linguistics, 15,* 87-105.

Giles, H. (Ed.). (1977). *Language, ethnicity and intergroup relations.* London: Academic Press.

Giles, H., Bourhis, R. Y., & Taylor, D. M. (1977). Towards a theory of language in ethnic group relations. In H. Giles (Ed.), *Language, ethnicity, and intergroup relations* (pp. 307-348). London: Academic Press.

Giles, H., & Byrne, J. L. (1982). An intergroup model of second-language acquisition. *Journal of Multilingual and Multicultural Development, 3,* 17-40.

Giles, H., & Hewstone, M. (1982). Cognitive structures, speech and social situations: Two integrative models. *Language Sciences, 4,* 187-219.

Giles, H., & Johnson, P. (1981). The role of language in ethnic group relations. In J. C. Turner & H. Giles (Eds.), *Intergroup behaviour* (pp. 199-243). Oxford: Basil Blackwell.

Giles, H., & Johnson, P. (1986). Perceived threat, ethnic commitment, and interethnic language behaviour. In Y. Y. Kim (Ed.), *Interethnic communication: Current research* (pp. 91-116). Newbury Park, CA: Sage.

Giles, H., & Johnson, P. (1987). Ethnolinguistic identity theory: A social psychological approach to language maintenance. *International Journal of the Sociology of Language, 68,* 69-99.

Giles, H., Mulac, A., Bradac, J. J., & Johnson, P. (1987). Speech accommodation theory: The first decade and beyond. In M. McLaughlin (Ed.), *Communication yearbook 10* (pp. 13-48). Beverly Hills, CA: Sage.

Giles, H., & Powesland, P. F. (1975). *Speech style and social evaluation.* London: Academic Press.

Giles, H., Rosenthal, D., & Young, I. (1985). Perceived ethnolinguistic vitality: The Anglo- and Greek-Australian setting. *Journal of Multilingual and Multicultural Development, 6,* 256-269.

Giles, H., & Ryan, E. B. (1982). Prolegomena for developing a social psychological theory of language attitudes. In E. B. Ryan & H. Giles (Eds.), *Attitudes towards language variation* (pp. 208-223). London: Edward Arnold.

Gudykunst, W. B. (1985). The influence of cultural similarity and type of relationship on uncertainty reduction processes. *Communication Monographs, 52,* 203-217.

Gudykunst, W. B. (Ed.). (1986). *Intergroup communication.* London: Edward Arnold.

Hall, B. J., & Gudykunst, W. (1986). The intergroup theory of second language ability. *Journal of Language and Social Psychology, 5,* 291-302.

Hewitt, R. (1986). *White talk black talk: Inter-racial friendship and communication amongst adolescents.* Cambridge: Cambridge University Press.

Hewstone, M., & Brown, R. (1986). Contact is not enough: An intergroup perspective on the 'contact hypothesis.' In M. Hewstone & R. Brown (Eds.), *Contact and conflict in intergroup encounters* (pp. 1-44). Oxford: Basil Blackwell.

Hewstone, M., & Giles, H. (1986). Social groups and social stereotypes in intergroup communication: A review and model of intergroup communication breakdown. In W. B. Gudykunst (Ed.), *Intergroup communication* (pp. 10-26). London: Edward Arnold.

Labov, W. (1972). *Sociolinguistic patterns.* Philadelphia: University of Pennsylvania Press.

Lambert, W. E., Hodgson, R., Gardner, R., & Fillenbaum, S. (1960). Evaluative reactions to spoken language. *Journal of Abnormal and Social Psychology, 60,* 44-51.

McKirnan, D. J., & Harmayan, E. V. (1984a). Speech norms and attitudes toward outgroup members: A test of a model in a bicultural context. *Journal of Language and Social Psychology, 3,* 21-38.

McKirnan, D. J., & Harmayan, E. (1984b). Speech norms and perceptions of ethno-linguistic group differences: Towards a conceptual and research framework. *European Journal of Social Psychology, 14,* 151-168.

Platt, J., & Weber, H. (1984). Speech convergence miscarried: An investigation into inappropriate accommodation strategies. *International Journal of the Sociology of Language, 46,* 131-146.

Romaine, S. (Ed.). (1982). *Sociolinguistic variation in speech communities.* London: Edward Arnold.

Ryan, E. B., & Carranza, M. (1975). Evaluation reactions of adolescents toward speakers of standard English and Mexican American accented English. *Journal of Personality and Social Psychology, 31,* 855-863.

Ryan, E. B., & Giles, H. (Eds.). (1982). *Attitudes towards language variation.* London: Edward Arnold.

Shockey, L. (1984). All in a flap: Long-term accommodation in phonology. *International Journal of the Sociology of Language, 46,* 87-96.

Simard, L. M., Taylor, D. M., & Giles, H. (1976). Attribution processes and interpersonal accommodation in a bilingual setting. *Language and Speech, 19,* 34-87.

Stephenson, G. M. (1981). Intergroup bargaining and negotiation. In J. C. Turner & H. Giles (Eds.), *Intergroup behavior*. Chicago: University of Chicago Press.

Street, R., & Giles, H. (1982). Speech accommodation theory: A social cognitive approach to language and speech behaviour. In M. Roloff & C. R. Berger (Eds.), *Social cognition and communication* (pp. 193-226). Beverly Hills, CA: Sage.

Tajfel, H. (1974). Social identity and intergroup behaviour. *Social Science Information, 13,* 65-93.

Tajfel, H. (1978). Social categorisation, social identity and social comparison. In H. Tajfel (Ed.), *Differentiation between social groups* (pp. 61-76). London: Academic Press.

Tajfel, H., & Turner, J. (1979). An integrative theory of intergroup conflict. In W. G. Austin & S. Worchel (Eds.), *The social psychology of intergroup relations* (pp. 33-47). Monterey, CA: Brooks/Cole.

Taylor, D. M., & McKirnan, D. (1984). A five-stage model of intergroup relations. *British Journal of Social Psychology, 23,* 291-300.

Thakerar, J., Giles, H., & Cheshire, J. (1982). Psychological and linguistic parameters of speech accommodation theory. In C. Fraser & K. R. Scherer (Eds.), *Advances in the social psychology of language* (pp. 205-255). Cambridge: Cambridge University Press.

Thibaut, J., & Kelley, H. H. (1959). *The social psychology of groups*. New York: John Wiley.

Trudgill, P. (1986). *Dialects in contact*. Oxford: Basil Blackwell.

Walker, I., & Pettigrew, T. F. (1984). Relative deprivation theory: An overview and conceptual critique. *British Journal of Social Psychology, 23,* 301-310.

Young, L., Giles, H., & Pierson, H. (1986). Sociopolitical change and perceived vitality. *International Journal of Intercultural Relations, 10,* 459-469.

8

Episode Representations
in Intercultural Communication

JOSEPH P. FORGAS • *University of New South Wales*

This chapter deals with the role of cognitive representation about interaction situations in intercultural communication. In the first half of the chapter, a sociocognitive approach to intercultural communication is proposed, and the links between communication and the cultural context are considered. It is argued that social episodes, defined as consensual cognitive representations about recurring interaction sequences, are crucial to successful interpersonal behavior and communication, and conflicting episode representations of interaction episodes are summarized. Recent work establishing the culture-specificity of episode cognition is also described. It is concluded that this approach to intercultural communication capitalizing on recent developments in cognitive social psychology offers a most fruitful avenue for further research.

Episodes of intercultural communication—encounters with people from cultures other than our own—represent an increasingly common, and often enlightening experience for growing numbers of people. Such encounters are also among the most fascinating examples highlighting the close interdependence between culture, communication, and individual social cognition. Research on intercultural communication has been of considerable interest to social scientists for a variety of reasons. It is in encounters with people from different cultures that the culture-bound, contextual character of our most flexible communication medium, language, becomes most apparent. Communication systems such as language "have a real existence only in the social and cultural settings in which they appear" (Wurm, 1976, p. 363), and knowing how to communicate presupposes far more than simply knowing a language (Hymes, 1967). As the meanings communicated through language are to

AUTHOR'S NOTE: *Financial support from the Australian Research Grants Scheme and from the German Research Foundation, and the collaboration of Stephanie Moylan and Michael Bond in some of the research reported here is gratefully acknowledged. Requests for reprints should be sent to Joseph P. Forgas, School of Psychology, University of New South Wales, P.O. Box 1, Kensington 2033, Australia.*

a considerable extent defined by the interlocutors' shared cultural knowledge of situational requirements (Clark & Wilkes-Gibbs, 1986; Isaacs & Clark, 1987), intercultural communication represents an exciting challenge to our usual taken-for-granted language rules (Forgas, 1985a). Much of nonverbal communication is similarly culture-bound (Forgas, 1985b; Weitz, 1978). The situation-specificity of language, and how such cultural knowledge is psychologically represented is, in turn, of growing interest to cognitive social psychologists (see Forgas, 1981b; 1983b; Herrmann, 1983).

Human communication in general, and verbal communication in particular, capitalizes on people's shared knowledge and understanding of the rules and norms governing recurring social encounters. Shared cognitive representations about such prototypical interaction situations are also the building blocks of culture (Mead, 1934). Intercultural communication is a case par excellence when shared situation representations, the basis of all successful communication, are themselves problematic or confused. In this chapter we shall offer a tentative theory of intercultural communication, based on contemporary research in cognitive social psychology on how consensual cognitive representations of social episodes evolve and are maintained and modified by cultural influences. In the second half of the chapter, empirical research on the cognitive representation of social episodes, and the influence of group, subcultural, and cultural variables on such representations, will be outlined.

TOWARD A COGNITIVE-CULTURAL CONCEPTUALIZATION OF INTERCULTURAL COMMUNICATION

A social-cognitive approach to intercultural communication rests on several propositions. These are summarized next, as a preliminary to a more detailed discussion, which follows.

(1) Culture and cognition are interdependent. This proposition asserts that culture is created and maintained as the result of the cognitive activity and representations of individuals. Correspondingly, culture does provide individuals with shared schemas to understand and regulate their everyday encounters, including communication episodes.

(2) Communication is based on shared cognitive representations about reality, which are by necessity culture specific. This proposition suggests that all forms of human communication, both verbal and nonverbal,

capitalize on the shared cultural understanding between the partners. Messages partly derive their meaning from the preexisting knowledge structures in the minds of individuals.

(3) Cognitive representations about social episodes are critical to successful communication. This proposition suggests that of all forms of cultural knowledge, it is implicit representations about social interactions that are most directly involved in regulating interpersonal communication. The proposition also implies the testable hypotheses that culture and other social variables have a major influence on cognitive representations about interaction episodes.

(4) Intercultural communication by definition involves the absence of wholly shared episode representations between the interactants. This proposition suggests that the critical issue in intercultural communication is that partners do not have matching and shared cognitive representations about encounters. Research on the nature and characteristics of such episode representations is thus central to a proper understanding of the cognitive processes involved in intercultural communication.

(5) The effectiveness of intercultural communication is directly related to the degree to which shared episode representations between the interactants are present. In other words, there exists a theoretical continuum from no shared episode representations to completely shared representations, which is positively correlated with the efficiency of intercultural communication.

Culture and Cognition

The central theme of this approach is that culture and cognition are inseparable. Culture exists in the minds of individuals, and it is individual perceptions, interpretations, and representations of culture, which in their innumerable daily manifestations, help to maintain or change our stable sense of the relevant knowledge structures shared by individuals. Cognitive social psychology is eminently equipped to undertake the task of quantifying and describing such implicit cultural knowledge. We must of course be very careful in considering what kinds of cognitive representations are most pertinent to regulating intercultural communication. We would like to suggest in this chapter that of all forms of cultural knowledge, none is more typical or important to understanding intercultural communication than our knowledge of the rules and norms governing recurring everyday interactions, or social episodes.

The role of such situational constraints in language use has been well recognized in linguistic research (Clark, 1985). Several early attempts to reliably classify and study communication situations were designed to deal with this problem. Firth (1957) sought to analyze situations in terms of such features as participants and objects. Gregory (1967) focused on such situational features as the medium (channel), the role (topic), and the addressee (relationships), while Poyatos (1976) and Hymes (1967, 1972) developed even more ambitious descriptive schemes. Others, such as Ervin-Tripp (1964, 1972), Brown and Fraser (1979), and Giles and Hewstone (1982) progressed toward constructing empirically based situational taxonomies. However, none of these classificatory schemes have led to substantial empirical research, and few of them enjoy universal acceptance.

One reason for this may be that many of the earlier attempts to deal with situational influences on communication were based on a priori, speculative schemes that tended to emphasize the most salient descriptive features of situations (such as setting, objects). As we shall see later, people's cognitive representations about social situations are in fact rarely based on such objective characteristics. Commonly, the connotative, subjective meaning of a particular situation is the major variable that determines how social situations are perceived and cognitively represented. (Battistich & Thompson, 1980; Forgas, 1979a; Pervin, 1976). In contrast to most earlier, descriptive approaches, cognitive social psychology offers a potentially very useful framework for understanding and empirically representing how social situations in general, and communication situations in particular, are implicitly perceived.

The Study of Social Episodes

One of the most obvious, yet often ignored features of everyday social life is that it largely consists of recurring, patterned activities and encounters. Much of our daily social life involves the cooperative acting out of well-defined, familiar interaction sequences. Having a chat with your spouse, visiting a doctor, eating in a restaurant, or attending a colloquium are examples of recurring interaction routines. In fact, it seems to be the very predictability and regularity of such social episodes that makes orderly interactions feasible (Mead, 1934). As Goffman (1974) observed, agreed-upon and shared representations of social encounters are the basis on which all social life, and our stable sense of identity and confidence in our dealings with others rests. There are many influential theorists in both psychology (Brunswik, 1956; Lewin, 1951; Murray, 1951) and in sociology (Goffman, 1974; Thomas, 1966; Wolff,

1964) who were deeply interested in the role such social situations play in regulating interpersonal communication and behavior, although empirical research on this topic is a fairly recent development (Forgas, 1979a). For our purposes, *social episodes* may be defined as "typical, recurring interaction units within a specified subculture, which constitute 'natural units' in the stream of behaviour, and about which members of a given subculture have a shared, implicit cognitive representation" (Forgas, 1983c, p. 145). In recent years, social psychologists have paid increasing attention to how cognitive representations about such interaction episodes may be empirically analyzed (Argyle, Furnham, & Graham, 1982; Forgas, 1979a, 1982; King & Sorrentino, 1983), and the way such interaction scripts influence memory, thinking, and information processing (Abelson, 1980; Bower, Black, & Turner, 1979). Indeed, related concepts such as "scripts," "action plans," "event prototypes" or "event schemata" (Abelson, 1980; Bower, Black, & Turner, 1979; Lichtenstein & Brewer, 1980) have much in common with our notion of social episodes.

One important difference between most earlier approaches and the present conceptualization is that most previous research focused almost exclusively on the information processing consequences of ad hoc episode "scripts." In contrast, we conceive of interaction episodes as real, sociocultural units in their own right, and not simply convenient vehicles for information processing experiments (Forgas, 1981b, 1983b). Consequently, we are interested mainly in the content and structure of people's implicit representations of social episodes as the cognitive reflection of their surrounding culture. Despite the growing interest in such episode representations, the influence of cultural variable on cognitive representations of interactions has received relatively little attention to date.

Until fairly recently, the accurate empirical representation and analysis of subjectively perceived episodes was methodologically problematic (Forgas, 1979b). During the past decade or so, several investigators succeeded in constructing reliable quantified models of episode domains. According to several studies, the number of social episodes that make up the interactive repertoire of most people may be quite limited, often consisting of less than 30 such common and recurring routines (Forgas, 1979a, 1982; Pervin, 1976). Research on the episode representations of American, English, Swedish, Australian, and German groups of students, housewives, academics, and sports teams yielded meaningful and reliable results (Battistich & Thompson, 1980; Forgas,

1976, 1979a, 1982; King & Sorrentino, 1983; Pervin, 1976). It appears that cognitive representations of interaction episodes are commonly based on a limited number of connotative rather than descriptive dimensions, such as self-confidence, intimacy, involvement, and formality.

Culture and Episode Representations

The links between the surrounding culture and people's perceptions of social episodes have also received relatively little attention to date. Yet the close interdependence of external cultural norms and values and internal cognitive representations of episodes has been well recognized at least since Thomas and Znaniecki's classic studies on cultural adaptation in the early 1920s. Mead (1934), in his symbolic interactionist theory, placed particular emphasis on the crucial role human symbolic capacities play in the construction of both cultural systems and individual personalities. Definitions of interaction situations are among the most important building blocks of a culture, directly influencing everyday behaviors (Triandis, 1972; Wolff, 1964). Ethnographers and linguists have long been aware that "all societies recognize certain communicative routines which they view as distinct wholes, separate from other types of discourse, characterized by special rules of speech and nonverbal behavior and often distinguishable by clearly recognizable opening and closing sequences" (Gumperz & Hymes, 1972, p. 17). The values, norms, expectations, and emphases in our culture and language cannot but shape the way we implicitly represent our social environment (Forgas, 1985b).

All social interaction is based on the shared understanding of the rules, norms, and goals of the encounter between the interactants: "for interaction to succeed, participants must essentially agree in their social situation definition" (Leodolter & Leodolter, 1976, p. 327). Intercultural communication may be characterized as a communication episode where by definition, there is some inconsistency or ambiguity about the implicit definition of the encounter between the partners. The considerable evidence for the situation-contingent use of alternative language codes in multilingual (Fishman, 1971) or multicultural environments is largely consistent with the present arguments emphasizing the role of episode representations in intercultural communication. Research indicating that the choice of particular language codes may have a major influence on how the situation and the communicator is perceived and interpreted is also consistent with this view (Bond, 1983). Investigations of the cognitive representation of social episodes thus offer a fruitful empirical approach to studying the exact nature of how such divergent cognitive representations of social episodes arise and their consequences in intercultural communication. Several empirical studies have been successful in quantifying and analyzing cultural and subcultural differences in episode cognition. We shall consider some of the relevant investigations next.

Subcultural Influences on Episode Representations

If cognitive representations of social episodes are indeed dependent on a person's cultural and subcultural background, it is of considerable importance that such a relationship be empirically demonstrated. Several investigations now exist that clearly indicate that subcultural and group membership may have a profound influence on the way people cognitively represent interaction episodes. Linguistic research has also clearly established that there exists something like an "ethnography of speaking"—people sharing a subcultural milieu may have their own specific communication codes—just as any social grouping, be it a small Norwegian village or a group of Burundi tribesmen, inevitably develop their own unique interaction and communication repertoires (Albert, 1972; Blom & Gumperz, 1972; Forgas, 1985a; Garfinkel, 1967). Since a person's subcultural milieus also generate their own particular ways of interpreting and representing social episodes.

In one directly relevant investigation, we sought (a) to compare the implicit episode representations of two different subcultural groups, (b) to describe empirically the kind of implicit dimensions used by each of these two subgroups to differentiate between social occasions, and (c) to assess the advantages of using categorical or dimensional representations of episode domains.

The two subcultural groups we studied were middle-class housewives in a British town and undergraduate students (N = 99; Forgas, 1976). This investigation consisted of two stages. In stage one, social episodes were elicited from a sample of subjects drawn from each of the two subcultures. These subjects were asked to write a detailed diary, recording all of their social interactions over a period of time, as well as noting common and recurring episodes that for some reason were not part of their social encounters during this time. The most frequently mentioned 25 social episodes were identified from these diaries, and were used as stimuli in stage two of the study. At this stage, a second sample of subjects from each subculture were presented with labels containing the description of the 25 target episodes, and were asked to sort these episodes into groups in terms of how similar they thought they were. This is one method for collecting similarity judgments about stimuli that are relatively complex. These data were then collated into a similarity matrix, reflecting the way these individuals implicitly differentiated between social episodes. The similarity matrices were used as input to a multidimensional scaling (MDS) analysis of the perceived episode space.

In essence, this analysis constructs a geometrical map that represents the way a hypothetical "typical" member of each group perceives social episodes. Results showed that for housewives, interaction episodes were implicitly differentiated in terms of three major features: (1) the degree of intimacy, involvement, and friendliness that an interaction entailed, (2) self-confidence, and (3) positive or negative evaluation they felt about each encounter.

These results are of considerable interest for the study of intercultural communication for several reasons. First, they show that it is possible to construct a meaningful and empirically accurate representation of the way people implicitly think about their interaction episodes. Second, this study also established that such episode representations are highly sensitive to the social and cultural background of the individuals studied. In the present case, our two subject groups, housewives and students, came from the same culture but quite different subcultures. The analysis nevertheless indicated quite large and meaningful differences between them in the way they represented social episodes. For example, interactions involving entertaining and socializing with friends were perceived with considerable self-confidence by students, yet the very same interaction episodes were located in a rather different region of the episode space of housewives, indicating a more ambivalent perception of such encounters in this subculture. We may conjecture that interpersonal communication in such episodes would be more likely to be fraught with difficulties between members of these two subcultural groups, than would communication in encounters in which perceptions of interaction episodes coincided. Of course, if minor subcultural differences can affect episode representations so profoundly, major cultural differences are likely to be even more important, with commensurate consequences for intercultural communication.

Group and Individual Variations in Episode Cognition

If episode representations are indeed sensitive to subcultural differences, as the study just mentioned clearly suggests, it may well be that smaller social units, such as groups, may also generate their own unique way of seeing social encounters. To look at this possibility, in one of our studies we compared the implicit episode domains of two small social groups that differed in their group cohesion and interaction style, but were comparable in terms of most other characteristics, such as the background, sex, status, intelligence, and education of their members. Subjects (N = 30) were members of two college rugby teams at the same university. One of the teams was a more successful, cohesive, and well-integrated unit than the other, but in other ways the groups were quite similar. We expected that the more cohesive, intimate, and involved group would have an episode space that was (a) cognitively better integrated, (b) more finely defined and differentiated, and (c) was perceived with a greater degree of consensus than the episode space of the more fragmented and heterogeneous group.

The differing cohesiveness and interaction style of the two groups was first carefully established in a pilot study (Forgas, 1981a). The social episodes of the two groups were elicited in a series of detailed interviews with members. Analysis of the episode representations was undertaken using Carroll and Chang's (1970) Individual Differences Multidimensional Scaling (INDSCAL) model, followed by a series of multiple discriminant analyses assessing the structural properties of the episode spaces and the differences between the two groups.

Carroll and Chang's (1970) INDSCAL model assumes that people use the same set of implicit dimensions to differentiate between a group of stimuli (in this case, social episodes), but they differ in how much they rely on each dimension in their perceptions. INDSCAL constructs a "group stimulus space," representing the way the group as a whole sees the stimuli and a subject space, where individual subjects are located in terms of their reliance on each of the stimulus dimensions. The analysis uncovers the implicit dimensions underlying judgments and constructs a multidimensional "episode space" showing the location of each episode relative to every other episode. Carroll and Chang (1970) suggest that INDSCAL dimensions need not be further rotated, and "should correspond to meaningful psychological dimensions in a very strong sense" (p. 196). In addition to providing a parsimonious representation of how subjects as a group cognitively represent a stimulus domain, the subject weights may also be used to statistically evaluate individual differences in perception.

Results showed that the more cohesive group in fact had a more complex and better differentiated episode space (three dimensions: friendliness, intimacy, and activity) than the more fragmented group (two dimensions: evaluation and friendliness). Interactions related to playing sport were a more closely integrated part of the episode space of the cohesive group, and there was also a greater degree of consensus between members of this team in how they perceived their interactions. This pattern of results suggests that the cognitive representations people have even of identical social encounters are to a considerable extent determined by their membership in various social groups or cultures. In the present case, even though the two groups were similar in terms of age, intelligence, education, socioeconomic background, sex, and so on, their implicit representations of social episodes nevertheless reflected subtle and measurable cognitive differences between them. These could be statistically assessed, and could be meaningfully related to the social milieu and interaction style of each group. The empirical demonstration of such a link between group membership and cognition is, of course, entirely consistent with many classical theories in social psychology (Mead, 1934), as well as some contemporary work on social cognition (Forgas, 1981a, 1981b; Tajfel & Forgas, 1981). This study indicates that it is in the course of direct face-to-face interaction within a group that primary representations of social episodes are shaped, which ultimately become crystallized in enduring cognitive representations of recurring interaction routines. Just as membership in a small group has such demonstrable cognitive consequences, membership in a culture is even more likely to shape a person's repertoire and perception of interaction episodes.

In order to investigate more precisely the role of group influences on episode representations, in a related study we looked at the role of an individual's status and position within a group on episode perceptions. Subjects were all members of a small and intensive academic research group (N = 16), and came from three distinct status categories: faculty members, research students, and other staff. We used methods similar to those just described to construct a reliable empirical model of this academic group's social episodes, which was defined by four characteristics: anxiety, involvement, evaluation, and socioemotional versus task-orientation (Figure 8.1). When we compared the importance of

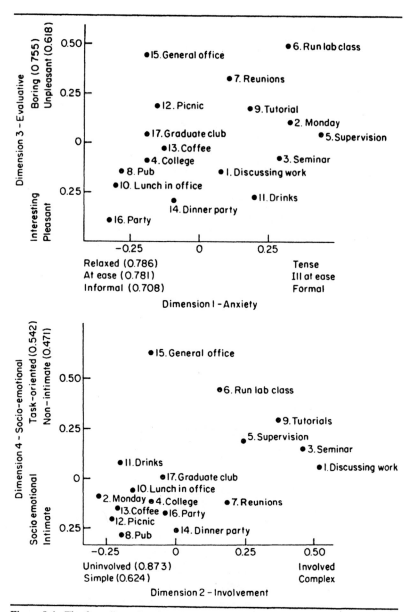

Figure 8.1 The four-dimensional model of the episode space.

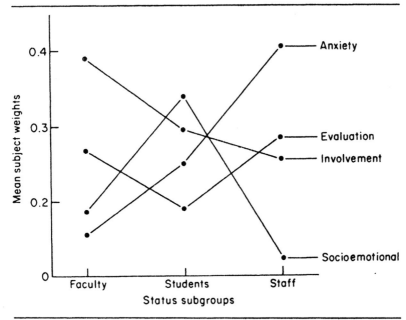

Figure 8.2 The relationship between status and episode perception style. (The mean dimension weights for each of three status subgroups—faculty, students, and staff—on four empirically constructed episode perception dimensions.)

these four episode characteristics to the implicit episode perceptions of the three status subgroups, we found that faculty, students, and staff indeed saw social episodes very differently (Forgas, 1978). Decreasing status was associated with the increasing role of anxiety in episode perceptions, involvement was used as a criterion mainly by faculty, and students were least evaluative but placed the greatest importance on task-orientation in their representation of episodes (Figure 8.2). We may deduce from this pattern that communication between members of these status subgroups would be most problematic in episodes that are perceived with the greatest degree of discrepancy. The results of this study also suggest that sociocultural variables such as status have a major role in influencing how people perceive social episodes and come to interact with each other (Forgas, 1978). This is precisely the kind of interdependence between episode cognition and communication that our model of intercultural communication would also predict.

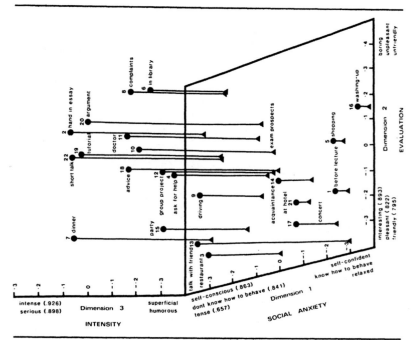

Figure 8.3 The three-dimensional representation of the perceived episode space. (The bipolar scales reflect the interpretation of each dimension.)

In addition to group influences, numerous individual characteristics also play a role in how people perceive social episodes. In one study, it was found that the level of social skill a person manifests was significantly related to their episode perception strategies (Forgas, 1983a). Figure 8.3 shows the perceived episode space of the group of students studied (N = 137), which was defined by three major episode characteristics: the evaluation, anxiety, and intensity of the encounter. It was found that highly socially skilled individuals saw episodes more in terms of the evaluation and intensity dimensions, while low socially skilled persons primarily relied on the anxiety dimension in their cognitive representations of social episodes (Figure 8.4). This again illustrates the kind of pattern of differences that one might expect to occur due to the different cultural background of individuals. Just as being socially skilled or not skilled may lead to different episode perception strategies, conflicting cultural backgrounds should also lead to the demonstration of differences in spisode representations and com-

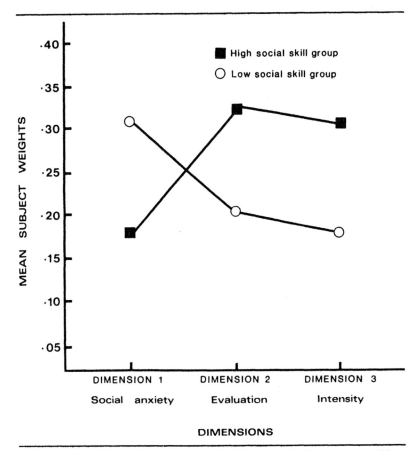

Figure 8.4 The relationship between social skills and episode perception. (Mean dimension weights are shown for high and low socially skilled subjects on each of the three empirically constructed episode perception dimensions.)

munication. There is now some direct evidence suggesting such cultural influences in episode perceptions, as we shall see next.

Cultural Influences on Episode Cognition

Intercultural communication does, almost by definition, involve different episode perceptions by the interactants. In order to empirically demonstrate such an interdependence, we shall have to look at the links between culture and episode cognition. This was the purpose of a recent cross-cultural study carried out with Michael Bond, comparing episode representations between Hong Kong Chinese and Australian subjects (Forgas & Bond, 1985).

As a prerequisite for evaluating the influence of culture on cognitive representations of interaction episodes, we must first have some way of measuring and comparing cultures. As Cattell and others have argued, if one wishes to establish empirical links between individual variables and culture patterns, it is necessary to have dimensions of both (Woliver & Cattell, 1981). Large-scale taxonomic studies of cultures were carried out both by psychologists (Cattell, 1949; Woliver & Cattell, 1981) and by sociologists and political scientists (Rummel, 1972; Russett, 1967; Sawyer, 1967). Perhaps predictably, studies of the first kind tended to focus on individual variables such as education, religion, and living conditions as distinguishing features of cultures, while those in the second category paid more attention to macrosocial variables such as class structure, trade patterns, and political systems.

Of considerably greater interest for our present purposes are studies that looked at the subjective, perceived norms and values that characterize different cultures. There can be little doubt that implicit cognitive processes, such as representations of interaction situations, are most likely to be influenced by such normative cultural variables (Triandis, 1972). One of the most comprehensive cross-cultural studies of cultural values was carried out by Hofstede (1980), who defined *culture* as "the collective mental programming of the people in an environment . . . it encompasses a number of people who were conditioned by the same education and life experience"(p. 43). Hofstede (1980) carried out a major, six-year research project attempting to describe the main criteria by which national cultures differ, based on the extensive analysis of survey data from 40 countries. Results suggested that national cultures differed along four major dimensions: (1) power distance, (2) uncertainty avoidance, (3) individualism-collectivism, and (4) masculinity.

On the basis of this research, the Hong Kong Chinese and Australian cultures selected for our study were found to be highly divergent on the power distance and individualism-collectivism dimensions, and moderately divergent on the other two dimensions (Hofstede, 1980). Chinese culture was characterized as accepting of high power distances and authority differences, and having a strongly collectivist social structure. Hofstede's (1980) research suggests that Chinese culture accepts inequality, and has a tightly knit social framework, with solidarity and acceptance of the immediate grou), family, or clan being an important value. This culture places empha ,is on the "we." In contrast, Hofstede (1980) found Australian cultur ; to be characterized by small power distance and strong individuali ,m, with low tolerance of inequality and authority, and a loosely knit social framework with a weak sense of communal obligations.

On the basis of such cultural differences, we expected that implicit representations of apparently identical interaction episodes would reflect those divergent value systems. Chinese should perceive episodes more in terms of communal values and acceptance of authority, while Australians were expected to place implicit emphasis on competitiveness and individualism in their representations. There is some evidence from previous research suggesting that cultural norms indeed influence such sociocognitive processes as, for example, person perception styles (Bond & Forgas, 1984). In addition to cultural differences, we also investigated the links between individual demographic and personality variables and episode perception in each culture. On the basis of some previous findings (see Forgas, 1982), we expected that the pattern of links between individual characteristics, such as age, sex, personality, and attitudes, and episode perception style would also be culture specific. In other words, age, sex, or personality would predict episode representations in both cultures, but the pattern of such links would also be culture-specific.

The study consisted of (a) the selection of a sample of social episodes equally familiar to both cultures, and relevant to the dimensions of power distance and individualism, followed by (b) the collection and multidimensional scaling (MDS) analysis of similarity ratings of these episodes, and (c) the analysis of cultural and individual differences in episode representations.

The social episodes were selected from interaction routines characteristic of the life routines of university students (see Battistich & Thompson, 1980; Forgas, 1976, 1982) and were further validated in interviews with students, such that these interactions were applicable to both cultures. Next, the episode pool was further narrowed by assigning each interaction to one of four groups defined by the power distance (equal versus unequal) and individualism (communal versus individual) dimensions. These criteria were selected on the basis of cross-cultural research indicating that Chinese and Australian cultures differ mainly in terms of these two variables (Hofstede, 1980; Kroger, Cheng, & Leong, 1979).

TABLE 8.1

1. Arguing with a waitress in the university cafeteria after she has given you the incorrect change. (U/I)
2. Having an intimate conversation with your boyfriend/girlfriend. (E/I)
3. Talking to a member of the administrative staff about the possibility of altering subjects or tutorial times. (U/I)
4. Giving moral support to a student who has recently failed an examination. (E/I)
5. Comparing marks with other students after they have been posted on a notice board. (E/G)
6. Working with other students on a group experiment. (E/G)
7. Writing an essay in the library. (E/I)
8. Eating lunch alone on the university grounds. (E/I)
9. Arguing/consulting with a lecturer about an extension or mark in an exam. (U/I)
10. Protesting to somebody who has cut in front of you in a queue. (E/I)
11. Having lunch with friends in the cafeteria. (E/G)
12. Arriving very late to a tutorial. (U/G)
13. Visiting a lecturer's house for an end of year party. (U/G)
14. Giving directions to someone who does not know his/her way around the university (E/I)
15. Studying with another student before an exam. (E/I)
16. Taking a friend of the opposite sex to the movies. (E/I)
17. Meeting a lecturer by chance on a bus/tram. (U/I)
18. Explaining a complicated psychological theory to a nonpsychology student. (U/I)
19. Consulting with a lecturer about the context of a recent lecture. (U/I)
20. Delivering a late submission to a lecturer or tutor and explaining why it is late. (U/I)
21. Acting as a subject in a psychology experiment. (U/G)
22. Going on an outing (concert, play, picnic, and so on) with university friends. (E/G)
23. Answering questions in a tutorial group after delivering a seminar or talk. (U/G)
24. Striking up a conversation with a stranger in the library, while waiting for a photocopying machine to become available. (E/I)
25. Arguing with your parents at home over some issue concerning the university (e.g. poor grades). (U/I)
26. Chatting with other students whilst waiting to be allowed into the examination room. (E/G)
27. Attending a rally/demonstration organized by university students. (U/G)

NOTE: a. U = unequal; E = equal; I = individual; G = group.

An equal power episode was defined as involving an interaction with someone of equal power or expertise, while unequal power episodes involved interactions with higher or lower status/expertise others. An individual episode involved interactions in which the person participates as an individual, while in communal episodes people interact as members of groups and communities. Altogether 27 episodes, equally characteristic of student life in both cultures, were identified using this process. While interactions often involve multiple elements, and the categorization of episodes in terms of these criteria is not always straightforward, this selection scheme was used to ensure that a varied and culturally relevant sample of interaction episodes is obtained. A summary of the episodes so selected and used as stimuli in the study is shown in Table 8.1.

Subjects (N = 138) were next asked to provide similarity judgments between the 27 episodes selected, using a multiple groupings procedure (see Forgas, 1979b; Kruskal & Wish, 1979). Once groups of episodes judged to be similar were created by subjects, they were asked to (a) write down their reasons for creating each group, (b) label that group of episodes, and (c) identify further subgroups of episodes *within* the groups already created that they saw as *most* similar to each other within each category. This two-step procedure resulted in a similarity matrix between the 27 episodes for each subject, in which the similarity between any two episodes could have the value of "2" (put within the same subgroup within a group), "1" (put within the same group), and "0" (not put within the same group). In addition, the interactions were also rated on a series of bipolar scales to aid the labeling of the MDS episode space.

Finally, a 50-item composite scale assessing attitudes, values, and personality variables was also administered to each subject. Items were selected from a number of published instruments so as (a) to be relevant and comprehensible to subjects from both cultures, while (b) measuring attitudes, personality variables, and values most likely to be relevant to the way interaction episodes are cognitively represented. Questions were selected from a variety of scales and measured (a) sociopolitical attitudes (Christie et al.'s (1969) New Left Scale; Comrey and New-meyer's (1965) Radicalism-Conservatism Scale); (b) personality characteristics; (Budner's (1962) Intolerance of Ambiguity Scale; Janis and Field's revised Feelings of Inadequacy Scale (Eagly, 1969); the abbreviated Rotter External-Internal Control Scale (Valecha, 1972); Neal and Seeman's (1964) Powerlessness Scale); (c) values (Withey's (1965) Dimensions of Values Scale; Levinson and Huffman's (1955) Traditional Family Ideology Scale); and (d) items from Crowne and Marlowe's (1964) Social Desirability Scale. A subsequent factor analysis of the 50 items derived from these instruments yielded four factors: conservatism, anxiety, I-E control, and social desirability.

The similarity matrices from Chinese subjects and Australian subjects were used as input to two separate sets of INDSCAL analyses. Each analysis was run to construct solutions ranging from 1 to 6 dimensions. The four-dimensional representation of the episodes appeared optimal for the Chinese and the Australian data. The empirical interpretation of these four-dimensional episode spaces was accomplished by fitting known bipolar scales to them (see Forgas, 1979b).

The Episode Space for the Chinese Subjects

For the Chinese subjects, the first INDSCAL dimension was most closely related to the unequal power/equal power, isolated/communal, and rare/commonplace scales, and was labeled *power distance.* This axis separated relatively rare, individual, and sometimes antagonistic interactions with superior status partners (lecturers, administrative staff) from interactions involving groups of equal status partners (e.g., studying or working together, chatting, or comparing marks). It is noticeable that this first dimension is relevant to both the individual/communal and equal/unequal power distinctions previously found to be characteristic of Chinese culture (Hofstede, 1980).

The second INDSCAL dimension, *social versus task orientation,* was related to the task oriented/social, ambiguous/unambiguous, and restrictive/free scales, separating work related situations seen as restrictive and ambiguous (e.g., answering questions in a tutorial, consulting with a lecturer) from casual, sociable encounters seen as unambiguous and free, such as chatting while waiting for the photocopier, going to movies, parties, and so on. The third dimension, labeled *evaluation,* was marked by the pleasant/unpleasant and interesting/boring scales, thereby separating disliked encounters (arguments, lonely episodes) from positively evaluated situations, such as explaining something to a partner or consulting with a lecturer. It seems that situations were judged positively because they were thought to be socially useful or valuable, rather than intrinsically enjoyable or rewarding by Chinese subjects. In other words, this evaluative dimension did not reflect hedonistic relevance as is common in Western cultures. Instead, it reflected the perceived social value and usefulness of an interaction. The fourth dimension was *involvement,* marked by the involved/uninvolved and intimate/nonintimate scales. Episodes involving superficially known others (giving directions, talking to a stranger) and friends (intimate conversation with boy/girl friend, party, and so on) were located at the opposite ends of this dimension.

The Chinese episode space shows the way an "average" member of this group thought about these interactions. Unlike in similar studies of student subcultures in the West (see Battistich & Thompson, 1980;

Forgas, 1979a, 1982; King & Sorrentino, 1983), the power distance and individualism/communalism dimension was apparently far more relevant to the episode representations of Chinese students (see Forgas, 1982). Further, the perception of episodes in terms of usefulness rather than pleasantness or enjoyability also appears to be a culture-specific feature of this episode domain. In a subsequent analysis, we specifically found that equal and unequal power episodes were indeed specifically separated from each other in the episode space. A further multiple discriminant analysis also showed that episodes designated as communal versus individual were also seen as significantly different within the episode space of Chinese subjects. These analyses confirm the impression that cultural differences in fact play an important role in how people cognitively represent social episodes.

Episode Perception by the Australian Subjects

Once again the four-dimensional episode space was found optimal. The first episode dimension was labeled *competitiveness,* separating antagonistic encounters (arguing with parents, protesting about marks) from cooperative situations (chatting with other students, comparing marks), marked by the cooperative/competitive, pleasant/unpleasant, and relaxed/anxious bipolar scales. The second dimension separated *social versus task oriented* episodes, and was marked by the task oriented/social, mental/physical, and unequal power/equal power scales. Episodes involving university work (studying, participating in an experiment) and socializing with friends (having lunch, going to the movies) are at the two extremes of this dimension. The third dimension was *involvement,* separating intimate and involved episodes from superficial encounters with strangers. The intimate/nonintimate and involved/uninvolved scales marks this axis. The fourth axis was *self-confidence,* marked by the self-confident/apprehensive and in control/not in control scales. This episode space is rather similar to data from earlier studies of Western student milieus.

Further analyses also showed that equal versus unequal power episodes were indeed well separated in this implicit episode space. Interactions involving unequal partners were seen as both more competitive and less self-confident than episodes involving equal partners. However, individualism/communalism did not have a significant effect on implicit representations. These results suggest that cultural differences (Hofstede, 1980) between the two subject groups had some marked effects on episode perceptions. A joint analysis of data from both groups of subjects confirmed this.

TABLE 8.2

	Chinese Subjects	Australian Subjects
	Coefficients for Canonical Variables	
Individual Differences Variables		
Demographic		
Age	.037	-.110
Sex	-.960	.007
Amount of work	.552	.839
Grades	.104	.395
Attitude and personality measures		
Conservatism	1.371	-.226
Anxiety	.228	.732
I-E Control	-.117	-.105
Social desirability	.639	.648
Episode Perception Variables (Subject dimension weights)		
Chinese subjects		
Dim 1. Equal/unequal power	1.138	—
Dim 2. Social/task	-.079	—
Dim 3. Evaluation	.496	—
Dim 4. Involvement	-.211	—
Australian subjects		
Dim 1. Competitiveness	—	.927
Dim 2. Social/task	—	.523
Dim 3. Involvement	—	-.109
Dim 4. Self-confidence	—	.010
Canonical correlation coefficient	.762*	.801*

*p < .01

These findings show that the Australian and Chinese subjects saw identical social episodes differently and that their judgments of these episodes on identical bipolar scales were also different. Only one dimension, reflecting the perceived social versus task oriented character of episodes, was equally applicable in both cultures. A direct statistical comparison of the individual judgmental styles of individual Chinese as against Australian subjects provided ultimate proof of the role of culture in episode representations. A multiple discriminant analysis comparing the mean dimension weights of Chinese versus Australian judges on each of the five INDSCAL dimensions showed that the cultural identity of the majority of subjects could be adequately determined on the basis of their episode perception styles alone. We also looked at the role of culture in mediating individual differences in episode cognition. A canonical correlation analysis of demographic and personality variables for each subject on the one hand, and episode perception measures (subject weights) on the other, indicated a significant but culture-specific link between these two groups of variables. These individual differences in episode judgments may be related to the different cultural values of the two societies. Chinese subjects saw episodes in terms of communality, collectivism, and social usefulness. The episode characteristics that Australian subjects weighted most highly are competitiveness, self-confidence, and freedom, as well as the hedonistic aspects of interactions. Table 8.2 provides a more detailed summary of the nature of the differences between the Australian and the Chinese groups.

The emergence of such clear and significant cultural differences in perceptions of social episodes is even more intriguing if we consider that subjects came from a subcultural milieu (university students) that is among the most homogeneous across cultures. The university systems of the two countries are similar in structure. Hong Kong students are exposed to many of the same Anglo-Saxon values and influences shared by Australians, and much of the everyday routine of university life is identical. Yet the way these students subjectively perceived and reacted to these identical perceptions appears to be profoundly different. Their judgments strongly reflected precisely those values that were independently found to be most characteristic of their broader culture (Hofstede, 1980).

These findings suggest that the subjective, implicit culture of people (Triandis, 1972) may be much more enduring and resistant to change than the superficial similarities in the external, objective environment in which they live may suggest. Student life in Hong Kong and Australia may not appear to be very different at first sight. What this study shows is that apparently very similar interaction episodes may have profoundly different meanings for people from these two cultures, with corresponding implications for intercultural communication. There is much anecdotal and descriptive evidence to support this point. The coexistence in Japan of the external behavior patterns consistent with an industrialized society, and a subjective culture that at times appears almost feudal in its complexity and hierarchical structure, is an interesting case in point. The present methods appear particularly promising in capturing and quantifying the subtle ways that culture is reflected in cognition, and ultimately comes to influence intercultural communication.

CONCLUSIONS

We have argued in this chapter that intercultural communication may be analyzed in terms of the cognitive representations of the individuals involved. Specifically, it was suggested that implicit cognitive representations about recurring interaction episodes play a critical role in intercultural communication. This orientation is based on important recent developments in cognitive social psychology (Forgas, 1981b, 1983b), as well as long-standing interest in the role of collaborative situation-definition processes in the study of language and communication (e.g., Clark & Wilkes-Gibbs, 1986; Forgas, 1985a). In order to make such an approach plausible, it is first necessary to establish how various cultural and subcultural influences do in fact shape a person's perception and understanding of social situations. This issue was addressed in the second half of the chapter, in which we reviewed a range of empirical studies demonstrating that the objective study of episode representations is not only possible, but also that such implicit episode spaces are highly sensitive to cultural, subcultural, and group influences.

Of course, the assumption underlying this approach that culture and cognition are interdependent is hardly new. Many classical theorists both in psychology and in sociology realized this (Mead, 1934; Thomas, 1966; Wolff, 1964). However, the precise demonstration of this interdependence remained methodologically problematic until recently. With the advent of sophisticated multidimensional scaling techniques, we now have a suitable way of describing such subtle and otherwise elusive cognitive domains as implicit representations of social episodes. Clearly, the work so far accomplished represents only an important first step toward the sociocognitive study of intercultural communication. The next stage must involve direct investigation of the consequences of conflicting episode representations in intercultural communication, both in the domain of verbal and nonverbal exchanges.

There are encouraging precedents for such an approach in social psychology. Investigations of nonverbal communication, for example, have been particularly effective in highlighting the role of cultural variables in many everyday communication strategies (Weitz, 1978). Language research also includes many examples illustrating the culture-sensitivity of communication in such fields as polyglossia, speech accommodation, or semantic choices (Forgas, 1985b; Giles & Hewstone, 1982; Herrmann, 1983). A study by Furnham (1982), for example, showed that situational features have a significant direct effect on the choice of various communication strategies. Furthermore, certain kinds of messages are much more situation-sensitive than others. Intercultural communication involves an adaptation of communication strategies in response to a perceived or actual conflict in the episode definitions of the interlocutors. We already have a range of suitable techniques for experimentally studying the kind of accommodation processes that take place when two people do not have a fully shared understanding about an encounter (see Forgas, 1985; Isaacs & Clark, 1987). What remains to be done is to link the kind of techniques for analyzing episode representations described here with experimental analyses of specific intercultural communication encounters. This chapter will, we hope, be successful in further promoting a cognitive social psychological approach in this exciting and important research area.

REFERENCES

Abelson, R. P. (1980). *The psychological status of the script concept.* (Cognitive Science Technical Report No. 2). New Haven: Yale University.

Albert, E. M. (1972). Culture patterning of speech behaviour in Burundi. In J. Gumperz & D. Hymes (Eds.), *The ethnography of communication.* New York: Holt, Rinehart & Winston.

Argyle, M., Furnham, A., & Graham, J. (1982). *Social situations.* Cambridge: Cambridge University Press.

Battistich, V. A., & Thompson, E. G. (1980). Students' perceptions of the college milieu. *Personality and Social Psychology Bulletin, 6,* 74-82.

Blom, J-P., & Gumperz, J. J. (1972). Social meaning in linguistic structures: Code-switching in Norway. In J. Gumperz & D. Hymes (Eds.), *The ethnography of communication.* New York: Holt, Rinehart & Winston.

Bond, M. (1983). How language variation affects inter-cultural differentiation of values by Hong Kong bilinguals. *Journal of Language, 1,* 41-53.

Bond, M., & Forgas, J. P. (1984). Linking person perception and behaviour intention across cultures. *Journal of Cross-Cultural Psychology, 15,* 337-352.

Bower, G. H., Black, J. B., & Turner, T. J. (1979). Scripts in memory for text. *Cognitive Psychology, 11,* 177-220.

Brown, P., & Fraser, C. (1979). Speech as marker of situation. In K. R. Scherer & H. Giles (Eds.), *Social markers in speech.* Cambridge: Cambridge University Press.

Brunswik, E. (1956). *Perception and the representative design of psychological experiments.* Berkeley: University of California Press.

Budner, S. (1962). Intolerance of ambiguity as a personality variable. *Journal of Personality, 30,* 29-50.

Carroll, D. J., & Chang, J. J. (1970). Analysis of individual differences in multidimensional scaling via N-way generalisation of 'Eckart-Young' decomposition. *Psychometrika, 35,* 283-319.

Cattell, R. B. (1949). The dimensions of culture patterns by factorization of national characters. *Journal of Abnormal and Social Psychology, 44,* 279-289.

Clark, H. H. (1985). Language use and language users. In G. Lindzey & E. Aronson (Eds.), *Handbook of social psychology* (Vol. I, pp. 179-231). New York: Random House.

Clark, H. H., & Wilkes-Gibbs, D. (1986). Referring as a collaborative process. *Cognition, 22,* 1-39.

Comrey, A., & Newmeyer, J. (1965). Measurement of radicalism-conservatism. *Journal of Social Psychology, 67,* 357-369.

Christie, R., Friedman, L., & Ross, A. (1969). *The new left and its ideology.* New York: Columbia University.

Crowne, D., & Marlowe, D. (1964). *The approval motive.* New York: Wiley.

Eagly, A. H. (1969). Sex differences in the relationship between self-esteem and susceptibility to social influence. *Journal of Personality, 37,* 581-591.

Ervin-Tripp, S. (1964). An analysis of the interaction of language, topic, and listener. In J. Gumperz & D. Hymes (Eds.), *The ethnography of communication.* New York: Holt, Rinehart & Winston.

Ervin-Tripp, S. (1972). On sociolinguistic rules: Alternation and co-occurrence. In J. Gumperz & D. Hymes (Eds.), *The ethnography of communication.* New York: Holt, Rinehart & Winston.

Firth, J. R. (1957). *Papers in linguistics.* London: Oxford University Press.

Fishman, J. (Ed.). (1971). *Advances in the sociology of language.* The Hague: Mouton.

Forgas, J. P. (1976). The perception of social episodes: Categorical and dimensional representations in two different social milieus. *Journal of Personality and Social Psychology, 33,* 199-209.

Forgas, J. P. (1978). Social episodes and social structure in an academic setting: The social environment of an intact group. *Journal of Experimental Social Psychology, 4,* 434-448.

Forgas, J. P. (1979a). *Social episodes: The study of interaction routines.* London: Academic Press.

Forgas, J. P. (1979b). Multidimensional scaling: A discovery method in social psychology. In G. P. Ginsburg (Ed.), *Emerging strategies in social psychology.* Chichester, England: John Wiley.

Forgas, J. P. (1981a). Social episodes and group milieu: A study in social cognition. *British Journal of Social Psychology, 20,* 77-87.

Forgas, J. P. (Ed.). (1981b). *Social cognition: Perspectives on everyday understanding.* London: Academic Press.

Forgas, J. P. (1982). Episode cognition: Internal representations of interaction routines. In L. Berkowitz (Ed.), *Advances in experimental social psychology.* New York: Academic Press.

Forgas, J. P. (1983a). Social skills and episode perception. *British Journal of Clinical Psychology, 22,* 26-41.

Forgas, J. P. (1983b). What is social about social cognition? *British Journal of Clinical Psychology, 22,* 129-144.

Forgas, J. P. (1983c). Cognitive representations of interaction episodes. *Australian Journal of Psychology, 35,* 145-162.

Forgas, J. P. (Ed.). (1985a). *Language and social situations.* New York: Springer.

Forgas, J. P. (1985b). *Interpersonal behaviour: The psychology of social interaction.* Oxford: Pergamon.

Forgas, J. P., & Bond, M. H. (1985). Cultural influences on the perception of interaction episodes. *Journal of Cross-Cultural Psychology, 11,* 75-88.

Furnham, A. (1982). The message, the context and the medium. *Language and Communication, 2,* 33-47.

Garfinkel, H. (1967). *Studies in ethnomethodology.* Englewood Cliffs, NJ: Prentice-Hall.

Giles, H., & Hewstone, M. (1982). Cognitive structures, speech and social situations: Two integrative models. *Language Sciences, 4,* 188-219.

Goffman, E. (1974). *Frame analysis.* Harmondsworth: Penguin.

Gregory, M. (1967). Aspects of varieties differentiation. *Journal of Linguistics, 3,* 177-198.

Gumperz, J. J., & Hymes, D. (Eds.). (1972). *The ethnography of communication.* New York: Holt, Rinehart & Winston.

Herrmann, T. (1983). *Speech and situation.* Berlin: Springer.

Hofstede, G. (1980). *Culture's consequences: International differences in work-related values.* Beverly Hills, CA: Sage.

Hymes, D. (1967). The anthropology of communication. *Social Research, 34,* 632-647.

Hymes, D. (1972). Models of the interaction of language and social life. In J. Gumperz & D. Hymes (Eds.), *The ethnography of communication.* New York: Holt, Rinehart & Winston.

Isaacs, E. A., & Clark, H. H. (1987). References in conversation between experts and novices. *Journal of Experimental Psychology: General, 116,* 1-23.

King, G. A., & Sorrentino, R. M. (1983). Psychological dimensions of goal-oriented interpersonal situations. *Journal of Personality and Social Psychology, 44,* 140-162.

Kroger, R. O., Cheng, K., & Leong, I. (1979). Are the rules of address universal? A test of Chinese usage. *Journal of Cross-Cultural Psychology, 10,* 395-414.

Kruskal, J. B., & Wish, M. (1979). *Multidimensional scaling.* Beverly Hills, CA: Sage.

Leodolter, R., & Leodolter, M. (1976). Sociolinguistic considerations on psychosocial socialisation. In W. McCormack & S. Wurm (Eds.), *Language and man.* The Hague: Mouton.

Levinson, D., & Huffman, P. (1955). Traditional family ideology and its relations to personality. *Journal of Personality, 23,* 251-273.

Lewin, K. (1951). *Field theory in social science.* New York: Harper.

Lichtenstein, E. H., & Brewer, W. F. (1980). Memory for goal-directed events. *Cognitive Psychology, 12,* 412-445.

Magnusson, D. (1971). An analysis of situational dimensions. *Perceptual and Motor Skills, 32,* 851-867.

McCormack, W. C., & Wurm, S. A. (Eds.). (1976). *Language and man.* The Hague: Mouton.

Mead, G. H. (1934). *Mind, self and society.* Chicago: University of Chicago Press.

Murray, H. A. (1951). Toward a classification of interaction. In T. Parsons & E. Shils (Eds.), *Towards a general theory of action.* Cambridge, MA: Harvard University Press.

Neal, A., & Seeman, M. (1964). Organizations and powerlessness: A test of the mediation hypothesis. *American Sociological Review, 29,* 216-225.

Pervin, L. A. (1976). A free response description approach to the study of person-situation interaction. *Journal of Personality and Social Psychology, 34,* 465-474.

Poyatos, F. (1976). Analysis of a culture through its culturemes: Theory and method. In W. McCormack & S. Wurm (Eds.), *Language and man.* The Hague: Mouton.

Rummel, R. H. (1972). *The dimensions of nations.* Beverly Hills, CA: Sage.

Russett, B. M. (1967). *International regions and the international system.* Chicago: Rand-McNally.

Sawyer, J. (1967). Dimensions of nations: Size, wealth and politics. *American Journal of Sociology, 73,* 145-172.

Tajfel, H., & Forgas, J. P. (1981). Social categorisation: Cognition, values and groups. In J. Forgas (Ed.), *Social cognition.* London: Academic Press.

Thomas, W. I. (1966). Situational analysis: The behaviour pattern and the situation. In M. Janowitz (Ed.), *W. I. Thomas on social organization and social personality.* Chicago: University of Chicago Press.

Triandis, H. C. (1972). *The analysis of subjective culture.* New York: John Wiley.

Valecha, G. K. (1972). Construct validation of an abbreviated 11-item I-E Control Scale. Ph.D. dissertation, Ohio State University.

Weitz, S. (Ed.). (1978). *Nonverbal communication.* New York: Oxford University Press.

Whorf, B. L. (1962). *Language, thought and reality.* Cambridge, MIT Press.

Withey, S. (1965). The US and the USSR. In D. Bobrow (Ed.), *Components of defense policy.* Chicago: Rand-McNally.

Wolff, K. H. (1964). Definition of the situation. In J. Gould & W. Kolb (Eds.), *A dictionary of the social sciences.* New York: The Free Press.

Woliver, R. E., & Cattell, R. B. (1981). Reoccurring national patterns from 30 years of multivariate cross-cultural studies. *International Journal of Psychology, 16,* 171-198.

Wurm, S. A. (1976). Summary of discussion. In W. McCormack & S. Wurm (Eds.), *Languages and man.* The Hague: Mouton.

9

Intercultural Conflict Styles
A Face-Negotiation Theory

STELLA TING-TOOMEY • *Arizona State University, Tempe*

This chapter investigates the relationship between facework maintenance and intercultural conflict styles. Specifically, the two dimensions of self-face concern and other-face concern, and negative face and positive face are used to develop a set of theoretical propositions that account for conflict communication style differences in individualistic, low-context cultures, and collectivistic, high-context cultures. It is proposed that cultures that are high in self-face concern and negative face need (dissociation need) will engage in a direct mode of conflict interaction. Cultures that are high in other-face concern and positive face need (association need) will engage in an indirect mode of conflict interaction. Implications of the face-negotiation theory to understand classes of problematic situations are discussed.

Conflict is a pervasive phenomenon that penetrates all forms of social and personal relationships in all cultures. Partners in a conflict situation typically bargain over many facets of the conflict process. They bargain over their goal differences, they bargain over the process, and they bargain over their situated identities. Conflict, as a class of threatening situations, poses threats to the situated identities of the negotiators. It is a communication process that involves different styles of interchanges between two interdependent negotiators who perceive incompatible needs or goals and perceive each other's potential interference in achieving those goals. More specifically, conflict is viewed, in this chapter, as a problematic situation that demands active facework management from the two interdependent conflict parties.

"Facework" and "conflict style," however, are two culturally grounded concepts. Culture provides the larger interpretive frame in which "face" and "conflict style" can be meaningfully expressed and maintained. The negotiators' predispositions toward the concept of "face," their face-need and face-concern levels, and their modes and styles of managing the conflict episode are, for the most part, influenced by the cultural premises from which they draw their values and norms. The cultural values and norms will influence and shape how members in a cultural system manage facework and, in turn, how they should appropriately handle and manage a conflict situation. While there has been a plethora of studies on interpersonal-organization conflict negotiation in the past 20 years (for example, Baxter, 1982; Blake & Mouton, 1964; Brown, Yelsma, & Keller, 1981; Donohue & Diez, 1985; Folger & Poole, 1984; Putnam & Jones, 1982a, 1982b; Rahim, 1983; Rahim & Bonoma, 1979; Sillars, 1980a, 1980b; Ting-Toomey, 1983; Thomas & Kilman, 1978), there is a paucity of studies addressing the critical role of culture and its effect on face-management and conflict negotiation style. Most conflict researchers have acknowledged the importance of studying conflict context, but the concept of "context" typically refers to the situational context rather than the cultural context. In addition, while most conflict studies have engaged in a critical examination of conflict styles in the U.S. culture, a theoretical explanation has not been fully articulated as to why individual members engage in certain conflict styles over others (for example, confrontational style over avoidance style, integrating style over obliging style).

Hence, the objective of this chapter is a general one: to explore the role of culture in both face-management and conflict style processes. Conflict is viewed as a face-negotiation process in which the "faces" or the situated identities of the conflict parties are being threatened and called into question. The relationships among culture, facework, and conflict style are analyzed in five sections: (1) the basic assumptions of the facework process will be introduced; (2) relevant cross-cultural conflict style studies will be reviewed; (3) the basic axioms of the conflict face-negotiation theory will be presented; (4) specific theoretical propositions that are derived from the conflict face-negotiation theory will be enumerated; and (5) the implications of the face-negotiation theory to the study of cross-cultural problematic situations will be discussed.

FACEWORK PROCESSES

Culture and Facework

According to the observations of cross-cultural researchers, "facework" is a ubiquitous concept that exists in all cultures (Brown & Levinson, 1978; Goffman, 1959, 1967, 1971; Katriel, 1986; Hill, Ide, Ikuta, Kawasaki, & Ogino, 1986; Ide, Hori, Kawasaki, Ikuta, & Haga, 1986; Hu, 1944; Okabe, 1983; Ting-Toomey, 1985). The concept of "face" has been defined variously as "something that is diffusedly located in the flow of events" (Goffman, 1955, p. 214), "a psychological image that can be granted and lost and fought for and presented as a gift" (Yutang, 1968, p. 199), and "the public self-image that every member of a society wants to claim for himself/herself" (Brown & Levinson, 1978, p. 66). Face, in essence, is a projected image of one's self in a relational situation. It is an identity that is conjointly defined by the participants in a setting. However, the degree to which one wishes to project an "authentic self" in a situation and the degree to which one chooses to maintain a "social self" in a situation varies in accordance to the cultural orientations toward the conceptualization of selfhood. In other words, a different degree of selfhood is being projected into this public self-image known as "face." In individualistic cultures, such as those of Australia, Germany, and the United States, the consistency between maintaining a private self-image and a public self-image is of paramount importance. An individual's public self-presentation of "face" should correspond to an invariant "core self" within an individual to a certain degree. In collectivistic cultures, such as those of China, Korea, and Japan, the "self" is a situationally and relationally based concept. In analyzing selfhood and otherness in Confucian thoughts in China, Tu (1985) pointed out that "a distinctive feature of Confucian ritualization is an ever-deepening and broadening awareness of the presence of the other in one's self-cultivation. This is perhaps the single most important reason why the Confucian idea of the self as a center of relationships is an open system" (p. 232).

The self, in the Chinese cultural context, is defined through an intersecting web of social and personal relationships. The self in most collectivistic cultures, in fact, is maintained and codified through the active negotiation of facework. Whereas in individualistic cultures, such as that found in the United States, however, the self is often defined as an intrapsychic phenomenon. The public "face," then, should ideally correspond to the internal states of the negotiators. Providing "face-support" to another person in a problematic situation means lending support and confirmation to his or her idealized sense of self, which in turn should be ideally consistent with his or her core "authentic self" (McCall & Simmons, 1966, p. 75). As Bellah, Madsen, Sullivan, Swidler, & Tipton (1985) commented in analyzing individualism and commitment in North American life: "In the absence of any objectifiable criteria of right and wrong, good or evil, the self and its feelings become our only moral guidance. . . . There each individual is entitled to his or her own 'bit of space' and is utterly free within its boundaries" (p. 76). From the collectivistic perspective of selfhood, the self is never free. It is bounded by mutual role obligations and duties and it is structured by a patterned process of give-and-take reciprocal facework negotiation. Facework, in this context, is focused on how to lend role-support to another's face and at the same time not to bring shame to one's own self-face. From the individualistic perspective of selfhood, the self is ideally a free entity—free to pursue its own personal wants, needs, and desires. Facework, in this context, is heavily emphasized on how one can preserve one's own autonomy, territory, and space, simultaneously respecting the other person's need for space and privacy.

Positive and Negative Face

Brown and Levinson (1978) developed an elaborate theory of politeness based on two underlying assumptions: (1) All competent adult members of a society have (and know each other to have) "face"— the public self-image that every member wants to claim for himself or herself. The "face" has two related components: (a) negative face—the basic claim to territories, personal reserves, rights to nondistraction, and (b) positive face—the basic claim over this projected self-image to be appreciated and to be approved by others; and (2) all competent adult members of a society have certain rational capacities and modes to achieve these ends (p. 66).

Negative facework means the negotiation process between two interdependent parties concerning the degree of threat or respect each gives to one another's sense of freedom and individual autonomy. Positive facework entails the degree of threat or respect each gives to one another's need for inclusion and approval. Negative facework (speech acts such as apology for imposition, prerequest ritual, compliance-resistance act, and command act) emphasizes the need for dissociation. Positive facework (speech acts such as self-disclosure, compliment, and promise) emphasizes the need for association. Both concepts (association and dissociation), in fact, have been extensively documented by cross-cultural researchers (Adamopoulos, 1984; Lonner, 1980; Triandis, 1972, 1977, 1978) as psychological universals that cut across cultural boundaries. However, while one might expect that both negative facework and positive facework are present in all cultures, the value orientations of a culture will influence cultural members' attitudes toward pursuing one set of facework more actively than others in a face-negotiation situation. Facework then, is viewed as a symbolic front that members in all cultures strive to maintain and uphold; while the modes and styles of expressing and negotiating face-need would vary from one culture to the next.

Types of Strategies

In addition to the concepts of "negative face" and "positive face," Brown and Levinson (1978) identified five levels of facework strategies that potentially threaten either the negative face or the positive face of the involved parties in a politeness situation. These face-threatening acts (FTA) are arranged in different hierarchical levels of direct to indirect verbal speech acts. Direct FTA are viewed as posing the highest threat to the negotiators' faces, and indirect FTA are viewed as posing the least threat, and hence the most polite verbal acts. Again, the correlations between the direct mode and the perceived threat level, and between the indirect mode and the politeness level would vary from one culture to the next. In cultures that foster a direct mode of interaction in everyday life (such as low-context cultures like those in Germany, Scandinavia, Switzerland, and the United States), a direct mode of behavior probably is perceived to be not so threatening as an ambiguous mode of interacting. In cultures that nurture an indirect mode of interacting (such as high-context cultures like those in China, Japan, Korea, and Vietnam), a direct mode of communicating can be perceived as highly threatening and unsettling to one's own face. While Brown and Levinson (1978) focused mainly on the concept of "face-threat," the concept of "face-respect" has not been explicitly dealt with in their politeness theory.

More recently, Shimanoff (1985, 1987) reconceptualized Brown and Levinson's FTA typology and identified four types of affective strategies in terms of the degree they respect or threaten the face-needs of the negotiators in a problematic situation. These four suprastrategies concerning facework negotiation are: (1) face-honoring (FH) type, (2) face-compensating (FC) type, (3) face-neutral (FN) type, and (4) face-threatening (FT) type. While the first three types represent respect strategies for other's face, the last type is viewed as a negative face-confronting strategy. Overall, Shimanoff (1985, 1987) reported that in the marital context, marital partners tend to use more face-honoring, face-compensating, and face-neutral strategies than face-threatening strategies. Baxter (1984), in studying politeness strategies between males and females, found that people tend to use more face-politeness strategies in close relationships than in distant relationships. Tracy,

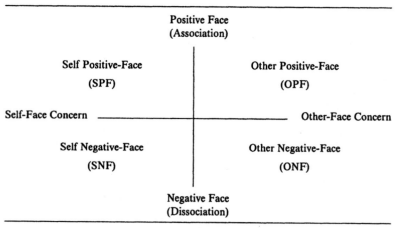

Figure 9.1 Two-dimensional grid of facework maintenance.

Craig, Smith, and Spisak (1984), in testing discourse strategies in multiple "favor-asking" situations, discovered that favor-asking messages varied in the degree to which they acknowledged the hearer's desire to be liked and appreciated (positive-face need) and the hearer's desire for autonomy and freedom of action (negative-face need). In addition, favor-asking messages varied in the attention they gave to the speaker's own positive face need. Finally, Leichty and Applegate's (1987) research analyzing individual differences in face-saving strategies revealed that actors are not overly concerned with intimate face-wants on relatively small requests, but that they give considerable attention to the intimate face-wants when substantial autonomy threat is involved. Also, speaker power, request magnitude, and relational familiarity all influence the degree to which the autonomy desire of the person being persuaded is attended to. Craig, Tracy, and Spisak (1986), and Leichty and Applegate (1987) recommended that a new theory of facework should make a clear distinction between strategies that threaten self-face and other-face, and also strategies that gear toward negative-face maintenance and positive-face maintenance.

A Model of Facework

The facework literature to date suggests that when two interdependent parties come together in a facework negotiation session, they negotiate over two implicit principles: (1) face-concern principle: self-face, other-face, or mutual-face, and (2) face-need principle: negative face (concern for autonomy), and positive face (concern for inclusion). Negative-face need cah be viewed as the need for autonomy or dissociation, and positive-face need can be viewed as the need for inclusion or association. These two principles are expressed through the two-dimensional grid in Figure 9.1.

Figure 9.1 consists of two conceptual dimensions: the self-concern and other-concern dimension and the positive-face and negative-face need dimension. The self-concern and other-concern dimension refers to the individual's orientation toward attention for self versus other. The positive-face and negative-face dimension refers to the individual's perceived need for association or dissociation. Self positive-face (SPF) maintenance means the use of certain communication strategies to defend and protect one's need for inclusion and association. Other positive-face (OPF) maintenance means the use of certain communication strategies to defend and support the other person's need for inclusion and association. Self negative-face (SNF) maintenance means the use of certain interaction strategies to give oneself freedom and space, and to protect self from other's infringement on one's autonomy. Finally, other negative-face (ONF) maintenance means the use of certain interaction strategies to signal respect for the other person's need for freedom, space, and dissociation. All four face types (SPF, OPF, SNF, and ONF) are subjected to differential treatments by the hearer in the negotiation process. The hearer can defend, respect, threaten, or confront the speaker's concern for self or other image, and the speaker's need for either positive face or negative face maintenance. While existing facework literature recognizes the functional importance of facework and the linguistic acts that accompany various face-needs and face-concerns, no study to date has explicated the critical role of culture in the facework negotiation process. In addition, there have been many interpersonal communication studies that used the concept of facework in compliance-gaining research, but no study has yet applied the face-negotiation concept in interpersonal conflict process. The rest of this chapter then will integrate the construct of facework with the conflict negotiation process.

To summarize, the basic assumptions of the facework negotiation process are: (1) members in all cultures negotiate over the concept of face; (2) the concept of face is especially problematic in uncertain situations (for example, request situation, complaint situation, embarrassment situation, and conflict situation) when the situated identities of the interactants are called into question; (3) all face-negotiation entails multiple-goal orientations (self-concern and other-concern, negative-face and positive-face); (4) all negotiators express a concern for self-face protection or other-face support (or both) in problematic situations; (5) all negotiators express a need for dissociation (negative face) and/or a need for association (positive face) in problematic situations; (6) the self-other orientation dimension and the association-dissociation dimension would be influenced by the relational variables (such as low-high familiarity level, low-high intimacy level), the situational variables (such as informal-formal level, public-private level) of the context, and the salience (such as topic magnitude, topic commitment) of the problematic issue; (7) the self-other dimension and the positive-face and negative-face need dimension would be influenced by the cultural interpretation and the cultural expectation levels of the context; and (8) while the four sets of suprastrategy—SPF, OPF, SNF, and ONF—are present in all negotiation settings in all cultures, certain sets of suprastrategy would be favorably preferred by members of a culture more often than others. The next two sections will develop along the lines of the last two assumptions in which the concept of facework is placed in the context of cross-cultural conflict situations.

CONFLICT STYLES

Interpersonal Conflict Styles

There have been many interpersonal and organizational communication studies that set out to test conflict communication styles in both relational and organizational settings. For example, Blake and Mouton (1964) used a two-dimensional framework: (a) the degree (low or high) of desire to meet personal needs or goals, and (b) the degree (low or high) of desire to maintain interpersonal needs. They analyzed the conflict process in terms of five styles: forcing, confronting, sharing, withdrawing, and smoothing. Putnam and Wilson (1982) concluded that these conflict styles can be clustered into three styles: (a) control style: acts that lead to direct confrontation, arguments, imposition of ideas on another person; (b) solution-oriented style: acts that aim to find solutions to the conflict and integrate the needs of both parties; and (c) nonconfrontational style: acts that entail indirectness, avoidance, and withdrawal. Ross and DeWine (1984) concurred with Putnam and Wilson's three-style approach, and came up with a forcing style, an issue style, and a smoothing style.

Rahim (1983), and Rahim and Bonoma (1979), however, in developing a conflict typology based on the dimensions of concern for self and concern for others, still maintained the importance of a five-style approach. The first dimension explains the degree (low or high) to which a person attempts to satisfy his or her own concern or own face-need. The second dimension explains the degree (low or high) to which a person wants to satisfy the concern of others or, in other words, satisfy others' face-need. Their conflict styles include: (a) dominating (high self-concern, low other-concern), (b) obliging (low self-concern, high other-concern), (c) integrating (high self-concern, high other-concern), (d) avoiding (low self-concern, low other-concern), and (e) compromising (intermediate self-concern and other-concern). Finally, Brown, Yelsma, and Keller (1981) discussed the importance of an individual's predispositions to conflict process. They suggested that researchers should pay close attention to conflict predispositional factors, such as an individual's range of affective feelings, task energy level, concern for self-uniqueness, concern for control, respect for others, and concern for one's community.

Unfortunately, amidst the enthusiastic debate between three-style versus five-style approach to conflict, interpersonal and organizational conflict researchers typically have failed to provide cross-cultural evidence for both their theoretical and methodological claims over the various styles of conflict negotiation. We may summarize that overall, for the U.S. sample, conflict styles have been developed by various researchers along the lines of concern for self or concern for other, issue-oriented or relationship-oriented, and conflict-approach or conflict-avoidance attitude. In relating various conflict styles with face-management process, the concern for self is related to the concern for self-face protection; the concern for other is related to the concern for other-face support. Issue-oriented approach is reflective of the need for control, for choices, and for negative face of autonomy; relationship-oriented approach is reflective of the need for connection, for approval, and for positive face of association. Finally, conflict-approach attitude leads to the use of either direct confrontational strategies or solution-oriented strategies. Conflict-avoidance attitude leads to the use of either passive obliging strategies or withdrawal-exit strategies. The concern for self-face protection, the issue-oriented approach, and the conflict-approach attitude leads to a direct mode of handling conflict. Finally, the concern for other-face violation, the relationship-oriented approach, and the conflict-avoidance attitude leads to an indirect mode of managing conflict. In most conflict situations, members in all cultures typically face a set of dialectical choices: between protecting self-face and preserving other-face, and between defending self-face and confronting other-face. In addition, they have to search for the balance point between negotiating for self-concern and other-concern, and between association need and dissociation need.

Cross-Cultural Conflict Styles

It is only in the past five years that intercultural researchers have become actively engaged in cross-cultural conflict style research. For example, Tafoya (1983) used a barrier perspective to study the relationship between conflict style and culture. He found that two types of cultural barriers—personal psychological barriers and interpersonal conflict style barriers—can detract from the functional conflict process. Wolfson and Norden (1984), using a Coordinated Management of Meaning (CMM) approach, found that Chinese subjects tend to use more passive strategies in handling conflict, while North American subjects tend to use more active strategies in managing conflict. In addition, Chinese subjects felt that they had a limited range of choices in handling teacher-student conflicts, while North American subjects perceived a wider range of behavioral options.

Cushman and King (1985), using a "national culture" approach, tried to explain conflict style differences in Japan, Yugoslavia, and the United States. They found that the Japanese culture values the importance of maintaining public face in the conflict process and would prefer the use of a collaborative style to resolve conflict. Yugoslavian culture values the equality norm in a conflict situation and would prefer a compromising style in handling conflict. Finally, the U.S. culture values the competitive norm in a conflict process, and would prefer a competitive style of conflict management. Nomura and Barnlund (1983), also using a "national culture" approach, found that Japanese subjects tend to use more passive, accommodating strategies in the interpersonal criticism process, while American subjects tend to use more active, confrontational strategies. Kumagai and Straus (1983), in examining Japanese and North American conflict style differences, presented similar findings to Nomura and Barnlund's (1983) study. Kagan, Knight, and Martinez-Romero (1982), in testing for conflict style differences between Mexicans and Anglo-Americans, found that Mexican subjects tend to use more passive, avoidance conflict strategies, while Anglo-Americans tend to use more active, confrontational strategies. In testing for Black and White differences in conflict styles, Ting-Toomey (1986) found that Black subjects tend to use more controlling style strategies than do White subjects, and that White subjects tend to use more solution-oriented style strategies than do Black subjects. Ross and DeWine (1986), in analyzing cross-cultural conflict styles in Denmark and the United States, discovered that North American subjects tend to prefer more issue-oriented strategies to manage conflict than do Danish subjects. As the cross-cultural conflict literature has indicated so far, conflict style is a cultural-relative construct. Research findings consistently point out that Whites in the U.S. culture tend to use two predominant styles of conflict: dominating (confrontation-oriented) style and integrating (solution-oriented) style. However, the reasoning behind the apparent conflict style differences in various cultures have not been satisfactorily addressed. Most cross-cultural conflict studies remain on a descriptive level of national culture differences, while the theoretical underpinnings of why cultural members choose certain conflict strategies over others remain thin and unpersuasive.

Moving beyond a "national culture" explanation, Nadler, Nadler, and Broome (1985), in examining conflict situations across cultures, used a negotiation perspective to the study of conflict style and culture. They proposed that the three most critical components in understanding cross-cultural conflict are: perspectives toward conflict (orientations and criteria toward conflict), personal constructs (such as fairness, trust, and power), and message strategies (such as the use of threats, promises, use of time, and decision-making style). Finally, Ting-Toomey (1985) and Chua and Gudykunst (1987) used Hall's (1976) low-context culture (LCC) and high-context culture (HCC) framework to study the relationship between conflict style and culture. They found that low-context members tend to prefer a direct mode of conflict style (such as the use of confrontational strategies or solution-oriented strategies), while high-context members tend to prefer an indirect mode of conflict style (such as the use of smoothing strategies or avoidance strategies). Rather than treating culture as a static variable, the cultural variability dimensions (individualism-collectivism dimension, low-context/high-context dimension) were used in these studies to explain the conflict style differences in different cultures. With the various cross-cultural conflict studies in mind the following section will present the cultural variability dimensions in relationship to the conflict face-negotiation theory.

FACE-NEGOTIATION THEORY

Individualism-Collectivism

Numerous cross-cultural studies in the last five years (Bond & Forgas, 1984; Chua & Gudykunst, 1987; Gudykunst & Nishida, 1986; Hui & Triandis, 1986; Hofstede & Bond, 1984) have provided empirical evidence that the theoretical dimension of individualism-collectivism is the primary dimension that differentiates different clusters of cultures from an international perspective. Hofstede (1980) analyzed organizational behaviors in 40 cultures identifying individualism-collectivism as one out of the four primary dimensions that links organizational life with culture. Cross-cultural studies (Gudykunst & Nishida, 1986) that have analyzed the relationship between interpersonal perception and culture also provide strong support for the critical role of the individualism-collectivism dimension in understanding communication style differences in different sets of cultures. Hui and Triandis (1986), after surveying cross-cultural anthropologists and psychologists from all parts of the world, concluded that the dimension of individualism-collectivism can be used as a powerful theoretical construct to explain the degree of interactional differences and similarities between cultures.

In sum, the terms *individualism* and *collectivism* refer to "a cluster of attitudes, beliefs, and behaviors toward a wide variety of people" (Hui & Triandis, 1986, p. 240). While individualistic cultures draw upon the "I" identity as the prime focus, collectivistic cultures draw upon the "we" identity. Individualistic cultures are concerned with the authenticity of self-presentation style. Collectivistic cultures are concerned with the adaptability of self-presentation image. Overall, individualistic cultures (such as that in Australia and the United States) emphasize individualistic goals over group goals, individualistic concerns over group concerns, and individual rights and needs over collective responsibilities and obligations. Collectivistic cultures (such as those in China and Japan), in contrast, value group goals over individual goals, group concerns over individual concerns, and collective needs over individual needs. While individualistic cultures are concerned with self-face maintenance, collectivistic cultures are concerned with both self-face and other-face maintenance. Individualistic cultures value autonomy, choices, and negative-face need, while collectivistic cultures value interdependence, reciprocal obligations, and positive-face need.

Low- and High-Context

In addition to the individualism-collectivism dimension, Hall's (1976, 1983) low-context culture and high-context culture (LCC-HCC) dimension serves as a good theoretical foundation to account for communication style differences across a range of cultures. While the individualism-collectivism dimension points to the underlying values of different clusters of cultures, the LCC-HCC dimension points to communication style differences across a set of cultures. Hall's LCC-HCC framework provides a conceptual grounding to understand groups of cultures from a communication perspective.

According to Hall (1983) and Ting-Toomey (1985), LCC system (cultures such as those in Germany, Scandinavia, Switzerland, and the United States) and HCC system (cultures such as those in China, Japan, Korea, and Vietnam) exist on a continuum of cultural communication differences. The LCC system (with the U.S. culture as the prime example) values individual value orientation, line logic, direct verbal interaction, and individualistic nonverbal style. The HCC system (with the Japanese culture as the prime example) values group value orientation, spiral logic, indirect verbal interaction, and contextual nonverbal style. Individualistic verbal and nonverbal communication style means intentions are displayed clearly and have direct correspondence with verbal and nonverbal patterns. Contextual verbal and nonverbal style means intentions and meanings are situated within the larger shared knowledge of the cultural context. While meanings in the LCC are overtly displayed through direct communication forms, meanings in the HCC are implicitly embedded at different levels of the sociocultural context.

Hence, in the LCC system, face-negotiation is an overt communication process. The face-giving and face-protection moves and counter-moves have to be overtly spelled out, and the arguments and the persuasions in a conflict situation would typically follow a linear logic pattern. Face-negotiation in the LCC system would be based on an immediate cost-reward-comparison model, whereas in the HCC system, face-negotiation is an accumulative, long-term process. Since members in the HCC system are interlocked in a group-value perspective, every face-support or face-violation act on another person will have larger social and group implications. The arguments and disagreements in a conflict situation would be ambiguously expressed and the face-giving and face-saving appeals would typically follow a spiral logic pattern. Face-negotiation in the HCC system would probably be based on a long-term, cost-reward-comparison model. In LCC systems, immediate reciprocity of face-giving and face-saving is important to the success of face-negotiation moves. In HCC systems, eventual reciprocity of face-honoring and face-compensating is important for the maintenance of both social and personal relationship developments.

The face-conflict axioms that are derived from both the individualism-collectivism dimension and the LCC-HCC dimension are posited as follows: (1) Both LCC and HCC systems have the concept of "face"— a public image that an interactant claims for himself or herself; (2) LCC members project the "I" identity in facework negotiation, and HCC members project the "we" identity in facework negotiation; (3) the "I" identity facework maintenance makes facework negotiation a competitive process, and the "we" identity facework maintenance makes facework negotiation a collaborative process; (4) the "I" identity orientation means interactants will focus more on self-face perseverance and other-face threat strategies, the "we" identity orientation means interactants will focus more on mutual-face perseverance and other-face honoring strategies; (5) members in both LCC and HCC systems negotiate both face types, negative-face and positive-face, with LCC systems focusing more on negative-face maintenance process, and HCC system focusing more on positive-face maintenance processes; (6) members in both LCC and HCC systems use all four types of face-maintenance suprastrategy: SPF, OPF, SNF, and ONF, however, LCC members tend to use more SPF and SNF strategies while HCC members tend to use more OPF and ONF strategies in interpersonal problematic situations.

THEORETICAL PROPOSITIONS

Altogether 12 theoretical propositions are derived from the preceding discussion of facework negotiation and cross-cultural conflict styles. The first two propositions are presented as follows:

Proposition 1: Members of individualistic, LC cultures tend to express a greater degree of self-face maintenance in a conflict situation than do members of collectivistic, HC cultures.

Proposition 2: Members of collectivistic, HC cultures tend to express a greater degree of mutual-face or other-face maintenance than do members of individualistic, LC cultures.

Members of individualistic cultures tend to operate from the "I" identity system and members from the collectivistic cultures tend to operate from the "we" identity system. The "I" identity system influences one's perception and attention toward "self" as the most important entity of choices. In the LCC system, the concept of "face" is fused with a strong sense of "I" image in the negotiation process. The "we" identity system influences one's perception and orientation to seek outward for connection and approval. In the HCC system, the concept of "face" is always an other-directed concept. Without the approval or disapproval of other people surrounding the self, the concept of "face" does not exist. The third and fourth propositions are as follows:

Proposition 3: Members of individualistic, LC cultures would tend to use more autonomy-preserving strategies (negative-face need) in managing conflict than would members of collectivistic, HC cultures.

Proposition 4: Members of collectivistic, HC cultures would tend to use more approval-seeking strategies (positive-face need) in managing conflict than would members of individualistic, LC cultures.

While privacy and autonomy are the trademarks of individualistic LC cultures, interdependence and inclusion are the hallmarks of collectivistic HC cultures. In a conflict uncertainty situation, face threat means, to members of LC cultures, threatening their need for autonomy and control over self and other. Face threat means, to the members of HC cultures, threatening their need for inclusion and approval by others. Face-violation acts, to the LCC members, would be communicative acts that violate their sense for independence and privacy. Face-violation acts, to the HCC members, would be communicative acts that violate their sense for interconnection and mutuality. Different cultural members, in a sense, would perceive different degrees of threat and different thematic variations of threat in a conflict situation. Propositions 5 and 6 are presented as follows:

Proposition 5: Members of individualistic, LC cultures would tend to use more self positive-face (SPF) and self negative-face (SNF) suprastrategies than would members of collectivistic, HC cultures.

Proposition 6: Members of collectivistic, HC cultures would tend to use more other positive-face (OPF) and other negative-face (ONF) suprastrategies than would members of individualistic, LC cultures.

Self positive-face and self negative-face strategies are defend-attack strategies that aim at protecting self-inclusion need and self-autonomy need while assaulting the face of the other conflict partner. Other positive-face and other negative-face strategies are pleasing and non-imposition strategies that aim, perhaps, at protecting one's self or face from the other's direct criticisms and rejections. Members in the LC cultures tend to use overt face-negotiation tactics, while members in the HC cultures tend to use functionally ambiguous face tactics. Overt face-negotiation tactics promote competition, ambiguous face-negotiation tactics aim at preserving group harmony. The seventh and eighth propositions are presented as follows:

> *Proposition 7:* Members of individualistic, LC cultures tend to use a greater degree of direct face-negotiation strategies than do members of collectivistic, HC cultures.
>
> *Proposition 8:* Members of collectivistic, HC cultures tend to use a greater degree of indirect face-negotiation strategies than do members of individualistic, LC cultures.

"Face" in LC cultures is a commodity that can be explicitly bargained and counter-bargained. "Face" in the HC cultures is a psychological-affective construct that ties closely with other concepts such as "honor," "shame," and "obligation." In the LC cultures, "face" exists only in the immediate time-space that involves the two conflict parties, unfortunately, "face" in the HC cultures involves the multiple faces of relatives, friends, and family members that are closely linked to the HCC interactants. "Face" is a relatively "free" concept in the LC cultures; "face" is an obligatory concept in the HCC system that reflects one's status hierarchy, role position, and power resource. The more one is in power, the more one knows how to bestow, maintain, honor, and destroy face. For LC cultures, the direct dealing with "face" in a conflict situation signifies an honest, up-front way of handling a problematic situation. For HC cultures, the indirect, subtle dealing with "face" in a conflict situation reflects good taste and tactfulness. The ninth and tenth propositions are proffered as follows:

> *Proposition 9:* Members of individualistic, LC cultures tend to use more dominating or controlling strategies to manage conflict than do members of collectivistic, HC cultures.
>
> *Proposition 10:* Members of collectivistic, HC cultures tend to use more obliging or smoothing strategies to manage conflict than do members of individualistic, LC cultures.

Dominating or controlling conflict strategies reflect the importance of self-face concern in individualistic, LC cultures. Obliging or smoothing conflict strategies reflect the other-face concern in collectivistic, HC cultures. In LC cultures, "control" of one's freedom, autonomy, and choices is of paramount importance to one's sense of ego. In HC cultures, "blending in" with other's wishes, desires, and needs is of utmost importance in upholding one's own face and at the same time not embarrassing the other person's face. From the HCC perspective, dominating or confrontational conflict strategies are viewed as posing a direct threat to the other person's face without leaving room for further negotiations and maneuvers in the conflict process. From the LCC perspective, the obliging or the roundabout way of handling conflict in the HCC system poses a direct insult to the face of the negotiators in the LCC conflict situation. While the LCC members would view the indirect way of handling conflict as a cowardly act, the HCC members would view the direct way of handling conflict as lacking in good taste. On both the verbal and nonverbal levels, LCC members would tend to use more direct speech acts (such as direct demands and direct compliance-gaining strategies) and direct, personalized nonverbal style to deal with the face-negotiation process, while HCC members would tend to use more indirect speech acts (such as indirect requests and indirect compliance-gaining strategies) and indirect, contextualistic, nonverbal style to deal with the conflict-confrontation process. The eleventh and twelfth propositions are presented as follows:

> *Proposition 11:* Members of individualistic, LC cultures would use a greater degree of solution-oriented conflict style than would members of collectivistic, HC cultures.
>
> *Proposition 12:* Members of collectivistic, HC cultures would use a greater degree of avoidance-oriented conflict style than would members of individualistic, LC cultures.

While members in the LC cultures can separate the conflict issue from the person, members in the HC cultures typically view conflict as an integration between the issue and the problem in the person. While LCC members are able to analyze the logic of conflict from a task-oriented viewpoint, HCC members typically combine the instrumental dimension with the affective dimension. Hence, for LCC members, while they can manage conflict face-negotiation from an instrumental, solution-oriented perspective, HCC members would typically take the conflict-

TABLE 9.1

**A Summary of Low-Context
and High-Context Face-Negotiation Processes**

Key Constructs of "Face"	Individualistic, Low-Context Cultures	Collectivistic, High-Context Cultures
Identity	emphasis on "I" identity	emphasis on "we" identity
Concern	self-face concern	other-face concern
Need	autonomy, dissociation, negative-face need	inclusion, association, positive-face need
Suprastrategy	self positive-face and self negative-face	other positive-face and other negative-face
Mode	direct mode	indirect mode
Style	controlling style or confrontation style, and solution-oriented style	obliging style or avoidance style, and affective-oriented style
Strategy	distributive or competitive strategies	integrative or collaborative strategies
Speech act	direct speech acts	indirect speech acts
Nonverbal act	individualistic nonverbal acts, direct emotional expressions	contextualistic (role-oriented) nonverbal acts, indirect emotional expressions

flight approach and try to avoid the conflict person at all costs. Table 9.1 presents the major characteristics of individualistic, LCC and collectivistic, HCC face-negotiation processes.

IMPLICATIONS

Five implications can be drawn from the face-negotiation theory: (1) The theory can be applicable to any intercultural problematic situations that entail active facework negotiation process; (2) the theory can be applied to situations that involve a high degree of threat (or uncertainty) to the face of the intercultural interactants; (3) the theory can be used in situations that demand a high degree of politeness between the intercultural interactants; (4) the theory can be used in conjunction with other speech act types (such as request act, compliment act, complaint act, and insult act); and (5) the theory can be used in relationship to other conceptual variables such as compliance-gaining, compliance-resistance, and communication competent behaviors.

The face-negotiation theory states basically that while all intercultural interactants come to a problematic situation with the need for facework management, their focus and orientation toward what aspects of the face need to be tend to vary from one culture to the next. In individualistic, low-context cultures, it is predicted that members would be more likely to turn to self positive-face management and self negative-face management strategies in resolving threat or uncertainty in a problematic situation. In collectivistic, high-context cultures, it is predicted that members would be more likely to use other positive-face strategies and other negative-face management strategies to satisfy the inclusion and approval need.

It is also predicted that because of the different concerns for either negative-face protection (concern for autonomy) or positive-face protection (concern for inclusion), these concerns will be translated to the actual choices of certain conflict styles over others. For LCC members, the concern for autonomy and freedom of actions would influence the LCC individuals to select controlling strategies to preserve distance between the two interactants, and to choose confrontational strategies to fend off opponents in their space-violation acts. For HCC members, the concern for inclusion and other-approval would influence the HCC individuals to select obliging strategies to seek approval for self-face from the other interactant, or to pick avoidance strategies to avoid the problematic issue altogether.

In continuing the theorizing process in intercultural, facework negotiation, future studies need to pay close attention to: (1) the basic taxonomies and metaphors that members use in different cultures that have direct or indirect bearing in the facework negotiation process; (2) the underlying logic and interpretation that cultural members have concerning the use of face-saving, face-violating, and face-honoring communication behaviors; (3) what classes of facework constitute face-threatening acts and what classes of facework constitute face-respecting acts; (4) the fundamental communication acts that are viewed as face-violation behaviors, face-honoring behaviors, and face-compensating behaviors; and (5) the face-negotiation patterns (such as symmetrical patterns or complementary patterns) that constitute optimal communication competence and performance in each culture.

The concept of "face" is viewed in this chapter as a symbolic resource that members in all cultures strive to maintain. However, while "face" is a transcultural concept that governs the active negotiation processes in all cultures, the nuances and subtleties that attach to different facets of facework management would vary from one culture to the next. The dimensions of individualism-collectivism and low-context and high-context have been used as a starting point to aid in the theorizing process of conflict face-negotiation. It is hoped that as more data emerge concerning the theory of face-negotiation, specific propositions concerning specific problematic situations in specific cultures can be systematically introduced and developed. This study provides the groundwork for more integrated efforts between researchers whose work is in language behavior, conflict styles, or interpersonal-intercultural communication competence process, to collaborate with and to contribute to a common understanding of the face-negotiation process in all cultures.

REFERENCES

Adamopoulos, J. (1984). The differentiation of social behavior: Toward an explanation of universal interpersonal structure. *Journal of Cross-Cultural Psychology, 15,* 487-508.

Baxter, L. (1982). Conflict management: An episodic approach. *Small Group Behavior, 13,* 23-42.

Baxter, L. (1984). An investigation of compliance-gaining as politeness. *Human Communication Research, 10,* 427-456.

Bellah, R., Madsen, R., Sullivan, W., Swidler, A., & Tipton, S. (1985). *Habit of the heart: Individualism and commitment in American life.* New York: Harper & Row.

Blake, R., & Mouton, J. (1964). *The managerial grid.* Houston: Gulf.

Bond, M., & Forgas, J. (1984). Linking person perception to behavior intention across cultures. *Journal of Cross-Cultural Psychology, 15,* 337-353.

Brown, C., Yelsma, P., & Keller, P. (1981). Communication-conflict predisposition: Development of a theory and an instrument. *Human Relations, 34,* 1103-1117.

Brown, P., & Levinson, S. (1978). Universals in language usage: Politeness phenomenon. In E. Goody (Ed.), *Questions and politeness: Strategies in social interaction* (pp. 56-289). Cambridge: Cambridge University Press.

Chua, E., & Gudykunst, W. (1987). Conflict resolution style in low- and high-context cultures. *Communication Research Reports, 4,* 32-37.

Craig, R., Tracy, K., & Spisak, F. (1986). The discourse of requests: Assessment of a politeness approach. *Human Communication Research, 12,* 437-468.

Cushman, C., & King, S. (1985). National and organizational cultures in conflict resolution: Japan, the United States, and Yugoslavia. In W. Gudykunst, L. Stewart, & S. Ting-Toomey (Eds.), *Communication, culture, and organizational processes* (pp. 114-133). Beverly Hills, CA: Sage.

Donohue, W., & Diez, M. (1985). Directive use in negotiation interaction. *Communication Monographs, 52,* 305-318.

Folger, J., & Poole, M. (1984). *Working through conflict: A communication perspective.* Glenview, IL: Scott, Foresman.

Goffman, E. (1955). On face-work: An analysis of ritual elements in social interaction. *Psychiatry: Journal for the Study of International Processes, 18,* 213-231.

Goffman, E. (1959). *The presentation of self in everyday life.* Garden City, NY: Doubleday.

Goffman, E. (1967). *Interaction ritual: Essays on face-to-face interaction.* Garden City, NY: Doubleday.

Goffman, E. (1971). *Relations in public.* New York: Harper & Row.

Gudykunst, W., & Nishida, T. (1984). Individualism and cultural influences on uncertainty reduction. *Communication Monographs, 51,* 23-36.

Gudykunst, W., & Nishida, T. (1986). The influence of cultural variability on perceptions of communication behavior associated with relationship terms. *Human Communication Research, 13,* 147-166.

Hall, E. T. (1976). *Beyond culture.* New York: Doubleday.

Hall, E. T. (1983). *The dance of life.* New York: Doubleday.

Hill, B., Ide, S., Ikuta, S., Kawasaki, A., & Ogino, T. (1986). Universals of linguistic politeness: Quantitative evidence for Japanese and American English. *Journal of Pragmatics, 10,* 347-371.

Hofstede, G. (1980). *Culture's consequences: International differences in work-related values.* Beverly Hills, CA: Sage.

Hofstede, G., & Bond, M. (1984). Hofstede's culture dimensions: An independent validation using Rokeach's value survey. *Journal of Cross-Cultural Psychology, 15,* 417-433.

Hu, H. C. (1944). The Chinese concept of "face." *American Anthropologist, 46,* 45-64.

Hui, C., & Triandis, H. (1986). Individualism-collectivism: A study of cross-cultural researchers. *Journal of Cross-Cultural Psychology, 17,* 225-248.

Ide, S., Hori, M., Kawasaki, A., Ikuta, S., & Haga, H. (1986). Sex differences and politeness in Japanese. *International Journal of the Sociology of Language, 58,* 25-36.

Kagan, S., Knight, G., & Martinez-Romero, S. (1982). Culture and the development of conflict resolution style. *Journal of Cross-Cultural Psychology, 13,* 43-59.

Katriel, T. (1986). *Talking straight: Dugri speech in Israeli Sabra culture.* Cambridge: Cambridge University Press.

Kumagai, F., & Straus, M. (1983). Conflict resolution tactics in Japan, India, and the U.S.A. *Journal of Comparative Family Studies, 14,* 377-387.

Leichty, G., & Applegate, J. (1987, May). *Social cognitive and situational influences on the use of face-saving persuasive strategies.* Paper presented at the International Communication Association convention, Montréal.

Leung, K., & Bond, M. (1984). The impact of cultural collectivism on reward allocation. *Journal of Personality and Social Psychology, 47,* 793-804.

Lonner, W. (1980). The search for psychological universals. In H. Triandis & W. Lambert (Eds.), *Handbook of cross-cultural psychology* (Vol. 1, pp. 143-204). Boston, MA: Allyn & Bacon.

McCall, G., & Simmons, J. (1966). *Identities and interactions.* New York: Free Press.

Nadler, L., Nadler, M., & Broome, B. (1985). Culture and the management of conflict situations. In W. Gudykunst, L. Stewart, & S. Ting-Toomey (Eds.), *Communication, culture, and organizational processes* (pp. 71-86). Beverly Hills, CA: Sage.

Nomura, N., & Barnlund, D. (1983). Patterns of interpersonal criticism in Japan and the United States. *International Journal of Intercultural Relations, 7,* 1-18.

Okabe, R. (1983). Cultural assumptions of East and West: Japan and the United States. In W. Gudykunst (Ed.), *Intercultural communication theory: Current perspectives* (pp. 21-44). Beverly Hills, CA: Sage.

Putnam, L., & Jones, T. (1982a). The role of communication in bargaining. *Human Communication Research, 8,* 262-280.

Putnam, L., & Jones, T. (1982b). Reciprocity in negotiations: An analysis of bargaining interaction. *Communication Monographs, 49,* 171-199.

Putnam, L., & Wilson, C. (1982). Communication strategies in organizational conflicts: Reliability and validity of a measurement. In M. Burgoon (Ed.), *Communication yearbook 6* (pp. 629-652). Beverly Hills, CA: Sage.

Rahim, A. (1983). A measure of styles of handling interpersonal conflict. *Academy of Management Journal, 26,* 368-376.

Rahim, A., & Bonoma, Y. (1979). Managing organizational conflict: A model for diagnosis and intervention. *Psychological Reports, 44,* 1323-1344.

Ross, R., & DeWine, S. (1984, November). *Interpersonal needs and communication in conflict: Do soft words win hard hearts?* Paper presented at the Speech Communication Association convention, Washington, DC.

Ross, R., & DeWine, S. (1986, November). *Cross-cultural conflict management: A comparison between United States and Denmark styles.* Paper presented at the annual meeting of the Speech Communication Association convention, Chicago.

Shimanoff, S. (1985). Rules for governing the verbal expression of emotions between married couples. *Western Journal of Speech Communication, 49,* 147-165.

Shimanoff, S. (1987). Types of emotional disclosures and request compliances between spouses. *Communication Monographs, 54,* 85-100.

Sillars, A. (1980a). Attributions and communication in roommate conflicts. *Communication Monographs, 47,* 180-200.

Sillars, A. (1980b). The sequential and distributional structure of conflict interactions as a function of attributions concerning the locus of responsibility and stability of conflict. *Communication yearbook* (Vol. 4) (pp. 217-236). New Brunswick, NJ: Transaction.

Tafoya, D. (1983). The roots of conflict: A theory and a typology. In W. Gudykunst (Ed.), *Intercultural communication theory* (pp. 205-238). Beverly Hills, CA: Sage.

Thomas, K., & Kilman, R. (1978). Comparison of four instruments for measuring conflict behavior. *Psychological Reports, 42,* 1139-1145.

Ting-Toomey, S. (1983). Coding conversation between intimates: A validation study of the intimate negotiation coding system. *Communication Quarterly, 31,* 68-77.

Ting-Toomey, S. (1985). Toward a theory of conflict and culture. In W. Gudykunst, L. Stewart, & S. Ting-Toomey (Eds.), *Communication, culture, and organizational processes* (pp. 71-86). Beverly Hills, CA: Sage.

Ting-Toomey, S. (1986). Conflict styles in black and white subjective cultures. In Y. Kim (Ed.), *Current research in interethnic communication* (pp. 75-89). Beverly Hills, CA: Sage.

Tracy, K., Craig, R., Smith, M., & Spisak, F. (1984). The discourse of requests: Assessment of a compliance-gaining approach. *Human Communication Research, 10,* 513-538.

Triandis, H. (1972). *The analysis of subjective culture.* New York: John Wiley.

Triandis, H. (1977). *Interpersonal behavior.* Monterey, CA: Brooks/Cole.

Triandis, H. (1978). Some universals of social behavior. *Personality and Social Psychology Bulletin, 4,* 1-16.

Tu, W. M. (1985). Selfhood and otherness in Confucian thought. In A. Marsella, G. DeVos, & F. Hsu (Eds.), *Culture and self: Asian and western perspectives* (pp. 231-251). New York: Tavistock.

Wolfson, K., & Norden, M. (1984). Measuring responses to filmed interpersonal conflict: A rules approach. In W. Gudykunst & Y. Kim (Eds.), *Methods for intercultural communication research* (pp. 155-166). Beverly Hills, CA: Sage.

Yutang, L. (1968). *My country and my people.* Taipai, Republic of China: John Day.

IV

INTERCULTURAL ADAPTATION

10

Network Theory in Intercultural Communication

JUNE OCK YUM • *State University of New York at Albany*

Network theory treats individuals as embedded in networks of social relationships influencing, as well as being influenced by, the structure and characteristics of those networks. Network theory also is concerned about the formation, expansion, maintenance, and dissolution of communication structures. Four main sources of network theory are discussed: role theory, exchange theory, action theory, and convergence theory. Based upon the assumption that intercultural communication is more heterogeneous than intracultural communication, six theorems are proposed. It is proposed that intercultural networks are more likely to be radial than interlocking, less dense, less likely to be multiplex, more likely to consist of weak ties than strong ties, to have weaker transitivity effects, and to have structures in which intermediary roles are more important than intracultural networks.

Interest in network analysis has been increasing across a variety of social science disciplines from communication, sociology, and anthropology, to political science in recent years. Whitten and Wolfe (1973) maintained that social network analysis in the 1970s was one of the important theoretical trends in all the social sciences since the 1940s. Network analysis, however, has been understood primarily as an analytic tool, rather than as a new theoretic endeavor. In the late 1970s and 1980s, we have seen significant improvement in the methodologies for analyzing networks often combined with new computer algorithms and mathematical formulations.

These advances in methodology have not been accompanied by the same degree of theoretical advancement. Aldrich (1982) argued that more often "treated as a method for displaying data than as a substantive approach, network analysis may actually have suffered from the ease with which investigators coopt its concept" (p. 281). Burt (1980) also suggested that the lack of network theory was the most serious impediment to the realization of the potential value of network models in empirical research. Some scholars, however, have argued that network analysis has a unique position as a social scientific theory

(Barns, 1972; Rogers & Kincaid, 1981). In this chapter, the following three topics will be covered: (1) the theoretical foundations of network analysis, (2) models of network concepts, and (3) network theory in intercultural communication.

THEORETICAL FOUNDATIONS OF NETWORK ANALYSIS

Before discussing the theoretical issues, it is necessary to specify the underlying assumptions basic to network analysis. The most commonly accepted premise of network analysis is that human behavior can be explained by analysis of the relationships established between and among individuals, as opposed to the characteristics of the individuals themselves. Such an assumption is "the basic Lockian idea that man is by nature a social creature experiencing an innate need to establish relations with others of his kind" (Noble, 1973, p. 7). Under this assumption, network theory can be applied to any group of individuals, and, in fact, such groupings are outcomes of human nature.

More important, network theory negates the assumptions the structural-functional approach makes about the nature of society and its members. Fundamentally, the structural-functional approach views society as a bounded group existing over time for a period long enough to enable the group to evolve its own characteristic culture (Noble, 1973). It also assumes that "the various parts of a social system make positive contributions to the whole and thereby produce equilibrium, adjustment, and order" (Blau, 1982, p. 273). Under such a societal view, human behavior is understood as compulsorily normative in character and people are perceived to be strictly limited in their pursuit of social actions and goals (Anderson & Carlos, 1976). Such a static model of society and human behavior was questioned seriously when social scientists encountered dynamic social situations such as migration, diffusion of innovations, and accelerated social change such as revolution, as well as people manipulating their environment to achieve their goals rather than following internalized normative mandates.

In network theory, the main focus is on positions and social relationships, rather than beliefs or internalized norms. Also, the focus is on series of interconnecting relationships rather than static, bounded groups or subgroups. Individual members of a social system are perceived as actively choosing, creating, and manipulating their networks and in turn being influenced by such networks.

Whitten and Wolfe (1973) suggested that the theoretical underpinnings of network analysis seem to be derived from three sources: role theory, exchange theory, and action theory. More recently, the convergence theory from the field of communication also provides an alternative theoretical foundation for network analysis.

Role Theory

The basic formulation of role theory is that individuals have to play many roles: they are role-bearers or role-performers, manipulating via their roles their network of social relationships (Banck, 1973). Each member of a society plays his or her roles relative to one another. By initiating a new role (such as chairperson) a person may establish new links and by terminating a role (by divorce, for example) one may free oneself from a number of other social-role links. Whitten and Wolfe (1973) questioned whether role theory can adequately establish a conceptual foundation for the analysis of social networks. Social network theory emphasizes the overall structure of interconnected relationships rather than an individual's role or roles in interacting with another individual. In networks, a new level of role allocation occurs, such as the role of bridge, isolate, liaison, broker, opinion leader, and gatekeeper. These roles, however, are positional roles within a network as a whole rather than socially prescribed as is the case in role theory.

Exchange Theory

A number of network theorists have suggested that exchange theory provides the best theoretical basis for network analysis. Whitten and Wolfe (1973) maintained that "without exchange theory the notion of network would appear quite abstract, divorced from the realities of human life, in specific social and cultural settings" (p. 52). Anderson and Carlos (1976) argued that exchange theory is an important source of input into a developing "theory of social networks." A number of network studies were explicitly based upon the notions of exchange theory (Burt, 1975, 1977; Kapferer, 1972, 1973; Marsden & Laumann, 1977).

Initially, exchange theorists were concerned about relatively isolated dyadic exchange relationships. Recently, there has been a shift in theoretical emphasis from a microlevel analysis to a macrolevel analysis of exchange systems. Cook (1982) suggested that "it is this shift in theoretical emphasis to larger systems of exchange or networks of connected exchange relations that holds promise for providing theoretical grounding for process of interest to network theorists" (p. 177). The building block of exchange theory is the *exchange relation,* which is defined as a "temporal series containing opportunities for exchange which evoke initiations which in turn produce or result in transactions" (Emerson, 1972, p. 59). Like network analysis, the exchange relation, not each individual behavior or single transaction between a pair of actors, is the unit of analysis (Cook, 1982). Exchange relations are perceived to form an exchange network if one exchange relation is affected by the other exchange relations. The concept of reciprocity is at the heart of exchange theory (Whitten & Wolfe, 1973). The concept of reciprocity has been refined as a continuum from "generalized reciprocity" through "balanced reciprocity" to "negative reciprocity."

Exchange theory provides a number of conceptual schemes such as exchange domains (relational contents), multiple domains (multiple exchange relations), an actual flow of resources, which can be translated to equivalent network concepts. Exchange theory suggests that the origins of a network are exchange and reciprocity and in turn, interpersonal networks connect individuals in a series of communicative, economic, manipulative, and other types of strands (Whitten & Wolfe, 1973).

Action Theory

Another theoretical foundation for network analysis is action theory. This theory postulates that social life is like a game involving continuous "scheming, struggling, and making decisions" (Cohen, 1969, p. 223). Action theorists argue that people take action to maximize their gain and to minimize their loss. People are perceived as political beings who manipulate their exchange relations rather than as people who are mostly manipulated by social norms or cultural imperatives.

Similarly, network theory is perceived as "network of relations into which a person is born and which he constructs, tries to manipulate and through which he is manipulated" (Boissevain, 1974, p. 7). Action theorists put emphasis on people actively pursuing their goals. More-over, it has been argued that "the social network approach seeks to reintroduce people into sociological analysis, from where they have been banished since Durkheim" (Boissevain, 1974, p. 9). Besides Boissevain, a number of other network theorists have based their analysis on action theory (Baily, 1968; Barth, 1963, 1969; Mayer, 1966; Whitten, 1970).

Convergence Theory

In the field of communications, the dominant theoretical paradigm has viewed communication as a linear, one-way act rather than as a cyclical, multidirectional process. Traditionally, it also has concentrated on the psychological effects of communication on separate individuals rather than on the social effects of communication on the relationships among individuals (Kincaid, 1979; Rogers & Kincaid, 1981). To redress these biases, Kincaid (1979; Rogers & Kincaid, 1981) developed a convergence theory of communication that defines communication as a process in which two or more people share information and converge toward greater mutual understanding (see also Kincaid's chapter in this volume). The emphasis is placed on the differences between individuals rather than on individuals per se. Communication is considered as a process made possible by differences among individuals as well as the process by which such differences are reduced by the cybernetic mechanism of feedback. Rogers and Kincaid (1981) extended this model to the social system level by combining it with network theory, referring to it as the network/convergence paradigm.

This paradigm treats individuals as embedded in networks of social relationships that are both created and maintained by the exchange of information. Communication networks are differentiated into local areas of relatively greater density of connections inside its boundaries than outside. Because the members of such locally bounded networks tend to share the same information over time (compared to those outside it), communication results in a convergence among members toward a state of greater uniformity. This basic theorem of communication is considered a prerequisite for self-organization and cultural evolution (Kincaid, 1987).

MODELS OF NETWORK CONCEPTS

Scholars have disagreed whether a set of statements can be put forward as a formal network theory (Whitten & Wolfe, 1973). Anderson and Carlos (1976) maintained that "there does not exist a theory of social networks that comprehensively explains the social and psychological bases of network interrelationships and bonding processes. In addition, we know very little, in a systematic way, about how networks emerge, are altered, maintained, or atrophy" (p. 28). Despite this skepticism, the number of empirical as well as theoretical studies has steadily increased. These theoretical works fit into three models: the first model treats network characteristics as independent variables, the second treats them as dependent variables, and the third treats them as intervening variables.

Networks as Independent Variables

A number of researchers has developed explanatory models of social behavior with network characteristics as the main independent variables. In a study of a Korean village, Kincaid and Yum (1976) found that the success of the village mothers' club, whose members maintained closely interconnected communication networks in the village, was closely related to the adoption of family-planning contraceptives. This finding was confirmed in a follow-up network study of 24 Korean villages (Rogers & Kincaid, 1981).

A follow-up network analysis of the Evans-Pritchard (1950) classic study of the Nuer political organization, Kapferer's (1969) analysis of conflict among industrial workers in Zambia, and Boissevain's (1974) study of personal networks in Malta all demonstrated the utility of applying network concepts to explain social behavior in diverse cultural settings. Other studies have found that network characteristics have significant effects on interethnic attitudes (Yum, 1983) and ethnic tolerance (Alba, 1978).

A substantial number of studies have incorporated network concepts in the study of migration and acculturation of immigrants and in the study of the diffusion of innovations. Network factors influence migration itself as well as the consequences of migration—adaptation and acculturation. People tend to migrate following previously established network lines. A person does not usually migrate from a rural to an urban area or from one country to another in a haphazard manner, but rather tends to follow certain network chains that create an urban village or ethnic enclave in a city. Once migration occurs, adaptation is facilitated by local networks that provide emotional support, instrumental information, and even material support (Yum, 1982). Mayer (1974) found that network patterns influence the acculturation process of urban migrants of Xhosa. The close-knit networks of certain Xhosa urban migrants encapsulated its members in urban enclaves and inhibited their acculturation into urban life. At the same time, the loose-knit networks of another group of Xhosa in the city facilitated their process of modernization and acculturation. A number of other studies demonstrated that network characteristics are important independent variables for explaining migration, adaptation, and acculturation (Abalon, 1976; Bar-Yoseph, 1968; Gans, 1962; Recio-Androdos, 1975).

From the very beginning, studies of the diffusion of innovations have found that interpersonal communication is essential in an individual's decision to adapt. Since the 1950s, there have been a number of studies conducted outside the United States that have examined the diffusion of new technology or ideas from one culture (or subculture) to another (Rogers, 1983). Many have demonstrated that the diffusion of innovation is very much influenced by interpersonal networks. Network analyses under the rubric of the diffusion of innovation have been conducted in India, Bangladesh, the Philippines, Mexico, Korea, China, Taiwan, and Nigeria, among others.

Besides contributing to the explanation of individual behavior, network variables have also been found to have significant effects on group or system performance. In their study of 24 Korean villages, Rogers and Kincaid (1981) found that the connectedness of the mothers' club leader in the village's family-planning communication networks and the degree of overlap between the family-planning and general communication network had a significant impact on the village rate of adoption of contraceptives. Studies by Guimaraes (1972) and Korzeny and Farace (1978) also demonstrated that a higher degree of connectedness in a system is related positively to the degree of behavior change at the system level. Diffusion studies in different cultures have also demonstrated the utility of the networks analysis across diverse cultural settings (Yum, 1984).

Networks as Dependent Variables

A number of researchers have been concerned with developing theoretical models to investigate how networks emerge, expand, and are maintained or dissolved. The most broad orientation is an evolutionary one that suggests that network formation is the result of some general active forces in social life (Whitten and Wolfe, 1973). For instance, Tonnies's notion of community change from Gemeinshaft to Geselleshaft involves a change from narrow, close-knit networks to loose-knit, radial ones. Yum (1985, 1987a) has proposed that differences in network patterns are the result of general cultural differences. In a comparison of East Asian and Western communication patterns, she suggested that as a result of East Asians' emphasis on social relationships, their societies have developed more closely knit networks with stronger boundaries between ingroups and outgroups. She also maintained that such network roles as intermediaries are much more important in East Asia than in North America. Cultural differences of network patterns were empirically tested with five ethnic groups in Hawaii (Yum, 1984).

Other variables that have been found to be important causes in determining networks are geographic mobility (Turner, 1967), physical propinquity (Moreno, 1953; Rogers & Kincaid, 1981), heterogeneity (such as the relative size of each ethnic group in a city; Rytina, 1982; Blau & Schartz, 1984), and original affinity (Moreno, 1953). Festinger, Schachter, and Back (1950) found that social conditions (such as having small children) and physical propinquity had interactive effects on the development of social networks. Boissevain (1973) suggested that environmental factors, such as urban-rural distinction, population density, and personal characteristics such as age, religion, and gregariousness interactively influence network size and patterns.

The transivity hypothesis has been suggested as one of the mechanisms through which networks are formulated and maintained (Davis, 1970). This hypothesis states that if A likes B and B likes C then A comes to like C. Modifying the transivity hypothesis, Anderson and Carlos (1976) argued that sentiment relations (such as transivity) matter most in the earliest phase of the development of network ties. Once a link has become established, on the other hand, its fate depends more on the positively or negatively valued outcomes of transactions between the group's members than on sentiment.

Based upon the exchange theory, power imbalance and dependency are also found to have significant effects on network formation and maintenance. Blau (1964) maintained that "by supplying services in demand to others, a person establishes power over them. If he regularly renders needed services they cannot readily obtain elsewhere, others become dependent on and obligated to him for these services" (p. 118). Such dependency and obligation relationships will function to establish networks and they remain active as long as such dependency relationships continue.

Even though network theory has developed as a "critique of the normative view of social action" (Anderson & Carlos, 1976, p. 38), it does not mean that networks are completely free of normative forces. More often than not, we keep certain network relations because of societal norms such as *uye-ri* (long-term faithfulness) in Korea (Yum, 1987c) or *mezia* (reciprocity) in Tunisia (Jangmans, 1973). Social norms can serve as powerful mechanisms for maintaining existing networks by regulating membership and group boundaries.

Networks as Intervening Variables

A number of researchers have demonstrated that network variables intervene between various independent and dependent variables of interest. While studying foreign immigrants' information levels, Yum (1982) found that communication diversity that was measured in part by network diversity intervened between the antecedent variables of social and cognitive capacity and the dependent variable of information acquisition. Kincaid (1972) found that among Mexican urban slum settlers, network variables had intervening effects between socioeconomic status and locus of control and family-planning adoption. Similarly, Burnstein (1976) found an indication that, in a national election in Israel, much of the impact of background variables operate through their impact on network ties to political parties. The results of these studies indicate that network variables often act as a mediating influence in determining how particular antecedents affect behavior/attitude change.

NETWORKS IN INTERCULTURAL COMMUNICATION

If we accept the basic premise that intercultural communication is an interaction process between people, groups, or organizations whose cultural origins are significantly different, then network theory is very appropriate for the investigation of such a phenomenon. The main strength of network theory over other theories of communication that emphasize explanation only with individual level variables is that it is context-based and automatically includes some aspect of the social environment. Increasing attention has been given to the effects of social context on intercultural communication. Hall (1976) applied the terms *high-context* and *low-context* communication and differentiated communication patterns depending upon how much information is embedded in the context. Bernstein (1972) argued that the particular form of a social relation acts selectively upon what is said, when it is said, and how it is said. He observed that context exercises major control over syntactic and lexical selection and that different forms of social relationships can generate very different speech systems or communication modes.

The structural-functional approach perceives people as first becoming socialized into social norms and then behaving in accord with their internalized norms. Such normative explanations, based on internalized motives for action, are ultimately individualistic (Wellman, 1982). It has been documented that the predominant value system of the United States is individualism while many other cultures place a greater emphasis on mutual dependency and harmonious social relationships (Bellah et al., 1985; Northrop, 1946; Yum, 1987a, 1987b). Therefore, when one investigates intercultural communication between the United States and other cultural groups that emphasize social relationships, one of the main differences expected would be their network patterns.

Diffusion studies conducted in cultures outside the United States, for example, contradicted the notion that adaptation is solely an individual decision as opposed to a process located in networks and involving group initiation, group pressure, and sometimes even group decision making. In intercultural communication situations, a normative analysis is not very helpful because members of different groups have a history of different socialization resulting in different norms. Such analysis would predict that only cultural misunderstanding would result rather than cultural adaptation and mutual understanding.

Intercultural communication provides very different communication situations than intracultural communication. Because culture is the sum total of learned behavior (Hall, 1959), members of different cultural groups "do not share the same set of communication rules, symbols, and behaviours, nor the manners in which individuals explicitly or implicitly address relational concerns" (Kim, 1986, p. 92). This does not mean that intercultural communication networks are impossible, but that they would be expected to have different patterns than intracultural communication networks.

Assumption 1: The variance between cultural groups is greater than the variance within each cultural group.

From a network structures' point of view, heterogeneity itself, regardless of the specific content (such as religion) of heterogeneity, makes a difference in network outcomes (Blau, 1982). Based on the basic assumption of relatively greater heterogeneity in intercultural communication than in intracultural communication, a number of differences in network patterns may be proposed.

Theorem 1: Intercultural network patterns will be more likely radial than the interlocking type compared to intracultural networks.

Theorem 2. Intercultural networks are less dense than intracultural networks.

A radial personal network is one in which an individual interacts with a set of dyadic partners who do not interact with each other. An interlocking personal network is one in which an individual interacts with a set of dyadic partners who interact with each other (Laumann, 1973; Rogers, 1973; Rogers & Kincaid, 1981). In a homogeneous group, one's friends tend to be friends with each other, thus constituting an interlocking personal network. However, in intercultural situations, the high level of heterogeneity would make it less likely that one's intercultural contacts would develop relationships with one's intracultural contacts. The density of a network is the ratio of actual direct links among members of a network to the total possible number of such links. According to this definition, interlocking networks should be more dense than radial ones.

Theorem 3: Intercultural networks are less likely to be multiplex than intracultural networks.

Multiplexity is the degree to which multiple message contents flow through a dyadic link between two individuals and hence the degree to which two individuals have multiple role relationships (Rogers & Kincaid, 1981, p. 133). Some authors refer to multiple links as "multistranded," or "multidomain." The converse is referred to as "unistranded" or "uniplex." Sometimes a network link functions as a conduit of diverse content such as sentiment, information exchange, advice- giving, and so forth. On the other hand, some network links may perform only one function such as material exchange.

Multiplex relationships require more time to establish than uniplex relationships, even within a single culture. Usually, intercultural relationships are initiated as uniplex links. A good example is the coworker or supervisor-subordinate relationship that may later expand into other types of relationships, such as friendship. However, developing multiplex relationships, especially of a personal nature, with members of different cultural groups are often perceived to be too difficult or undesirable (Kim, 1986). As a consequence, if it is at all possible to find a substitute for certain relational needs within one's own cultural group, then intracultural links are more likely to be used than intercultural networks. Velzen studied the coalition process of Tansanian tribe compartments and found that multiplex relations would grow and develop between persons within the same compartment rather than with persons outside those compartments (Velzen, 1973).

The uniplexity of intercultural network ties has important implications for the strength of such ties.

Theorem 4: Intercultural network ties are more likely to be weak ties than strong ties.

The "strength of weak ties" hypothesis formulated by Granovetter (1973) proposes that the informational strength (especially problem-solving information, such as where to find a better job) of a network comes from its weaker ties. Since this hypothesis was first proposed, a variety of operational definitions of the strength of ties has been proposed. Granovetter (1973) simply considered close friendship relationships to be strong ties compared to much weaker acquaintance ties. Other researchers have elaborated on this initial definition by including recency of contact (Lin, 1982), frequency of interaction, kinship ties, and geographical propinquity as additional indicators of network strength.

If intercultural contacts are more difficult to develop into close friendships and thus tend to remain uniplex links, it follows that such links are more likely to be weak than strong. Granovetter (1973) pointed out that "there is empirical evidence that the stronger the tie connecting two individuals, the more similar they are, in various ways" (p. 1362). Conversely, we can hypothesize that the more different or "heterophilous" they are (which is the case in intercultural communication), the weaker the tie connecting two individuals.

Two network studies of culturally encapsulated populations (Mexican and Black) confirmed that intracultural groups are almost completely dominated by strong ties (Granovetter, 1982). Granovetter argued that the heavy concentration of social energy in strong ties has the affect of fragmenting communities of the poor into encapsulated networks with poor connections between these units. He further argued that what they need are more weak ties that would connect these encapsulated cultures. Karweit and others (1979) applied this hypothesis to school settings, arguing that it is more beneficial to encourage the establishment of weak ties between different racial groups in school (black and white students) to connect black and white cliques than to encourage strong biracial friendship ties, which has been the most common strategy. The "strong ties" strategy has not been very successful possibly because of the difficulty of establishing strong intercultural ties, and hence the greater likelihood of maintaining strong ties within one's own cultural group, as suggested in Theorem 3.

Theorem 5: The roles of liaison and bridge will be more prevalent and more important for network connectedness in intercultural networks than in intracultural networks.

In network analysis a *liaison* is defined as an individual who links two or more cliques in a system, but who is not a member of any clique, and a *bridge* is defined as an individual who links two or more cliques in a system from his or her position as a member of one of the cliques (Rogers & Kincaid, 1981). Both roles are perceived to be intermediaries or brokers. Given that intercultural networks are more heterogeneous than intracultural networks, it follows that it would be more difficult to interact directly with members from different cultures than to interact indirectly. A person with bicultural or multicultural skills (linguistic skills or experience in the other culture) is more likely to be used to connect two culturally different groups. Aldrich (1982) suggested that intermediary or broker roles are a natural result of actors' attempts to minimize transaction costs. Connecting two culturally different groups would cost more than connecting similar cultural groups and, therefore, connecting roles such as liaisons and bridges will play much more important functions in intercultural network structures than in intracultural network structures.

Most members of one culture usually do not have intercultural communication skills or the opportunities to develop them. The group as a whole, therefore, has to depend upon intermediaries to make intercultural contacts. Bilingual social workers who help recent immigrants, for example, have been found to function not only as information disseminators but more importantly as the connection points which link immigrant groups to the host society. The intercultural research literature describes an increasing number of multicultural persons who are capable of dealing with multiple cultures without conflicts (Adler, 1976; Bochner, 1982). One of the characteristics of multicultural persons is that they do not maintain any clear boundaries between themselves and their various cultural contexts (Adler, 1976). Therefore, they seem to be the ideal type who function as liaison or bridge in intercultural networks.

Theorem 6: Transivity will play a much smaller role in creating intercultural networks than intracultural networks.

Transivity operates when my friend's friends are my friends and my friend's enemies are my enemies. Such an extension of loyalties and the transfer of obligations assumes normative sanctions against those who do not conform. Within a homogeneous group that shares a common cultural value system, one is likely to extend one's networks of assistance and to join in discrimination against a friend's enemies. On the other hand, in intercultural situations where people do not share as many cultural values, where relationships tend to be uniplex rather than multiplex, and are weak rather than strong, such strong normative sanctions and strong emotional obligations would not be expected to form.

Anderson and Carlos (1976) suggested that events, transactions, and relationships in many networks are public events. In other words, "a public 'score' of a person's debits and credits in exchange is kept by network members-at-large in many social networks" (Anderson and Carlos, 1976; p. 38). Therefore, a person's willingness to extend his or her loyalties and obligations would not depend so much on personal sentiments and dependency relationships as on his or her anticipated interactions with other persons in the group (Anderson and Carlos, 1976). Because this score-keeping is readily visible among more homogeneous groups and the anticipated transactions with within-group members are higher, it follows that transivity as a mechanism of network extension and maintenance is stronger in intracultural networks than in intercultural networks.

CONCLUSION

Network theory provides an important alternative to the dominant communication theories that focus on the individual and on psychological effects rather than on groups and social effects. The field of intercultural communication is more sensitive to both process and relationship issues than other communication fields because of the nature of the topic itself. For this reason, network theory can make a valuable contribution to the study of intercultural communication. For instance, under network theory, acculturation can be treated as network formation, maintenance, and expansion. For the study of the persistence or dissolution of ethnic groups, Barth (1969) argued that the focal point of investigation should be "the ethnic boundary that defines the group, not the cultural stuff that it encloses" (p. 14). Communication network analysis offers a powerful methodology for measuring and studying ethnic boundaries, and network theory is relevant to the phenomenon. Barth further proposed that "the persistence of ethnic groups in contact implies not only criteria and signals for identification, but also a structuring of interaction which allows the persistence of cultural differences" (p. 16).

The basic assumption of network theory and the six theorems developed here provide an initial theoretical framework to test network theory in intercultural communication in comparison to intracultural communication. These theorems permit the examination of the structure and processes of intercultural communication. They are applicable to intercultural communication situations in general.

If one wants to investigate intercultural networks between specific cultures, one needs to take additional steps. First, we need to understand the cultural rules that regulate and place a higher value on certain network patterns and processes than others.

In East Asian cultures, for instance, Confucianism provides the fundamental ethics and rules for social relationships (Yum, 1985, 1987a, 1987b). Confucian ethics define what is the proper relationship in particular contexts and how different relationships should be handled. It should be possible to find a similar basis for the norms for social network formation in Islamic and Judeo-Christian ethics.

Each culture also has a different "network vocabulary" (Anderson & Carlos, p. 48) to conceptualize different social network relations. The *oybun-kobun* relationship (head-follower relationship) in Japan or the *sunbai-hoobai* relationship (senior-junior relationship, especially in school) in Korea have important implications for networks in those two cultures. It is necessary to have some understanding of such network vocabularies to analyze accurately any intercultural networks in which a mixture of such vocabularies coexist. Along these same lines, the use of kinship terms for nonkin members has been observed in very closely knit, intracultural networks (Lomitz, 1977; Stack, 1974). Many cultural groups do use fictitious kinship terms for close associates. Understanding such practices would enhance our comprehension of intercultural networks in which such terms exist and evolve over time. We also need to learn what the most important factors are for network formation and maintenance within various cultures in order to understand what happens when intercultural communication occurs among them. For instance, in Korea, school relations, especially from high school, create the most enduring networks (Yum, 1987c), whereas in Japan, besides school relations, shared employment in a large corporation often creates the most enduring networks (Vogel, 1963). Such differences has strong implications for the strength of weak ties hypothesis. Even though two network links are the same in terms of frequency or recency of interaction, if one link was originally established by means of a strong network tie (such as classmates), we would expect that link to persist longer than the other link. Even in intercultural networks, if the link is initially established through such a mechanism as a school tie (say, for a Korean and American), we would expect for that link to have a higher probability of remaining strong compared to links established through frequent office or neighborhood contacts. Such an analysis goes beyond the immediate communication behavior of an existing intercultural network and examines the original cultural foundations upon which they may have been established.

Another important issue is the time period required to create and maintain networks within different cultures. Hall (1959) did the pioneering work on the cultural differences in the concept of time. For certain cultures, it may take a much longer time to form a network than another, yet once formed such a network may endure for a much longer time than similar networks formed in other cultures. This issue raises the question of what effect two different time perspectives would have on networks when members from the cultures that hold them interact. We need to understand how long a period of examination is necessary to understand fully the structure and process of development of such intercultural communication networks.

Intercultural communication network theory is still in its initial stage of development, but it promises to extend our knowledge of intercultural communication beyond what is now being gained from the perspective of dyadic interpersonal communication. It should be clear by now that intercultural communication networks are made up of interpersonal relationships, but that the analysis and related theory goes beyond the dyadic level of analysis to the level of triads, cliques and subgroups, and intact social systems. As more research is conducted, we expect to see intercultural network theory and research enrich the interpersonal perspective and vice versa. There are several important contexts in which intercultural communication networks can be studied and the theory further developed: communities with a mixture of ethnic subcultures, societies with substantial immigration from different cultures, the relocation of industrial/commercial organizations from one culture to another, and, of course, large university campuses with an influx of significant numbers of foreign students. Each of these situations involve intercultural communication networks that endure for long periods, and thus attain a sufficient degree of stability for analysis.

REFERENCES

Abalon, J. (1976). The social organization of an urban Samoan community. In E. Gee (Ed.), *Counterpoint: Perspectives on Asian Americans.* Los Angeles: Asian American Studies Center, University of California.

Adler, P. S. (1976). Beyond cultural identity: Reflection on cultural and multicultural man. In L. Samovar & R. Porter (Eds.), *Intercultural communication: A reader* (2nd ed.). Belmont, CA: Wadsworth.

Alba, N. (1978). Ethnic networks and tolerant attitude. *Public Opinion Quarterly, 42,* 1-16.

Aldrich, H. (1982). The origins and persistence of social network. In P. Marsden & N. Lin (Eds.), *Social structure and network analysis.* Beverly Hills, CA: Sage.

Anderson, B., & Carlos, M. L. (1976). What is social network theory? In T. Burns & W. Buckley (Eds.), *Power and control.* London: Sage.

Baily, F. G. (1968). Parapolitical system. In M. Swartz (Ed.), *Local-level politics.* Chicago: Aldine.

Banck, G. A. (1973). Network analysis and social theory. In J. Boissevain & C. Mitchell (Eds.), *Network analysis: Studies in human interaction.* The Hague: Mouton.

Barns, J. A. (1972). *Social networks.* Reading, MA: Addison-Wesley.

Barth, F. (1969). *Ethnic groups and boundaries.* Boston: Little, Brown.

Barth, F. (1963). *The role of the entrepreneur in social change in Northern Norway.* Bergen: Norwegian University Press.

Bar-Yoseph, R. (1968). Desocialization and socialization: The adjustment process of immigrants. *International Migration Review, 2,* 27-45.

Bellah, R., Madsen, R., Sullivan, W., Swidler, A., & Tipton, S. (1985). *Habits of the heart: Individualism and commitment in American life.* New York: Harper & Row.

Bernstein, B. (1972). A sociolinguistic approach to socialization; with some reference to educability. In J. Gumperz & D. Hymes (Eds.), *Directions in sociolinguistics: The ethnography of communication.* New York: Holt, Rinehart and Winston.

Blau, P. (1964). *Exchange and power in social life.* New York: John Wiley.

Blau, P. (1982). Structural sociology and network analysis. In P. Marsden & N. Lin (Eds.), *Social structure and network analysis.* Beverly Hills, CA: Sage.

Blau, P., & Schwartz, J. (1984). *Crosscutting social circles.* New York: Academic Press.

Bochner, S. (1982). The social psychology of cross-cultural relations. In S. Bochner (Ed.), *Cultures in contact: Studies in cross-cultural interaction.* Oxford: Pergamon.

Boissevain, J. (1973). An exploration of two first-order zones. In J. Boissevain & J. Mitchell (Eds.), *Network analysis: Studies in human interaction.* The Hague: Mouton.

Boissevain, J. (1974). *Friends of friends: Networks, manipulators, and coalitions.* Oxford: Blackwell.

Burnstein, P. (1976). Social networks and voting: Some Israeli Data. *Social Forces, 54,* 833-847.

Burt, R. (1975). Corporate society: A time series analysis of network structure. *Social Science Research, 4,* 271-328.

Burt, R. (1977). Power in social topology. In R. Liebert & A. Imershein (Eds.), *Power, paradigms and community research.* Beverly Hills, CA: Sage.

Burt, R. (1980). Models of network structure. *Annual Review of Sociology, 6,* 79-141.

Cohen, A. (1969). Political anthropology: The analysis of the symbolism of power relations. *Man: Journal of the Royal Anthropological Institute of Great Britain and Ireland, 4,* 215-235.

Cook, K. (1982). Network structures from an exchange perspective. In P. Marsden & N. Lin (Eds.), *Social structure and network analysis.* Beverly Hills, CA: Sage.

Davis, J. (1970). Clustering and hierarchy in interpersonal relations. *American Sociological Review, 35,* 843-851.

Emerson, R. (1972). Exchange theory, Part I: A psychological basis for social exchange. In J. Berger, M. Zelditch, & A. Anderson (Eds.), *Sociological theories in progress* (Vol. 2). Boston: Houghton Mifflin.

Evans-Pritchard, E. (1950). *The Nuer.* Oxford: Clarendon.

Festinger, L., Schacter, S., & Back, K. (1950). *Social pressures in informal groups: A study of a housing project.* New York: Harper & Row.

Gans, H. (1962). *The urban villagers.* New York: Free Press.

Granovetter, M. (1973). The strength of weak ties. *American Journal of Sociology, 78,* 1360-1380.

Granovetter, M. (1982). The strength of weak ties: A network theory revisited. In P. Marsden & N. Lin (Eds.), *Social structure and network analysis.* Beverly Hills, CA: Sage.

Guimaraes, L. L. (1972). *Communication integration in modern and traditional social systems: A comparative analysis across twenty communities of Minas Gerais.* Doctoral dissertation, Michigan State University.

Hall, E. (1959). *The silent language.* New York: Doubleday.

Hall, E. (1976). *Beyond culture.* New York: Doubleday.

Jangmans, D. G. (1973). Politics on the village level. In J. Boissevain & J. Mitchell (Eds.), *Network analysis: Studies in human interaction.* The Hague: Mouton.

Kapferer, B. (1969). Norms and the manipulation of relations in a work context. In J. Mitchell (Ed.), *Social networks in urban situations.* Manchester, England: Manchester University Press.

Kapferer, B. (1972). *Strategy and transaction in an African factory.* Manchester, England: Manchester University Press.

Kapferer, B. (1973). Social networks and conjugal roles in urban Zambia: Towards a reformulation of the Bott's hypothesis. In J. Boissevain & J. Mitchell (Eds.), *Network analysis: Studies in human interaction*. The Hague: Mouton.

Karweit, N., Hansell, S., & Ricks, M. (1979). The conditions for peer associations in school. (Report No. 282). Baltimore, MD: Johns Hopkins University, Center for Social Organization of Schools.

Kim, Y. Y. (1986). Understanding the social context of intergroup communication: A personal network approach. In W. Gudykunst (Ed.), *Intergroup communication*. London: Edward Arnold.

Kincaid, D. L. (1972). Communication networks, locus of control, and family planning among migrants to the periphery of Mexico City. Doctoral dissertation, Michigan State University.

Kincaid, D. L. (1979). The convergence model of communication. Paper 18, East-West Communication Institute, Honolulu.

Kincaid, D. L. (1987). The convergence theory of communication, self-organization and cultural evolution. In D. Kincaid (Ed.), *Communication theory: Eastern and Western perspectives*. New York: Academic Press.

Kincaid, D. L., & Yum, J. O. (1976). The needle and the ax: Communication and development in a Korean village. In D. Lerner & W. Schramm (Eds.), *Communication and change: The last ten years—and the next*. Honolulu: University Press of Hawaii.

Korzeny, F., & Farace, R. (1978). Communication networks and social change in developing countries. *International and Intercultural Communication Annual, 4,* 69-94.

Laumann, E. (1973). *The bonds of pluralism: The force and substance of urban social networks*. New York: John Wiley.

Lin, N. (1982). Social resources and instrumental action. In P. Marsden & N. Lin. (Eds.), *Social structure and network analysis*. Beverly Hills, CA: Sage.

Lomitz, L. (1977). *Networks and marginality*. New York: Academic Press.

Marsden, P., & Laumann, E. (1977). Collective action in a community elite: Exchange, influence resources, and issue resolution. In R. Liebert & A. Imershein, (Eds.), *Power, paradigms, and community research*. London: Sage.

Mayer, A. (1966). The significance of quasi-groups in the study of complex societies. In M. Banton (Ed.), *The social anthropology of complex societies*. New York: Praeger.

Mayer, P., with Mayer, I. (1974). *Townsman or tribesman: Conservatism and the process of urbanization in a South African city* (2nd ed.). Cape Town: Oxford University Press.

Moreno, J. (1953). *Who shall survive? Foundations of sociometry, group psychotherapy, and sociodrama*. Beacon, NY: Beacon House.

Noble, M. (1973). Social network: Its use as a conceptual framework in family analysis. In J. Boissevain & J. Mitchell (Eds.), *Network analysis: Studies in human interaction*. The Hague: Mouton.

Northrop, F.S.C. (1946). *The meeting of East and West*. New York: Macmillan.

Recio-Androdos, J. (1975). Family as a unit and larger society: The adaptation of the Puerto Rican migrant family to the mainland suburban setting. Doctoral dissertation, New York University.

Rogers, E. (1973). *Communication strategies for family planning*. New York: Free Press.

Rogers, E. (1983). *Diffusion of innovations*. New York: Free Press.

Rogers, E., & Kincaid, D. L. (1981). *Communication networks: Toward a new paradigm for research*. New York: Free Press.

Rytina, S. (1982). Structural constraints on intergroup contact: Size, proportion, and intermarriage. In P. Marsden & N. Lin (Eds.), *Social structure and network analysis.* Beverly Hills, CA: Sage.

Stack, C. (1974). *All our kin.* New York: Harper & Row.

Turner, C. (1967). Conjugal roles and social networks: A reexamination of an hypothesis. *Human Relations, 20,* 121-130.

Velzen, T. (1973). Coalitions and network analysis. In J. Boissevain & J. Mitchell (Eds.), *Network analysis: Studies in human interaction.* The Hague: Mouton.

Vogel, E. (1963). *Japan's new middle class.* Berkeley: University of California Press.

Wellman, B. (1982). Studying personal communities. In P. Marsden & N. Lin (Eds.), *Social structure and network analysis.* Beverly Hills, CA: Sage.

Whitten, N. (1970). Network analysis and processes of adaptation among Ecuadorian and Nova Scotian Negros. In M. Frelich (Ed.), *Marginal natives: Anthropologists at work.* New York: Harper & Row.

Whitten, B., & Wolfe, W. (1973). Network analysis. In J. Honigman (Ed.), *The handbook of social and cultural anthropology.* Chicago: Rand McNally.

Yum, J. O. (1982). Communication diversity and information acquisition among Korean immigrants in Hawaii. *Human Communication Research, 8,* 154-169.

Yum, J. O. (1984a). Network analysis. In W. Gudykunst & Y. Kim (Eds.), *Methods for intercultural communication research.* Beverly Hills, CA: Sage.

Yum, J. O. (1984b). Social networks of five ethnic groups in Hawaii. In R. Bostrom (Ed.), *Communication yearbook 7.* Beverly Hills, CA: Sage.

Yum, J. O. (1985, May). *The impact of Confucianism on communication: The case of Korea and Japan.* Paper presented at the 35th Annual Conference of the International Communication Association, Honolulu.

Yum, J. O. (1987a). *Asian perspectives on communication.* Paper presented at the 37th Annual Conference of the International Communication Association, Montréal, Canada, May.

Yum, J. O. (1987b). *Korean philosophy and communication.* In D. Kincaid (Ed.), *Communication theory: Eastern and Western perspectives.* New York: Academic Press.

Yum, J. O. (1987c). The practice of uye-ri in interpersonal relationships in Korea. In D. Kincaid (Ed.), *Communication theory: Eastern and Western perspectives.* New York: Academic Press.

Yum, J. O., & Wang, G. (1983). Interethnic perception and communication behavior of five ethnic groups in Hawaii. *International Journal of Intercultural Relations, 7,* 285-308.

11

A Theory of Adaptation
in Intercultural Dyads

HUBER W. ELLINGSWORTH • University of Tulsa

This chapter describes a theory of task-oriented intercultural dyads in which individual adaptation is the central variable in completing tasks and minimizing cultural differences. The Dubin method is employed to generate units, laws, and propositions that describe the participants, setting, purpose, process, and outcomes and to predict circumstances under which successful adaptation will occur. As a result of participation, changes are also predicted in the attitudes and cognitions of participants, forming the basis for future encounters.

As the study of intercultural communication study expands and matures, new themes emerge that focus the attention of scholars. A predominant concept of the 1980s is *adaptation*—those changes that individuals make in their affective and cognitive identity and in their interactive behavior as they deal with life in a new cultural environment. Accelerated in-migration, particularly into the United States and Britain, has heightened interest in the experiences of immigrants. The flow of longer-term sojourners such as foreign students continues together with a growing number of technical, professional, management, and sales representatives engaged in international commerce. The length of sojourn is usually for a definite period known in advance by the visitors and often by their associates in the host country.

The time dimension thus operates as a strong factor in motivating the nature and extent of adaptation. The immigrant, especially the refugee, often literally cannot go home again, and his or her incentive to adjust productively to the new environment is conditioned by a permanent lack of alternatives. In addition, the burden of adaptation is placed clearly with the newcomer. Programs by government and private sponsors may ease on-arrival difficulties, but in the longer-term, adaptation must occur primarily in the individual, and not in the host society. The host response may indeed range from positive to neutral or aloof to actually negative (Phizacklea, 1984). As for sojourners, the extent of adaptation is likely to be conditioned by the knowledge of a planned return home, and the amount of adjustment above a minimum survival level will result largely from individual motivation, opportunity, and ability to change.

With both the immigrants and longer-term sojourners, research attention by anthropologists, sociologists and communication scholars often has focused on some dimension of cultural assimilation, a stage that emerges after the initial stages of intercultural contact.

The group or community has been the focus for much of this body of inquiry. An example of anthropological investigation is the study of changes in personality type among North American Indians as part of assimilation into the dominant culture (Spindler, 1955). Majority-minority group relationships have attracted considerable attention, focusing on such matters as group identity, language demands, stratification, competition, and segregation (Blalock, 1952; Glazer & Moynihan, 1970, 1975; Spiro, 1955). Still other sociological investigation has employed ethnographic methods to examine self-perceptions of alienation (Gallo, 1974) and patterns of community life (Gans, 1962) within ethnic groups.

The individual also has been used frequently in the past few decades as a unit of analysis in investigating the experiences of both immigrants and sojourners in developing and maintaining psychological well-being. Kim (1979) has associated communication behavior with acculturation. Collectively, the body of research on group and individual assimilation represents a challenging basis for theorizing. As will be seen, however, little of this research can be brought to bear on the theoretic problem that will be examined.

In the theory that follows, adaptation is defined in a narrower, more focused sense. It concerns potentially observable behaviors that occur when a hypothetical, culturally different dyad undertakes some task that one or both members wish to see completed. Such dyads occur throughout intercultural contact, whether involving immigrants, long-term sojourners, or short-term visitors. Brislin (1981) reports a common pattern of adaptive difficulties by a variety of sojourners, as does Torbiorn (1982). The effects of face-to-face adaptation, functional or nonfunctional, represent part of each individual's learning experience, thus partially conditioning the nature of future cross-cultural contacts with the same or different people. Not all cultural adaptation occurs in such miniencounters. Other extra-time factors, such as introspection, reaction to physical and social environment, use of mass-media, and the like, will together shape the total pattern. But the task-oriented dyad may represent a microcosm of the larger experience of adaptation. It lends itself readily to investigation, both by observation and through anecdotal accounts by participants.

FOUNDATIONS OF THEORY

Theoretical Approach

The theory presented here is based upon earlier work by the author, first presented in 1980 at a convention of the International Communication Association. At that time, it was observed that the development of intercultural communication as a field of study was based upon teaching, training, shared anecdotes, conferences, and a relatively small body of research, much of it descriptive or single-variable and with considerable disparity in definition and methodology. Publication of journal or semijournal theories derived from research thus necessarily was limited in quantity and scope. A volume titled *Intercultural Communication Theory* was published under the editorship of William B. Gudykunst (1983). The appearance of that book signaled that at least some scholars in the field were ready to undertake the role of theoretician. The production of a second volume five years later is indicative of further formalization and maturation of intercultural communication study. This latest work is in part a test of whether a sufficient body of knowledge has been created to support a variety of research-derived formal theory. In the case of face-to-face adaptation, the answer is marginally affirmative. Although the volume of sojourner research has increased considerably, there is still very limited attention to dyadic interaction. This revised adaptive theory is somewhat less speculative than its original form (Ellingsworth, 1983). It relies on rational generation, with some research and anecdotal support. Its goals are description and prediction; it stops short of the traditional aim of control associated with deterministic theory. Of the various formal systems of theory-building, the author continues to rely on the work of Robert Dubin (1969) as most appropriate to the task.

Dubin (1969), a sociologist, has presented an extensive methodology for theory construction. He stresses the importance of both rational and empirical contributions to theory construction and is concerned jointly with description and prediction to further the goal of understanding. Dubin's methodology is complex and comprehensive, but an abstracting of key elements—units, laws, propositions, and system state—provides a suitable basis for producing a focused theory of adaptive intercultural communication.

Elements of Theory

The most basic element of the Dubin method is the *thing*. Things are nominal entities that populate and make up a system. As Dubin states, "My thing can be anything," so long as it can be shown as part of the system. So the initial task in building a theory is to identify the things: people, events, objects, or whatever is relevant to describing the circumstances of the system chosen. Since these will produce clutter in their entirety, some evaluation and winnowing will be necessary before the final choice of things is completed.

After the things have been specified, next comes the *unit*, "a property of a thing." A thing can never be a unit, but a unit must arise from a thing. A unit is a repeated event or behavior capable of being assigned a value that at a given time may range from "absent" to "present in some degree," and can be described as "changed" or "unchanged" from the previous observation. A unit is, in a quite literal sense, a *variable*. It goes beyond attention to simple variation and takes its meaning from changes relative to changes in other units. At least two units are necessary for a theory, and the chosen number will depend on the complexity of the system being theorized about and the theorist's judgment about how much of the system can be meaningfully included. Units are connected by *laws of interaction* specifying how the units are related. Laws are not predictive, but arbitrarily describe the ongoing relationships of units. Within these lawlike relationships occur possibilities for predictive, correlative statements called *propositions*. Propositions are phrased in logical combinations of unit values—relationships labeled "more," "less," and "the same." Thus, propositions predict "the more of something... the less of something else," "the less... the more," "the less ... the same," and so forth for a total of nine possibilities. Not all of these are equally functional, because a change in one unit associated with no change in another may indicate the lack of a relationship.[1] Because it is not situation-based, a proposition is not directly testable by empirical methods, but can be analyzed into two or more testable hypotheses phrased according to the problem being investigated.[2]

One additional concept, *system state,* is employed to describe the constellation of all unit values as they exist at a particular time. The system state thus provides a summative judgment of the overall system functioning. In addition to this abridged apparatus of theory building, the other requisite before proceeding is a statement that defines and describes the system to which the concepts are to be applied.

System Definitions

The present adaptive, dyadic theory to follow employs a number of technical terms, which are first defined and then presented in the system description.

Foreignness is a concept central to the identification of intercultural interaction. It is the initial perception by one participant that the other is from a background different from his or hers, based on superficial observation of physical appearance, name, manner of speaking, dress and adornment, and other external tokens of cultural identity. Interaction will later reinforce or mitigate the initial perception of degree of foreignness. The term is entirely relative and nonprejudicial. It focuses on one person's perception of the other as culturally different.[3]

Communication style describes the individual's accustomed coding behavior in symbolic interaction, including verbal pattern (ranging from voice quality, vocal volume, and articulation through word choice and statement structure to accustomed use of a particular dialect or language) and nonverbal behavior (kinesic and proxemic mode and contact rituals).

Beliefs in this description are defined by Rokeach (1969, pp. 121-125) as "any simple proposition, conscious or unconscious, inferred from what a person says or does, capable of being preceded by the phrase 'I believe that . . .'" Cognitive beliefs represent a person's knowledge and the degree of agreement or disagreement with that knowledge. Affective beliefs underlie degree of arousal about an object or concept. Behavioral beliefs predispose to action. The three are inseparable and interactive.

As Rokeach describes it, the belief system is the total cognitive universe of a person's beliefs about the social world and about himself or herself.

In the description being presented, beliefs are asserted to have a cultural base growing out of nurture and conditioning (Rokeach, 1973). It is not assumed that each person from a particular culture has identical beliefs, but rather that similarity of beliefs is one of the things shared by members of a culture. When individuals from different cultures interact, they may become aware that some of the beliefs invoked by the other are drawn from a culture-based belief system different from their own and are not simply a matter of individual difference.

Adaptive behavior is any attempt to accommodate substantively and behaviorally to the perceived foreignness of the other participant. When this adaptation is regarded by others as sensitive, complimentary, and supportive, it will prove to be "functional." If it is perceived as gauche, compromising or even insulting, it can be labeled "nonfunctional" and may have an even more negative effect than an absence of effort to adapt. Because adaptive behavior is so central to this theory, it will be discussed in greater detail than will the other terms. The probable need for adaptive behavior is signaled by initial perception of foreignness. Adaptive behavior is a high-risk activity, especially in the initial stages of encounter when limited information about the other is available, yet it cannot be avoided or delayed very long.

The author recalls cases of adaptive behavior, both functional and nonfunctional. In a country with a strong religious orientation, he needed to see a government official. A convenient time in his travel schedule was Friday afternoon, when all government offices were closed for weekly religious observances. The sojourner suggested an appointment then, but quickly observed that it would probably not be convenient to the official because the latter would have to forego the scheduled worship. It happened that the official was a nonpracticing religionist who took the adaptive suggestion as a reproach of his lapsed piety. The appointment never took place. On another occasion, the sojourner opened an interview by praising the city architecture, and in particular a magnificent mosque that dominated the city center, which subsequent conversation revealed as the central railway station. The interaction continued, but now the burden of adaptation clearly became the responsibility of the visitor.

Another remembered and nonfunctional attempt at adaptation involved food preference. The author was responsible for the conduct of multinational training programs in the United States. This job included arranging for physical facilities. At a new venue, he met with the chef to explain the nature of the group and their dietary needs. Since many of the participants were from rice cultures, it was explained that a quantity of rice would be needed at each meal. The chef was eager to comply and the first lunch featured several large pans of Spanish rice, a dish including tomatoes, peppers, and spices, which went unrecognized. At a postlunch conference, the chef explained defensively that he knew these people were foreigners, that Spaniards were foreigners, and that fortunately he had a foreign rice recipe. A participant rice advisory committee was formed and the result was a satisfactory adaptation, after a notably nonfunctional beginning.

Some adaptive efforts are indeterminate in advance. In sojourns in Latin America and Southeast Asia, the author's use of inelegant but workable host-country language or expressions often was countered with requests to proceed in English, even when the host's competence in it was severely limited. Some people perceived the visitor's initiative as a pejorative reflection on their English ability; still others appeared pleased at the effort, but indicated that they preferred to practice their English.

Perhaps the most consistently appreciated adaptation was the sojourner's acceptance of local food, drink, and ritual beginnings. This can be a challenge when the opening custom is the ubiquitous powdered coffee made with lukewarm water and mixed equally with sweetened condensed milk. The most demanding experiences included the consumption of *durian*, a delicious tropical fruit with the odor of a pigpen and *balut*, a fertile duck egg just short of hatching. The Filipino hosts believed that only a "true Filipino at heart" could eat and enjoy *balut* and were gratified by the visitor's willingness. Another adaptation perceived as functional was prior knowledge of and expressed interest in historical and cultural sites not known as obvious tourist attractions and not associated with the colonialist past.

Participants are those who join in a task-oriented dyad. Because the encounter is not casual or fortuitous, one individual will have been the "initiator" of the contact and the other the "respondent."

Intercultural communication must be defined formally and also operationally with enough detail to identify cases for study. A simple and useful starting point is: "An interpersonal encounter may be designated as intercultural when the participants act as though they believe it is intercultural." Using prior accustomed intracultural communication style as a baseline, if a participant now alters communication style slightly (such as speaking more loudly and clearly) to markedly (such as switching to another dialect or language) he or she is indicating that the other individual appears "foreign" and that some adjustment in accustomed style is necessary in order for contact to be made. If the other also shows efforts at adaptive behavior, then the necessary condition for initiation of intercultural communication has occurred. Descriptive research is needed to determine what cues adaptive behavior and the extent to which cueing is normative or idiosyncratic. If cueing can be specified, then occurs the more sophisticated question of whether perceived degree of foreignness is correlated with magnitude of adaptive behavior. With this discussion, the initial definition may be more precisely stated as: "An interpersonal encounter is identifiable as intercultural while the participants are undertaking adaptive behavior based on their estimates of the foreignness of the other." If mutual adaptive behavior persists during the real-time encounter, then the whole interaction is classifiable as intercultural. If the participants discover that they share a communication style that is common to both, the situation will not become intercultural except as culture-based differences in belief are invoked and are adapted to. If adaptation in style and beliefs is needed, but one or both cease to make the effort, the situation is no longer within the bounds of intercultural communication as defined for these purposes.

System Description

The key elements of an interpersonal communication system are *participants, setting, purpose, process,* and *outcomes.* These are the *things,* in Dubin's (1969) terminology, from which events arise and can be specified as units. It is particular characteristic of these things in some situations that make them potentially intercultural.

Participants. An individual can be foreign only relative to someone else. The two must appear to one another as sufficiently different for a mutual cueing of foreignness. In addition, the participants will share some linguistic code at a level sufficient to make symbolic interaction possible. (The definition does not include translated or mediated situations, which require their own description and theory.) The effects of using a shared language that is primary to one and secondary or tertiary to the other will be discussed next as a part of Setting.

While such things as appearance and manner of speaking are observable tokens of cultural identity, intercultural communication is clearly more than a mutual alteration of style, because of the possibility of misunderstanding and disagreement arising from the latent belief systems of the participants.

If purposeful interpersonal communication is the acknowledgement of similarities and differences between participants and the symbolic negotiation of those differences that are related to the agenda of purposes, the same is also true of intercultural contacts. But in the latter case, tensions are increased when culture-based beliefs are invoked. Sources of ambiguity include possible erroneous identification of the "kind" of foreigner, incomplete or inaccurate knowledge of the cultural stereotype with which the other has been correctly identified, and the extent to which the individual actually conforms to the cultural stereotype. When the association is ongoing, there is repeated opportunity for learning, and then uncertainty about the other's style and beliefs will decline. The analysis presented here focuses on first-time encounters, which are less predictable and whose outcomes determine in part whether contact will be renewed. With a first-time encounter, adaptation will include a sensitive verbal probing of beliefs related to task or purpose to identify areas of commonality and of disagreement. This should occur before they are defensively invoked and become manifest problems. The invocation of culture-based beliefs is an important concern of this theory. It can be illustrated as follows. The author was involved for several years in an exit seminar for sojourners from many countries about to return home after a year or more in the United States. The major theme of the seminar involved cultural, social, and professional reentry by sojourners, with the goal of facilitating their role as agents of change. Discussion of these matters revealed a wide range of attitudes toward all the matters under consideration, including such classic culture-based values as time, fatalism, the place of the individual in society, and the possibility and desirability of change. In the climate of openness promoted by the seminar, discussion was usually temperate and productive. Occasionally, participants would spontaneously make strongly evaluative comments in response to statements of others, which would in turn produce nonverbal withdrawal, accompanied by the words "In my country . . ." This was often preliminary to a formal description of the virtues of the home society. Seminar staff members came to realize that the invocation signaled an end to productive discussion on the point at hand and that it would then be necessary to redirect the group to something else.

To summarize the discussion about participants, the intercultural system is composed of two persons, mutually perceptible as "foreign," whose communication styles signal that they possess underlying belief systems drawn from differing cultures.

Setting. Participants in intercultural communication come together in an environment that is both physical and social. In a perfect world they would meet as true peers, devoid of social role differences and power inequity, and at cultural parity, to achieve mutually developed equitable purposes. The contact would happen in a location neutral to both and be conducted in a language not native to either. If such settings do occur, they are probably rare enough not to be useful as a basis for theory. Most cases of intercultural communication occur in settings that contribute to inequity between participants, growing out of social role differences, language of choice, perceived power and influence, and locale. Setting disparity will probably be present when the language of choice is primary to one and secondary or tertiary to the other, and when one is physically on home ground and the other is a visitor. The net effect of such disparities will tip the balance of the relationship from equity toward hierarchy and influence both the process and its outcomes.

Purpose. This theory is about encounters that are purpose-related rather than fortuitous or casual. Consequently, purpose has existed for one or both participants before the encounter. The fact of cultural or national difference will often be a factor in initiating the encounter. Purposes arise from needs for cooperation, participation, or agreement in such areas as commerce, manufacturing, defense, education, science, technology, politics, agriculture, medicine, the arts, and scholarly research. As with interpersonal communication generally, the initiator will have in mind a purpose for seeking contact and the respondent will have in mind a reason for agreeing to participate. In intercultural communication, purpose and setting are interactive elements. If the initiator has an advantage in status or the potential for exercising power, he or she may be able to summon the other and state his or her purpose as a directive, and thus place the burden of adaptation on the respondent. If a potential respondent has a resource badly needed by the initiator, the respondent is in a power position and may impose the major obligation of adaptation on the initiator. If each has something the other needs, if their goals are separate and noncontradictory, or if there is a commonality of purpose that must be jointly pursued, adaptive responsibility will approach parity, and the most manifest cases of intercultural communication will occur.

Process. The process (or in Dubin's term, the *system state* at any particular time) of intercultural communication centers on adaptation. When things are going well—when style adaptation is functional and work is proceeding—latent belief differences are less likely to be manifested. Nonfunctional style adaptations may be followed by the invocation of belief-based disagreement. Another dynamic dimension of the system state is the use of communication strategies that grow out of relative congruence of purpose. When the parties agree that their interests are mutual or noncontradictory, cooperative strategies of work and adaptation will occur. When one needs something the other is reluctant to supply, persuasive strategies will appear, accompanied by increased adaptive behavior by the persuader. When there is considerable disparity in status or power, the strategy may become coercive and the burden of adaptation may shift from the "stronger" to the "weaker" to the point that intercultural communication is no longer occurring.

Outcomes. Interpersonal communication has both purpose-related and personal outcomes. Some involve the achievement, modification, or thwarting of original purposes and some concern the effects of the experiences on the participants. In intercultural communication the latter has special dimensions. Participants will have been responding not only to the other as an individual, but also to preexisting beliefs about what that group of "foreigners" is like. Thus an important outcome will be reinforcement or modification of prior cultural stereotypes and this learning will become a part of the cognitive resources for future encounters. Whether such learning later proves to be functional or nonfunctional will depend on the extent to which the next such "foreigner" conforms to the stereotype. Thus experience does not necessarily increase competence in intercultural communication, though it has the potential for doing so. Another important outcome of intercultural interaction is self-examination. Adaptation involves confronting not only the other, but also the self. In this process, the personal cultural stereotype is reinforced or modified, and this learning also becomes part of the background of the individual's future intercultural encounters.

Purpose-related outcomes in encounters in which cultural difference is present do not differ significantly from those of interpersonal communication in general, but their achievement may require more time and energy because of the potential need for adaptive behavior.

Theory Development

Before presenting the details of this adaptive theory, it is appropriate to review the abbreviated Dubin (1969) system in context. The things that make up the field are (1) two hypothetical *participants* who, at the time of the encounter, perceive one another as "foreigners," based on superficial observation of the other's appearance and manner of speaking; (2) the presence of some *purpose* for the encounter in the mind of at least one participant, or of both, though the purposes need not be identical; (3) the assumption of an ongoing *process* that changes as the interaction continues; (4) the assumption of outcomes that reflect the initial purpose(s) in some form, either modified or unmodified; and (5) the assumption of personal changes that have occurred in the participants as a result of the interaction.

The *units* are properties of these things that are capable of taking on values ranging from "absent" to "present in some amount." The units, therefore, must be expressible in nominal-level data terms to make possible the specification of changes in a unit that can be observed relative to changes in other units. The author has chosen nine units, two each related to context, adaptation, purpose, and strategy, plus one process unit.

The next step is generation of lawlike statements that specify which units are related to others in a causal or reciprocal way. A definitive body of research would be helpful here; in its absence, rationality, experience, and a measure of common sense must be employed. For eight units there are many arithmetic possibilities if both double and multiple combinations are considered. From this inventory of the possible, a selection of the most plausible has been made, resulting in seven laws for the theory.

Choice of units and laws fulfills the descriptive goal of the theory; for prediction, it is additionally necessary to generate propositions that assert the nature and direction of effects associated with changes in unit values. The number of propositions that can be logically generated from seven laws is indeterminate, because laws can produce more than one proposition. Here the process was related to the overall purpose of the theory, and 11 propositions were finally selected.

ADAPTATION IN INTERCULTURAL DYADS

As previously noted, this is a theory about potentially observable, real-time behaviors of a hypothetical, culturally different dyad oriented to some task that one or both wish to see completed. The range of possible circumstances or settings is very large and is minimally suggested by such encounters as a new immigrant wishing to buy an article of clothing, a tourist with passport or customs difficulties, an industrial representative who needs an appointment with an important government official, an academic researcher who plans to establish a research team in another country, a student sojourner meeting on arrival with an adviser to plan a degree program, a visitor who has unwittingly violated a local regulation or custom, a consular representative in initial contact on a trade agreement, a foreigner seeking medical treatment, or a U.S. Peace Corps volunteer arriving in the assigned village. At a substantive level, these are very different encounters; at another level, they share marked similarities that can be examined by a theory of adaptation.

Units

In the beginning, it is assumed that the minimal condition for an intercultural encounter—a mutual perception of foreignness by participants—has occurred. The following units then become relevant:

(1) *Status-Power*—the extent to which an imbalance in status or power is invoked during the task as an alternative to adaptive behavior.

(2) *Territorial behavior*—because the interaction will usually occur on the "turf" of one or the other participant, territorial behavior refers to the physical or psychological invoking of cues pointing to control of the environment.

(3) *Adaptation of communication style*—extent of alteration in normative coding behavior in order to meet assumed needs of the other. This alteration ranges in scope from vocal pattern through choice of another language or dialect and includes changes in kinesic and proxemic modes.[4]

(4) *Invocation of culture-based beliefs*—extent to which tension, frustration, or disagreement stimulates more general statements implying cultural superiority or inferiority.

(5) *Dyadic purpose*—extent to which participants discover their purposes to be mutually supportive or noncontradictory, as in a "nonzero-sum" game where both can win.

(6) *Individual purpose*—extent to which participants discover that one can gain only at cost to the other, as in a "zero-sum" game.

(7) *Purpose-related outcome*—a measure of task completion.

(8) *Participant-related outcome*—an indication of change in participants as a function of levels of adaptation during the interaction.

(9) *Process-related unit*—a summative estimate of the interaction of the various units at any given time, which provides an indicator of how things are going.

The eight units (not including the process-related unit) are next linked by laws. As might be expected in a theory on this theme, the adaptation of communication style unit is the central focus, with relationships shown between it and each of the other seven.

Laws

As previously noted, in the Dubin system, units are linked by statements that stipulate which units are centrally related and whether the relationship is directional or reciprocal. Laws form the basis for other predictions about changes in the system when there is an alteration in unit values.

In constructing this theory of dyadic intercultural adaptation, we are searching for relationships among variables that are reliable enough to be called laws. Although an examination of dyadic research has provided some guidance, much of it has focused on the solution of laboratory problems by peers, as contrasted with field situations in which the problems are real and are being negotiated by culturally different persons under varying conditions of setting and status. As noted before, the intercultural communication rubric likewise provides a limited research base. Yet if laws cannot be set down, formal theory cannot proceed.

The laws that follow were drawn largely from the author's field experience in Latin America while a researcher at Michigan State University, in South Asia as a researcher at the East-West Center, as a consultant with UNESCO, and through extensive individual travel to Europe and China. These ideas have been discussed with a number of experienced colleagues, notably Robert Worrall of the Population Council and Francis C. Byrnes and Mason Miller of Winrock International. These contacts have indicated that the assertions are not idiosyncratic and are sufficiently well-validated by experience to be called laws for purposes of theory generation.

Law 1. Adaptation of communication style is related to achievement of purpose.

When need for adaptation becomes apparent, the extent and functionality of such adaptation will have an important effect on how productive the interaction proves to be. This is true whether the interaction involves bargaining in a bazaar or negotiating a binational trade agreement.

Law 2. Adaptation of communication style is related to invocation of culture-based beliefs.

The goal of a purposive dyad is obviously the smooth completion of the agenda. Adaptation enables the dyad to remain focused on the task at hand and to minimize the possibility of a shift to the perceptions of major cultural difference between participants. But if tension or misunderstanding arises, each person has a convenient cultural bastion from which to invoke "In *my* country . . ." statements. Such utterances usually precede pronouncements of beliefs arising from the cultural system. In the process, the initial focus on task can be diluted or lost. So adaptation that keeps the invocation of differences in belief to a minimum is central to productive fulfillment of purpose.

Law 3. Compatible on noncontradictory purpose is related to the sharing of adaptive responsibility.

This law states that when a dyad must work together in order to achieve a mutually rewarding purpose, each member will equitably contribute to adaptive behavior. The same is true if the goals are reciprocal and noncompetitive.

Law 4. When one dyadic participant wants something that the other sees as being of little or no personal benefit and no quid pro quo emerges, then the adaptive burden remains with the initiator.

That is, unless the initiator can define the situation in terms of some shared or direct advantage to the other, adaptation remains firmly the responsibility of the individual who will benefit.

Law 5. When one participant holds the territorial advantage, the other has the burden of adaptation.

A home or workplace is a clear example of an area "owned" by one participant. This control may be mitigated by the host's behavior, such as moving away from a desk or work station or even adjourning to a cafe, but the host-visitor relationship will always be present to some extent and in productive dyads the visitor will continue to acknowledge his or her responsibility as primary adaptor.

Law 6. When one member of a dyad is clearly superior to the other in terms of status or power, the burden of adaptation will remain with the inferior throughout the interaction.

This seems to be true in both intracultural and cross-cultural situations. A motorist who has been stopped by a policeman and a foreign traveler passing through customs both display adaptive style unlike their normal communicative behavior with other strangers or with peers. North American professors and overseas students often experience some initial discomfort if the North American insists on a degree of informality in excess of what the student has been conditioned to expect from a person in that role.

In a reverse situation, North American visitors may believe that their home status will be transferred without loss into other environments or are simply unaware of the greater importance of status difference in some cultures. In summary, status/power difference defines the burden of adaptation, and a violation of this law can generate additional problems in task completion.

Law 7. Adaptation of communication style is related to changes in the participant's cognitions, self-image, and future perception of those from the other represented culture.

It is probably true that all human interaction is synonymous with change in the participants. If this is the case, then the effect is intensified in a bicultural dyad, especially where adaptation has been displayed. In the experience of working to fulfill a purpose, each person will learn more about how the other regards such cultural basics as time use, values, social organization, and ethics. As a result of contrastive interaction about some of these matters, each will also learn more about the system he or she represents. If adaptation is necessary for task completion, some changes will occur, both in self-perception and perception of the other, as the manifest parts of the culture are assigned greater or lesser importance. For example, status difference or the expected time needed to complete the task may eventually be perceived as having greater or lesser significance than was originally thought.

Propositions

Once a system has been described, defined, and bounded by laws, the basis has been laid for the theoretic predictions about the effect of changes within the system. When formulated, laws are assumed to possess external validity. By contrast, propositions are speculative statements about what might happen to a unit if a change occurred in another unit. Here the process is national, but subject to refinement. Two units related by one law can generate nine logical propositions, because each unit can take on values of "more," "unchanged," or "less." When the content is examined, however, it will be seen that two-thirds of the propositions are contradictory, since it is pointless to predict that an increase in Unit A will simultaneously produce an increase in Unit B, an unchanged condition in Unit B, and less of Unit B. Consequently it is necessary to inject field information in the form of research findings or experience to assess which of the predictions is most likely. In making the following choices, this theorist has relied mostly on his own experiences. The law from which the proposition arises is specified.

Proposition 1. An increase in amount of functional adaptive behavior will be accompanied by accelerated progress toward task completion (Law 1).

Once the need for adaptation has been recognized and undertaken by one or both participants, then the more that occurs the more progress will be made. This statement raises the logical question of whether adaptation can become excessive. The answer is that it probably is self-regulating. If it reaches the point of obsequiousness or servility by one party, it probably will have become nonfunctional and an invitation to exploitation by the other. This proposition generally predicts that more adaptation is better and will speed task completion.

Proposition 2. When adaptive behavior occurs and proves to be nonfunctional, the other participant will respond by invoking culture-based differences in belief (Law 2).

In an intracultural dyad, when one participant behaves in ways perceived by the other as gauche or condescending, the response may be to ignore or minimize, to respond in kind, or to accelerate emotional tension. Intercultural dyads in general tend to operate with more formality, and so personalizing the conflict is less likely. This proposition acknowledges that in an intercultural dyad, there is an additional response that can be employed. This response is to make statements that carry implied criticism and evaluation about the cultures represented. This response is predicted to be the most likely.

Proposition 3. The appearance of belief statements by one participant will be followed by accelerated adaptive behavior by the other (Law 2).

When nonfunctional behavior by one person is followed by an "in my country" response from the other, the first person will now attempt to make amends by increasing adaptive activity in an effort to compensate. If this is successful, the focus will narrow and the dyad will get on with the task. If not, little progress will occur.

Proposition 4. A shift from inequity toward parity in adaptive behavior will accelerate progress toward task completion.

When most or all of the adaptive effort is being displayed by one person, system functioning will depend on that person's ability to keep things moving. If the other now displays a willingness to assume some responsibility by adapting cognitively and stylistically, the work will move ahead more rapidly.

Proposition 5. When participants share a purpose, they will move toward equity in adaptation, regardless of status difference or territorial advantage (Law 3).

The motivation of wanting the same thing is predicted to generate willingness to adapt, even when one party holds an advantage in status/power or setting.

Proposition 6. When interaction reveals that only one person will benefit from task completion, that person will accelerate adaptive behavior (Law 4).

Two persons may undertake a task in which the outcome appears mutually beneficial. Further activity may reveal that this is not the case. The beneficiary, both to compensate and to achieve the purpose, will step forward as the principal adaptor.

Proposition 7. When one person has a territorial advantage, it will have limited effects on adaptation unless invoked; then the other person will display an increase in adaptation (Law 5).

The effect of "owning the turf" remains a latent factor, but when verbally or symbolically invoked it signals the other to increase adaptation.

Proposition 8. When the initiator has more status/power than the respondent, he or she will initially use that advantage as a substitute for adaptive behavior and may continue to do so throughout the interaction (Law 6).

This prediction is that the effect of difference in status is always present, whether or not it is openly invoked.

Proposition 9. The more adaptation displayed by a participant, the more change will occur in attitudes and perceptions concerning the other culture represented.

In the process of working out adaptive strategies, a person becomes more sensitized to the other culture and may become more aware of elements that he or she likes or dislikes.

Proposition 10. The more adaptation displayed by a participant, the more change that will occur in that person's perceptions of self and the culture he or she represents (Law 7).

In working out adaptive strategies, a person becomes more aware of liking or disliking elements that he or she represents. Thus learning and cultural awareness are a product of adaptation, for the self.

Propositon 11. As a summative prediction about the system state, invocation of culture-based beliefs will constitute the principal disruptive element; in its absence, functional adaptive behavior will compensate for status and territorially and mitigate the effects of problems with purpose.

DISCUSSION

As suggested earlier, this theory was developed to focus attention on the real-time, face-to-face dyad that constitutes a central locus for intercultural contact. Just as adaptation is a major factor in immigrant and sojourner experience, so adaptation as defined here is central to productive work in a dyad. Adaptation also represents a learning laboratory that will feed information into future intercultural contacts. At the first level, this theory is *descriptive*. It proposes the existence of an hypothetical, tasked-oriented dyad in which there is a mutual perception of foreignness leading to the realization that differences must be adapted to or compensated for. Who will do this, and how, is linked to purpose, setting, and status/power. If things go wrong, a recourse is to retreat into statements about the relative merit of the two cultures. Eventually the task is completed, or not, and the participants are changed to some degree. This description also offers some explanation of the system and how it has been observed to operate.

As a sojourner and a teacher-trainer of the subject, the author has felt the need for a cognitive structure that could be used for both participation in and observation of dyads. This was the motivation for proposing and developing the theory. The descriptive elements are potentially useful as a model for short-term, intensive training programs. It would be possible to simulate a variety of the conditions described, both live and videotaped, and encourage the development and evaluation of coping strategies. A structured training activity that begins with attention to mutual perception of foreignness and proceeds through several stages in which purpose, setting, and status are manipulated can simulate the conditions described and predicted in the theory. Conditions can be specified as involving any two specific cultures or as a culture-general contact. Such a training program needs little in the way of facilities or instrumentation and could be operated with almost any number of trainees.

Aside from didactic applications in observation and instruction, this theory also has heuristic potential for research and further theory development. Descriptive research is needed for such concepts as foreignness, adaptation, and individual change. For more formal research, the propositions invite hypothesis generation and testing. Since this is a generic theory of adaptation, it can open the possibility of more specific adaptive theories focusing on code, context, attribution, and phenomenology. The author knows of no published research that has been attributed directly to this theory, but he and some students have examined initial intercultural encounters in professional social work in Hawaii. The reported time for perception of foreignness ranges from 30-60 seconds; voice quality, skin color, and nonverbal cues were the most frequently identified elements in perception of foreignness. Further possibilities for research include attempting to index relative amount of foreignness, relative degree of adaptation, parameters of functional and nonfunctional behavior and the levels of intensity generated by them, the kinds of activity that occur when nonfunctional adaptation has taken place, and the ways that intracultural dyads differ from intercultural pairs on some of the indicated dimensions.

In summary, research published since 1980 has lent some support to the original concept of real-time adaptive theory, but the idea remains more rational than data-based, partly because adaptation is predominantly defined and researched as changes made by an individual in a new environment, rather than as a shared or shifting responsibility involving two participants. It appears that the theory has potential utility as a structure for teaching and training, as an impetus to further research, and as a beginning point for more specialized theorizing.

NOTES

1. For example, given the units of "time spent in watching U.S.-produced situation comedies" and "use of U.S. idiomatic expressions" a proposition would predict that the more time spent by a non-American in watching U.S. situation comedies, the more idiomatic expressions would be used in conversation with an American visitor.

2. If the research problem were related to the diffusion of idiomatic U.S. Black English by means of television, an hypothesis might specify particular video programs in which most of the actors were black.

3. This concept is akin to George Simmel's idea of "The Stranger" employed by William B. Gudykunst and Young Y. Kim (1984). It should be rendered as "strangerness" and differs from Simmel in that each party is a stranger to the other, while Simmel describes the stranger as a newcomer to a community. The members view him as a stranger but he does not call them strangers, because they are on home ground.

4. The author is indebted to the late Ralph Cooley and to Vernon E. Cronen and Robert Shuter whose criticism of the 1983 version of this theory noted the limited attention to code as a significant element in style adaptation. See Cooley (1983) and Cronen and Shuter (1983).

REFERENCES

Blalock, H. M. (1982). *Race and ethnic relations*. Englewood Cliffs, NJ: Prentice-Hall.
Brislin, R. (1981). *Cross-cultural encounters*. New York: Pergamon.

Cooley, R. (1983). Codes and contexts: An argument for their description. In W. Gudykunst (Ed.), *Intercultural communication theory* (pp. 241-252). Beverly Hills, CA: Sage.

Cronen, V. & Shuter, R. (1983). Forming intercultural bonds. In W. Gudykunst (Ed.), *Intercultural communication theory* (pp. 89-118). Beverly Hills, CA: Sage.

Dubin, R. (1969). *Theory-building.* New York: Free Press.

Ellingsworth, H. (1983). Adaptive intercultural communication. In W. Gudykunst (Ed.), *Intercultural communication theory* (pp. 195-204). Beverly Hills, CA: Sage.

Gallo, P. J. (1974). *Ethnic alienation: The Italian Americans.* Cranbury, NJ: Farleigh Dickinson University Press.

Gans, H. J. (1962). *The urban villagers.* New York: Free Press.

Glazer, N., & Moynihan, D. P. (1970). *Beyond the melting pot.* Cambridge, MA: MIT Press.

Gudykunst, W. (Ed.). (1983). *Intercultural communication theory.* Beverly Hills, CA: Sage.

Gudykunst, W. & Kim, Y. (1984). *Communicating with strangers.* New York: Random House.

Kim, Y. Y. (1979). Toward an interactive theory of communication-acculturation. In D. Nimmo (Ed.), *Communication yearbook 3* (pp. 435-455). New Brunswick, NJ: Transaction.

Landis, D. & Brislin, R. (Eds.). (1983). *Handbook of intercultural training* (Vol. 2). New York: Pergamon.

Phizacklea, A. (1984). A sociology of migration or 'race relations'? A view from Britain. *Current Sociology, 32*(3), 199-209.

Rokeach, M. (1969). *Beliefs, attitudes and values: A theory of organization and change.* San Francisco: Jossey-Bass.

Rokeach, M. (1973). *The nature of human values.* New York: Free Press.

Spindler, G. D. (1955). *Sociological and psychological processes in Menomini acculturation.* Berkeley: University of California Press.

Spiro, M. E. (1955). The acculturation of American ethnic groups. *American Anthropologist, 57,* 1240-1252.

Torbiorn, I. (1982). *The nature of human values.* New York: Free Press.

12

The Convergence Theory and Intercultural Communication

D. LAWRENCE KINCAID   •   *Johns Hopkins University*

A general, convergence model of communication is presented in which the cyclical process of information sharing among two or more individuals is described. The relationship among the physical, psychological, and social aspects of communication is delineated. The convergence principle and the basic cybernetic process involved in information processing are used to deduce two complementary, general theorems of communication. The theorems specify the conditions under which intercultural communication will lead to a convergence between members of the cultures involved, producing a state of greater cultural uniformity within both cultures as a whole. Empirically testable hypotheses are developed that apply to the convergence between an immigrant subculture and its host culture, to convergence within the immigrant culture, and to divergence between the immigrant culture and its original culture over time. Mathematical representations are proposed for the first two hypotheses, and tested with data from a previous study of Korean immigrants in the United States. And finally, the implications of the convergence theory for the field of intercultural communication and for the study of acculturation are discussed.

In Dostoyevsky's classic novel, *Crime and Punishment,* near the end of the story, Raskolnikov has a vivid dream while recovering from a severe illness in a prison hospital. In the dream, a horrible plague descends upon all of Europe, a plague that affected the mind and drove everyone insane.

> But never had men considered themselves . . . so completely in possession of the truth . . . their decisions . . . their moral convictions so infallible. . . . All were excited and did not understand one another. . . . Each thought he alone had the truth. (Dostoyevsky, 1866/1950, p. 528)

The social system disintegrated rapidly. Soldiers called to restore order attacked one another. Farmers abandoned their fields. All commerce came to a halt

because everyone proposed his own ideas . . . and they could not agree. . . .
Men met in groups, agreed on something, swore to keep together, but at
once began on something quite different from what they had proposed.
(p. 529)

This dream has important implications for the study of human
communication, especially for intercultural communication. First,
good literature has important insights for the human sciences. Second,
the story reveals how absolute certainty renders communication
inoperable, resulting in some of humankind's greatest inhumanity
toward itself, a point so eloquently made by J. Bronowski (1974) in
Ascent of Man. At times intercultural communication seems to
approach this extreme, when the intercultural assumptions are so
divergent and the intracultural certainty so high that communication is
very ineffective or does not seem to work at all.

And finally, the dream itself describes a world in which the
communication process as we know it ceases to function. In this sense
the dream is analogous to the physical world with the force of gravity
removed: Stones roll uphill as well as downhill, nothing stays in its
place, and nothing works as it did before. Such an analogy suggests that
there must be some basic principle of communication without which it
simply would not function as we know it.

In this chapter we will examine such a principle, the *principle of
convergence.* It is a fundamental principle of human communication in
the same sense as "light travels in a straight line" is a basic principle of
geometrical optics (Toulmin, 1960, pp. 83-85). To give up such a
principle would involve abandoning the study as well as the practice of
communication as we know it. Hence, it is not open to empirical
falsification in any straightforward way.

A diagram of communication as a convergence process was introduced in 1975 (Kincaid & Schramm, 1975). A complete model of
communication as convergence soon followed (Kincaid, 1979, Rogers &
Kincaid, 1981). A mathematical theory of communication and cultural
convergence appeared in Volume 7 of this annual (Barnett & Kincaid,
1983), followed by an empirical test of the theory with Korean
immigrants in the United States (Kincaid, Yum, Woelfel, & Barnett,
1983). Since then the implications of the principle of new communication technology and cultural diversity (Kincaid, 1983), and for self-
organization and cultural evolution (Kincaid, 1987) have been
articulated.

The main objectives of this chapter are to reformulate the basic concepts, principles, and propositions of the convergence theory and to reexamine its implications for intercultural communication. All the terms of the theory are defined. Theoretical propositions are derived from key terms and basic principles, but not in an axiomatic or logical-deductive form. It is the *terms* themselves in statements at one level, not the statements made at other levels (Toulmin, 1960, p. 85). And finally, the theory will be applied to the acculturation of Korean immigrants in the United States.

BASIC CONCEPTS OF THE CONVERGENCE THEORY

At the highest level of abstraction, the theory rests upon the intuitive, presupposed principle of convergence. "Convergence" implies that at least two or more "things" are moving toward one point, toward one another, toward a common interest, or toward uniformity. Movement implies both process and time. Movement *toward* a point does not imply meeting at that point—only the direction of change is implied. In actual communication, this is the direction of change which is normally expected, and is very often its result. The principle of convergence states that if two or more individuals share information with one another, then over time they will tend to converge toward one another, leading to a state of greater uniformity. "Toward one another" and "greater uniformity" do not mean perfect identity or absolute uniformity. They describe only the direction of movement and a level of greater uniformity relative to a previous state in the process.

On what alternative principle or expectation could a theory of communication be built? The logical possibilities are few: divergence, random or chance fluctuations, contingency upon outside factors, and ignorance. The first implies that communication itself is a process that creates differences rather than reduces them. The second implies unpredictability or chaos, that communication is not subject to any regularity of outcome. The third implies that the outcome of communication is contingent upon factors outside the process of communication itself. The last possibility implies no knowledge, or perhaps an unwillingness to make even an informed guess.

Successful theory development requires that the most likely alternative be assumed so that its logical consequences can be derived and tested. The convergence theory proposes that communication theory be based upon the principle of convergence, and then developed by discovering which conditions facilitate or impede convergence, rather than the other way around.

With the principle of convergence as an initial assumption, the following terms may be defined:

Definition 1: *Process* is a change of state over time that leads toward a particular result.

Definition 2: *Information* is a physical difference that affects uncertainty in a situation in which a choice exists among a set of alternatives.

Definition 3: To *share* is to experience something with someone else.

Definition 4: *Convergence* is a process of movement toward one point, toward one another, toward a common interest, or toward uniformity.

Convergence of two objects toward one another implies simultaneous divergence of these two objects from any other objects not involved in the process. It also implies a prior divergence of the two objects at some point in their history.

These first four terms plus the convergence principle may be combined to produce a general definition of communication which is applicable to intercultural communication:

Definition 5: *Communication* is a process in which two or more individuals share information and converge toward a state of greater uniformity.

The convergence model was developed to describe the stages or steps involved when individuals experience the same information, in other words, when they communicate with one another about the same topic (Kincaid, 1979; Rogers & Kincaid, 1981). A modified version of this model is presented in Figure 12.1.

One of the unique features of this model is that it shows the relationship among the three levels of reality involved in the process of communication. *Reality* is presupposed in this discussion, and like the terms *movement* and *point* is assumed. The meaning of the three types of reality, however, may be inferred from the components that comprise them. The psychological aspects of communication consist of the subprocesses of perceiving, recognizing, understanding, and believing.

Information already has been defined as a physical difference. Such differences take the form of shapes or patterns created in any physical medium, such as sound waves in speech; those involved in audio or visual media such as radio, telephones, television, cinema; and so forth.

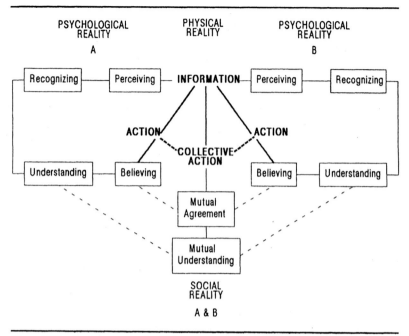

Figure 12.1 Basic components of the convergence model of communication.
(Adapted from Kincaid, 1979; Rogers & Kincaid, 1987)

Such a definition is broad enough to include all nonverbal information as well, from differences in the way one touches another person to the form of physical gestures. As the model suggests, information and action form a unity because all action is informative to the extent that it is a physical difference or pattern that has the potential of being perceived, recognized, interpreted, believed, and acted upon.

Definition 6: *Perceiving* is the process of becoming aware of a physical difference (information) through one's senses.

Definition 7: *Recognizing* is the process of identifying a previously known form or pattern (information) that has been perceived.

Definition 8: *Interpreting* is the process of understanding the meaning of a form or pattern (information) that has been recognized.

Definition 9: *Believing* is the process of accepting a particular interpretation as valid.

Definition 10: *Mutual understanding* is a state in which two or more individuals share to some degree a similar interpretation of information that they have shared.

Definition 11: *Mutual agreement* is a state in which two or more individuals to some degree jointly accept as valid a mutual understanding that has been reached.

Definition 12: *Action* and *collective action* are the overt behavior of an individual and the coordinated, overt behavior of two or more individuals, respectively.

Perceiving, recognizing, interpreting, and believing are all decision processes that take place under some degree of uncertainty. A complete discussion of each component may be found in Kincaid (1979) and Rogers and Kincaid (1981). In the simplest possible terms, each decision subprocess may be conceived as a decision that reduces uncertainty in the previous stage. A physical difference (pattern) beyond some threshold creates uncertainty in an observer that poses the question, "Is something there?" Detection of a sound, for example, would make one wonder if someone had actually spoken or not. Answering the question, "yes," reduces that uncertainty, but *at the same time* it creates uncertainty about *what* was said. This next level of information processing is a problem of pattern recognition. The fact that more than one alternative is possible creates uncertainty, and requires another choice. Supposing that the answer to the question, "What was spoken?" is the phrase, "excuse me," then uncertainty is reduced about what it was (by a decision), creating at the same time a new level of uncertainty about what it means.

Understanding what something means is the resolution of semantic uncertainty. "Excuse me" has a variety of possible interpretations. Although uncertainty about which one applies can be left unresolved (perhaps to avoid making a mistake), usually some choice is necessary to take an appropriate action. Answering the question, "What does it mean?" reduces semantic uncertainty, immediately posing a question (raising uncertainty) about whether that interpretation is valid: "Is that a valid interpretation?" An affirmative answer constitutes belief in that interpretation as opposed to others. As the model suggests, one acts on one's interpretations and beliefs about the world, or more precisely, on one's *information* about the world. Action itself involves uncertainty ("What should I do or say about it?"), which is resolved by taking action.

Thus far, the model has described a series of purely individual, psychological processes. Communication, however, is social behavior. Moreover, the decisions reached by each individual are usually tentative approximations. That is, residual uncertainty remains. If this residual uncertainty is still too high to act upon, additional information is sought. Continuing with the preceding simple example, one can respond (act) by directly asking the other person, "Excuse you for what?" Or, in general, "What do you mean by that?" The answer constitutes new information that is processed through the same steps as before. The other way to obtain more information is to act on one's best estimate of what was said, and to see if that decision is confirmed or not. Both of these actions initiate another cycle of information processing *in coordination with* the other person.

Several such coordinated cycles of information processing are often experienced in communication. Some of the new information generated in each cycle functions as feedback that is used to further reduce residual uncertainties. Some of the new information may also increase uncertainty, or introduce new uncertainty about a different topic, which then becomes subject to the same processes of reduction.

According to the convergence model, then, communication is a cybernetic process in which two or more individuals share information with one another, reducing each one's own uncertainty not only about what the other person means but also about what one means oneself. From the perspective of two or more persons taken *collectively,* the initial number of alternative interpretations, beliefs, and behavior among them is expected to diminish over time as a result of this cyclical process of information sharing. A state of greater uniformity, or the successive reduction of diversity, is the result toward which the process of communication leads (see Definition 1). Feedback is much more than "knowledge of results." It is a process crucial to all forms of communication.

> Definition 13: *Feedback* is a diminishing series of under-and-over corrections converging on a goal.

The goal referred to in the definition of feedback may or may not be consciously pursued. Reducing error or uncertainty is inherently part of information processing. If one is actively attempting to interpret what someone says, one is automatically involved in an effort to reduce alternatives (hence, uncertainty), and arrive at the "correct" or most appropriate one. The collective outcome is convergence over time toward a state of greater uniformity or less diversity.

Sharing, uniformity, and *diversity* are all familiar terms in most definitions of culture. To extend the convergence model from the microlevel analysis of dyadic or small group communication to the level of communities, societies, or cultures requires some mediating phenomena as well as additional conceptual tools. Communication "networks" provide that necessary bridge.

Definition 14: "A *communication network* consists of interconnected individuals who are linked by patterned flows of information." (Rogers & Kincaid, 1981, p. 75)

Although individuals live in large communities and societies, at an intermediate level they are embedded within interpersonal networks that are created and maintained by communication. If extended indefinitely, a whole community, whole society, and even the entire global community may be conceived of as one communication network. In actuality, these large-scale networks are always reducible to regional and local subnetworks of greater density characterized by a flow of the same information *within* their local boundaries greater than *between* them.

Mass communication has become one of the important sources of information for such local networks. In fact, members of the same local networks tend to share exposure to, and the content of, the same mass media. Hence, the mass media can be included as extensions of such local networks and one of the means by which they share information.

At present, these local networks consist of the three principal (overlapping) forms of human organization: organizations, communities, and cultures. *Organization* itself tends to be defined as a "complex pattern of communication and relationships in a group of human beings" (Simon, 1976, p. xvii). A community is usually thought of as an interacting population of individuals living in a particular area with a common history and common interests. Given the close relationship between communication and culture, it is not surprising that both types of collectivities—organizations and communities—are considered to have their own "cultures."

Culture probably has been defined in more ways by more scholars than any other term in the social sciences, and it is also the principal concern of the humanities. Culture is used by some as a process identical to communication, by others as equivalent to a group of people, and by others as a set of artifacts of a group of people. Recently, the trend has shifted from material, extrinsic artifacts to intrinsic aspects.

Definition 15: *Culture* consists of the meanings, beliefs, values, sentiments, and behavior that are shared by a group of people and transmitted from one generation to the next.

A key attribute of culture, often overlooked, is that it is not a property of individuals: It is something *shared* to some degree by a *collectivity* of individuals. If everyone shares the same understandings to the same degree, we refer to it as a uniform culture. If not everyone shares the same understandings or shares them to a different degree, we refer to it as a diverse culture. All real cultures are somewhere between perfect uniformity and diversity. Thus one of the most important aspects of any culture is the statistical distribution of meanings, beliefs, values, and behavior shared by its members. The distribution of a strong, relatively uniform culture is characterized by a low statistical variance. This low variance within cultures is not a fixed property; it fluctuates over time. The shape of its distribution is a result of communication. Regardless of the strength of a collectivity's culture, by definition it will have a higher degree of internal homogeneity *within* itself than between it and other distinct cultures.

The delineation of the boundaries separating local networks, communities, and cultures is usually imprecise and sometimes arbitrary, but meaningful, nevertheless, for the layperson and social scientist alike. Fewer connections and lower communication between such units is one indication of their relatively separate identities.

Definition 16: *Intercultural communication* is communication between members of relatively diverse cultural groups.

This definition is consistent with that proposed by Sarbaugh (1979; see Sarbaugh's chapter in this volume). The study of intercultural communication is concerned with the problems, as well as with the differences, in communication that are created by that relatively higher degree of diversity. The particular problems that have been studied include language, nonverbal patterns, perceived similarity, self-disclosure, adjustment and acculturation, global homogenization, conflict, stereotypes, and competence and effectiveness.

THE CONVERGENCE THEORY AND INTERCULTURAL COMMUNICATION

One of the rarely articulated assumptions of the study of intercultural communication is that the initial differences that affect communication between members of different cultures are expected to diminish over time with frequent contact. Observation of this phenomenon worldwide has generated some anxiety over the possibility of a gradual homogenization of global culture. As suggested here, this is a problem of maintaining the boundaries between the communication networks of distinct cultures. To protect local (ethnic) cultures, Barth (1969) suggested that boundaries or a set of prescriptions must be established to control communication between them in order to insulate parts of their respective cultures from confrontation, modification, and eventual convergence. Levi-Strauss (1956) specified three ways to prevent convergence: (1) have each one deliberately introduce differences within its own group, (2) bring in new parties from outside whose diversities are different, and (3) allow antagonistic political and social systems to block or reduce communication across cultural boundaries.

The suggestions to protect cultural diversity imply that once the boundaries restricting communication between members of distinct cultures are relaxed or removed, then cultural convergence is inevitable. Such an implication is consistent with our basic definition of communication as a cybernetic process of convergence. The theory involved can be clearly stated by specifying ideal conditions in which the boundaries around the participants are relatively closed and communication within the boundaries is either completely restricted or unrestricted (Kincaid, 1987; Kincaid et al., 1983).

Theorem 1: In a relatively closed social system in which communication among members is unrestricted, the system as a whole will tend to *converge* over time toward a state of greater cultural *uniformity.*

Theorem 2: In a relatively closed social system in which communication among members is restricted, the system as a whole will tend to *diverge* over time toward a state of greater cultural *diversity.*

Together the two theorems make explicit the assumptions of intercultural contact described here. At the dyadic level of communication, these theorems are consistent with the principle of convergence and the cybernetic process.

For diverse cultural groups in contact, the statistical measure of variance is an appropriate measure of the degree of uniformity or diversity. Computation of variance around a mean requires continuous measures of the beliefs, values, and behavior of a particular culture. For discrete, discontinuous measures, statistical entropy can be used (Kincaid, 1987). Diversity corresponds to higher levels of entropy and uniformity to lower levels of entropy. The formula for statistical entropy is identical to Shannon and Weaver's (1949) formula for information. Greater uncertainty in their formulation corresponds to a higher aggregate level of diversity, lower uncertainty to a lower aggregate level of diversity.

In more familiar terms, in relatively strong, homogeneous cultures one can be more certain about what values, beliefs, and behavior to expect. In communication within a uniform culture, a smaller number ,of beliefs, values, and behaviors are expressed by a greater proportion of members compared to communication within a diverse culture or between cultures. In studies of cultural evolution, this factor is referred to as a "frequency-dependent bias." It is considered as one of the main causes of cultural evolution (Boyd & Richerson, 1985).

In the case of the immigration of some members of one culture into the local community of another culture, conditions are created that approach the ideal conditions specified in Theorem 1. Therefore, a hypothesis may be constructed that can be empirically tested.

> Hypothesis 1: If communication between members of an immigrant cultural group and the host culture is unrestricted, then over time, the values of the immigrant group and the host culture will converge toward a state of greater uniformity.

The change is expected to be inversely proportional to the relative sizes of their respective populations. Thus we would expect much greater movement of the immigrant group toward the values of the host culture than vice versa. The initial impact of the input of a proportionately small number of immigrants into a culture is to increase the overall level of diversity in the host culture. The proportionately greater number of members from the host culture, the frequency-dependent bias that that implies, and the general convergence principle of communication combine to reduce this initial diversity over time. This outcome is expected to the extent that communication is relatively unrestricted between members of the two cultures, and communication is relatively restricted between members of the immigrant culture and their original culture. The latter condition simply reiterates that the immigrants become part of the relatively bounded society of the host culture.

These conditions apply to a greater extent to the children of immigrants than to their parents. Thus one would hypothesize that convergence among the second generation would be greater than among the first generation. This amounts to a restatement of the "melting pot" theory of assimilation, but with the conditions for homogenization specified as well as the conditions required to maintain cultural diversity. Communication among the first generation of immigrants themselves is usually greater than that between the immigrants and the host culture. Language similarity, geographical proximity, and pre-existing social networks facilitate communication within the immigrant culture and discourage (but do not completely restrict) intercultural communication. Thus while sufficient conditions for convergence exist between the two cultures, the relatively bounded nature of the immigrant group allows them to continue for some time as a relatively distinct subculture within the host culture. If this is the case, then we would also predict some cultural convergence within the immigrant culture, and divergence between the immigrant culture and its original culture.

Hypothesis 2: If communication within a relatively closed immigrant group is unrestricted, then over time the values of the immigrant group will converge toward a state of greater uniformity.

Hypothesis 3: If communication between an immigrant group and its former culture is restricted, then over time the values of the immigrant group will diverge from its original culture.

Together Hypotheses 2 and 3 describe the process of cultural evolution by means of migration. Historically, groups that migrated to other geographical regions became isolated from their original culture and thereafter evolved a distinct culture of their own. This phenomenon is the source of most of the diversity found in the world today. Today almost all migration is into a larger, preexisting host culture rather than into unoccupied territory. Thus the two processes of convergence operate side by side:

(1) convergence between immigrants and the host culture, and
(2) convergence within the immigrant culture and divergence between the immigrant culture and its former culture.

In the next section, mathematical representations of the theory are presented that correspond to the first two hypotheses. Then they will be tested with empirical data from the study of Korean immigrants to the United States. No data were available from Korea with which to test the third hypothesis.

APPLICATION OF THE CONVERGENCE THEORY
TO THE ACCULTURATION OF IMMIGRANTS
TO THE UNITED STATES

Convergence of Immigrants to the Host Culture

The convergence theory of communication was expressed mathematically by Barnett and Kincaid (1983) as a mechanical analogy of a damped harmonic oscillator, such as that constituted by a spring, mass, and dashpot (Hypothesis 1). Given a means of measuring the aggregate conceptual or value configuration of two cultures in a metric multidimensional space, and the means to compare the overall difference between them in terms of a metric distance measure, then it is possible to apply this mathematical model to the motion of one culture relative to the other. In its simplest form the process may be modeled by the equation

$$m\ddot{x} + C\dot{x} + kx = 0 \qquad [1]$$

where the m is the concept's mass, C is a velocity-dependent linear damping force, k is a linear restoring force, x is the position of the concept measured from an equilibrium position, and $\dot{x}$ and $\ddot{x}$ are, respectively, the first and second derivatives with respect to time of the displacement from equilibrium, corresponding to the velocity and acceleration of the concept. The equation is of homogeneous form (set equal to 0), and thus represents a closed system with no forces acting on the converging system.

The equation describes the motion of an object oscillating about an equilibrium point, and hence is suitable for the description of a subculture converging toward an equilibrium point represented by the host culture. In the equation, m, C, and k are constants whose values are measured empirically. The coefficient m (mass) represents the extent the subculture resists acceleration, that is, changes in its rate of convergence toward the host culture. C represents a linear damping force that functions as a resistance to change, like friction. The linear restoring force, k, indicates the strength of the forces compelling the subculture toward the position of the host culture. In the case of a physical object distended from a spring, k is the restoring force produced by extending the spring by one unit. In the case of acculturation, k represents the forces of change produced by intercultural communication between the subculture and host culture.

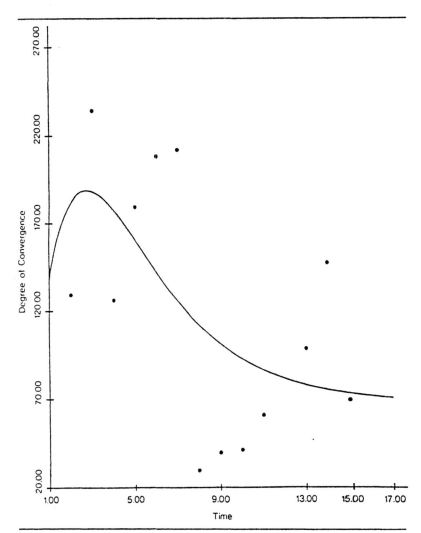

Figure 12.2 Degree of convergence by time in the United States. (Source: Kincaid and others, 1983)

Kincaid and associates (1983) tested this model on the acculturation of Korean immigrants in Hawaii (see also Kincaid & Yum, 1987; Yum, 1982, 1984). Values of Koreans and the host culture were measured by means of direct magnitude estimates of the differences among eight Eastern and Western values—success, happiness, individual freedom, saving face, sense of authority, family, children, and divorce—and three personal points of reference—me, Americans, and the term for one's own ethnic identity (Koreans, Japanese, Caucasians, and so on). Their relative configurations were scaled in metric multidimensional space by means of the Galileo (TM) computer program (Woelfel & Fink, 1980). The collective value configuration of the host culture was used as the equilibrium position toward which the values of the immigrant group were expected to converge according to the model (equation 1). In this test, the host culture was composed of Caucasians, Japanese, Filipinos, Samoans, and Koreans weighted in proportion to their populations. The value configuration of the Korean immigrant group was broken into 15 subgroups according to the number of years they had lived in the United States (1-15 years). The overall distance between Koreans and the host culture was calculated year by year, and the results were treated as a form of motion analogous to damped harmonic motion.

Depending upon the relative values of the coefficients in the equation, the equation could have three different solutions. If the linear damping force, C, is great relative to m and k ($C^2 > 4mk$), then the system is overdamped. If the product of the mass and restoring force is large relative to the linear damping force ($C^2 < 4mk$), then the system is underdamped. And finally, if the linear damping force is equal to m and k ($C^2 = 4mk$), then the system is critically damped.

The equations representing each of these possibilities were tested against the data using a nonlinear curve-fitting program (APPL:SSQFIT) that minimizes the sum of the squared errors of the curve from the data. The plot of the underdamped model (with an intercept of 65) is shown in Figure 12.2. This was the best fitting model with the most reasonable assumptions. It accounted for 40% of the variance over the 15-year period, which, for purposes of comparison, was 15 percentage points, or 60% higher than a simple linear regression model. The results are described in greater detail in Kincaid et al. (1983).

Convergence Within an Immigrant Culture

An alternative form of the convergence theory was developed that is applicable to Hypothesis 2, convergence within an immigrant culture (Kincaid, 1987). The model was originally expressed in terms of statistical entropy, S, as measured by the classical formula, $S = -\Sigma p_i \log_n p_i$, for discontinuous measures of culture. The statistical measure for variance, $V = \Sigma (X_i - \overline{X})/N - 1$, is also an appropriate measure of entropy of diversity within a culture when continuous

TABLE 12.1
Average Coefficient of Variation
of Each Value for Korean Immigrants
after 1-7 and 8-15 Years of Acculturation

Value	1-7 Yrs. (N = 255)	8-15 Yrs. (N = 35)	Difference	% Decrease
Individual freedom	1.17	0.78	-0.40	-33.9
Americans	1.11	0.73	-0.38	-34.6
Family	1.49	1.09	-0.41	-27.1
Me	1.26	0.94	-0.32	-25.6
Koreans	1.13	0.85	-0.29	-25.2
Success	1.25	0.95	-0.29	-23.8
Children	1.56	1.19	-0.37	-23.8
Saving face	1.06	0.83	-0.23	-21.7
Happiness	1.51	1.20	-0.31	-20.3
Divorce	1.03	0.90	-0.13	-12.3
Sense of authority	0.98	0.88	-0.10	-10.3
All values	1.23	0.94	-0.29	-23.6

measures are used. According to Theorem 1 and its application in Hypothesis 2, intracultural communication among immigrants themselves will lead to a convergence of cultural values over time toward a state of greater uniformity. Greater uniformity is indicated by a reduction in variance. From one state to another, A to B, this change can be expressed simply as

$$V_B \leq V_A \qquad [2.1]$$
$$V_B - V_A \leq 0 \qquad [2.2]$$

where the variance, V, of state B is less than or equal to the variance of a prior state, A, or the difference in variance between state B and state A is less than or equal to zero. When time is treated as continuous, the same relationship may be expressed in terms of the differential equation:

$$\dot{V} \leq 0 \qquad [2.3]$$

where the first derivative of the variance, $\dot{V}$, with respect to time is less than or equal to zero; that is, decreases with time toward complete uniformity.

This proposition was tested with the data from the study of Korean immigrants just noted. For Hypothesis 2, an analysis was conducted of the variance of 55 paired-comparison judgments of the distances among the 11 values. The total sample was divided into two groups, immigrants that had been in the United States for 1-7 years, and those who had been here for 8-15 years. For Hypothesis 2 to be confirmed, the variances for the group that has been in the United States longer should be lower than for the group that has spent less time in the United States.

To control for changes in the means from the first time period to the second, the coefficient of variation (standard deviation divided by the mean) was used in place of the variance itself. The results are shown in Table 12.1. The average coefficient of variation for each value is shown for both time periods followed by the difference and percentage decrease from state A to state B. On the average, the diversity of judgment of each value's relation to the other 10 declined. "Individual freedom" showed the greatest decrease, followed by "Americans." The least decrease was for "Divorce" and "Sense of Authority." The average diversity of all 55 value judgments decreased 23.6%, from 1.23 to 0.94.

CONCLUSION

A general, convergence model of communication was presented in which the cyclical process of information-sharing among two or more individuals was described. The relationship among the physical, psychological, and social aspects of communication was clearly delineated. The convergence principle and the basic cybernetic process involved in information processing were used to deduce two complementary, general theorems of communication. The theorems specify the conditions under which intercultural communication will lead to convergence between members of the cultures involved, producing a state of greater cultural uniformity within both cultures as a whole. Empirically testable hypotheses were developed that apply to the convergence between an immigrant subculture and its host culture, to convergence within the immigrant culture, and to divergence between the immigrant culture and its original culture over time. Mathematical representations were proposed for the first two hypotheses, and tested with data from a previous study of Korean immigrants to the United States. The results confirmed the first two hypotheses. No data were available from Korea to test the third hypothesis.

The convergence theory of communication satisfies the demand from the discipline for a theory that captures the dynamic nature of human communication. The field of intercultural communication would benefit greatly from a theory that clearly describes communication as a process and focuses upon changes over time between members of diverse cultural groups. The convergence theory provides a general perspective with which to study intercultural communication at the dyadic level and above. The empirical tests of the first two hypotheses had some limitations. The most important was the use of cross-sectional data to test a time-series hypothesis. This limitation also made it impossible to determine to what extent the social system of the immigrants in the United States was relatively closed, especially to information from the original culture. It should be pointed out, however, that the most likely direction of impact of information from the original culture during the 15-year period studied would be to impede the convergence process, not to enhance it.

The actual communication patterns of the immigrant group within its own boundaries and between it and the host culture were not taken into account. Most observers of immigrant ethnic groups, however, have noted the strong tendency of their members to live in close proximity and interact more frequently with one another than with members of the host culture immediately after migration, and the tendency for this pattern to decline as time goes by. So, this was not an unreasonable assumption in the empirical test.

The empirical tests described in this chapter served primarily as an illustration of how the theory can be applied and as an example of some of the empirical methods that can be used. The illustration also indicates one of the important contexts in which to study intercultural communication. The acculturation of immigrants by means of intercultural communication is important not only for the members of the immigrant group, but also for the development and well being of the host culture.

REFERENCES

Barnett, G. A., & Kincaid, D. L. (1983). Cultural convergence: A mathematical theory. In W. B. Gudykunst (Ed.), *Intercultural communication theory: Current perspectives* (pp. 171-194). Beverly Hills, CA: Sage.

Barth, F. (1969). *Ethnic groups and boundaries: The social organization of cultural differences.* Boston: Little, Brown.

Boyd, R., & Richerson, P. J. (1985). *Culture and the evolutionary process.* Chicago: University of Chicago Press.

Bronowski, J. (1974). *The ascent of man.* Boston: Little, Brown.

Dostoyevsky, F. (1950). *Crime and punishment.* New York: Random House. (Original work published 1866)

Kincaid, D. L. (1979). *The convergence model of communication* (Paper 18). Honolulu: East-West Communication Institute.

Kincaid, D. L. (1983). Communication technology and cultural diversity. *Informatologia Yugoslavica, 15,* 5-7.

Kincaid, D. L. (1987). The convergence theory of communication, self-organization, and cultural evolution. In D. L. Kincaid (Ed.), *Communication theory from Eastern and Western perspectives* (pp. 209-221). New York: Academic Press.

Kincaid, D. L., & Schramm, W. (1975). *Fundamental human communication.* Honolulu: East-West Center Modular Text.

Kincaid, D. L., Yum, J. O., Woelfel, J., & Barnett, G. A. (1983). The cultural convergence of Korean immigrants in Hawaii: An empirical test of a mathematical theory. *Quality and Quantity, 18,* 59-78.

Kincaid, D. L., & Yum, J. O. (1987). A comparative study of Korean, Filipino, and Samoan immigrants to Hawaii: Socioeconomic consequences. *Human Organization, 46,* 70-77.

Levi-Strauss, C. (1975). Race and history. In L. Kuper (Ed.), *Race, science, and society.* New York: Columbia University Press. (Original work published 1956)

Rogers, E. M., & Kincaid, D. L. (1981). *Communication networks: Toward a new paradigm for research.* New York: Free Press.

Sarbaugh, L. (1979). *Intercultural communication.* Rochelle Park, NJ: Hayden.

Shannon, C., & Weaver, W. (1949). *The mathematical theory of communication.* Urbana, IL: University of Illinois Press.

Simon, H. A. (1976). *Administrative behavior* (3rd ed.). New York: Free Press.

Toulmin, S. (1960). *The philosophy of science.* New York: Harper & Row.

Woelfel, J., & Fink, E. L. (1980). *The measurement of communication processes: Galileo theory and method.* New York: Academic Press.

Yum, J. O. (1982). Communication diversity and information acquisition among Korean immigrants in Hawaii. *Human Communication Research, 8,* 154-169.

Yum, J. O. (1984). Social networks of five ethnic groups in Hawaii. *Communication yearbook 7* (pp. 574-591). Beverly Hills, CA: Sage.

13

Intercultural Transformation
A Systems Theory

YOUNG YUN KIM ● *Governors State University*
BRENT D. RUBEN ● *Rutgers University*

This chapter proposes a theory that focuses on the process of intercultural transformation, a gradual change that takes place in the internal conditions of individuals as they participate in extensive intercultural communication activities. In this process of internal change, the individuals' cognitive, affective, and behavioral patterns are viewed to develop beyond their original, culturally conditioned psychological parameters. Grounded in the holistic, interactive perspective of General Systems Theory on the nature of human behavior, the present theory explains why and how intercultural transformation occurs. At the center of this theoretical explanation is the stress-adaptation-growth dynamic, viewed to be present in the intercultural communication experiences of most people and acting as the "mover" of individuals toward increasing intercultural attributes.

We live in the midst of rapid cultural change and increasing intercultural connectedness. Impressive development in communications and transportation technology moves us closer to the vision of a "global village." Even in our own society, our relationship to our personal and collective past is increasingly remote, making us cultural strangers in our own society. The tempo of change toward increasing interculturalness in global as well as domestic realities is felt in almost every facet of human affairs and in virtually all societies, large and small.

To be a successful business manager in a multinational company, one cannot be highly ethnocentric. To be an effective diplomat, one must communicate with great sensitivity and understanding, and with the social skills of the local culture. To be a good teacher in a multiethnic urban school, one must be able to deal with children and their parents whose cultural attributes are different from one's own. To be a fully

AUTHORS' NOTE: Some of the ideas in this chapter have been discussed in our previous works, particularly in Gudykunst and Kim (1984), Kim (1985a, 1985b, in press), and Ruben (1975, 1980, 1983, 1988).

functioning member of an educational organization, one must be able to understand and adapt to the changing cultural and technological dynamics and the implications thereof.

Indeed, the intercultural "predicament" demands from each of us a conscious decision—a conscious decision concerning our basic attitudes toward ourselves and toward our relationships to otheis and the world at large. We need to be more aware of and more capable of dealing with the diversity of cultures and subcultures interlaced beneath the surface of every international and domestic affair.

When faced with new circumstances, however, most people prefer to continue in their old cultural ways without a clear intercultural vision and without a readiness to embrace the different and the unfamiliar. Even though effective managing of intercultural situations demands an orientation that goes beyond any one cultural perspective, we invariably struggle to put new circumstances into old frameworks. After all, our lifelong cultural habits are difficult to break. As Barnlund (1982) wrote, "One acquires a personality and a culture in childhood, long before [s]he is capable of comprehending either of them" (p. 14). Yet it is crucial that we work toward becoming intercultural if we are to be functional and effective in our intercultural environment.

This chapter proposes a way of viewing the process of becoming intercultural. Based on the fundamental principles of human behavior stipulated by General Systems Theory, we present a set of laws and propositions that we think are helpful for describing and explaining the process through which an individual grows beyond the psychological parameters of a given culture.

REVIEW OF LITERATURE

An increasing number of attempts have been made to explore ideologies and worldviews that are larger than national and cultural interests and that embrace all humanity. As early as 1946, Northrop (1946/1966), in *The Meaning of the East and the West,* proposed an "international cultural ideal" to provide intellectual and emotional foundations for what he envisioned as "partial world sovereignty." Among contemporary critics of culture, Thompson (1973) explored the concept "planetary culture" in which Eastern mysticism was integrated with Western science and rationalism. Similarly, Capra (1975), in *The Tao of Physics,* showed an essential harmony between these two complementary manifestations of the human mind.

Additional philosophical ideas have been proposed by Gebser (see Feuerstein, 1987), who projected "integral consciousness" as an emerging mode of experiencing reality. In this mode, the "rational," "mythical," "magical," and "primal" modes are simultaneously present and integrated. Elgin's (1981) idea of "voluntary simplicity" echoes Gebser, portraying an emerging "global common sense" and a practical life-style to reconcile the willful, rational approach to life of the West and the holistic, spiritual orientation of the East. Other concepts such as "international" (Lutzker, 1960), "universal" (Walsh, 1973), "multi-cultural" (Adler, 1982), and "marginal" (Lum, 1982) have been presented to project similar images of personhood, with varying degrees of descriptive and explanatory value.

Paralleling these philosophical and ideological visions of intercultural personhood, many behavioral scientists have investigated experiences of individuals extensively exposed to foreign cultures. Stimulated by the post-Second World War boom in student exchange and international migration, the Peace Corps movement in the 1960s, the expansion of multinational trade, and the increase in civil and military government personnel, extensive literature has approached the investigation. Studies of the intercultural communication experiences of sojourners and immigrants can be broadly categorized into two approaches—the "intercultural communication-as-problem" approach; and the "inter-cultural communication-as-learning/growth" approach, as briefly reviewed next.[1]

Intercultural Communication-as-Problem Approach

Because encounters with alien cultural environments present surprises and uncertainties (in varying degrees depending on the severity of cultural dislocation experiences), there have been ample discussions, essays, and empirical studies dealing with this phenomenon. The concept *culture shock,* has been used by anthropologists, communi-cation researchers, sociologists, and psychologists, among others, to explain many of the frustrations encountered in the early part of the sojourner's stay abroad. Many writers have described the various psychological, social, and physical reactions associated with culture shock. Other similar terms also have been employed to refer to variations of such "shock" experiences, including *role shock* (Byrnes, 1966; Higbee, 1969), *language shock* (Smalley, 1963), *culture fatigue* (Guthrie, 1966, 1975), and *transition shock* (Bennett, 1977). Essentially, culture shock has been used to refer to "a form of personality maladjustment which is a reaction to a temporary unsuccessful attempt to adjust to new surroundings and people" (Lundstedt, 1963, p. 8) and a natural consequence of the state of a human organism's inability to interact with the new and changed environment in an effective manner (Bennett, 1977). Taft (1977) identified a number of common reactions to cultural dislocation: (1) "cultural fatigue," as manifested by irritability, insomnia, and other psychosomatic disorders; (2) a sense of loss arising from being uprooted from one's familiar surroundings; (3) rejection by the individual members of the new environment; and (4) a feeling of impotence from being unable to competently deal with the environmental unfamiliarity. Similarly, many immigrant studies have looked into the phenomena related to "mental illnesses" of immigrants. Descriptions of encounters with the Southeast Asian refugees in mental health settings have appeared in the literature (see Kinzie, Tran, Breckenridge, & Bloom, 1980; Williams & Westermeyer, 1986). In each of these cases, the features associated with environmental change are the "shock" effects involving heightened emotions and intense suffering.

Closely related to the studies of culture shock are studies examining the process of individual adjustment in unfamiliar cultural environments. Many attempts have been made to identify the "stages" of adjustment that individuals go through in a foreign environment. Oberg (1960), for instance, described four stages: (1) a "honeymoon" stage characterized by fascination, elation, and optimism; (2) a stage of hostility and emotionally stereotyped attitudes toward the host society and increased association with fellow sojourners; (3) a recovery stage characterized by increased language knowledge and ability to get around in the new culture; and (4) a final stage in which adjustment is about as complete as possible, anxiety is largely gone, and new customs are accepted and enjoyed.

Others have depicted the stages of adaptive change individuals go through in "curves." These curves indicate the patterns of change over time in the degree of satisfaction in living in the alien environment. Some empirical support has been found, for instance, for what has been described as a U curve of adjustment (Lysgaard, 1955), depicting the initial optimism and elation in the host culture, the subsequent dip or "trough" in the level of adjustment, followed by a gradual recovery to higher adjustment levels. Gullahorn and Gullahorn (1963) extended this curve further and proposed a W curve, indicating that sojourners often undergo a reacculturation process (a second U curve in their home environment similar to that experienced abroad). (See Church, 1982, for a detailed review.)

A common viewpoint in these studies of culture shock and adaptation has been that life is difficult in foreign lands. These studies also shared a common concern for minimizing the psychological difficulties and maximizing effective performance in an unfamiliar environment. Few agreements exist, however, as to patterns and processes of adaptive changes that can be determined from the existing studies. Adjustment stage models also present inherent conceptual difficulties in classifying individuals. As Church (1982) pointed out, the existing models do not adequately address crucial questions, such as "Is the order of stages invariant?" and "Must all stages be passed through or can some be skipped by some individuals?"

Nor is there conclusive or generalizable support for the U curve hypothesis (see Becker, 1968; Breitenbach, 1970, Spaulding & Flack, 1976). Not all students, for example, have been observed to begin their sojourn with a "honeymoon phase" or with a period of elation and optimism (Klineberg & Hull, 1979). Even those studies supporting the hypothesis have shown marked differences in the time parameters of the curve, making the U curve description too flexible to be sufficiently useful.

International Communication-as-Learning/Growth Approach

Countering the preceding "problem-oriented" studies, an alternative approach was proposed by Adler (1987) who viewed culture shock in a broader context of intercultural learning and growth. In Adler's view,

> Culture shock is thought of as a profound learning experience that leads to a high degree of self-awareness and personal growth. Rather than being only a disease for which adaptation is the cure, culture shock is likewise at the very heart of the cross-cultural learning experience. It is an experience in self-understanding and change. (p. 29)

Similarly, Ruben (1983) questioned the problem-oriented perspective as he discussed the results of a study of Canadian technical advisers and their spouses on two-year assignments in Kenya (Ruben & Kealey, 1979). In this study, the intensity and directionality of culture shock was found to be unrelated to patterns of psychological adjustment at the end of the first year in an alien culture. Of still greater interest was the finding that, in some instances, the magnitude of culture shock was positively related to social and professional effectiveness within the new culture. These findings suggested implications that directly contradict the problem-oriented perspective on the nature of culture shock.

In the intercultural communication-as-learning/growth approach, then, culture shock experiences are viewed as the core or essence, though not necessarily the totality, of the cross-cultural learning experience. The culture-shock process is regarded as fundamental in that the individual must somehow confront the social, psychological, and philosophical discrepancies one finds between his or her own internalized cultural disposition and that of the new environment. The cross-cultural learning experience, accordingly, is viewed in large part as a transitional experience reflecting a "movement from a state of low self- and cultural awareness to a state of high self- and cultural awareness" (Adler, 1972/1987, p. 15).

Based on this perspective, Adler (1975) described five phases of encompassing and progressive changes in identity and experiential learning. Briefly, the five phases are: (1) a *contact phase* characterized by excitement and euphoria during which the individual views the new environment ethnocentrically; (2) a *disintegration phase* marked by confusion, alienation, and depression, during which cultural differences become increasingly noticeable; (3) a *reintegration phase* characterized by strong rejection of the second culture, defensive projection of personal difficulties, and an existential choice to either regress to earlier phases or to move closer to resolution and personal growth; (4) an *autonomy stage* marked by increasing understanding the host culture along with a feeling of competence; and (5) a final *independence stage* marked by a cherishing of cultural differences and relativism, creative behavior, and increased self- and cultural awareness.

Adler's model of cultural learning and of psychic growth contributes significantly to broadening the traditional, problem-oriented perspective on intercultural communication experiences. As such, it has provided important insights for the present theorizing.

TOWARD A SYSTEMS THEORY
OF INTERCULTURAL TRANSFORMATION

Although existing research has been useful in focusing attention on the intercultural communication experiences of sojourners and immigrants, it is generally post hoc and descriptive in nature. The inconsistent descriptions of the stages and patterns of adjustment over time are at least partly due to the lack of a comprehensive, coherent system of theoretical principles: Few existing models have systematically articulated the theoretical relationship between intercultural encounters, culture shock experiences, and adaptive transformation. The present theory attempts to address this existing need. It integrates the culture shock phenomenon and adaptive changes in individuals within a single theoretical framework that is designed to provide a systematic explanation for the process of intercultural transformation. In this framework, culture shock is viewed as neither "positive" nor "negative" necessarily, but as an integral and inevitable part of the process of becoming intercultural. It is seen as a process of individual transformation—a value-neutral phenomenon that occurs "naturally" through intercultural communication experiences.

In theorizing the process of intercultural transformation, we recognize that not all individuals are successful in productively managing intercultural stress and making adaptive transformations. We know from the literature, as well as from our own observation, that certain immigrants and sojourners experiencing intense and extensive environmental challenges have been too overcome by stress to wholly able to cope. Some have become subject to severe psychological disturbances, and others simply have given up and returned to the original culture. Such extreme cases are in the minority, however, and do not alter the common experiences of intercultural adaptation by the majority.

Definitions

Intercultural communication is defined as the communication process that takes place in a circumstance in which communicators' patterns of verbal and nonverbal encoding and decoding are significantly different because of cultural differences. Although many intercultural experiences occur indirectly through being exposed to messages that we read, see, and hear in mass media (including books, journals, magazines, movies, television programs, and newspapers), we are primarily concerned here with communication situations of direct, face-to-face encounters between individuals of differing cultural backgrounds. The term *culture* is used broadly and inclusively to refer to the collective life patterns shared by people in social groups such as national, racial, ethnic, socioeconomic, regional, and gender groups. Communication situations are considered intercultural to the extent that the participants carry different cultural and subcultural attributes. The more the participants differ in their cultural and subcultural attributes, the more intercultural the communication is (see Gudykunst & Kim, 1984; Ruben, 1983; Sarbaugh, 1979).

Intercultural transformation refers to the process of change in individuals beyond the cognitive, affective, and behavioral limits of their original culture. As a process, the concept implies differential levels of *interculturalness*. The term *intercultural* is preferred here to other similar terms such as *multicultural, universal,* and *marginal*. Simply projecting a personhood that transcends any given cultural group, the term is not bounded by any specific cultural attributes.[2]

These specifications of terms collectively define the present *theoretical domain,* limiting it to the *internal changes* that occur in individuals as they participate in interpersonal encounters with people whose cultural attributes differ significantly from their own. Further, the present theory is a *culture-general* (culture-free, universal) theory because its implications are not tied to particular time- and space-bound entities such as specific nations, societies, ethnic groups, and relationships between communicators. At least some of the internal transformations postulated in the theory are viewed to occur for anyone who participates in intercultural communication activities.

The theory explicated next generally follows the theory-building methodological principles set forth by Dubin (1969), and is based on concepts and principles of General Systems Theory. First, a set of systems concepts and principles will be identified. Second, these concepts will be applied to the situations of intercultural communication, and a set of *principles* (or *laws* in Dubin's terminology) will be postulated to explain the general nature of relationships between concepts. These laws will then be the basis on which a number of *propositions* will be explicated to explain the specific nature of the process of intercultural transformation.

The General Systems Perspective: Assumptions

General Systems Theory is a conceptual network, or a perspective, on a "higher" abstraction level than a theory about a specific phenomenon.[3] This abstract nature of the theory enables theorists to use some of its concepts and principles as metatheoretical assumptions in developing a content-specific theory such as the present one. Further, the theory emphasizes the holistic nature of any system and its functions and assumes the dynamic interactions among its parts and with its environment.

The basic building block of General Systems Theory, of course, is the *system.* The term refers to any entity or whole that consists of interdependent parts. For the present purpose, individuals are viewed as systems and are understood to function through ongoing interactions with the environment and its inhabitants. In this perspective, *communication* refers to the process of information decoding (receiving, processing, and transforming) and encoding (expressing verbally and nonverbally) necessary to function in a given environment. Through communication, an individual is linked with the environment informationally. This continual give-and-take process of communication is necessary to the emergence and survival of all humans as social beings. As such, each person is viewed as an *open system.*[4]

Like all other living systems, humans are characteristically *homeostatic,* attempting to hold constant a variety of variables in our internal meaning structure to achieve an ordered whole. When individuals receive messages that disrupt their existing internal order, they experience *disequilibrium.* In this state of disequilibrium, *stress* confronts the individual, and he or she struggles to regain internal equilibrium. Stress, then, is a manifestation of a generic process that occurs whenever the capabilities of an open system are not totally adequate to the demands of the environment. In stressful situations, the so-called defensive mechanism is activated in individuals as an attempt to hold the internal structure constant by some kind of psychological maneuvering. People attempt to avoid or minimize the anticipated or actual "pain" of disequilibrium and stress by self-deception, denial, avoidance, and withdrawal (Lazarus, 1966, p. 262).

When the environmental challenges continue to threaten internal equilibrium, individuals by necessity continue to strive to "meet" and manage the challenge through their *adaptive activities* of acting on the environment as well as of responding to it. Unlike animals that commonly respond to environmental challenges with passivity, human adaptive activities include both alteration of internal conditions and alteration of environmental conditions (Chomsky, 1972). With the "reflexive" and "self-reflexive" capacities of the human mind that reviews, anticipates, generalizes, analyzes, and plans, individuals are capable of creatively transforming their internal as well as external conditions. This uniquely human adaptive capacity is called by Jantsch (1980) "self-organizing," and is viewed as the key to internal growth. "We live, so to speak, in co-evolution with ourselves, with our own mental products" (p. 177).

Through iterative communication processes between the inner and outer world, individuals' internal structures evolve and grow. They learn to see a situation "with new eyes." This self-organizing (or reflexive and self-reflexive) characteristic of human systems enables human thought to generate more adaptive alternatives than lower animals are capable of generating. More meanings can be attributed to objects, and a greater number of connections between meanings arise, and, thus, a greater number of outcomes. Whereas the myth has no alternative when faced with a light and immediately flies toward it, a person engaging in complex thought processes can perceive a stimuli in many ways and can consider many ways of interrelating these perceptions for adaptive purposes.

The *stress-adaptation-growth* process is cyclic and continual. Once an environmental threat propels the system into disequilibrium, the person acts to restore harmony by restructuring his or her internal communication system in order to accommodate the challenge. Internal equilibrium is thus regained until the system is confronted by new environmental challenges. Implicit in this view is the notion that there is simply no way to derive the benefits of growth without the concomitant experiences of stress. This principle presents the unity in which stress and growth are integrated in the adaptation process because neither occurs without the other, and each occurs because of the other.

The dynamic tension between stress and adaptation and the resultant internal growth essentially characterizes the life processes of humans (as well as all living systems). It is this tension that is necessary for the continued existence of individuals facing environmental challenges. It is the resolution of stressful difficulties that promises the qualitative transformation of a person toward a greater internal capacity to cope with varied environmental conditions. The increased internal capacity, in turn, facilitates the subsequent handling of stress and adaptation.

The foregoing systems concepts and principles can be summarized as follows:

Assumption 1: A person is an open communication system that interacts with the environment through input and output of information.

Assumption 2: A person has an inherent homeostatic drive to maintain his or her internal equilibrium.

Assumption 3: A person's internal equilibrium is disturbed when the person-environment symmetry is broken.

Assumption 4: When internal equilibrium is disturbed, a person experiences stress.

Assumption 5: Most individuals are capable of reducing stress and regaining internal equilibrium by adapting to a changed environment.

Assumption 6: Stress and growth are inseparable as aspects of adaptation. Both are necessary to define the nature of a person's internal growth.

Assumption 7: The internal growth of a person facilitates his or her subsequent adaptability.

Applying these principles of human systems to situations of intercultural communication, a number of theoretical axioms and propositions that explain the process of intercultural transformation are presented in the following section.

FROM CULTURAL TO INTERCULTURAL: AXIOMS AND PROPOSITIONS

As human infants grow, they adapt to a cultural environment composed largely of the symbols and objects whose meaning and significance are the product of the communication activities of other humans. Over time, individuals develop and internalize the cognitive, affective, and behavioral attributes that are commonly shared by people in the cultural milieu. Such attributes, in turn, serve as necessary means of communication in managing themselves and their environment.

In this process, the individuals become cultural beings. Cultural attributes become a large part of their unconscious patterns of communication, particularly the cognitive patterns of categorizing and sorting information from the environment. As cultural persons, they are further conditioned by the collective ways of feeling and behaving. Humans, thus, have limited freedom in experiencing what is beyond the borders of their cultural consciousness.

The internalized cultural imprinting that governs individuals' internal conditions remain largely unrecognized, unquestioned, and unchallenged until they encounter people with different cultural attributes. As Boulding (1956/1977) stated, the human nervous system is structured in such a way that the patterns that govern behavior and perception come into consciousness only when there is a deviation from the familiar (p. 13). Intercultural encounters provide such situations of deviation from the familiar as individuals are faced with things that do not follow their hidden program.

The Intercultural Stress-Adaptation-Growth Process

In communicating interculturally, people inevitably experience a multitude of difficulties as they experience communication patterns that challenge their taken-for-granted assumptions. Individuals who are seriously engaged in intercultural encounters (such as immigrants and sojourners who must by necessity operate effectively in an alien environment) are challenged to change at least some of their culturally conditioned ways of thinking, feeling, and behaving. The extent of such challenges of intercultural communication are at least partly dependent on the degree of heterogeneity of the participants' cultural attributes in a particular encounter. The more incongruent and heterogeneous the cultural attributes of the communicators, the more intercultural their communication experiences will be.[5]

As such, intercultural communication experiences are inherently stressful. Understanding and being understood interculturally often involves a substantial challenge, which introduces internal disequilibrium and stress in participants. Confronted with situations in which assumptions and premises acquired in childhood are called into question, the communicators experience uncertainty and conflict. In the case of immigrants who have moved to an alien culture, there will be a dramatic increase in symbolic as well as physical challenges. Conservative estimates suggest that, within the first year in a new culture, an individual may experience nearly one third of what Holmes and Rahe (1967) considered the 43 most significant life changes.

This phenomenon is what is commonly referred to as culture shock, typically viewed, as we pointed out earlier, as a negative, problematic, and undesirable phenomenon to be avoided. Viewed in the present system's terms, however, culture shock is a manifestation of a generic process that occurs whenever the capabilities of a living system are not sufficiently adequate to the demands of an unfamiliar cultural environment. It is a necessary precondition to change and growth, as individuals strive to regain their inner balance by adapting to the demands and opportunities of the intercultural situation.

In facing culture shock situations, then, individuals must, at least temporarily, alter some of their existing cultural patterns of communication in order to make communication work as they intend. To put it differently, such situations require us to suspend or change some of the old cultural ways and accommodate some of the new cultural ways. This necessity is commonly met with conscious or unconscious resistance of the individuals engaged in intercultural communication, which adds to the stress they already experience. Yet insisting on the old cultural ways and trying to avoid stress is like "wanting to have one's cake and eat it, too."

Culture shock—or the generic intercultural stress—is, indeed, part and parcel of the intercultural adaptation cycle. New and unfamiliar environmental conditions of culture differences naturally produce strain in individuals' internal systems as they strive to adapt. The psychological movements of individuals into new dimensions of perception and experience often produce forms of temporary personality disintegration, or even "breakdown" in some extreme cases. Intercultural stress is therefore viewed as the internal resistance of the human organism against its own cultural evolution.

To the extent that stress is said to be responsible for suffering, frustration, and anxiety, it also must be credited as an impetus for learning, growth, and creativity for the individual. Temporary disintegration is thus viewed as the very basis for subsequent growth in the awareness of life conditions and ways to deal with them. Jourard (1974) described this dynamic process as integration—disintegration-reintegration:

> Growth is the dis-integration of one way of experiencing the world, followed by a reorganization of this experience, a reorganization that includes the new disclosure of the world. The disorganization, or even shattering, of one way to experience the world, is brought on by new disclosure from the changing being of the world, disclosures that were always being transmitted, but were usually ignored. (p. 456)

Similarly, Hall (1976), in proposing a psychic growth of individuals beyond their own cultural parameters, calls this process "identity-separation-growth dynamism." (See, also, Dabrowski, 1964, for a similar view.)

The stress-adaptation-growth process lies at the heart of intercultural communication experience in a forward-upward movement of a cycle of "draw-back-to-leap." Each stressful experience is responded to with a "draw back," which then activates one's adaptive energy to "leap forward." (See Figure 13.1.) The shifting between the breakup of the old internalized cultural system and the creation of a new system enables the individual to be better adapted to subsequent intercultural encounters. Ultimately, the intercultural communication experiences of individuals contribute to the evolution of the social systems of which they are a part.

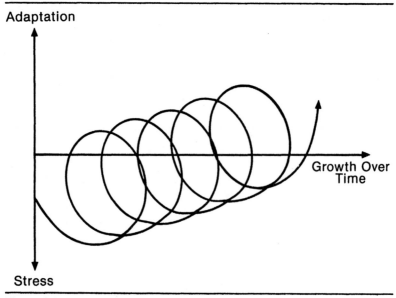

Figure 13.1 Stress-adaptation-growth dynamics of the process of intercultural transformation.

This process of growth is strongly evidenced in numerous immigrants, refugees, and missionaries, who, of necessity, have had to incorporate within themselves the communication patterns of the new environment and thus have restructured their internal conditions. When possible, they have also managed the conditions of the host environment in accordance with their prior cultural attributes. Through continuous intercultural stress-adaptation-growth experiences stimulated by the environmental challenges, they have expanded their internal capacities to function in the changed environment.

Empirical research has provided some supportive indication, although indirect and rudimentary, that the stresses in adapting to a different culture indeed lay the groundwork for subsequent adaptive growth. For example, Eaton and Lasry (1978) reported that the stress level of more upwardly mobile immigrants was greater than those who were less upwardly mobile. Among Japanese-Americans (Marmot & Syme, 1976) and Mexican-American women (Miranda & Castro, 1977), the better adapted immigrants had a somewhat greater frequency of stress-related symptoms (such as anxiety and need for psychotherapy) than the less adapted group. Additionally, some of the findings from the study of

Ruben and Kealey (1979) suggested that the Canadians in Kenya who would ultimately be the most effective in adapting to a new culture underwent the most intense culture shock during the transition period. Other acculturation studies of immigrants and foreign students in the United States have shown that, once the initial phase has been successfully managed, individuals demonstrate an increased cognitive complexity, positive orientation toward the host environment and themselves, and behavior capacities to communicate with the natives (see, for example, Coelho, 1958; Kim, 1976, 1978, 1980).

Readers must be reminded, at this point, that not all individuals are successful in making transitions toward becoming intercultural. Certain individuals, although in the minority, may strongly resist such internal change, thereby increasing the stress level further and making the stress-adaptation-growth cycle intensely difficult. Some may not be able to cope with intense stress experiences because of a lack of psychological resilience. Others may find themselves in intercultural situations that present too severe a challenge to manage. *Most* individuals in *most* circumstances, however, are viewed to undergo the stress-adaptation-growth cycle as just postulated.

Consequences of Intercultural Transformation

As has just been explained, the process of becoming intercultural—of personal transformation from cultural to intercultural—is a process of growth beyond one's original cultural conditioning. One consequence of extensive communication experiences and the subsequent internal transformation is the development of a cultural identity that is far from being "frozen." An intercultural person's cultural identity is characteristically open to further transformation and growth. This does not mean that a highly intercultural person's identity is culture-free or cultureless. Rather, it is not rigidly bound by membership to any one particular culture. Adler (1982), in his explication of "multicultural" person, characterizes this unique identity:

> The identity of multicultural man [woman] is based, not on "belongingness" which implies either owning or being owned by culture, but on a style of self-consciousness that is capable of negotiating ever new formations of reality. In this sense multicultural man [woman] is a radical departure from the kinds of identities found in both traditional and mass societies. He [She] is neither totally *a part of* nor totally *apart from* his [her] culture; he [she] lives, instead, on the boundary. (p. 391)

A second consequence of extensive intercultural communication experiences and adaptive change is a cognitive structure that enables a broadened and deepened understanding of human conditions and cultural differences and a view of things that are larger than any one cultural perspective. Yoshikawa (in press) described such cognitive growth in intercultural communication as a creative process that shares an analogous structural relationships with the scientific discovery process and the religious enlightenment process. In this view, Yoshikawa postulated the developmental stages as a movement from an ethnocentric (or dualistic) perception to a nondualistic, "metacontextual" perception. At this stage of cognitive development, a person is able to experience the dynamic and dialogical interaction between the original culture and the new culture.

The increased cognitive depth and breadth is, in turn, likely to facilitate corresponding emotional and behavioral capacities as well. The inherent drive toward internal balance (or harmony) in individuals as open systems will lead to a congruence between cognitive, affective, and behavioral domains of an individual's internal system. In the moment of calm and relaxation, the process of what we may call the *inner alchemy* takes place: As the "old" person breaks up, the intercultural knowledge, attitudes, and behavioral capacities construct a "new" person at a higher level of integration.

Thus the intercultural person who has benefited from extensive intercultural communication and adaptive transformation often possesses an affirmative (or accepting) attitude toward cultural differences, as well as the emotional and behavioral openness and capacity to participate in the other person's experiences. Even when the person is not aware of the cultural customs of the other person, a highly intercultural person is likely to have the affective and behavioral flexibility to adapt to the situation and creatively manage or avoid conflicts that could result from inappropriate switching between cultures. Houston (1981), a Japanese-American writer, spoke of her personal interculturalness as follows:

> Now I entertain according to how I feel that day. If my Japanese sensibility is stronger, I act accordingly and feel OK. If I feel like going all American, I can do that too and feel OK. I've come to accept the cultural hybrid of my personality and recognize it as a strength, not as a weakness. Because I am culturally neither pure Japanese nor pure American ... does not mean that I am less of a person. It seems that I have been enriched by the heritages of both.

As has been pointed out, it is our view that this internal growth beyond the parameters of any one culture characterizes an "intercultural person." As such, an intercultural person achieves what Harris (1979) referred to as an "optimal level of communication competence." At this stage, one achieves the maximum capacity to communicate with individuals who are significantly different in cultural backgrounds, and are able to make deliberate choices of actions in specific situations rather than simply being dictated by the normative courses of action in a given culture. Becoming intercultural, therefore, can be viewed as a process of reaching out beyond culture for a full blossoming of the uniquely human adaptive capacity.

The discussion thus far on the nature of intercultural communication and the process of becoming intercultural can be summarized in the following axioms:

Axiom 1: Intercultural communication experiences are inherently stressful, in varying degrees, owing to participants' cultural differences.

Axiom 2: The stress of intercultural communication experiences facilitates participants' adaptation.

Axiom 3: An outcome of intercultural stress-adaptation experiences is an intercultural transformation in internal conditions.

Axiom 4: Intercultural transformation is reflected in an increased cognitive, affective, and behavioral capacity.

Axiom 5: The increased cognitive, affective, and behavior capacity, reduces the amount of stress in subsequent intercultural communication experiences.

From these principles of intercultural communication and the process of intercultural transformation, we may explicate a number of specific propositions for empirical testing.

Proposition 1: The more cultural differences between individuals in an intercultural communication situation, the more stress they are likely to experience.

Proposition 2: The more stress individuals experience in intercultural communication situations, the more intercultural transformations are likely to take place in them.

Proposition 3: As individuals become increasingly intercultural, their cultural identity becomes increasingly flexible.

Proposition 4: As individuals become increasingly intercultural, their cognitive capacity to understand cultural differences increases.

Proposition 5: As individuals become increasingly intercultural, their affective capacity to affirm and participate in the experiences of culturally different individuals is likely to increase.

Proposition 6: As individuals become increasingly intercultural, their behavioral flexibility to manage cultural differences increases.

Proposition 7: As individuals become increasingly intercultural, the level of stress in their intercultural communication experiences decreases.

CONCLUSION

The focal idea in the proposed theory has been the stress-adaptation-growth dynamic of intercultural communication experiences. This dynamic process speaks of profound human pliability and resilience. Except for a small portion, most of us have an impressive capacity to manage intercultural encounters successfully without damaging our overall psychological health and integrity. As has been demonstrated amply by numerous immigrants and sojourners who have successfully overcome severely stressful situations and transformed themselves adaptively, the process of becoming intercultural is not only a philosophical ideal but also an empirical phenomenon.

The present approach contains both the intercultural communication-as-problem approach and the intercultural communication-as-learning/growth approach within a single theoretical framework. It shows the interrelatedness of the stress and growth aspects of intercultural communication based on the adaptive principles of human systems. Stress, thus, is recognized as generic to all intercultural encounters and as the necessary condition for intercultural transformation toward increased clarity, flexibility, and competence in dealing with culturally different individuals.

As noted earlier in this chapter, the present theory is limited in its domain to the changes that occur *within* intercultural communicators. This means that various factors external to individuals—such as the nature of larger social and political contexts in which they communicate, the specific cultural attributes of the participants, and the nature of their relationships, as well as their individual idiosyncrasies—have not been considered in examining the general relationship between intercultural communication experiences and the process of intercultural transformation. For a more elaborate theoretical description and explanation of the process of becoming intercultural, these external conditions need to be specified.

We also need to look into the question of the limits of human systems capacities and the individual differences thereof in the process of becoming intercultural. Some individuals, although small in percentage, are by innate temperament or by circumstantial conditions extremely susceptible to ill effects from any change or trauma. In principle, these limits and individual variations define the parameters of stability of human systems in coping with intercultural stress. Stability, in turn, is limited by the degree of coupling with the environment and, therefore, we must examine the nature of intercultural communication environment as well in considering the limit of human resilience in coping with intercultural stress.

Given these limitations, the seven propositions explicated in this theory await empirical testing. In testing the propositions, we stress the importance for a series of intensive, naturalistic inquiries of individuals for a prolonged period before the key concepts can be operationalized into valid and reliable quantitative measurements. The holistic and interactive nature of an individual's cognitive, affective, and behavioral system, and the complex and intricate nature of the process of intercultural communication, and of becoming intercultural, demand careful "qualitative" insights. In-depth case studies using such research methods are participant observation and intensive interviewing over an extended period should help us obtain such insights.

Along with the research implications of the proposed theory is its potential practical value. Intercultural personhood is an aspiration that promotes individual "fitness" in our intercultural world. Although the theory itself has been developed independent of this practical utility, we believe that the process of becoming intercultural is a process in which individuals continually integrate new cultural elements of life. In this process, they are likely to become increasingly open to the dynamics of intercultural encounters and to attitudes that are less ethnocentric, less prejudging, less rejecting of other cultures and peoples, and more embracing of their differences with a clearer, more acute, and more tolerant mind, a heightened emotional sensibility, and a more flexible behavioral repertoire.

Most people who struggle to find their way into intercultural encounters are quite likely to "profit" by that struggle. In becoming intercultural, there is a special privilege to think, feel, and behave beyond the parameters of any single culture. This accomplishment, regardless of the accompanying psychological and social "cost," has an intrinsic merit in dealing with our increasingly complex intercultural world. In this frame of mind, the tension, stress, and effort necessarily present in overcoming intercultural difficulties can be more willingly accepted and endured.

It is this almost limitless human capacity for adaptation and self-organization—our ability to learn and integrate new experiences, altered perceptions, and flashes of insights—that gives life to the present theory. The "uncommitted potentiality for change" (Bateson, 1972, p. 497) is in each of us, and the present theory is simply a way to point in that direction.

NOTES

1. See, for example, Adler (1975), Brislin (1981), Church (1982), Furnham (1984), Furnham & Bochner (1986), and Kim (1988) for more thorough literature reviews in this area.

2. The present term *intercultural personhood* is preferred because it is more general and inclusive than other similar terms without implying any specific cultural attributes. It portrays personal characteristics that transcend any given cultural group. Unlike the term *multicultural person,* it does not imply that the individual necessarily "possesses" characteristics of more than one culture. Unlike the term *universal person,* it does not suggest an awareness and appreciation of all groups of the world. The term *international person* focuses on the expanded psychological orientation beyond a national boundary, but it does not emphasize numerous ethnic, racial, and other subcultural groups within a nation. The term *marginal person* suggests a sense of inferiority or alienation, which is not considered an attribute of intercultural personhood.

3. The term *higher* emphasizes the greater generality and abstraction, rather than a greater importance or value of systems concepts in relation to the concepts in other conceptualizations of intercultural communication.

4. For discussions of human communication based on the General Systems perspective, see Boulding (1977) and Ruben & J. Kim (1975).

5. In theorizing the adaptation process of immigrants and sojourners in the host culture, Kim (1979; 1988) has taken the individual background factors, relationship factors, and host environmental factors into account.

REFERENCES

Adler, P. S. (1975). The transition experience: An alternative view of culture shock. *Journal of Humanistic Psychology, 15*(4), 13-23.

Adler, P. S. (1982). Beyond cultural identity: Reflections on cultural and multicultural man. In L. A. Samovar & R. E. Porter (Eds.), *Intercultural communication: A reader* (pp. 389-408). Belmont, CA: Wadsworth.

Adler, P. S. (1987). Culture shock and the cross-cultural learning experience. In L. F. Luce & E. C. Smith (Eds.), *Toward internationalism* (pp. 24-35). Cambridge, MA: Newbury. (Original work published in 1972)

Barnlund, D. (1982). Communication in a global village. In L. Samovar & R. Porter (Eds.), *Intercultural communication: A reader*. Belmont, CA: Wadsworth.

Bateson, G. (1972). *Steps to an ecology of mind.* New York: Ballantine.

Becker, T. (1968). Patterns of attitudinal changes among foreign students. *American Journal of Sociology, 73,* 431-442.

Bennett, J. (1977). Transition shock: Putting culture shock in perspective. In N. Jain (Ed.), *International and Intercultural Communication Annual, 4,* 45-52.

Boulding, K. E. (1977). *The image: Knowledge in life and society.* Ann Arbor: The University of Michigan Press. (Original work published in 1956)

Breitenbach, D. (1970). The evaluation of study abroad. In I. Eide (Ed.), *Students as links between cultures.* Paris: UNESCO.

Brislin, R. W. (1981). *Cross-cultural encounters.* Elmsford, NY: Pergamon.

Byrnes, F. C. (1966). Role shock: An occupational hazard of American technical assistants abroad. *Annals, 368,* 95-108.

Capra, F. (1975). *The Tao of physics.* Boulder, CO: Shambhala.

Chomsky, N. (1972). *Language and mind.* New York: Harcourt, Brace, Jovanovich.

Church, A. T. (1982). Sojourner adjustment. *Psychology Bulletin, 91*(3), 540-572.

Coelho, G. V. (1958). *Changing images of America: A study of Indian students' perceptions.* New York: Free Press.

Dabrowski, K. (1964). *Positive disintegration.* Boston: Little, Brown.

Dubin, R. (1969). *Theory building.* New York: Free Press.

Eaton, W. W., & Lasry, J. C. (1978). Mental health and occupational mobility in a group of immigrants. *Science and Medicine, 12,* 53-58.

Elgin, D. (1981). *Voluntary simplicity.* New York: Bantam.

Feuerstein, G. (1987). *Structures of consciousness: The genius of Jean Gebser: An introduction and critique.* Lower Lake, CA: Integral.

Furnham, A. (1984). Tourism and culture shock. *Annals of Tourism Research, 11*(1), 41-57.

Furnham, A., & Bochner, S. (1982). Social difficulty in a foreign culture. In S. Bochner (Ed.), *Cultures in contact.* Elmsford, NY: Pergamon.

Furnham, A., & Bochner, S. (1986). *Culture shock: Psychological reactions to unfamiliar environments.* London: Methuen.

Gudykunst, W. B., & Kim, Y. Y. (1984). *Communicating with strangers: An approach to intercultural communication.* New York: Random House.

Gullahorn, J. T., & Gullahorn, J. E. (1963). An extension of the U-curve hypothesis. *Journal of Social Issues, 19*(3), 33-47.

Guthrie, G. M. (1966). Cultural preparation for the Philippines. In R. B. Textor (Ed.), *Cultural frontiers of the Peace Corps.* Cambridge: MIT Press.

Guthrie, G. M. (1975). A behavioral analysis of culture learning. In R. W. Brislin, S. Bochner, & W. J. Lonner (Eds.), *Cross-cultural perspectives on learning.* New York: John Wiley.

Hall, E. T. (1976). *Beyond culture.* New York: Doubleday.

Harris, L. M. (1979, May). *Communication competence: An argument for a systemic view.* Paper presented at the annual conference of the International Communication Association, Philadelphia.

Higbee, H. (1969). Role shock—A new concept. *International Educational and Cultural Exchange, 4*(4), 71-81.

Holmes, T. H., & Rahe, R. H. (1967). The social readjustment rating scale. *Journal of Psychometric Research, 11,* 213-218.

Houston, J. W. (1981, May). *Beyond Mansamar: A personal view on the Asian-American womanhood.* Lecture presented at Governors State University, University Park, IL. (audio recording available)

Jantsch, E. (1980). *The self-organizing universe: Scientific and human implications of the emerging paradigm of evolution.* New York: Pergamon.

Jourard, S. (1974). Growing awareness and the awareness of growth. In B. Patton & K. Giffin (Eds.), *Interpersonal communication.* New York: Harper & Row.

Kim, Y. Y. (1976). Communication patterns of foreign immigrants in the process of acculturation. *Human Communication Research, 4*(1), 66-77.

Kim, Y. Y. (1978). Toward a communication approach to the acculturation process. *International Journal of Intercultural Relations,* 192-224.

Kim, Y. Y. (1979). Toward an interactive theory of communication-acculturation. In B. D. Ruben (Ed.), *Communication yearbook 3* (pp. 435-453). New Brunswick, NJ: Transaction Books.

Kim, Y. Y. (1980). *Psychological, social, and cultural adjustment of Indochinese refugees.* In *Indochinese refugees in the State of Illinois* (Vol. IV of 5 volumes). Chicago: Travelers Aid Society of Metropolitan Chicago.

Kim, Y. Y. (1985a). Communication, information, and adaptation. In B. D. Ruben (Ed.), *Information and behavior* (Vol. 1. pp. 324-340). New Brunswick, NJ: Transaction Books.

Kim, Y. Y. (1985b). Intercultural personhood: An integration of Eastern and Western perspectives. In L. A. Samovar & R. E. Porter (Eds.), *Intercultural communication: A reader* (4th ed., pp. 400-410). Belmont, CA: Wadsworth.

Kim, Y. Y. (1988). *Communication and cross-cultural adaptation.* Clevedon, England: Multilingual Matters.

Kinzie, J. D., Tran, K. A., Breckenridge, A., & Bloom, J. L. (1980). An Indochinese refugee psychiatric clinic: Culturally accepted treatment approaches. *American Journal of Psychiatry, 137,* 1429-1432.

Klineberg, O., & Hull, W. F. (1979). *At a foreign university: An international study of adaptation and coping.* New York: Praeger.

Lazarus, R. S. (1966). *Psychological stress and the coping process.* New York: McGraw-Hill.

Lum, J. (1982). Marginality and multiculturalism. In L. Samovar & R. Porter (Eds.), *Intercultural communication: A reader* (3rd ed.). Belmont, CA: Wadsworth.

Lundstedt, S. (1963). An introduction to some evolving problems in cross-cultural research. *Journal of Social Issues, 19*(3), 1-9.

Lutzker, D. (1960). Internationalism as a predictor of cooperative behavior. *Journal of Conflict Resolution, 4*(4), 426-430.

Lysgaard, S. (1955). Adjustment in a foreign society: Norwegian Fulbright grantees visiting the United States. *International Social Science Bulletin, 7*(1), 45-51.

Marmot, M. G., & Syme, S. L. (1976). Acculturation and coronary heart disease in Japanese-Americans. *American Journal of Epidemiology, 104*(3), 225-247.

Miranda, M. R., & Castro, F. G. (1977). Culture distance and success in psychotherapy with Spanish speaking clients. In J. L. Martinez Jr. (Ed.), *Chicano Psychology* (pp. 249-262). New York: Academic Press.

Northrop, F. (1966). *The meeting of the East and the West.* New York: Collier. (Original work published in 1946)

Oberg, K. (1960). Cultural shock: Adjustment to new cultural environments. *Practical Anthropology, 7,* 170-179.

Piaget, J. (1977). Problems of equilibriation. In M. Appel & L. Goldberg (Eds.), *Topics of cognitive development.* New York: Plenum.

Ruben, B. D. (1975). Intrapersonal, interpersonal and mass communication process in individual and multi-person systems. In B. D. Ruben & J. Y. Kim (Eds.), *General systems theory and human communication* (pp. 164-190). Rochelle Park, NJ: Hayden.

Ruben, B. D. (1978). Communication and conflict: A system-theoretic perspective. *The Quarterly Journal of Speech, 64*(2), 202-210.

Ruben, B. D. (1980, March). *Culture shock: The skull and the lady—reflections on cultural adjustment and stress.* Paper presented at the annual conference of the Society for Intercultural Education, Training, and Research, Mount Pocono, PA.

Ruben, B. D. (1983). A system-theoretic view. In W. B. Gudykunst (Ed.), *Intercultural communication theory* (pp. 131-145). Beverly Hills, CA: Sage.

Ruben, B. D. (1988). *Communication and human behavior* (2nd ed.). New York: Macmillan.

Ruben, B. D., & Kealey, D. J. (1979). Behavioral assessment of communication competency and the prediction of cross-cultural adaptation. *International Journal of Intercultural Relations, 3*(1), 15-47.

Ruben, B. D., & Kim, J. Y. (1975). *General systems theory and human communication.* Rochelle Park, NJ: Hayden.

Sarbaugh, L. (1979). *Intercultural communication.* Rochelle Park, NJ: Hayden.

Smalley, W. A. (1963). Culture shock, language shock, and the shock of self-discovery. *Practical Anthropology, 10,* 49-56.

Spaulding, S., Flack, M. J., & Associates (1976). *The world's students in the United States: A review and evaluation of research on foreign students.* New York: Praeger.

Taft, R. (1977). Coping with unfamiliar cultures. In N. Warren (Ed.), *Studies in cross-cultural psychology* (Vol. I, pp. 121-153). London: Academic Press.

Thompson, W. (1973). *Passages about earth: An exploration of the new planetary culture.* New York: Harper & Row.

Walsh, J. E. (1973). *Intercultural education in the community of man.* Honolulu: University of Hawaii Press.

Williams, C. L., & Westmeyer, J. (1986). Psychiatric problems among adolescent Southeast Asian refugees: A descriptive study. *Pacific/Asian American Mental Health Research Center Newsletter, 4*(3/4), 22-24.

About the Authors

JAMES L. APPLEGATE is Associate Professor and Chair of the Department of Communication at the University of Kentucky. He was a University Fellow and received his Ph.D. from the University of Illinois in 1978. His doctoral dissertation, Examining Communication Abilities of Children and Adults, received a Golden Anniversary Award from the Speech Communication Association. He is the author of numerous articles, book chapters, and research reports examining factors affecting communication ability. He has been invited to present his research at meetings throughout the United States, Canada, and Mexico. Recently, he edited (with Howard E. Sypher) *Communication by Children and Adults*. He is currently Vice President of the Southern Speech Communication Association.

VICTORIA CHEN received her M.A. in 1985 from the University of California, Santa Barbara, Department of Communication. She is a doctoral candidate in the Department of Communication, University of Massachusetts, Amherst. She has presented papers on topics of cross-cultural communication and communication theory. Her current research interests include the relevance of ethnography to the development of communication theory. Her continuing project is field observations on the adjustment to middle age by American professors.

MARY JANE COLLIER is an Associate Professor of Speech Communication at California State University, Los Angeles. She received her doctoral degree in communication theory and research from the University of Southern California in 1982. Her research interests include cultural identification, and cultural and intercultural communication competence in interpersonal relationships and instructional communication settings. Her work has appeared in *Communication Yearbook, The International Journal of Intercultural Relations,* and *Communication Quarterly.*

NIKOLAS COUPLAND is Lecturer in Sociolinguistics and Founding Director of the Centre for Applied English Language Studies at the University of Wales Institute of Science and Technology, Cardiff, Wales. He received his Ph.D. from the University of Wales. He is author of *Dialect in Use: Sociolinguistic Variation in Cardiff English* (University of Wales Press, 1987) and editor of *Styles of Discourse* (Croom Helm, 1988). Other published work, principally in the areas of dialectology and dialect stylistics, has appeared in journals such as *Language in Society, International Journal of the Sociology of Language,* and *Language and Communication.* With Howard Giles, he codirects an interdisciplinary research program titled, "Communication and the elderly." Other current activities include coediting *The Handbook of Miscommunication and Problematic Talk and English in Wales: Diversity and Development* (Multilingual Matters Ltd.).

VERNON E. CRONEN received his Ph.D. in 1970 from the University of Illinois, Urbana, Department of Speech Communication. He is a Professor at the University of Massachusetts, Amherst, Department of Communication. His published work appears in various journals of communication and psychology. He has contributed a number of chapters to books in communication, psychology, and family therapy and is coauthor of *Communication, Action, and Meaning.* His current research interests include family interaction, moral judgment, and social change, in addition to intercultural communication. His continuing project is the ongoing defiance of middle age.

HUBER W. ELLINGSWORTH is Professor of Communication at the University of Tulsa. He received his doctorate in speech from Florida State University. His career-long interest is in the uses of communication for development and in the effect of cultural variables in the communication process. He has written on these themes in the ICA *Yearbook* and *Intercultural Communication Annual.* He is coauthor of *Communication and Social Change in Latin America* and *Administration of Family Planning Programs in the Philippines and Malaysia,* and is a research consultant with UNESCO and Winrock International.

JOSEPH P. FORGAS received his doctorate in psychology from Oxford University in 1977. He is Professor of Psychology at the University of New South Wales, Sydney, Australia. He is a former Professor of Psychology at the University of Giessen, West Germany, and spent several periods at Stanford University. His research interests focus on interpersonal behavior, social cognition, and verbal and nonverbal communication. His publications include several books (*Social Episodes*, 1979; *Social Cognition*, 1981; *Language and Social Situations*, 1985; *Interpersonal Behaviour*, 1985), and numerous journal articles and chapters dealing with the links between culture, cognition, and social behavior.

ARLENE FRANKLYN-STOKES received her B.Sc. from the University of Bristol, England, where she is conducting doctoral research on the topic of suspension from school. She has been involved in published work with Howard Giles and Miles Hewstone in the areas of communication and intergroup contact, respectively, and, with the former, is coauthor of a chapter for the forthcoming *Handbook of Intercultural Communication*.

CYNTHIA GALLOIS obtained her Ph.D. in social psychology from the University of Florida in 1976. She has since lived in Australia and is now a Senior Lecturer in Psychology at the University of Queensland. Her research and teaching interests lie mainly in the social psychology of communication, especially in intercultural and intergroup communication, nonverbal communication and the expression of emotion, and assertive communication. She is coauthor (with Victor Callan and Patricia Noller) of the Australian text *Social Psychology* (Harcourt Brace Jovanovich, 1986), and her research articles on communication have appeared in the *Journal of Personality and Social Psychology, Journal of Cross-Cultural Psychology, Journal of Nonverbal Behavior,* and *Journal of Language and Social Psychology,* among others.

HOWARD GILES is Professor of Social Psychology and Founding Director of the Center for Communication and Social Relations at the University of Bristol, from which he received his Ph.D. With Peter Robinson, he has organized three International Conferences on Language and Social Psychology at Bristol (1979, 1983, & 1987) and together they are editing the forthcoming *Handbook of Social Psychology* (John Wiley). He has published widely in areas concerned with language and ethnic identity/values, language and perceptions of the social structure, interethnic interaction, ethnic language attitudes, and second language acquisitions. With John Wiemann he is conducting a program of cross-national studies on beliefs about talk.

WILLIAM B. GUDYKUNST is Professor of Communication at Arizona State University. His research focuses on explaining uncertainty reduction processes across cultures and between members of different groups. His most recent books include *Intergroup Communication* (Edward Arnold) and *Cross-Cultural Adaptation* (coedited with Y. Y. Kim, published by Sage). He recently completed *Culture and Interpersonal Communication* with S. Ting-Toomey and E. Chua (Sage), and is working on *Strangeness and Similarity: A Theory of Interpersonal and Intergroup Communication* (Multilingual Matters), and has coedited with M. Asante the *Handbook of Intercultural and Development Communication* (Sage).

YOUNG YUN KIM is Professor of Communication at Governors State University, University Park, Illinois. She received her M.S. degree from the University of Hawaii and Ph.D. from Northwestern University. The main area of her research and writing has been the communication phenomena in cross-cultural adaptation of immigrants and sojourners. She has written many journal articles and book chapters, is coauthor, with W. B. Gudykunst, of *Communicating with Strangers* (Random House, 1984) and *Communication and Cross-Cultural Adaptation* (Multilingual Matters, 1988), and has edited *Methods for Intercultural Communication Research,* with W. B. Gudykunst (Sage, 1984); *Interethnic Communication* (Sage, 1986); and *Cross-Cultural Adaptation,* also with W. B. Gudykunst (Sage, 1987).

D. LAWRENCE KINCAID received his Ph.D. from Michigan State University and is Senior Research Advisor and an Associate of the Department of Population Dynamics of Johns Hopkins University. Formerly he was Research Associate at the East-West Communication Institute in Honolulu and Associate Professor at the State University of New York, Albany. His major interests are in communication theory and research methodology. His work with Everett Rogers on the convergence theory of communication was published in *Communication Networks: Toward a New Paradigm for Research* (Free Press, 1981). He recently edited *Communication Theory from Eastern and Western Perspectives* (Academic Press, 1987).

W. BARNETT PEARCE is Professor and Chair of the Department of Communication at the University of Massachusetts, Amherst. He received his B.A. from Carson-Newman College and his M.A. and Ph.D. from Ohio University. His most recent book is *Development as Communication: A Perspective on India* (Carbondale: University of Southern Illinois Press, 1986), with Uma Narula. His next book will be *Communication and the Human Condition,* also from SIU Press. His major unfinished project is learning to grow old gracefully!

BRENT D. RUBEN is Professor and Director of the Ph.D. Program, School of Communication, Information, and Library Science, Rutgers University. He is the author of *Communication and Human Behavior* (1984, 1987) and the author/editor of *Interdisciplinary Approaches to Human Communication* (1979), *Beyond Media* (1979), *General Systems Theory and Human Communication* (1975), among other books and articles. He was also Founding Editor of the International Communication Association's *Communication Yearbook* series.

LARRY E. SARBAUGH received his Ph.D. from Michigan State University in Communication in 1967. He is Professor Emeritus in the College of Communication Arts and Sciences at Michigan State University. His scholarly interests are intercultural communication, communication and change, and teacher education. He is author of *Intercultural Communication* and *Teaching Speech Communication.*

HOWARD E. SYPHER is an Associate Professor in the Department of Communication at the University of Kentucky. He received his Ph.D. from the University of Michigan in 1979. His research has been published in national and international psychological and communication journals and he is coeditor of a new communication series published by Guilford Press. Dr. Sypher has served as a consultant to numerous organizations and as a Visiting Professor in Australia.

MILT THOMAS received his M.A. in Interpersonal Communication from the University of Montana and is a graduate student in speech communication at the University of Washington. He is interested in intra- and intercultural conflict, the ethnography of communication, and hermeneutics. He is also interested in the philosophy of dialogue, and is coauthor, with John Stewart, of an article in *Bridges Not Walls* (4th edition) on dialogic listening.

STELLA TING-TOOMEY, who received her Ph.D. in interpersonal-intercultural communication from the University of Washington, is Associate Professor of Communication at Arizona State University. She has been elected with Felipe Korzenny of San Francisco State University to coedit the *International and Intercultural Communication Annual,* Volumes 13-16. Her publications have appeared in *International Journal of Intercultural Relations, Human Communication Research,* and *Communication Monographs,* among others. Her research interests are in conflict face-negotiation across cultures and interpersonal-intergroup relationship development.

JUNE OCK YUM, who received her Ph.D. from the University of Southern California, Annenberg School of Communication, is Assistant Professor of Communication at the State University of New York at Albany. Her primary research interests are in intercultural communication and interethnic relations, stereotyping, and Asian perspectives of communication. She has published articles in *Human Communication Research, Communication Yearbook, Human Organizations,* and *International Journal of Intercultural Relations,* among others.